An Unholy Traffic

An Unholy Traffic

Slave Trading in the Civil War South

ROBERT K.D. COLBY

OXFORD
UNIVERSITY PRESS

Oxford University Press is a department of the University of Oxford. It furthers
the University's objective of excellence in research, scholarship, and education
by publishing worldwide. Oxford is a registered trade mark of Oxford University
Press in the UK and certain other countries.

Published in the United States of America by Oxford University Press
198 Madison Avenue, New York, NY 10016, United States of America.

© Oxford University Press 2024

All rights reserved. No part of this publication may be reproduced, stored in
a retrieval system, or transmitted, in any form or by any means, without the
prior permission in writing of Oxford University Press, or as expressly permitted
by law, by license, or under terms agreed with the appropriate reproduction
rights organization. Inquiries concerning reproduction outside the scope of the
above should be sent to the Rights Department, Oxford University Press, at the
address above.

Portions of Chapter 4 were adapted from the article, "'Negroes Will Bear Fabulous Prices':
The Economics of Wartime Slave Commerce and Visions of the Confederate Future," originally published
in the *Journal of the Civil War Era*, Volume 10, Number 4, December 2020. Copyright © 2020 the
University of North Carolina Press. Used by permission of the publisher. www.uncpress.org

You must not circulate this work in any other form
and you must impose this same condition on any acquirer.

Library of Congress Cataloging-in-Publication Data
Names: Colby, Robert K.D., author.
Title: An unholy traffic : slave trading in the Civil War South / Robert K.D. Colby.
Other titles: Slave trading in the Civil War South
Description: New York, NY : Oxford University Press, [2024] |
Includes bibliographical references and index. |
Identifiers: LCCN 2023053720 (print) | LCCN 2023053721 (ebook) |
ISBN 9780197578261 (hb) | ISBN 9780197578285 (epub) | ISBN 9780197578292
Subjects: LCSH: Slave trade—Southern States—History—19th century. |
Slavery—Economic aspects—Southern States. | Slave trade—United States—
History—19th century. | Slavery—Economic aspects—United States. |
United States—History—1849–1877.
Classification: LCC E442 .C67 2024 (print) | LCC E442 (ebook) |
DDC 306.3/620973—dc23/eng/20231205
LC record available at https://lccn.loc.gov/2023053720
LC ebook record available at https://lccn.loc.gov/2023053721

DOI: 10.1093/oso/9780197578261.001.0001

Printed in Canada by Marquis

The manufacturer's authorised representative in the EU for product safety is
Oxford University Press España S.A. of El Parque Empresarial San Fernando de Henares,
Avenida de Castilla, 2 – 28830 Madrid (www.oup.es/en or product.safety@oup.com). OUP España
S.A. also acts as importer into Spain of products made by the manufacturer.

For Erin
and
for Jane, Daniel, Margaret, and Adam

Contents

Acknowledgments	ix
Introduction	1
1. "No Money, and No Confidence": Slave Trading, Secession, and the Panic of 1860	17
2. The "Uncongenial Air of Freedom": Union Occupation and the Slave Trade	45
3. "Old Abe Is Not Feared in This Region": The Revival of Confederate Slave Commerce	78
4. "Negroes Will Bear Fabulous Prices": Inflation, Speculation, and the Confederate Future	108
5. "Liable to Be Sold at Any Moment": State-Making, Continuity, and the Slave Trade	133
6. Sold "Far Out of the Way of Lincoln": Emancipation and Counterrevolutionary Slave Commerce	160
7. "Broke... All Up": The Ends and Afterlives of the Wartime Slave Trade	189
Epilogue	212
Notes	217
Select Bibliography	325
Index	337

Acknowledgments

Success, proverbially, has many fathers, leaving failure an orphan. In the hopes that this book registers as the former, I want to recognize the many people who can rightfully claim a share in its paternity. If it is the latter, the responsibility is my own.

Academic life is inherently peripatetic, but I repeatedly have been blessed in where mine has taken me. This book began at the University of North Carolina, Chapel Hill, where it benefited immeasurably from Harry Watson's sage advice, encouragement, and patient but firm refusal to accept the eighty-page chapter drafts I tried to foist on him. For offering that elusive advisorial blend of independent inquiry and critical refinement, I owe Harry much. I likewise incurred debts to Joe Glatthaar and Bill Barney, whose encyclopedic knowledge, sharp critiques, and perpetual cheer make UNC an unrivalled place to study the Civil War. Ed Baptist, Peter Coclanis, Thavolia Glymph, and Ben Waterhouse offered critical insights into this book in its earliest stages. I hope they see their influence on the resulting work.

At Christopher Newport University, Liz and Nathan Busch have created a wonderful home for people studying and teaching the American experiment. I am deeply grateful to them for bringing me to the Center for American Studies as a postdoctoral fellow. From a chance encounter in an archive, Jonathan White has become a mentor, sounding board, and dear friend. Brent Cusher, Frank Garmon, Ben Lynerd, Jeffry Morrison, Lynn Shollen, and many others made McMurran Hall a perpetually welcoming place. Thank you as well to my Junior Fellows and Summer Scholars, especially Mazie Clark, Trevor Cogan, and Nyla Lewis.

I have been privileged to finish this book at the University of Mississippi. My thanks to Jesse Cromwell, Darren Grem, Zack Kagan-Guthrie, Frances Kneupper, Alex Lindgren-Gibson, Becky Marchiel, Jared Pack, Paul Polgar, Sean Scanlon, Susan Stearns, Doug Sullivan-Gonzalez, and Jeff Watt for thoroughly lining the Velvet Ditch. Chuck Ross and Noell Wilson have generously and enthusiastically supported this project, for which I am grateful. A student of the Civil War could hardly ask for a more intellectually invigorating context in which to work than in the Center for Civil War Research and in close collaboration with April Holm. I also benefited from the support of the Neff Memorial Fund in producing this volume; I hope the result honors John's memory.

Though we spend much time working alone, historians' projects are hardly solitary endeavors. Long before this book existed, Gary Gallagher and Michael Holt opened my eyes to what it meant to be an historian, introduced me to the nineteenth century, and exemplified all that faculty ought to be. Jessica Auer, Adam Domby, Evan Faulkenbury, Ashton Merck, Isabell Moore, Melanie Sheehan, Mary Elizabeth Walters, Garrett Wright, Mishio Yamanaka, and Pearl Young are models of collegiality. Regular writing sessions with Melissa DeVelvis, Jonathan Jones, Lucas Kelley, Aubrey Lauersdorf, Caroline Newhall, and Alexandra Stern have sharpened this book. And to Eric Burke, Brian Fennessy, Joshua Lynn, Robert Richard, Joe Stieb, and Joshua Tait: sometimes it actually is about the friends we make along the way.

The Institute for Humane Studies generously supported a manuscript workshop that significantly advanced this book. One could not ask for more thoughtful readers than Rick Bell, Alexandra Finley, Joshua Lynn, Joshua Rothman, Andrew Slap, and Amy Murrell Taylor. I am grateful to each of them for their probing insights and exacting critiques. Participants in the Nau Center Civil War Seminar, CUNY Early American History Seminar, Southern Historical Association Junior Scholars Workshop, and CNU College of Social Sciences Research Seminar further refined this project. I have also benefited from comments from and conversations with Martha Hodes, Will Kurtz, Susan O'Donovan, Jaime Amanda Martinez, Caleb McDaniel, Sharon Ann Murphy, Ryan Quintana, Calvin Schermerhorn, and Aaron Sheehan-Dean.

A Clein Family Fellowship and a Raymond J. Faherty Award from UNC's History Department enabled early research for this project, as did a Dissertation Completion Fellowship from the UNC Graduate School. Additional support came from an Archie K. Davis Fellowship from the North Caroliniana Society, a William and Madeline Smith Research Travel Award from the University of Texas's Dolph Briscoe Center for American History, a Mellon Research Fellowship from the Virginia Museum of History and Culture, a Summer Research Grant from UNC's Center for the Study of the American South, a Library Fellowship from the John L. Nau III Center for Civil War History at the University of Virginia, and a Short-Term Fellowship from the Rose Library at Emory University. Brian and Paige Hrubik, Rick and Shannon Campanelli, Adam Domby, Rob Jefferson, Dave McWhorter, Chris

Rohde, and Cortlandt Schoonover welcomed me into their homes on my research travels.

A project as archivally fragmented as this one would have been impossible without constant assistance from archivists and librarians—a reality brought home during the COVID-19 pandemic. Matt Turi in the Southern Historical Collection and Jason Tomberlin in the North Carolina Collection went above and beyond in sharing materials and pointing me in productive directions. The staff of CNU's Trible Library did yeoman's work to make materials available in the heart of the pandemic. John McClure and the research team at the VMHC as well as the staffs of the Briscoe Center, Albert and Shirley Small Special Collections Library, and Rose Library graciously hosted extended research visits. I am also grateful to the many archivists who digitized materials I could not access in person.

Oxford University Press has provided an excellent home for this book, thanks in no small part to the editorial precision of Susan Ferber. I am grateful for her close reading and careful refinement of the argumentation and prose of this book, and for her deft guidance through the publication process. Robert Gudmestad and an anonymous reader for OUP offered trenchant comments that broke new paths in my thought and offered clear direction in rethinking the work. Thank you as well to Gabe Moss for creating the maps that illuminate the following pages. Elements of Chapter 4 appeared in the *Journal of the Civil War Era* and are reproduced in part with the permission of the University of North Carolina Press.

Above all, I share this volume with my family. My siblings, Douglas, Shelby, Brian, and Paige, have been fonts of encouragement and companionship. My father- and mother-in-law, Mark and Carol Hrubik, have unceasingly backed this book and have contributed quietly to it in ways too numerous to count. Their love has meant more to me than I can say. My parents, Bob and Kim Colby, have loved me in every way imaginable. They have given me my passion for the past, my education, and as firm a foundation as anyone could desire. I hope this makes them proud. This project predates all my children but is infinitely less beloved and delightful. Jane, Daniel, Margaret, and Adam are the joys of my life. There is, moreover, one person who has lived as long and as closely with this book as I have. It, therefore, belongs to Erin as thoroughly as it does to me. She has endured multiple moves and suffered the precarity of academic life without complaint or doubt. I could not have written a sentence without her abiding faith, hope, and love. She is my companion and my best friend. I owe it all to her.

Introduction

On the afternoon of April 2, 1865, fifty bedraggled men, women, and children stumbled out of cells in Robert Lumpkin's Richmond, Virginia slave jail. Congregating in the prison yard, they furtively pooled their observations regarding the great events unfolding around them. For while their confinement obscured their vantage, something was clearly afoot. Over and above the normal hubbub of a city swollen by Confederate bureaucrats, military officials, and refugees, a new and growing tumult sounded. Wagons rumbled. Locomotives whistled. Tramping feet and frantic shouting suggested that Richmond's entire populace had taken to the streets. Atop the noxious atmosphere of Lumpkin's creek bottom jail, notorious within Virginia's Black community as "the Devil's Half Acre," hung an acrid smoke tinged with niter, ammonia, and (ever so faintly) alcohol.

As the enslaved eagerly discussed the meaning of these portents, Lumpkin threw open the gate leading from his jail onto Wall Street, an alley running through Shockoe Bottom toward the landings, warehouses, and depots on the James River. Like its New York City counterpart, Richmond's Wall Street housed an array of speculators. Its traders, however, dealt in people rather than in stocks and bonds. Slave traders' offices and auction rooms lined the street, interspersed with those of the doctors, lawyers, and merchants who catered to them. Hotels grand and seedy housed their clientele, while jails like Lumpkin's confined the people in whom buyers and sellers came to transact. The business enslavers conducted there was so robust that even nonslaveholders watched the city's slave market for insight into the broader cotton economy. For as one observer had noted only a few years earlier, "there is no slave market in the country—and probably not in the world—where the business is carried on so briskly as in Richmond."[1]

The names and backgrounds of the men and women assembled in Lumpkin's yard that day are lost to history, though enslavers' descriptions of others they hoped to confine there offer some clues. They included men like Lewis, a burly twenty-four-year-old who, a few weeks earlier, an enslaver had sold to Greensboro, North Carolina. Lewis promptly fled, at which point his enslaver enlisted Lumpkin's aid in recapturing and jailing him. Others resembled Jane, whose enslaver hoped to imprison her after she vanished into the overcrowded capital. The packed facility probably also held Black Union soldiers like Charles Dice, men captured in the battles for Richmond and exposed to sale by a Confederate state that denied their claims to freedom and manhood.[2] Whatever their backgrounds, all those held in the Devil's Half Acre were people rendered into property, incarcerated on an enslaver's whim (whether that enslaver be a private individual or the slaveholding state), and made available for purchase and sale.

If any slave merchants cried their human wares that afternoon, however, the collective roar of what one witness labeled "thousands of the half-starved and half-clad people of Richmond" drowned them out. Only a few hours earlier, General Robert E. Lee had informed Confederate authorities that US advances would soon force him to evacuate the defenses ringing nearby Petersburg, leaving the Rebel capital defenseless. In response, panicked officials began evacuating gold, government records, and other valuables from Richmond, barreling from their offices around the Capitol down Shockoe Hill to the railroad depots at its foot. Detachments of soldiers set arsenals, munitions, factories, stores of food and drink—anything the invaders might desire—aflame. As word of the coming surrender coursed through the city, civilians thronged the streets seeking sustenance and plunder amid the wreck of the Confederacy.[3]

Into this melee stepped the denizens of Lumpkin's jail, bound not for liberty but for continued captivity. Up Wall Street Lumpkin drove them, the chains on their legs and shackles on their wrists impeding their ability to dodge the men and horses careening through the streets and preventing them from melting away into the churning crowds. Their destination, the depot of the Richmond & Danville Railroad, stood a few hundred yards to the south. The railroad offered Lumpkin a lifeline, a means of retaining the enslaved in bondage and preserving the value stored in their persons. Upon arriving, his captives watched with trepidation as Lumpkin wheedled railroad officials for space on a departing train. If they denied him, advancing US forces soon would liberate the bondspeople. If he prevailed, they would hurtle southward behind the cover of Lee's retreating forces to ongoing enslavement in the surviving Confederacy. They would be carried far from family and friends and, very likely, would be sold in unfamiliar places. They would remain, in short, property, to be disposed of as Lumpkin and subsequent purchasers desired.[4]

After a furious but brief debate, the train's operators denied Lumpkin's request. Overburdened with government traffic, they could spare nothing for a slave trader's private needs.[5] Lumpkin led the coffle back to the Devil's Half Acre, the jailer deflated, his captives brimming with excitement. Another night of terror still lay between them and freedom as fires sparked by retreating Rebels and fanned by a brisk wind swept within blocks of the slave trading district. Lumpkin and several of his slave-dealing neighbors fled before the conflagration, throwing open the doors to their jails and disappearing into the night. The next day, Union forces marched through the drifting ashes to claim the city. Led by a contingent of United States Colored Troops (USCTs), they liberated the inhabitants of jails like Lumpkin's, sending multitudes—thousands, in USCT chaplain Garland White's telling—"out shouting and praising God and father or master Abe, as they termed him" and embracing the freedom dawning (as a Black journalist put it) like "a pleasant dream."[6]

One could hardly imagine a more evocative encapsulation of the changes wrought by the Civil War than the sputtering failure of what contemporary writer Charles Carleton Coffin termed "the last slave-coffle of the Confederacy, the last vestige of its corner-stone." Both Coffin's contemporaries and subsequent students of the conflict embraced this symbolism. White, who had himself been sold through Richmond before the Civil War, was "overcome with tears," and "could not stand up under the pressure of such fulness of joy in my own heart," not least after he and his mother reunited amid the city's ruins. Generations of historians have similarly celebrated this moment, making Lumpkin's efforts emblematic of the liberation enslaved people achieved during the Civil War.[7]

When Lumpkin sought to salvage the dozens of enslaved people held in his facility, however, he had no intention of their being either his or the Confederate States of America (CSA)'s last coffle, much less a harbinger of slavery's demise. Rather, he hoped to preserve his chunk of the Confederacy's cornerstone, to continue chaining and selling people, and was foiled only when the new birth of freedom at last overtook slave capitalism. This last-ditch effort at human trafficking was the logical outcome of a life, a society, and a proto-nation defined by slavery. Nearly sixty in 1865, Robert Lumpkin had dedicated his adult years to the business of slavery. He entered the trade in the mid-1830s and for more than a decade personally carried and shipped people from Virginia to the Deep South. In 1841, forty-three of the captives who seized the slave ship *Creole* had been consigned to the

Figure I.1 Richmond, Virginia, April 1865, looking westward. Robert Lumpkin's jail is visible just left of center. Library of Congress, LC-DIG-ppmsca-08222.

vessel by Lumpkin, while a less remarkable 1849 venture profited him $3,370 on the sale of twenty-eight men, women, and children. By the late 1840s, Lumpkin had largely transitioned from personally buying and selling people to facilitating others' slave dealing as a middleman in the wider world of slave commerce. His Shockoe Bottom complex became a major locus of Richmond's burgeoning traffic in humanity, a place where buyers and sellers met and haggled over human property, where enslavers incarcerated fugitives from bondage and people awaiting sale, where traders lodged before moving south, and where terrified enslaved men and women awaited their fates.[8]

All this left Lumpkin, in one observer's words, a " 'good natured fat man, professional-looking,' always 'neatly dressed and swinging a slender gold-headed cane.' " By the 1850s he resembled, said another, nothing so much as a "prosperous physician," flaunting the respectability slave dealing provided.[9] Lumpkin acquired more than wealth and status through his work. Among the enslaved people who passed through his gates was a woman named Mary, whom Lumpkin bought at some point in the 1830s. In the ensuing decades, she became his sexual partner, the mother of his five children, and,

Figure I.2 Lumpkin's jail, as depicted in Charles H. Corey, *Richmond Theological Seminary, With Reminiscences of Thirty Years' Work Among the Colored People of the South* (Richmond, VA: J. W. Randolph Company, 1895), 47. Albert and Shirley Small Special Collections Library, University of Virginia.

ultimately, the heir to the portion of his slave trading fortune that survived the war.[10] Lumpkin had built an entire world—wealth, position, and family—on commerce in humanity. Small wonder, then, that he joined hundreds of thousands of Confederates in doing all they could to prevent the advent of a world without it.

Robert Lumpkin's career traced the apex of two and a half centuries of American slave trafficking. From the outset of colonization, settlers in British North America sold hundreds of thousands of people imported from Africa or the Caribbean in Atlantic seaports.[11] By the time of the American Revolution, a rudimentary internal slave trade supplemented the trans-Atlantic trade, allowing enslavers and traders to disseminate imported men and women into the backcountry.[12] This internal slave trade boomed in the independent American republic. Treaty and conquest opened Native lands in the trans-Appalachian Southwest to American settlers at the very moment that Congress shuttered US ports to the Atlantic slave trade and limited the available supply of enslaved laborers to those already in the country. Still more critically, cotton—a crop ideally suited to the soil and climate of the American South—simultaneously emerged as the world's premier industrial input.[13]

Surging global demand for cotton sent American enslavers into a mad scramble for lands and for laborers to work them. Members of wealthy slaveholding families sometimes migrated—first to South Carolina and Georgia, then Alabama, Mississippi, Louisiana, and, eventually, Arkansas and Texas—with portions of their existing workforces in tow. Increasingly, however, enslaved people moved south and west in the hands of a growing class of professional slave traders, who sought the profits lodged in the margins between the prices available for people in the Upper South and in the Cotton Kingdom. As the years passed, these traders developed intricate business partnerships, improved their access to American and Atlantic financial networks, and exploited the nation's expanding transportation and communication infrastructure to deal ever more people ever more efficiently.[14]

Between the Revolution and the Civil War, enslavers sold more than half a million people to traders who carried them from the Upper South to the Lower South. These sales devastated enslaved lives and communities, breaking up perhaps one in every three enslaved marriages and removing a parent from a similar proportion of enslaved households.[15] The slave trade, moreover, ensnared far more people than those who endured the long journey south. For every person who made the trek to the Cotton Kingdom in the company of a slave trader, enslavers sold at least one more within a city, county, or state.[16] Though the demographic and economic effects of these local sales register less clearly in the documentary record of slavery than do those of their long-distance cousins, they nevertheless rippled through enslaved people's lives. Sale even at a few miles' distance profoundly disrupted families and communities and injected hardship and uncertainty into their experiences. Thus, while the slave trade conjures images of coffles tramping steadily southward, the scope and influence of what we might term slave commerce—the sale, purchase, and exchange of people, both interregionally and locally—had significantly broader effects.

By the end of the antebellum period, the influence of this commerce in the enslaved not only defined the institution of slavery but engaged virtually all denizens of the American South. By permitting enslavers to commodify and transfer laborers, it rejuvenated slavery in the United States and made cotton one of the nation's premier economic outputs. Its existence implicitly and explicitly created enormous wealth for enslavers. Not only did individual slaveholders and slave dealers sell thousands of people in return for millions of dollars annually, but the mere possibility of sale imbued each and every enslaved person with a price, a dollar figure derived from the estimated value he or she might produce through his or her labor and the birth of new generations of bonded workers.[17] By 1860, enslavers valued the four million men, women, and children they held captive at a combined $3 billion. This staggering sum, which surpassed the total value of the nation's railroads, the capital held in its banks, and its growing industries, swelled as enslavers recirculated it as slave-backed loans, mortgages, and securities.[18] While slave ownership grew increasingly concentrated in the hands of the wealthiest Southerners as the 1800s passed, as much as 30 percent of the South's white population remained directly invested in economic gains realized from slavery, with the remainder deriving nonmonetary advantages from the less tangible privileges of race-based enslavement. Slave commerce thus offered something to all white Southerners, whether or not they ever actually set foot in a slave market. Bondspeople fought constantly to nullify this commerce's effects, manipulating their sales to avoid brutal enslavers, keep families intact, and sometimes to negate them entirely. Nevertheless, the power of purchase and sale fueled slavery's vitality and strengthened enslavers' political and psychological hold over the South.[19]

Historians of American slavery long downplayed the domestic slave trade's influence on the trajectory of the institution of slavery. Some considered it predominantly a figment of the abolitionist imagination, others a tragic but ultimately ancillary aspect of American bondage.[20] Over the last three decades, however, historians have demonstrated slave commerce's centrality to the institution. They have broken new ground on its scope, scale, and significance and placed it at the heart of the economic, cultural, and political landscape of the American South. They have revealed the trade's impact on the emergence of American capitalism, the deeply gendered nature of its operations, and its shattering effects on enslaved communities.[21] As historian Walter Johnson, writing in the vanguard of these studies, argued, "The history of the antebellum South is the history of two million slave sales"; if anything, recent examinations of slave commerce and its myriad penumbra have only broadened the scope of that assertion.[22]

A significant subset of these sales, however, have long gone all but unnoticed: those that occurred during the Civil War.[23] Scholars have overlooked them for reasons both epistemological and evidentiary. Recent histories of the trade in the enslaved have focused heavily on its role in the emergence of cotton capitalism. Given that the South's staple crop economy collapsed at the beginning of the war, Fort Sumter becomes a natural endpoint for scholars of slavery, cotton, and capitalism, with any wartime trafficking in people seemingly an addendum to a story already told. For historians of slavery and emancipation, meanwhile, the fact that African Americans continued to face the threat of sale amid the conflict troubles historical narratives that once emphasized the inexorable advance of freedom. Civil War historians, for their part, have focused alternately on the arc of campaigns and battles, wartime politics, the trials of life on the homefront and the conflicts stemming therefrom, and emancipation writ large. Glimpses of the slave trade appear in many of these studies, but the fragmentary nature of the evidence means that it predominates in none.

A close look at almost any cache of sources from the conflict, however, clearly reveals a vigorous, ongoing trade in enslaved people. African Americans subjected to the trade relayed their experiences of sale to Union soldiers, government officials, and newspaper correspondents. Confederate soldiers and civilians debated the merits of acquiring or disposing of people as the market fluctuated and the war reshaped their lives. Periodicals scrutinized the state of the market in humanity and guessed at what its activity augured for the course of the conflict. In an offhand reference here or a vignette there, the slave trade appears in thousands of moments buried in hundreds of archives and reams of documents. Individually, they can easily be overlooked. Once one begins to see them, however, they are impossible to ignore.

The mosaic cohering from these fragments shows that from Fort Sumter to (and in some cases beyond) Appomattox enslavers bought and sold thousands of men, women, and children. How many people, precisely, suffered this fate during the Civil War is impossible to know for certain. Historians have traditionally relied on several sources to estimate the numbers of people subjected to the slave trade. These include demographic data drawn from census records, manifests detailing the shipment of enslaved people along the coasts, notarial and conveyance records from New Orleans recording the transfer of enslaved property, and accounts left by individual traders. Even when available, however, these sources permit only a rough assessment of the numbers of people bought and sold, unless confined to a very specific area.[24]

For a period as cataclysmic as the Civil War, however, these records are either absent or inapplicable. Not only did the 1870 census undercount the Black population as a whole, but it occurred after a period of unprecedented African American movement. As one Tennessee official of the Bureau of Refugees, Freedmen, and Abandoned Lands (better known as the Freedmen's Bureau) noted, "the colored population" of his region "ha[d] increased somewhat since the war," partially due to the fact that "many of those who had been sold south before" and during "the war, have since returned to their relatives and friends."[25] Taken alongside the high level of noncommercial movement the war initiated, using the census to estimate the number of people moved via the wartime slave trade is impossible, especially at five years' remove from the conflict's end.[26] Secession and the Union blockade of the CSA eliminated the coastwise traffic and the resulting need for manifests, while the slave trade all but ceased a year into the war in New Orleans, home to the most fastidiously kept records documenting human property. No traders' records survive that span more than half the conflict. The research on which this book rests uncovered formal documentation—bills of sale, receipts, conveyance records, and account books—detailing more than two thousand transactions in enslaved people. Anecdotal evidence, however, indicates that this is only the tip of the iceberg (one Mississippian claimed that he alone bought and sold hundreds of people "even to the surrender"). Civil War enslavers almost certainly bought and sold several thousand people. No more precise figure can be given.[27]

Looking beyond the numbers of people sold and scrutinizing the survival of slave trafficking during the Civil War—the reasons underlying these thousands of transactions and their effects on the people bought and sold—brings together several major threads in the study of the American past that often stand apart. Specifically, it provides avenues for simultaneously exploring the entwined histories of slavery and capitalism, the ways in which Americans experienced the Civil War, and the tangled unfolding of emancipation in the United States. In recent years, scholars of slave commerce have broken new ground in the study of slavery's ties to capitalism, demonstrating the significance of commodified human beings as laborers in the expanding Cotton Kingdom, as drivers behind the industrial revolution, and as commodified abstractions in Atlantic finance.[28] But the system that Walter Johnson terms "slave-racial capitalism" required more than simply lucrative markets for slave-produced commodities for its survival. It required a state and an ideology structured around the preservation of a form of property fully capable of rising up and destroying the society constructed around it.[29] American slavery thus rested upon the twin pillars of economic profitability and active state support. Historians have focused predominantly on the former, but scrutinizing the wartime slave trade demonstrates the latter's outsized role.

As economist Karl Polanyi has argued, bolstering trade and rendering human labor commodifiable demands significant government intervention.[30] The domestic slave trade required the same, with local, state, and, to a lesser degree, national governments not only regulating slave commerce but defending enslavers' right to property in man.[31] States and localities surveilled virtually every aspect of enslaved life, including enslaved peoples' ability to assemble, read, engage in commerce, or worship. Slave patrols, sheriffs, magistrates, judges, and jails stood arrayed to ensure their subordination.[32] While the Constitution contained latent antislavery potential, it long offered enslavers significant practical protections, from the fugitive slave clause to the electoral bulwark embodied in the three-fifths clause to the Fifth Amendment's defense of property rights. For much of the nineteenth century, therefore, slaveholders found ready allies in government in retaining their human property.[33] Even though scholars of slavery have conceded the state's role in regulating trade, coercing markets, expropriating, surveying, and selling indigenous lands, and suppressing slave revolts, they do so with an emphasis on the emergence of cotton capitalism. With the Cotton Kingdom accomplished, the state fades from view and market forces assume explanatory power.[34]

A close look at the wartime slave trade recenters the essential role of the state in enabling transactions in man. Though the cotton complex collapsed during the Civil War thanks to a financial panic and Union blockade, Confederates nevertheless bought and sold thousands of people on the assumption that the Confederate state could and would perpetuate their right to hold them as property. For most of the war, in most of the Confederacy, this proved to be a sound bet. Wherever the CSA held sway, slave commerce continued. Where it lost its hold, the slave trade crumbled. US occupation could quickly neuter massive markets. But in the protected Confederacy, trading hubs flourished. Indeed, the protection of slavery, even within diminishing enclaves, rendered slave commerce a vehicle for the slaveholding state's power, a tentacle that could reach out and snatch African Americans away from the freedom that beckoned to them. Wherever the slaveholding state survived, wherever it remained able to reduce people consistently into property, it incubated slave commerce.

Many Confederates expected this state protection would ensure the revitalization of slave capitalism in the war's aftermath and used the wartime slave trade to invest accordingly. They saw the war's devastation of their staple crop economy as a temporary setback and assumed that when the Confederacy prevailed, cotton would once more be king. This made enslaved people a tempting speculation, particularly as the pressures of the war diminished the real prices sellers asked for them. Convinced that slavery would be safe for generations to come in an independent Confederacy, many zeroed in on acquiring young women and children. Their value during the war might be minimal, but their worth in an independent slaveholding republic would be immense. The survival of the slave trade during the Civil War thus demonstrates the profound hold cotton capitalism exercised on white Southerners, their anticipation that it would survive the conflict, and their reliance on state power to sustain it.

The need for a strong Confederate state and existence of a citizenry convinced of its eventual success in sustaining the slave trade bonds the study of slave capitalism with critical questions in the study of the Civil War itself. Civil War historians have long debated the strength and persistence of Confederate unity and whether it ultimately proved a help or a hindrance for the CSA. Although divisions and disillusionment emerging along lines of class, gender, and race unquestionably riddled the wartime South, the survival of a "national" traffic in enslaved people affirms the existence of a powerful and resilient nationalism that infused many Confederates until the moment of surrender.[35] Whether buoyed by a belief in the superiority of Southern civilization, the battlefield prowess of Confederate armies, or a simple inability to imagine a world without slavery, "diehard rebels" (as historian Jason Phillips terms them) maintained their faith in the survival of the Confederate nation and of the slave system it fought to preserve until the bitter end.[36] For such men and women, the domestic slave trade offered a means of buying shares in Confederate victory and the slaveholding future it would secure. The continued purchase and sale of people into the war's final days thus underscores Rebels' unflagging allegiance to their nation and to human bondage.

A close examination of the wartime slave trade also reveals the myriad ways in which slave commerce shaped the experience of the conflict for all inhabiting the Confederacy and informs our understanding of the lived realities of the conflict. The war wreaked havoc on the Confederate economic and monetary systems, sparking widespread hyperinflation.[37] Enslavers reacted by investing depreciating currency in people. The Confederacy's rapid, forced industrialization, meanwhile, relied heavily on slave commerce as a means of controlling and redistributing labor.[38] Slave commerce thus became a vehicle through which enslavers used the enslaved to construct the very state that kept them as captives. The slave trade's endurance simultaneously proved a boon for those caught flat-footed by the war's devastation. These men and women bought and sold people to buffer themselves against shortages of cash, food, and the many necessities of life made unavailable by the conflict and to mitigate rifts opening among Confederates through the bodies of those they fought to enslave. They also traded people to insulate themselves against the innumerable, often highly personalized, crises spawned by the conflict.[39] By helping both the Rebel state and individual Confederates weather the war, slave commerce abetted enslavers' pursuit of independence.

The persistence of the slave trade also profoundly influenced the process by which enslaved people sought their freedom during the Civil War. The war put enslavers under unprecedented pressure from the people they held captive and the armed emissaries of a US government hostile to slavery. They fought back through the slave trade. As they sold people away from freedom, enslavers offset the financial losses emancipation threatened to inflict upon them, frustrated captives' longings for freedom, and made terrible examples of those who tried but failed to attain it. The surviving slave trade not only provided slaveholders with a means to counter transgressions against the antebellum racial order but bound exposed Confederates to the remaining power and authority of the slaveholding state. In doing so, it injected a powerful undertow into the currents pushing many toward freedom.

The wartime slave trade was thus a critical part of emancipation's unfolding in the United States. Its endurance into the Civil War's last days undercuts straightforward narratives of freedom's unbroken progress during the war. As scholars of emancipation have shown, slavery's demise was unevenly distributed and shot through with uncertainties and pitfalls that plagued African Americans as they fought free from bondage. Even as they forced a reluctant US government to concede to them expanding degrees of liberty, they confronted abuse, neglect, starvation, and disease. They also faced reprisals from a Rebel state that vociferously denied each and every freedom claim they made.[40] The slave trade constituted a key vehicle for delivering such reprisals, abetting Confederate efforts to retain enslaved laborers and threatening to extract those who had escaped from their presumed safety.

The wartime slave trade did much to determine the attainability of freedom for the enslaved. Those closest to liberty found themselves, perversely, especially vulnerable to sale and separation from family and friends. The thousands sold away found themselves in deepened bondage, lacking even the mitigating effects of community to offset captivity's horrors.[41] The prospect of sale, however, also inspired bids for freedom. Many of those threatened with sale decided to seize their chance for liberty rather than accept the certainty of separation. Others fled following sales that deprived them of those whom they held most dear. Even though universal emancipation arrived in the immediate aftermath of these wartime sales, the separations they imposed could easily be lifelong. Decades after Appomattox, Black families continued pursuing members who had disappeared into the Civil War slave trade in hopes of healing some of the wounds it had caused.[42]

Understanding the long-term pain and trauma the wartime domestic slave trade inflicted upon African Americans is essential to ongoing reassessments of the Civil War's human costs. In recent years, scholars have not only increased estimates of the conflict's death toll but have broadened the geographical and chronological bounds of its impact by examining the environmental, epidemiological, and psychological effects it had upon participants for decades thereafter.[43] Brian Matthew Jordan argues in the context of combat veterans that the war's "human longitude"—the lingering aftershocks of the conflict in individuals' lives—meant that "an hour in the Civil War could . . . last fifty years" or more.[44] This was as true for enslaved people as it was for soldiers, especially when wartime ordeals built upon years of oppression. The freedom that ultimately emerged from the conflict existed alongside and was shaped by the redounding impact of wartime slave sales. In the vein of historian Nell Irvin Painter's call for movement toward a "fully loaded cost accounting" of slavery's effects, an examination of the wartime slave trade shows that that balance must include the psychological craters the institution left on the wartime and postbellum lives of those formerly held in bondage.[45]

In exhuming the Civil War slave trade, this study necessarily relies on enslavers' correspondence, diaries, and accounts, as well as on communications by Union soldiers, US and Confederate governmental records, and the documents slave traders themselves produced. Recovering the story of Civil

War slave commerce from the vantage point of those who were themselves bought and sold (or who lost loved ones to the traffic), however, requires an expanded source base. Their voices appear in their own published accounts, newspaper interviews, correspondence with Freedmen's Bureau agents, advertisements in postwar periodicals, and even, on occasion, notes embedded within enslavers' correspondence. The voices of people once enslaved can also be heard in interviews conducted by agents of the Works Progress Administration in the late 1930s. While scholars continue to debate their overall reliability (and the power dynamics reflected in their production), many historians have accepted these interviews as essential windows into enslaved life. This study does the same, but with the caveat that it exclusively relies on recollections the interviewees affirmatively placed in the war years.[46]

The story of the domestic slave trade during the Civil War necessarily begins in the years leading up to that conflict. In the late antebellum period, enslavers and slave traders constructed an intricate traffic in enslaved people that incorporated advances in the nation's transportation, communication, and financial networks. Their success expanded the scale and scope of American slave commerce, but also overinflated the prices placed on the enslaved. The 1850s also saw increased contention over the protections the national government owed enslavers—including the legitimacy of the internal slave trade. These tensions came to a head with the election of Abraham Lincoln. The ensuing secession of many slaveholding states severely inhibited the trade in humanity—though it did so less because nascent Confederates feared for slavery's future than because the resulting financial panic punctured the bubble in slave prices and reduced enslavers' ability to traffic in humanity.

Subsequent chapters explore the evolution of the slave trade during the war itself. With secession accomplished, the trade in enslaved people stabilized, albeit at levels below its antebellum peak. Where the Confederacy could protect it, slave commerce continued. But from the war's outset and with particular alacrity in the spring and summer of 1862, the United States conquered and occupied many of the CSA's largest slave trading hubs: Alexandria, Norfolk, Memphis, Nashville, Natchez, and, above all, New Orleans. While slavery remained formally legal in many of these cities, enslaved people's contestation of their bondage and US forces' growing unwillingness to maintain people as property gradually made enslaved people too risky an investment and all but erased the trade in these markets, demonstrating the key role of state power in preserving the slave trade.

In the Confederate interior, however, the story was entirely different. Charleston, Savannah, Atlanta, and especially Richmond offer a potent counternarrative to the experiences of US-occupied cities. While Union successes reduced Confederates' willingness to buy and sell people, the CSA's resurgence in the summer of 1862 drove a revived traffic in humanity. In sheltered cities, Confederates bought and sold people as investments in a cotton economy they hoped would soon thrive again, as hedges against inflation, and to meet the needs created by the war. The latter factor particularly drove robust localized demand as Confederates offloaded the crises of the conflict onto the shoulders of those whom they fought to keep enslaved. As the war ground on in late 1863 and early 1864, Confederates continued trading to maintain the state on a war footing, to offset shortfalls in food and other goods, to settle debts, to raise cash, and to fill the spreading cracks along lines of class and gender.

From the war's first days to its last, the threat of enslaved flight drove innumerable transactions in humanity. The final chapters explore these transactions, trace the slave trade at the close of the war, and uncover its effects in the conflict's aftermath. As enslaved people seized the chances the war presented and pressed the boundaries of their captivity, slaveholders sold them in droves to prevent their attaining freedom. These sales continued up until Appomattox and attached a high cost to the bids for liberty enslaved people continually made. The net effect of the thousands of sales undertaken during the conflict did much to shape African Americans' conceptions and experiences of freedom after the Civil War's conclusion. For many, the end of commodification and sale—an experience to which they and their loved ones had been subjected during the conflict—defined the results of the war. Freedom might be laggard in other areas, but the end of the slave trade was a sea change in and of itself. As they fought for broadened freedoms, the legacies of the slave trade shaped their actions and provided a powerful rhetorical weapon for the battles in which they engaged.

Robert Lumpkin's effort to smuggle fifty enslaved people out of falling Richmond was, in many ways, the Civil War in microcosm. It reflected a generations-deep investment in human chattel slavery and an inability to comprehend a world shorn of that institution. It demonstrated an overwhelming desire to retain Black people as property and to profit from them without regard to the costs this inflicted on their bodies, psyches, and communities. It defied emancipation's unfolding and displayed a desperate faith in the power of the Confederate state to preserve a world in which humans were commodities. For decades, the slave trade has served as the incisive vehicle for understanding the peculiar institution and the society and economy constructed upon it. Focusing on this commerce in the crucible of war reveals the lengths to which those invested in slavery would go to defend it and demonstrates the sacrifices and endurance required to escape from it.

1

"No Money, and No Confidence"

Slave Trading, Secession, and the Panic of 1860

As a sultry North Carolina day faded into night in June 1860, Ned extinguished the lights of the Hermitage, the house in which he had labored for most of his twenty-one years. As on most evenings, he passed through the great hall and slipped out the back door. But that night, Ned did not return to the Hermitage's slave quarters. Instead, skirting the outbuildings flanking the house, he struck out for freedom. Perhaps he stowed himself aboard a train on the North Carolina Railroad as it passed through nearby Graham. Perhaps he crept through the longleaf pine forests that blanketed Alamance County. Regardless of how he traveled, within three days he had arrived on the outskirts of Raleigh, the state capital. Ned now faced a difficult choice. Should he sneak onto a train heading north, the fastest route to freedom? Should he make for the coast and seek help from the state's Black maritime communities? Or should he cloak himself in the anonymity offered by Raleigh's mixed slave and free Black workforce?[1]

Ultimately, the choice would not be his. A farmer discovered Ned hiding on his property, jailed him, and sought further instructions from Ned's enslaver, the eminent jurist Thomas Ruffin.[2] Already sclerotic, the seventy-two-year-old Ruffin fumed over Ned's flight. Amid the acclaim he had won for his legal mind and decades of service on North Carolina's Supreme Court, Ruffin had also earned notoriety for upholding slaveholders' absolute authority over their human chattels. Unsurprisingly, the man who had once declaimed from the bench that "the power of the master must be absolute to render the submission of the slave perfect" ruled his own enslaved workforce with (in the words of one scholar) "fear and the lash" and reacted harshly to the escape of one of his own.[3] Deciding that Ned's flight threatened his broader slaveholding interests, Ruffin determined to sell him. If all Ruffin sought from Ned's sale were profits, he could have turned to Raleigh's modest slave market, minimizing the time and costs associated with the transaction. A local slave trader, however, warned him that doing so might permit Ned to remain in North Carolina. To ensure that Ned served as an example to the others he enslaved, Ruffin turned to Richmond's Dickinson, Hill & Co., one of the largest slaving firms in one of the South's biggest slave markets, believing they would surely sell Ned in "a <u>distant</u> market."[4]

Thus, less than two weeks after fleeing the Hermitage, Ned boarded a northbound train bound not for freedom but to the destination enslaved people feared most: the slave market. And while he sold Ned primarily for spite, Ruffin hardly could have chosen a more remunerative moment in which to do so. In the summer of 1860, the prices offered in American slave markets peaked after a decade-long ascent.[5] Just before Ned's arrival, Dickinson, Hill & Co. informed their trading partners that it was "a very good time" to send in enslaved people for sale. Prices for the men whom the firm categorized as "No. 1 negroes"—the agricultural laborers whom enslavers could exploit most profitably—had soared past $1,500, and the firm assured sellers like Ruffin that they could obtain the "highest market prices."[6]

When Ned arrived in Richmond, a porter—possibly an enslaved man like himself—extracted him from the multitude that flowed daily to the city's slave markets and escorted him through the offices, auction rooms, and private prisons clustered in Shockoe Bottom to Dickinson, Hill & Co.'s jail.[7] There, their operatives dressed Ned in new clothes and fed him substantially if not nutritiously before inviting prospective buyers to examine him. Among the clients thronging the firm's auction space, which one observer described as a "long, damp, dirty-looking room . . . profusely decorated with tobacco stains," the firm found a buyer.[8] Perhaps due to scarring from a childhood disease, perhaps because of his known penchant for flight, or perhaps because he actively undermined the efforts to sell him, Ned brought only $855, a relatively low price for a man of his age. For that sum, Dickinson, Hill & Co. fulfilled their promise to Ruffin, dispatching Ned into parts unknown and placing the proceeds—less their 2.5 percent commission and the costs of Ned's confinement—at the Bank of Virginia to Ruffin's account.[9]

Much of this process would have been quite familiar to Thomas Ruffin. In the 1820s, even as he climbed North Carolina's legal ladder, he partnered with a slave trader named Benjamin Chambers to buy people in North Carolina and sell them in South Carolina and Georgia.[10] Chambers daily enacted the triumph of property rights in man over enslaved people's natural rights while Ruffin gave them legal sanction, overriding from the bench localized legal practices that sometimes offered enslaved people protection from their captors.[11] Ruffin thus flexed the authority of an American state arrayed in

Figure 1.1 "Old Slave Market." Dickinson, Hill & Co. occupied this facility in the 1850s and 1860s. Virginia Museum of History & Culture (2002.301.55).

support of slavery, from the land offices that converted Native territory into cotton fields to the slave patrols, militias, and federal agents that enforced pro-slavery legal codes.

If Ned's sale resembled uncounted others that Ruffin had either participated in personally or enabled from the bench, it also augured changes on the horizon. Ruffin believed that Ned had fled under the "seduction of a white man from a Northwestern state" who had convinced him that "he was escaping to a free state."[12] Neither Ruffin nor Ned said any more on the subject, leaving the identity—or actual existence—of this shadowy figure ambiguous.[13] The man in question could have been a passing traveler. He also could have been a figment of Ruffin's imagination, an archetypal "Yankee peddler" injected into this drama.[14] It is possible, however, that when Ruffin alluded to this man, he was obliquely referencing contemporary politics. Even as he wrote, Abraham Lincoln, a son of the Old Northwest, accepted the antislavery Republican Party's nomination for the presidency. Thousands of men and women like Ned had watched Lincoln's rise avidly; Booker T. Washington remembered awakening in the night to his mother's fervent prayers for Lincoln, for, he recalled, even "the slaves on our far-off plantation, miles from any railroad or large city or daily newspaper, knew what the issues involved were" in the brewing conflict between the slaveholding and non-slaveholding states.[15]

Ned's flight thus lay simultaneously at the intersection of escalating political tensions and the enduring struggle between enslaver and enslaved. As Ned looked to a man like Lincoln—perhaps to Lincoln himself—for aid, Ruffin's slaveholding compatriots watched with trepidation the Railsplitter's march toward Washington. Fearing what such a man might do given the powers of the presidency, they laid plans to break away from the United States and form an independent slaveholding republic. Such an entity, they hoped, would enable them to preserve a world built on slavery. One in which men like Ruffin could freely exercise dominion over people like Ned. One rooted in the commodification and sale of the enslaved. One that their best laid plans would eventually hasten to its downfall.

If Ned rejoiced and Ruffin fretted at the idea that the slave system might be under threat, the operators of Dickinson, Hill & Co. could be forgiven for doubting such a crisis existed at all. That summer, Richard H. Dickinson and his partners, brothers Nathaniel B. and Charles B. Hill, stood at the pinnacle of a business that had seldom showed so much promise. The trials of the sectional crisis swirled around them—congressional battles over slavery's westward expansion, violence in Kansas, the Supreme Court's controversial *Dred Scott* ruling—but thus far, the nation had weathered them just as it had previous conflicts over slavery. Indeed, if the slave market was any indication, these crises were ephemeral. None of them had diminished the prices offered for enslaved people in the slightest.[16] For Dickinson, Hill & Co., the troubled 1850s had proved a bonanza. In 1856, rumors circulated that the firm had sold enslaved people worth a whopping $2 million; by 1860, their revenues put it in a tax bracket by themselves, though competitors like Hector Davis were not far behind.[17]

The slave trade in which Dickinson, the Hills, and Davis engaged had evolved considerably across the nineteenth century. At its core, it rested on the continuing reality that white Southerners could assign prices to African Americans, acquire them in one place, and sell them in another for a higher figure. The intermediary steps through which they did so had, however, changed in subtle but significant ways. In the decades between the Revolution and the Civil War, the slave trade evolved from an intermittent, ad hoc means of redistributing enslaved people imported from Africa to a regular, coherent business and a pillar of the American economy. Slave traders refined their business practices, escalating their activities to meet surging demand, taking advantage of the increased availability of financing, and co-opting improvements in transportation and communication infrastructure to modernize their trading and maximize the returns they received for Black bodies.

Nothing reshaped the slave trade more dramatically than the cotton revolution that swept the Atlantic world beginning in the 1790s. Cotton occupied a central place in burgeoning textile industries, themselves critical parts of the unfolding industrial revolution. With mills from Massachusetts to Manchester clamoring for fibers and finding themselves possessed of a climate and soil uniquely suited to its cultivation, Southern slavers soon found cotton (as one traveler noted) "infinitely more lucrative than" anything else they could produce. Better processing technology, including the cotton gin, and repeated confiscations of Native lands fueled a boom in American cotton production.[18] Between 1794 and 1798, US cotton outputs doubled; within six years, they octupled again. In 1819, 48,000 bales left New Orleans, the nation's leading cotton port. A decade later, fully 426,000 cleared the Mississippi's mouth, a figure that continued to climb across ensuing decades.[19]

Demand for cotton paced demand for enslaved laborers and spawned a robust trade in people. As Mississippi Territorial Governor William Claiborne reported in 1801, "the culture of Cotton is so lucrative that Common Negro Fellows will generally Command five hundred dollars per head," at which price, he anticipated, the region's slave markets would soon be "overrun."[20] To fulfill this prophecy, South Carolinians briefly and brutally reignited the Atlantic slave trade, but in 1808, an alliance of New Englanders and Upper South representatives banned this traffic (the latter fully cognizant their states would thereby attain a domestic monopoly on enslaved laborers).[21] An internal slave trade arose to take its place. Before long, an identifiable class of domestic slave dealers emerged in cities like New Orleans, while other traders prowled the Upper South for people to sell.[22] Their victims understood the reasons for their sale clearly. Maryland's Charles Ball, who also lost his mother and father to traders, knew that "prime hands" like him were in "high demand" because "cotton . . . had not been higher for many years."[23] Lucinda Key, meanwhile, mourned the sale of her children to "slave traders to the Cotton States."[24] Such brokers did unrelenting damage to enslaved communities. As Frederick Douglass remembered, in his native Maryland, "scarcely a month passed without the sale to the Georgia traders, of one or more lots" of human property.[25]

Typical of such men was James Mitchell, who departed Virginia's Southside in the fall of 1834 with thirty-one people in tow. Stopping periodically to purchase the bacon and other supplies required to keep the coffle moving forward, they transited the Blue Ridge Mountains, crossed the New and Clinch Rivers, and marched through central Tennessee—a harsh journey, as evidenced by Mitchell's regular payments to doctors to protect his human investments. The new year found the sorry procession in Mississippi. There, Mitchell's purchases pivoted from meat and meal to clothes, hats, and whiskey, goods designed to show his human chattels to their best advantage and to ply potential buyers. His efforts paid off. Within two weeks, he had sold every person he had brought south and, eighteen thousand dollars richer, he bought a horse and set out for Virginia to begin the process again.[26]

On his return journey, he might well have seen evidence of a revolution taking place in his line of business. Not long after Mitchell's coffle crossed the New River, an English traveler found encamped on its banks a group of Mississippi-bound captives fully ten times its size, the human property of John Armfield.[27] A decade earlier, Armfield's trading had been indistinguishable from Mitchell's. It changed when, in the late 1820s, he partnered with Isaac Franklin and formed an eponymous firm that would transform the business of slavery.[28] Franklin & Armfield debuted at an auspicious moment for American slavers. The 1830s saw cotton prices soar to the highest levels yet, even as Indian removal opened new lands and Andrew Jackson's bank war flooded the country with easy money. Amid this free-for-all Franklin and Armfield systematized their slave trading, imposing economies of scale on the traffic and using their close ties to financial institutions (up to and including the Second Bank of the United States) to bankroll a network of itinerant traders that swarmed the Upper South. These agents purchased hundreds of people annually. Armfield gathered them in his Alexandria, Virginia jail and dispatched them either overland to Natchez or by sea to New Orleans in one of the firm's custom-built slaving vessels. Franklin then sold these people to the cotton and sugar planters who thronged their slave markets and sent cash northward to fund renewed purchases.[29]

Franklin & Armfield's success attracted competitors and imitators, expanding the scale and scope of the American slave trade and spawning subsequent generations of slave merchants. Among those drawn by the profits they exhibited were Robert Lumpkin, Silas Omohundro, and a young Richard

H. Dickinson.[30] The scion of a modestly prominent Virginia family (his father served as a state legislator in the 1830s), Dickinson came to Richmond early in that decade. He threw himself into slave commerce, working as an agent for Henry N. Templeman, a rival of Franklin & Armfield's Richmond partner, Rice Ballard, before striking out on his own. By 1838, Dickinson embodied the contradictions of the young American republic, publicly toasting "the 4th of July '76" and prophesying, "may the tree of Liberty that was then planted flourish until it shades the world" just before he advised Virginia's governor on how best to sell enslaved convicts from the state penitentiary.[31]

Though the Panic of 1837 diminished both cotton prices and the demand for enslaved laborers and forced Dickinson and his peers to diversify their businesses, rising prices in the 1840s drew new participants into human trafficking.[32] Hector Davis succeeded Dickinson as Templeman's associate, while Nathaniel and Charles Hill arrived from King William County and established themselves in the business. Self-inflicted problems initially troubled the Hills. In 1845, a credit reporter labeled Nathaniel a man of "habits wild," "small means," and, eventually, a "failed auctioneer." He and Charles were "Not known to have prop[erty]," nor were they "of the choicest char[acter]"—a fact exemplified by their willingness to "sell neg[roe]s sometimes." Nathaniel's timely marriage to a fellow slave dealer's wealthy widow rescued the brothers, leaving them, by the early 1850s, "well off." Wealth swiftly obscured their earlier disreputability. Nathaniel ascended in the city's Democratic circles, winning election to the city council and to several civic and corporate boards, while Charles served as a justice of the peace.[33]

In the 1850s, the gravity of the Cotton Kingdom still drew thousands of men, women, and children south each year, but it did so through a slave trade undergoing yet another set of subtle transformations. These included shifts in the business practices of the large auction houses. High demand created competition among dealers. A Pennsylvanian who visited Richmond's slave market around that time counted between fifty and one hundred traders at a single auction, one of at least six he attended during a mere three days in the city. A Virginian put things more bluntly. Writing in late 1853, he marveled that Richmond was "full of niggers," such that the city's array of brokers were "selling them at wholesale." Traders thus worked to streamline their businesses. Prior to 1854 the Hills had competed with Dickinson, often holding rival auctions from their respective corners on Franklin Street. That December, however, they merged their resources and created Dickinson, Hill & Co. They also adopted new trading practices. Like Franklin & Armfield,

Dickinson, Hill & Co. and their ilk both bought and sold people directly and maintained networks of smaller-scale traders who purchased on their behalf. Unlike their predecessor, however, the newer firms also operated as commission merchants, taking custody of people owned by others (as in the case of Ned), selling them, and pocketing 2 to 3 percent commission and expenses before passing on the proceeds.[34]

Whatever their mode of trading, these dealers benefited from transportation and communication improvements that smoothed core aspects of slave commerce. A wave of roads, canals, and railroads emanating outward from Southern cities strengthened these centers' ties to their hinterlands and allowed both individual enslavers and itinerant traders to move people quickly to urban markets. This accelerated the process of sale and reduced the chance that injury, illness, or flight might diminish the value of the enslaved people in question.[35] As a result, one Richmonder noted in the late 1840s, "not a canal boat or stage scarcely comes to this place that does not bring negroes for sale."[36] References to "the cars" filled traders' correspondence, and Dickinson and N. B. Hill even joined the boards of railroads linking their markets to the rest of the Commonwealth.[37]

Better transportation also reoriented movement within the slave trade. Coasting vessels and coffles still carried people south for sale, but increasingly traders moved chattels in smaller groups along the rails and aboard riverine steamers. When, for example, Jourden Banks's enslaver sold him in the 1850s, Banks traveled to Richmond via the Virginia Central Railroad in company with four other people consigned thence. Once sold, he passed by rail through the Carolinas and Georgia to Montgomery, Alabama, where he boarded a steamer that carried him to his final destination.[38] Traditional termini of the trade like New Orleans and Natchez thus remained major markets, but interior cities on rivers and railroad lines grew in importance. Cities like Atlanta, Augusta, and Macon in Georgia, Nashville and Memphis in Tennessee, and Montgomery, Alabama all increased their portions of the traffic in the late antebellum period, as did Texas ports like Galveston and Houston, gateways to the farthest reaches of the cotton frontier.[39]

As lines of transportation reached into the Southern backcountry, they rendered the slave trade less linear than it had once been, especially as they strengthened communication networks throughout the South. Whether via mail borne along the rails or the telegraph lines humming alongside them, improved communications knit the slave trade into an ever more efficient

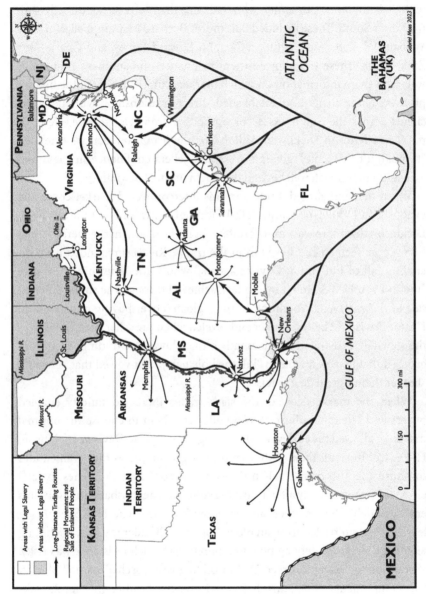

Figure 1.2 The domestic slave trade in 1860. Mossmaps.

and unified market.[40] Dickinson, Hill & Co., for example, maintained regular contact with New Orleans traders who kept them abreast of the news from that bellwether market. In the 1850s, they established additional connections with peers in other cities, men who had once themselves dealt directly with the Lower South. These included Baltimore's Bernard M. Campbell, Norfolk's William W. Hall, Washington, DC's John Edward Robey, and Charleston's Ziba Oakes. These ties allowed them to finance one another's trading, as well as to share information on which markets currently offered the highest prices.[41] Large firms also established direct relationships with potential clients across the South. As a correspondent from Oglethorpe, Georgia, put it in a letter to Dickinson, Hill & Co., the firm's connections extended "throughout this state," giving buyers and sellers confidence in them and extending their reach well beyond their own immediate vicinities.[42]

When demand surged, traders in this interconnected market competed viciously. In 1856, Lynchburg's Seth Woodroof wrote his longtime ally R. H. Dickinson that there was "more excitement in the negro market here... than I have ever seen since I have bin in the trade." Rivals surrounded him, including "all of Pulliam & Davises agents," who were "determined to" give "me and you Hell & Rub it in"—a task achieved through the subjection and sale of the enslaved. Woodroof, in turn, gloated over buying a man whom Hector Davis sold below market and reveled when the seller sued Davis over the shortfall. Frustrated by rheumatism that slowed his trading, Woodroof groused that he was unable to "kill the hole party," but vowed that he would "bother them a great deal as it is."[43]

When the market slowed, the slave trade's increased fluidity enabled buyers and sellers to adjust. Beyond allowing them to choose the optimal market, it allowed the enslavers who consigned people to Davis or Dickinson, Hill & Co. to recall them if they could not get the prices they wanted and to return them to market when times improved.[44] Bethany Veney experienced this when, shortly after a Virginia court sold her husband to resolve his enslaver's debts, her enslaver put her on the "cars" to Richmond. She quickly learned "certain tricks" from an older woman to "hinder my sale," including feigning illness and defying potential purchasers. Such resistance was risky. Woodroof, for example, urged Dickinson to give a "raschal" named Marion "my compliments" then "turn he[r] coat over her head & give her 25 licks well laid on he[r] naked Ass." But it spared Veney. Another woman took her place on the auction block as her enslaver withdrew her to the Shenandoah Valley.[45]

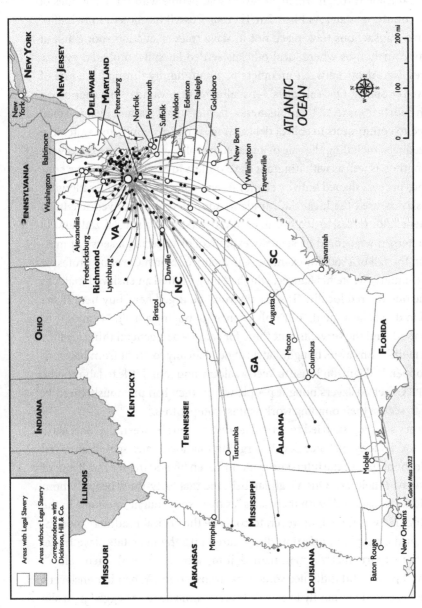

Figure 1.3 Dickinson, Hill & Co. Correspondence, June–December 1860. Drawn from letters held in the Library of Congress, American Antiquarian Society, Minnesota Historical Society, and Tufts University, this map shows the depth and breadth of Dickinson, Hill & Co.'s connections in the South on the eve of the Civil War. Mossmaps.

While traders and enslavers found the highest returns in the interstate slave trade, alongside it flourished a less notorious but equally potent local trade through which enslavers sold people within the confines of a city, county, or state. As historian Thomas Russell has noted, fully half of all slave transactions took place not in slave traders' auction rooms but at county courthouses where local officials settled lawsuits, probated estates, and resolved debts between members of a community through the sale of enslaved property. On "sale days"—usually the first Monday of a month, on which courts transacted their business—farmers, lawyers, and businessmen flocked to county seats to collect debts, swap stories, resupply, and watch the proceedings, including the sale of enslaved people. Local buyers jostled with one another as well as with itinerant slave traders to acquire people in a contentious process shaped both by economic and communal considerations.[46]

Enslavers used the local slave trade to address their perceived needs: to augment labor forces, to acquire an enslaved person for a specialized task, to find a person who could be sexually exploited, or to secure a sense of mastery. In the fall of 1860, for example, University of North Carolina professor John Kimberly wrote his fiancée, who had long desired an enslaved maid, to pursue one offered locally. "If she suits you," he urged her, "buy her." If she failed to do so, he argued, "our only chance" of buying a maid "would be in Richmond, and the servants sent there for sale are as a general thing sent for some fault."[47] Enslavers bought Patrick Snead locally to profit from his work as a cooper, Williamson Pease to keep a saloon, and John Little to labor in the fields.[48] Other enslavers bought people whom they had previously hired in order to secure their ongoing work against competitors.[49]

Slavery's apologists tried to articulate distinctions between the local slave trade and its long-distance cousin, arguing that local sales spared enslaved people the abuses of the interstate trade and even offered them a modicum of control over their fate. One Virginian believed that forty-three people whom he sold were "satisfied" with their sales "as they were bought by people in the country." He was forced, however, to concede the critical modifier "mostly." Some of the people in question disappeared into the interstate slave trade, and others (particularly a man named Tom) were angry with their sales.[50] Enslaved people did influence some local transactions. When her enslaver's decease exposed her family to sale, Virginia's Ann Clement begged men she knew to ensure that her children would be purchased by someone from a neighboring county rather than a lurking slave trader. Another Virginian rejoiced when her husband's enslaver acquired her in a local sale, while in

Mobile, Lucy Fearn and Daphne secured the former's purchase by a city resident rather than a New Orleans-bound dealer.[51]

Try as enslavers might to distinguish between the local and long-distance trades and to deny their culpability for slave commerce more broadly, they remained inseparable. One enslaver argued that local sales came down to the question of whether "the negros will be sold at the highest bider or chuse their masters"—a framing that overstated enslaved people's agency and implicitly acknowledged the looming threat of the interstate trade.[52] The long-distance trade always cast a coercive shadow on nominally local sales, eroding what paltry independence enslaved people possessed. In June 1860, for example, trader William S. Deupree asked his counterpart Samuel R. Fondren to purchase Josh Motley for him from Hector Davis. Deupree believed Motley, a fiddler, would be "of much service," perhaps by entertaining his clients in the market. He implied that he would honor Motley's preference regarding whether he "wants to live with us." The threat of what would happen if Motley declined remained implicit.[53]

The relative scale of the local slave trade remains difficult to quantify given that local transactions did not register in census or shipping records as long-distance slave trading did. But, as historian Herbert Gutman argues, they almost certainly equaled or exceeded the number of long-distance sales.[54] Enslaved people's testimony underscores their omnipresence. Before being sold from Kentucky to New Orleans, Henry Bibb experienced at least two local sales.[55] In only a few short months, Henry Box Brown watched enslavers sell his wife three times in and around Richmond, while various slaveholders sold R. S. W. Sorrick at least four times near Hagerstown, Maryland.[56] These local sales' effects could be less shattering than those of interstate transactions, but this offered small comfort to the enslaved. Each time a person stood exposed to sale, the threat of separation reared its head. Moreover, even relatively proximate transactions could be devastating for people only able to travel one day per week (if that). Thus, when Frederick County, Virginia's Dan Josiah Lockhart watched an enslaver from nearby Winchester acquire his wife, Maria, he reckoned the eight miles this carried her away "too far" and began engineering his own sale to overcome the distance.[57]

The long-distance and local slave trades thus melded relatively seamlessly under the broader umbrella of slave commerce: the commodification and sale of enslaved people. The compass of this umbrella was truly massive. All told, in the decades before the Civil War, the better part of one million enslaved people endured forced journeys from the Upper to the Lower South, with at least another million likely sold locally.[58] Through these transactions, slave dealers, enslavers, and the financiers who underwrote them forged a unified market in human chattels and quite literally made the Cotton Kingdom. The ability to sell enslaved people, whether next door or in distant markets, underpinned mortgages and securities, facilitated local credit networks, and ultimately made enslaved people one of the leading concentrations of wealth in the United States.[59] Local sales allowed enslavers to use people to settle debts, expand their businesses, and exploit the malleability of enslaved labor to meet an array of personal purposes. The slave market also became a space in which slaveholders could perform racial knowledge, display their mastery, and enact their paternalistic self-conceptions while simultaneously acquiring the labor essential to their economic and social visions. Without the slave trade, then, American slavery—and the socioeconomic systems resting upon it—could not function.[60]

As the 1850s came to an end, the prices offered for the enslaved soared thanks to robust cotton prices, the multiplying ways in which enslavers could put the enslaved to work, and a broader surge in commodity prices driven by an influx of California gold into the economy.[61] In politics, slaveholders' Democratic allies consistently held the presidency, while the *Dred Scott* decision seemingly secured the expansion of slavery. Agricultural reformer, slaveholder, and ardent disunionist Edmund Ruffin nevertheless took to the pages of the influential *De Bow's Review* to warn its readers that the rising anti-slavery Republican Party threatened the foundations of Southern society. In addition to inspiring the enslaved to insurrection and galvanizing opposition to slavery within the South, Republicans' preferred policies menaced the political and constitutional order upon which slavery rested. They could block slavery's expansion into the territories and forestall would-be slave states' entry into the Union. They could abolish slavery in the District of Columbia and use patronage to seed the South with anti-slavery sleeper agents. Republicans could also invoke Congress's power over interstate commerce to end the domestic slave trade. This alone, Ruffin claimed, would be sufficient to destroy slavery's political security and economic viability, hastening it "toward its doomed extinction."[62]

Radical Republicans certainly articulated a desire to implement this program. Despite Ruffin's warnings, however, by the measure of the slave

Figure 1.4 "The Popular Prejudice and the Blindness of the People on the U.S. Constitution." As this cartoon derisively illustrates, white Southerners considered both slavery (and the slave trade) constitutionally protected institutions and believed that Lincoln and the Republicans threatened them. Originally published in the *New York Illustrated News*. C. Fiske Harris Collection, Providence Public Library.

market, Southerners moved through the sectional crisis remarkably confident in slavery's future.[63] Even the Panic of 1857 scarcely dismayed enslavers, many of whom took its modest effects in the South as evidence of the slave system's relative strength.[64] As the decade closed, a North Carolinian stopped to marvel that even "as the agitation increases," the "value" attributed to the enslaved "does not decline."[65] One trader, meanwhile, ridiculed a competitor for making panicked sales after John Brown's 1859 raid on Harpers Ferry. The slave trade had inspired at least one participant in Brown's expedition: Dangerfield Newby, whose wife had recently informed him, "Master is in want of money if so I know not what time he may sell me"—a fate that would leave "all my bright hops of the futer . . . blasted." Having failed to raise the price demanded for his family, Newby perished in the attempt to rescue them. The high prices that proved fatal to Newby provoked only rejoicing from slave brokers. On the day of Brown's execution, Richmond's E. H. Stokes reported that "negroes still sell well . . . in spite of Brown & his clan" and expressed his hope that Brown's hanging would drive prices up.[66] "Times are indeed squally," one Virginian wrote another. "But the real danger" for enslaved property "is not yet."[67]

Indeed, the first days of 1860 proved remarkable mostly for the scale of white Southerners' investment in enslaved property. The dawn of a new year traditionally brought a wave of sales as enslavers settled debts and prepared for another planting season.[68] That January, however, the soaring prices and vigor of the trade stunned observers across the South. In Florence, South Carolina, a man urged his father to sell their enslaved property, for "they are bringing the most enormous prices." "I hardly think they can pay such prices for negroes to plant Cotton," he marveled, but "the demand seems to be increasing every day."[69] From his Richmond office, Hector Davis affirmed this. 1859 had been an extraordinary year for Davis, who sold at least 900 men, women, and children for a whopping $2.6 million.[70] 1860 promised to be still more lucrative. Prices, Davis informed a client in January, were "as high or higher than I ever saw them." That month alone, he sold 235 people for more than $125,000 and assured buyers, "You cannot go wrong in buying good grown negroes."[71]

Such predictions confounded some white Southerners. For most of the nineteenth century, slave prices had roughly followed cotton prices. In the late 1850s, however, the two decoupled, with slave prices soaring well past the underlying value of cotton. As a stunned purchaser watching prices ascend in a Dickinson, Hill & Co. auction exclaimed, "D—n it . . . how niggers has riz."[72] The cautious saw a bubble in the making. One Virginian predicted when the inevitable crunch came, "cotton, sugar, land and negroes are bound to be reduced in price" and advised a friend "do not be too eager to purchase," especially given that "Negroes are too high in our market."[73] Dickinson, Hill & Co. later conceded that "the speculations and extravagancies of the last three years have put up prices of lands, negroes, and crops, to such a height that it could not be maintained."[74] As one newspaper succinctly put it, a "negro fever" had swept through the South, one that needed to be treated with "truth and soberness" for its manic effects.[75]

Few saw the need for such introspection in the winter and spring of 1860. Given that slave prices had risen constantly since the late 1840s, many shared Davis's belief that the boom times would continue. This impulse drove a Virginian emigrant to Mississippi to seek a loan from his mother to buy people. "My chief desire," he informed her, "is to become a wealthy cotton planter." Neither high prices nor sectional strife deterred him. Enslaved people were "worth four times the amount" currently asked and in the long term "I shall want all the negroes I can get."[76] The *New Orleans Daily Crescent*, meanwhile, found "the high price of negroes" to be "a matter of continual mark and no little wonderment." "The great demand for slaves in the Southwest," it suggested, would surely keep slave traders busy in the coming year.[77] For some, this frenzy augured hope for the future amid the sectional crisis. From his post at the Louisiana State Seminary and Military Academy, Ohioan William T. Sherman wrote that if disunion were likely, "the price of negroes" would not now be "higher than ever before."[78]

With slave prices booming in 1860, would-be traders begged established firms for opportunities, while experienced dealers jockeyed for market share.[79] New Orleans's Charles Hatcher had previously closed his slave depot during the summer to avoid the epidemics that frequently swept the city. The profits attainable in 1860 encouraged him to keep it open through the stifling summer months.[80] Several Richmond dealers, including Robert Lumpkin, Hector Davis, Charles Hill and Dickinson, Hill & Co. junior partner John B. Davis, William Deupree, William Betts, Solomon Davis, and Samuel Fondren, pursued a form of vertical integration by incorporating the Traders' Bank of Richmond. They hoped this would provide consistent capital for their enterprises and allow them to profit from the extensive financing slave dealing required. Such a move represented an investment in slavery's and slave trading's boundless future.[81]

As spring turned into summer, cracks in the American political landscape became crevasses. In April, the Democratic Party shattered under Southern delegates' demand for a federal code protecting slavery in the territories. Without this, schismatics argued, slavery would wither on the vine in those regions. Northern delegates refused this ultimatum and nominated Stephen Douglas, while Southern Democrats put forth John C. Breckinridge. The two Democrats and the Constitutional Union Party's John Bell faced Lincoln, with the divided field increasing the Republican's odds of winning office and bringing Ruffin's prophecies to pass.[82]

The increasing likelihood of this eventuality gradually eroded the slave market's heretofore irretrievable ebullience. As the presidential field took shape in June, a trader reported that enslaved people had begun carrying a "political price," though he hoped that this was only temporary.[83] 1860 would ultimately see fewer enslaved people sold in the benchmark entrepôt of New Orleans than had 1859, but elevated prices persisted through the summer and rose even after Lincoln's nomination. As Dickinson, Hill & Co. reported in July, "prices rule high for good negroes, which are scarce and much wanted."[84] Some enslavers entered the market undeterred by rumblings of political turmoil. A South Carolina trader hoped to purchase at least thirteen people in Richmond, a Floridian thirty more.[85] This continuing robust demand suggests that while political events added uncertainty to the market, white Southerners remained ambivalent about slave prices' ultimate trajectory through the summer of 1860.[86]

Only as Lincoln's election became imminent did fear thoroughly pervade the slave market. In mid-September, Betts & Gregory noted, "the presidential election is having considerable effect on the market." The firm hoped conditions might still improve, but conceded, "how it will go no man can tell."[87] A Tennessee trader, meanwhile, reported that "the storm in this political excitement" meant there was "nothing in the way of trade going."[88] Henry F. Peterson, a long-time New Orleans dealer, sold people successfully in September and October, but, by November, embraced a similar pessimism. Ten days removed from his last sale, and with prospective buyers lacking, he sounded the alarm to Dickinson, Hill & Co. Not "many negros will be sold," he warned, urging them to limit their purchases accordingly.[89] The weeks leading up to the election were, a would-be Richmond seller concluded, "a most unfavorable time for selling negros," and many buyers and sellers decided to avoid the market until after the results were in.[90]

Lincoln's election drove the slave trade into a still deeper depression. In New Orleans, prices fell several hundred dollars (as much as 30 percent) from their summer highs and continued declining as first South Carolina and then six more states seceded in December and January.[91] New Orleans's market paced the rest of the South. While a Virginian's January 1861 complaint that enslaved people were worth only a third of what they had been the previous spring was surely an exaggeration, their decline was indisputable. Betts & Gregory found only "flatness and inactivity" across the state. Another Richmond commission firm reported "very few" people "now being sold."[92] As a North Carolinian succinctly put it, "Negroes have fallen & people have got afraid of them as an investment."[93] Even Lincoln's repeated assurances that he had (as he put it to a North Carolina congressman) "no thought of recommending the abolition of . . . the slave trade among the slave states" did little to arrest the panic then underway.[94]

For all that Southerners feared the effects of Lincoln's election on slavery, the collapse of the slave market was rooted in a larger financial catastrophe unleashed by the election and resulting secession movements. Slave prices fell, but they did so more because secession destroyed the infrastructure on which they rested rather than because enslavers lost confidence in the institution. Perpetually cash-strapped, enslavers (especially large planters) relied on credit extended by banks, factors, and mercantile houses against the succeeding year's crops to purchase food, clothing, agricultural implements—everything needed to keep their operations going. When prices fell or crops failed, they rolled their debts over and borrowed more to cover the difference. Slowly but surely, most found themselves beholden to cotton factors and merchants, many of whom owed their own debts to Northern or European creditors.[95]

Enslavers depended on this credit to purchase the people on whose labor everything ultimately rested. Sometimes they borrowed small amounts over short-terms.[96] But large-scale purchases demanded substantial sums extended for longer terms. In November 1860, future Confederate Secretary of War James Seddon and a business partner bought nearly one hundred people from Virginia Whig patriarch William Cabell Rives. Seddon paid 20 percent down and promised an additional 20 percent (plus interest) annually in each of the next four years. He planned to send these people to a newly acquired Mississippi property where they would grow enough cotton to pay his debts and then some. Seddon followed a path long trodden by ambitious slaveholders.[97] Indeed, one observer noted, "the majority of planters... would always run in debt... for negroes, whatever was asked for them." In doing so, they "were going ahead risking everything, in confidence that another year luck would favor them." Slave dealers catered to these ambitions by offering "excessive credit" on the assumption that "the higher the price of cotton the higher is that of negroes."[98]

These speculative efforts fed twin bubbles in slaves and cotton, especially as slave prices outstripped those of cotton in the late 1850s. Following Lincoln's election, however, what one Louisianian called a "state of excitement & dread of the future" pierced the nation's credit markets and punctured both bubbles, the collapse of which radiated outward through the Southern economy.[99] As New Orleans cotton factor Moses Greenwood wailed, "Stop cotton... & it stops everything."[100] With cotton prices falling and the future opaque, overextended financial institutions throughout the South called in their loans. Many refused to honor their obligations to Northern creditors, with some seeing secession as a means of obviating their debts altogether.[101] This left Yankee financiers unwilling to extend credit even to those who had not yet repudiated their debts.[102] Liquidity thus drained from the Southern economy.[103] In New Orleans, the South's financial hub and leading banking center, the amount of money circulating fell by a third between September 1860 and January 1861.[104] Dozens of mercantile houses succumbed. As these collapsing houses called in their own loans, the maelstrom expanded. As one observer stated in early 1861, virtually everyone "has broke or is breaking." With "merchants of the highest standing . . . suspending every day," a Louisianian added, "all commercial interests" were "entirely destroyed."[105]

The repercussions were immediate, devastating, and ubiquitous. One Richmond merchant complained that "stocks of all kinds are down & can hardly be sold at all" while another bewailed "extensive failures" among that city's mercantile houses.[106] "The present panic and commercial trouble," a Savannah merchant warned, "is only a beginning of what you are to see." The mounting problems led a Louisianian to denounce secessionists bitterly as the source of the "great difficulty" he experienced in "negotiating exchange," while even a pro-secession Alabamian conceded, "We are in the midst of a crisis in money matters. . . . No money, and no confidence in any one's ability to pay."[107]

Such concerns proliferated in correspondence between a New York mercantile firm, Benjamin Blossom & Son, and its longtime client, South Carolina's Daniel Jordan. As secession loomed, Blossom & Son chastised Jordan and his fellow Carolinians for having failed to anticipate the consequences of their actions. "Without any light ahead in political matters," they pointed out, "you cannot suppose we would feel very much like any new or large business operations." Secession and the threatened severing of business relations endangered both the national economy and the interests of Southern planters. As Blossom & Son castigated Jordan, Carolinians should have stayed in the Union, for there lay "your only safety for your property" — including the enslaved. While the economic crisis itself did not immediately threaten slavery, it undercut the value of enslaved property by curtailing enslavers' ability to buy and sell. As soon as South Carolina threatened disunion, Blossom & Son pointed out, "your landed & negro property depreciated 50 per cent" because "all trade & commerce" had been "killed for no one knows how long." For the sake of "evils having occurred which will prove probably to a great extent imaginary," Southerners injured the value of their property to the tune of "millions of doll[ar]s." Political and economic matters thus converged, depriving enslavers of credit and undermining confidence in business's resurrection.[108]

With slaveholders in desperate financial straits and would-be purchasers wary of taking on new obligations, slave dealers throughout the South struggled to make sales during the secession winter. In November, a Missouri trader working his way toward New Orleans complained to his wife that he had not yet sold a single person. "Banks are suspending and business men failing on all sides," he reported, rendering "trade of almost every kind stagnant." Times were so hard that when he appealed to her for a letter, he grimly joked that receiving one "would relieve us (nearly) as much as the sale of a negro."[109] Things were no better in his intended destination, where Moses Greenwood noted that "negroes are of course low and must go lower." Greenwood attributed this reality to the lack of money available. "No House in the city," he reported, could extend the credit necessary to purchase them.[110]

Those who tried to trade against these headwinds struggled mightily. One trader reported spending all winter trying to sell just two or three people, while in December 1860, Alabama slave dealer A. J. Rux complained, "it has been so long since I saw a man that wanted to buy a negro that I would not know what to say to him."[111] Silas Omohundro's efforts to sell William on Daniel Jordan's behalf bore this out. With the slave market stalled, William bounced for months among Richmond's slave jails. He became sick enough to be hospitalized, at which point he attempted to escape out of an upper-story window. Omohundro—he of three decades' experience in the slave trade—labeled William "the biggest Rascal of a Negro that I have ever had anything to do with in all the course of my trading." Dickinson, Hill & Co. eventually sold him for a paltry $250, and, under the circumstances, Omohundro considered Jordan "lucky" to get that.[112]

The panic, moreover, seemed likely to linger. Dickinson, Hill & Co. warned their agents they would be hard pressed to cover credit already drawn on them, much less to extend further loans as their own creditors reported shortfalls.[113] As 1860 closed, the firm informed their clients that the hard times were only beginning. "The financial crisis," they noted, "still rages and is not likely to abate for some months." With "any political change which will give peace and confidence in commercial matters" unlikely, Richmond's largest slave trading concern warned, prices for the enslaved would probably not regain their antebellum heights for some years to come.[114]

Enslavers feared the long-term implications of Lincoln's election enough to secede, but it was the broader economic collapse that immediately impaired slave commerce in 1860 and 1861. Indeed, slaveholders rarely voiced concern for slave property's long-term prospects during this period. When they complained about declining prices, they overwhelmingly attributed them to the widening economic gyre. A nephew of South Carolina's James Henry Hammond complained to his famous uncle that while "negroes have depreciated very much," Charleston financiers were also bracing for the worst economic downturn since the Panic of 1857.[115] One newspaper, meanwhile, blamed the president-elect for falling slave prices, but noted that while "Lincoln is chargeable for this," so was "the depression in the Northern market."[116] That other forms of property collapsed alongside the enslaved gave credence to this perspective. As one planter put it, "political disturbances, connected with the secession of the Cotton growing states, have greatly deranged the business affairs of the country and impaired the value of all property," a view shared by a Virginia merchant who likewise concluded that "All kinds of property have fallen very much."[117]

Environmental factors, particularly an extended drought and severe storms that damaged the 1860 cotton crop, compounded the South's spiraling economic crisis. An Alabama trader complained to E. H. Stokes that "the short crops and the fuss about Lincoln's election has frightened the people so much, they will not buy negroes at any price."[118] Another Alabamian bewailed the combined weight of "short crops & the political troubles of the country," which rendered "provisions as scarce as money."[119] It is unsurprising that slaveholders would not acquire people whom they could scarcely feed, much less afford. Elevated prices for food and other necessaries also consumed scarce resources that might otherwise have been invested in human property.[120] When added to the widespread reports of planned slave insurrections, the secession winter seemed an inauspicious time to invest in humanity.[121]

Some enslavers nevertheless pointed to transactions that did take place as evidence of the relative strength of the institution writ large. New Orleans trader Thomas Foster's successful sale of twenty-eight people in January 1861—undertaken as the states of the Deep South departed the Union— convinced many that "the value of slaves" had "suffered no diminution as yet from the disturbed condition of our financial and political affairs."[122] A traveler in Charleston gained a similar impression. Suggesting that "the highest former market prices" pervaded "in the face of this outcry of danger," he considered this "the best possible practical evidence of the public confidence in the tenure of slavery."[123] Three South Carolinians expressed that faith directly to Lincoln himself, offering to buy from him the allegedly mixed-race

Vice President Hannibal Hamlin, if the president would only send his running mate to Richmond's slave market.[124] The traffic in slaves thus suffered less from a lack of confidence in the institution's future than from turmoil in the wider economy with which slave trafficking was bound up.

Even a diminished slave trade proved catastrophic to those whom traders obtained. In November 1860, Miranda Plummer's enslaver abruptly sold her to an interstate dealer, who, in turn, tried to extort her purchase price from her family and community. When they could not meet his demands, he sold her south. Plummer managed to get a letter home to her family from New Orleans in May, but the looming war offered her neither comfort nor prospects for escape. She considered their separation permanent, informing her mother "Though I may hear from you yet, I never expect to see you again," while enjoining her not to "forget that I am still alive." Plummer would be one of the last people whom traders shipped from the Chesapeake to New Orleans, though this was small comfort to someone whose only solace was the hope of meeting her family in the Hereafter "to part no more."[125]

Others joined Plummer in slave markets as the secession mania raged. Adam and Eugene Pinkwood may have shared Miranda's Alexandria captivity before their sale to Richmond in February 1861.[126] Taylor Jackson, born near Baltimore and sold that winter, recalled spending three months in a New Orleans slave pen, his sale likely delayed by low prices.[127] Octave Johnson, enslaved by Arthur Thiboux in the same city, found himself sold to St. James Parish, where he labored as a cooper until he could escape.[128] Enslavers sold Allen Allensworth, later a political and religious leader among the freedmen, north to Kentucky.[129] That white Southerners continued to buy men and women puzzled Betty Simmons, whom a trader carried to New Orleans from St. Louis during the secession winter. If, as enslaved people widely believed, the looming war would result in their freedom, then why were so many enslavers seeking to buy them? As she later put it, "Us t'ink it too funny dey kep' fillin' up w'en dey gwinter be emtyin' out soon."[130]

The chaos in the market and the uncertainty of the future allowed enslavers to read into the slave market their preferred outcomes. For some, speculative impulses drove interest in men and women like Simmons. In January 1861, Moses Greenwood noted that with all commodities in flux, slave property was "as safe or more so" than any other investment, though he conceded that relatively few enslaved people were actually selling in New Orleans.[131] Expectations that good times would soon return inspired others to either retain or expand their slaveholdings. A North Carolina newspaper

Figure 1.5 Betty Simmons. Simmons recalled being perplexed that during the secession crisis anyone would consider it wise to purchase or sell enslaved people. Library of Congress, LC-USZ62-125348.

accurately captured slaveholders' prevailing attitude. It acknowledged that Lincoln's election had produced a crash in "property generally," for "a panic runs like fire in dry stubble." Nevertheless, it maintained, "*slavery in the States is in no danger*" and was, in fact, destined to expand. Given this reality, "it would ... be unwise to rush slave property into market at a sacrifice on account of Lincoln's election."[132] A Vicksburg newspaper, meanwhile, challenged anyone who doubted the validity of enslaved property to "purchase a few likely hands, that he may be convinced of his error."[133]

As would be the case in the years to come, many enslavers saw opportunity in falling slave prices. As prices fell, enslaved people—the ticket to wealth and status in the American South—became more affordable than they had been in several years.[134] Some large slaveholders expanded their operations at bargain prices. William Mercer, who enslaved dozens of people in and around Adams County, Mississippi, bought a blacksmith in New Orleans in February 1861.[135] Smaller-scale operators also jumped into the market. John Kimberly believed that the crisis would permit him to "buy anything I want at any price I may choose to give."[136] A Mississippian hoped to purchase at least two enslaved people if he could "collect my money that is due me," while a delegate to Virginia's secession convention wanted to purchase the family's first enslaved woman, reasoning that "they are cheaper now than they will be after a while."[137] Catering to these sorts of buyers, a slave trader operating near Warrenton, Virginia alerted his network to "a good many" enslaved people "in this neighborhood that can be bought quite low just now."[138]

Other enslavers anticipated slave commerce's swift rejuvenation. A Lynchburg, Virginia slaveholder, for example, in February 1861 expressed frustration that Richmond's Davis, Deupree & Co. had not yet sold an enslaved man for him. Conceding that he reposed "less confidence in the value of such property in Va than I had a week ago," he nevertheless asked them to reinvest the eventual proceeds in another enslaved person—specifically an enslaved girl "of good character, sprightly, and healthy."[139] Another Virginian took off the market seventeen people—but only "till next year."[140] A Georgian similarly delayed a sale until political matters were "more settled," while a South Carolinian hoped that "when the skies brighten," a boy named Sancho whom he had purchased "will be worth $2000"—nearly twice the price then prevailing for enslaved people.[141]

Many of those who chanced the slave market regretted having done so. One sufferer of buyer's remorse begged Betts & Gregory for short-term relief. Having bought "on the eve of the decline," he moaned, "when I bought right it was wrong before I could sell." A. J. Rux found selling in Alabama "the most up hill business now that a man can undertake" and feared there wouldn't "be any market this winter to do any good."[142] As enslavers' finances collapsed, some undertook emergency sales, either to pay off debts suddenly due or to alleviate acute cash shortages. Richmond merchant Samuel Mordecai, for example, hearing his brother had sold some fifty people, congratulated him on having "reduced your trouble on satisfactory terms."[143]

The establishment of the Confederacy as an independent slaveholding republic in February 1861 encouraged some enslavers to resume commerce in slaves, not least because several aspects of the CSA's founding bore directly on the trade. Despite years of agitation by South Carolina firebrands, the CSA's constitution maintained the ban on the Atlantic slave trade, keeping the market for enslaved property domestic and offering what one Carolinian termed "an inducement to the border states to join our Confederacy." It was probably a necessary one. As the governor of North Carolina warned his Georgia counterpart, "I am firmly convinced that No. Ca. and Va. . . . will never join a Southern Confederacy unless its Constitution prohibits the importation of Africans," for those two states "furnish Slaves for the Southern market, and the value of their property would be greatly affected by new importations." The upstart constitution, however, also implicitly threatened those Upper South states that tarried in the Union by allowing for a ban on the importation of enslaved people from the United States. This was not an idle threat. Georgia Secession Commissioner Henry Benning warned an outraged Virginia Convention, "I do not hesitate to say to you, that in my opinion, if you do not join with us but join with the North, that provision would be put in force."[144]

Following the formation of the Confederacy, prices rose in New Orleans's benchmark market by about 10 percent between January and April. They did not regain their 1860 peaks, but they approached the high prices of the late 1850s—though the raw number of people sold in the Crescent City remained considerably below the levels reached just before the war.[145] In Richmond, Davis, Deupree & Co. reported that the "negro market ha[d] improved much," while Betts & Gregory descried an "upward tendency."[146] If hesitant states like Virginia, moreover, joined the nascent Confederacy and secured the slave trade's integrity, one observer argued, "the rise in all descriptions of property would be unprecedented."[147]

As a result, even though secession had thrown their operations into chaos, slave traders enthusiastically supported first disunion and then the Confederacy.[148] Prior to Virginia's April secession, N. B. Hill, for example, planted a palmetto tree in his yard in a show of solidarity with South Carolina.[149] Slave dealers also played an integral role in a mass demonstration that raised a similar banner over the Virginia capitol.[150] Their motivations were straightforward. With the Union sundered, one newspaper predicted, "Negro trading is at an end, and will never be revived, unless the South is victorious." If cut off from the Confederacy, or if the haven it provided for slavery were destroyed, slave traders could lose everything. They knew that "upon the success of [the Confederate] cause, depends, now and forever, the continuance of their unholy traffic."[151]

On April 12, 1861, Confederate forces in Charleston Harbor opened fire on Fort Sumter, one of the United States' few remaining toeholds in the slaveholders' republic. Mere blocks from the batteries on the tip of Charleston's peninsula, enslaved people huddled in jails dotting Broad, Chalmers, and Queen Streets.[152] Among them might have been Henry Olmstead, his wife, and their five children. A month earlier, they had lived freely in New York, working on a steamer operating between Manhattan and Richmond. While moored in the latter city, they had been lured to a hotel, robbed, and sold to Charleston in an action that foreshadowed Confederates' use of the slave trade to reaffirm the unbreakable tie between blackness and bondage.[153] As artillery echoed across the water and through the predawn air, the Olmsteads and the other enslaved men and women sat at the Rebellion's ground zero. They knew better than most the intimate connections between the slave trade and the war.[154] But how long the conflict would last, what it would cost, and what its ultimate result would be remained unknown to all.

By the time Virginia seceded on April 17, 1861, leading the final four Rebel states into the Confederate fold, the prices offered for people like the Olmsteads had plummeted once again. A week after Fort Sumter's surrender, one of E. H. Stokes's cousins worried over an unsold person, "If I don't get my money out of the negro now I don't know when I can get it."[155] From Mobile, a broker wrote to Dickinson, Hill & Co. that while the arms trade might be "buoyant," all other "business" was "at a dead lock"; the few people who sold there did so below even the diminished prices available in Richmond.[156] Seth Woodroof knew that all his neighbors were "anxious for a fight," but not the information that defined his livelihood: what they would give for an enslaved man. As a result, he and other would-be sellers pelted traders like Dickinson, Hill & Co. with letters asking whether human property would sell for "any price."[157]

Many enslavers hoped that this crisis would prove temporary. Indeed, Stokes chose the very moment of secession to establish himself in Richmond as a permanent trader, taking over for Betts & Gregory, whom the crisis had bankrupted.[158] An Albemarle County slaveholder recalled people he had sent to Dickinson, Hill & Co., but planned to return them "as soon as the market gets so they can be sold."[159] Another commission firm conceded that selling that spring or summer was not wise, but predicted prices would rise again in the fall.[160] A Georgian cut off from his normal fruit trade, on the other hand, invested several thousand dollars in enslaved property.[161] A Virginian hoped to do the same, assuming, he half-joked to a friend, "Old Abe does not ruin us."[162]

This was the crucial question. Eleven states had departed the Union for fear of what "Old Abe" might do to their right to hold enslaved property and formed a new country for its protection. As nation struggled against nation, brother against brother, enslaved against enslaver, the commerce in slaves became both a sinew of war and an indicator of its course. It reflected enslavers' confidence in their fledgling republic and served as a support to it. It was a means of fighting the conflict, equipping its armies, and waging the homefront battles the enslaved almost immediately inaugurated. The survival of the slave trade, which for generations had enmeshed people of African descent, would define the conflict over the ensuing four years of war.

2
The "Uncongenial Air of Freedom"
Union Occupation and the Slave Trade

Shortly after midnight on May 24, 1861, Union soldiers posted in and around Washington, DC surged across the Potomac River and established beachheads in the new Confederate frontier: the Commonwealth of Virginia. Less than a day earlier, in a virtual fait accompli, white Virginians had overwhelmingly ratified the ordinance of secession passed a month earlier by a state convention, making ground only a few hundred yards from the White House enemy territory. In response, as soon as Virginia's secession became official, a mixed force of US Army regulars and volunteers crossed the Aqueduct and Long Bridges, boarded a fleet of steamers, and secured the approaches to Washington.[1]

Among the troops entering the Virginia port city of Alexandria that night were the men of the 1st Michigan Infantry. As they advanced west to take the terminus of the Orange & Alexandria Railroad, they found Confederate cavalry encamped around a fortified structure on Duke Street. After a brief skirmish, the regiment captured and confined thirty-five prisoners in the building.[2] These prisoners became merely the latest of thousands of people to be held there, for the structure in question turned out to be the slave pen once operated by Franklin & Armfield. Its current tenants—James H. Birch, notorious for kidnapping Solomon Northup two decades earlier, and his partner, Charles M. Price, a *bête noire* of the local Black population—had remained active in the trade up to the brink of the invasion; Price had recently dispatched four people to Dickinson, Hill & Co., and when his facility fell, was in Maryland searching for others.[3]

Most of Price's and Birch's fellow Alexandria slave traders abandoned their facilities and fled just ahead of the advancing Federals.[4] But when the Michiganders entered the Duke Street pen, they found (depending on which report one believes) one, three, or a throng of enslaved people confined there. Among them was George C. Smith. Born around 1839 just east of the District of Columbia in Prince George's County, Maryland, Smith had been sent by his

Figure 2.1 Exterior of Price, Birch & Co. Slave Pen, Alexandria, VA. Library of Congress, LC-DIG-ppmsca-11746.

enslaver (unnamed in the historical record) to Price, Birch & Co. in the weeks preceding the invasion. With US forces flocking to the nation's capital, this slaveholder feared for the security of his human property, even though the federal government remained, as yet, committed to maintaining slavery. Not trusting Lincoln's newly installed administration, he dispatched Smith across what would soon be an international border, banking on Price, Birch & Co.—and, by extension, the fastness of their jail, the laws of Virginia, and sale at a distance from interfering soldiers—to ensure Smith's continued bondage.[5]

The efforts required to keep Smith in slavery reproduced in miniature slaveholders' constant reliance on support from both private actors like Price, Birch & Co. and public authorities to maintain people as property. For all their fears, however, white Southerners had some reason to believe this would continue even under a Republican regime. Only two months earlier, Lincoln had vowed that he had neither the intention nor the power, "directly or indirectly, to interfere with the institution of slavery in the States where it exists" and had even endorsed a proposed Thirteenth Amendment abjuring considerable Federal power over slavery.[6]

Not trusting these assurances, however, Smith's nameless enslaver turned to the slave trade to put Smith beyond the reach of the Civil War's revolutionary potential. In doing so, he enabled his bondsman's liberation. Within a few minutes of entering Price, Birch & Co.'s jail, the 1st Michigan's orderly-sergeant found its keys and released Smith. When his now-former enslaver made a final bid to reclaim him, the regiment closed ranks, and "hustled" the interloper "off alone amid the jeers of the Michigan men."[7] Smith had begun the war as property in the eyes of both his enslaver and the US government. He would conclude it as an agent of that government, fighting as a member of the 1st Michigan Colored Infantry (later the 102nd USCI) against the institution of slavery.[8]

White Southerners' willingness to buy and sell men like Smith rested on two pillars. First, such transactions had to be economically worthwhile, broadly profitable in the short or long term. Second, enslavers had to believe that the people they bought and sold were likely to remain property.[9] Backed by state support (implicit or explicit), the slave trade ensured the

Figure 2.2 Interior of Price, Birch & Co. Slave Pen, Alexandria, VA. Library of Congress, LC-DIG-stereo-1s04354.

survival of slave property, for it was the trade that imbued enslaved people with value, a price—realized or theoretical—that empowered slaveholders to turn an economic gain on them. If governing authorities could not secure enslavers' property rights in man, however, the value they reposed in the enslaved would vanish.[10] Enslavers bought and sold people with the understanding that the government would recognize them as property—that it and its agents would affirm enslavers' right to hold them in captivity, would back the right to transfer their ownership, would prevent their escaping bondage, and would refrain from using its powers over taxation or trade to attack their value or commerce in them.[11]

Contemporary observers easily discerned the intimate ties between the slave trade, the institution of slavery writ large, and their need for government protection. Lauding the Compromise of 1850's ban on the slave trade in Washington, DC, Charles Sumner argued that slavery rested on two major "props and stays... the *slave trade* and the *lash*": the power to render people into property, and the power to compel their labor. "By these," he believed, "the whole monstrosity is upheld." Banning even a portion of the slave trade thus represented a major step in "preparing the way for that complete act of Abolition."[12] Frederick Douglass put things still more simply. For decades, he believed, Southern states had pleaded with the national government, "We must have a market for human flesh, or we are ruined." Because national leaders had, "whenever slave property was decreased in value, opened new markets for human flesh, and raised its price," they had helped the institution survive.[13] Unsurprisingly, when antislavery men sought to put an end to the institution, they emphasized the pressure that could be applied by clamping down on slave trading, particularly through Congress's power over interstate commerce. As one Universalist minister explained (including in a proposal made to Abraham Lincoln), "the fact that slaves cannot be sent from one State to another... will make the system so unpopular and unprofitable, that the anxiety among slave-holders will be to get rid of this description of property as easily and early as possible."[14]

Recognizing the need to protect enslaved property, enslavers erected a hedge of state-backed defenses around it. They propagated laws that rendered slavery hereditary and racial and put official imprimatur to the purchase and sale of the enslaved. Other laws constrained enslaved people's mobility, prevented their accruing property, regulated their family relationships, barred unsupervised assemblies, and punished those who challenged or fled their captivity. Almost any member of the white community could enforce these edicts, which fostered racial solidarity.[15] Finally, by offering enslaved people nominal legal protections, slave codes provided enslavers with rhetorical defenses, fig leaves of theoretical amelioration that partially obscured their growing power in the early years of the American republic.[16]

Slaveholders enforced these laws through outsized influence in seats of American government. They dominated their nonslaveholding neighbors at the local and state levels, often through disproportionate representation in government.[17] They leveraged their undemocratic advantages to preserve the value of their human property, fighting tooth and nail against not only anything tending toward emancipation but also against more innocuous measures like *ad valorem* taxation of the enslaved.[18] Taken as a whole, as historian Harry Watson concisely puts it, "slavery everywhere undergirded a pattern of political and economic privilege which seemed to discriminate" in enslavers' favor.[19] The state reinforced these privileges with force. Sheriffs and slave patrols policed enslaved people's movements and activities, hunted fugitives, and sought out arms and other contraband. Public and private jails opened to receive those apprehended in violations of the laws of slavery. And when rumors of insurrection swirled, enslavers called out the militia to support them.[20] Even enslaved people's labors on public works and infrastructure projects expanded the reach and capacity of the very state that maintained them as property.[21]

Enslavers fighting to replicate these efforts on the national level utilized the advantage of the three-fifths clause, an expansive conception of the protections owed them, and weaknesses in the government's federal structure to do so.[22] State agents forced Native Americans from the most promising cotton country, then surveyed, subdivided, and sold it, thereby expanding the reach of American slavery.[23] American envoys defended slavery abroad, demanding the return of fugitives who slipped the bounds of the United States and alerting enslavers to plans for abolition in the Atlantic world. The US military undertook punitive expeditions against those who sheltered Black refugees and stood ready to quash slave rebellions.[24] Slaveholders also used national authority to coerce their fellow citizens into supporting human bondage through mandates like the Fugitive Slave Act.[25]

Enslavers inaugurated the Civil War largely for fear that Republicans would turn these same levers of governmental power against the slave trade and slave property more broadly.[26] In April 1861, Jefferson Davis warned the Confederate Congress that having seized control of the "administration of the government," Republicans planned to undercut slavery's protection and expansion, "thus rendering the property in slaves so insecure as to be comparatively worthless, and thereby annihilating in effect property worth thousands of millions of dollars."[27] As George C. Smith's enslaver learned, however, the struggle to preserve enslaved property could also accelerate its demise. The act of rebellion exposed the Confederacy to substantial pressures—economic, social, and, above all else, military—amid which enslaved people leveraged US power against their enslavers' authority by their flight or their collaboration.[28] As the war dragged on, the friction of repeated encounters among enslaved people, soldiers, and a slave society gradually swung the power of the state behind the enslaved, eventually allowing them to make expanding claims on the nation itself and, where the Union held sway, making their purchase and sale impossible.[29]

Between the summer of 1861 and the summer of 1862, the Confederacy's slave markets reeled under these pressures. A Union blockade, Confederate cotton embargoes, and the ensuing collapse of the CSA's staple crop economy turned the secession-sparked monetary crisis into a full-blown financial disaster. These economic travails diminished but did not destroy the traffic in enslaved people. Indeed, between Fort Sumter and the Seven Days battles in June 1862, white Southerners purchased and sold thousands of people. Slave traders throughout the South plied their human wares, sundering Black families as mercilessly as they had during the antebellum years. These transactions continued because a surviving Confederate state—and Confederate states—guaranteed enslavers' right to hold men and women as property across the vast majority of the CSA's territory and protected the slave markets ensconced therein. This left many Confederates free to acquire people, while those looking to divest themselves of human chattels could find buyers.

When US forces occupied Alexandria in the war's first month, however, they demonstrated clearly how military advances could upend this calculus. During the conflict's first calendar year, similar scenes played out in market after market. Norfolk, Nashville, Memphis, Natchez, even New Orleans—the one-time "mistress of the trade"—disappeared from the slave trade as Union soldiers conquered them.[30] Even where slavery remained nominally legal (as in many of these cities, even after Union occupation), the abrasive effects of enslaved resistance and the Federal presence persistently undercut enslavers' ability and willingness to deal in people. Enslaved people's aspirations for liberty and the military's growing unwillingness to back enslavers' claims on them disincentivized investment in human property wherever the United

States could project power. Where it did so successfully, the slave market withered.

On April 26, 1861, a boy named Nelson departed Hector Davis's Richmond jail. Unlike most of those who exited the pen, Nelson did not face a lengthy trip south. His journey covered only a few blocks to the slopes of Shockoe Hill and the city's African Burying Ground. Nelson had come to Richmond three weeks earlier, sent to Davis for sale by his enslaver, J. J. Payne. He arrived with an older man, also named Nelson, and a woman named Melinda; while they were not the only people Payne sent Davis that month, it seems probable that they represented one of the many families cast adrift into the slave trade. The Richmond into which they entered was in turmoil. The very day of their arrival, Virginia's secession convention rejected disunion by nearly a two-to-one margin. In the ensuing weeks, during which they sat confined, the guns barked at Fort Sumter, Lincoln called for 75,000 troops to put down the Rebellion, and white Virginians cast caution aside and embraced disunion.

If secession fever raged beyond the walls of Davis's slave pen, other pestilences pervaded within them. Slave jails were notoriously virulent; not long before, the famous fugitive Anthony Burns found Lumpkin's "more foul and noisome than the hovel of a brute," filled with "loathsome creeping things" that "multiplied and rioted in the filth"—a perfect breeding ground for disease.[31] Throughout April, Dr. Robert Cabell, Davis's preferred physician for tending to his human property, was a regular presence in the pen. Among those he tended were both Nelsons and Melinda. These ministrations did little for the elder Nelson, who succumbed on April 22; Davis failed to record his malady but noted the $7.25 it cost to bury him. That same day, the trader bought medicine for Melinda and the younger Nelson in the hopes of preserving the money their lives represented. Cabell returned two days later to treat Melinda, but with little effect. On April 26, the pair received draughts of brandy, a stimulant considered capable of resuscitating patients in dire straits.[32] The gambit likely failed to revive Melinda (she disappeared thereafter from Davis's accounts) and did nothing for Nelson. The boy's final appearance in the historical record came in the form of the $3.50 Davis billed Payne for his burial, precisely the sum he had spent only recently on shoes and clothing to aid the boy's sale.[33]

Nelson lingered those three weeks in Davis's jail because the CSA's birth pangs had disrupted the trader's business. In April 1860, Davis had sold, on his own account, sixty-two people for nearly $60,000. During the same month in 1861, his sales fell to forty people for less than $30,000, a dismal prelude to a summer in which he would struggle mightily to find buyers.[34] For the people Davis hoped to sell, this translated into miserable, extended stays in a dim, poorly ventilated jail where they subsisted for weeks, if not months, on meager rations of meal and bacon. Indeed, when Nelson passed away in late April, Hannah, Armstead, and Davy had been in the jail since February.[35] Enslavers withdrew some people from Davis's custody in the face of diminishing prices and prospects. Following the older Nelson's death, for example, Payne recalled Almira, Joe, Willis, Newton, Wilson, and Jack.[36] Enslavers expected, however, that this retreat would be temporary. As one enslaver assured Dickinson, Hill & Co., he would return the people he had withdrawn "as soon as the market gets so they can be sold."[37] Nelson's fate shows that for all too many even this temporary reprieve came too late. Mary, Priscilla, Peter, and "Henrietta's child" also perished in Davis's jail that month.[38]

Just a day before Nelson's passing, Hector Davis paid $16.95 for a "secession flag" that he could fly over his property.[39] This was only the first of many gestures he made signaling his support for the fledgling Confederacy. A day after burying Nelson, Davis impulsively gave $10 to a passing soldier; two weeks later, he threw a dinner party for Louisiana troops arriving in Richmond (a fit of generosity perhaps inspired by his New Orleans slave trading connections). By the end of the year, his facility had become a rendezvous point for materiel sent by civilians to soldiers in the field and, occasionally, served as a hostel for Confederate troops bound for the front.[40] Day by day, his secession flag flew alongside the red cloth square that signified an impending sale of slaves, the twin standards of the new Confederacy.[41]

Though the establishment of the Confederacy and the onset of war dispersed some of the political fog enveloping the slave market, the first months of the war challenged the slave trade in new ways. Fears raised by the war combined with the ongoing financial crisis to amplify pre-existing tendencies within slave commerce in the spring and summer of 1861. Even in times of peace, the lucrative long-distance slave trade was highly seasonal, falling off during the spring and summer and expanding in the fall and winter as enslavers, relatively flush following the harvest, built out their workforces in preparation for the coming year.[42] As James Henry Hammond reminded Confederate Treasury Secretary Christopher Memminger, even under normal circumstances, economic activity would have slowed that summer as during that season slaveholders generally lacked the money needed "to purchas[e] more lands and negroes."[43]

The summer of 1861, however, was anything but normal, thanks in no small part to the ongoing demise of the CSA's financial infrastructure. Hector Davis's accounts underscore its aberrant nature. He and other slave brokers traditionally financed their dealing with a mixed array of credit and currency, including checks, banknotes, and drafts drawn on both Southern and Northern banks and financiers. By the spring of 1861, the latter had all but disappeared from his records, leaving only assorted Southern notes of indeterminate value. This dubious currency was also in short supply, to the point that Davis personally advanced several buyers funds to cover the people they purchased from him.[44] Credit remained tight, money scarce, and hope for a swift resolution limited. As a North Carolinian complained in April, "I don't think I have yet known a more general stagnation in business and a greater scarcity in money matters then we have . . . here now." "Scarcely anything we have," he worried, "will bring money," with "want of confidence . . . the principle cause of it."[45]

What scarce resources they could muster enslavers devoted to maintaining their existing operations. Many would have agreed with North Carolina's Charles Pettigrew: "We must stay at home and endeavor to live on what we can make and if we get any money send it to assist in driving these lawless Yankees beyond the border."[46] Unable to sell cotton, Mississippi's Richard Thompson Archer found that he possessed "nothing that will bring money except hay & corn that we can spare," and that he quickly "exhausted all my resources in supplying salt, sugar, and molasses for the subsistence of the negroes." Lacking the funds either to produce crops or pay his taxes, he desperately sought a loan from a man who had stood security for him in the past.[47] But former creditors could not always be relied upon. A Tennessee planter found that a Memphis firm capable of selling 17,000 bales of cotton in 1860 could not, a year later, repay even the $250 it owed him.[48] Enslavers thus lacked the resources necessary to purchase people and were unwilling to take on debts in the present that would come due in an opaque future.[49]

The removal of a large percentage of the men aged eighteen to thirty-five into the Confederate army further weakened the infrastructure supporting the slave trade. Not only did military-age men represent a significant number of the buyers and sellers in individual transactions, but they comprised the bulk of the agents on whom large slave dealers depended to acquire and move people between markets. As historian Joseph Glatthaar has shown, men personally invested in slavery joined the military in disproportionately high numbers early in the war, and slave traders seem to have been no exception. Atlanta trader Zachariah Rice joined Georgia politician Thomas R. R. Cobb's personal Legion, while North Carolina dealer Elias Ferguson served at Fort Fisher at the mouth of the Cape Fear River. Nathan Bedford Forrest, soon to be the most famous slave trading Confederate, had withdrawn to his Mississippi plantation in early 1860 following the literal collapse of his Memphis slave mart (through which perhaps 3,800 people had passed during his career). Secession cut short his retirement; within a week of Tennessee's secession in June 1861, he had joined a cavalry unit to protect the world that he had built through the slave trade.[50]

These factors—what one newspaper called "the crushing weight of civil commotion and rebellion"—merged with the impending contest of arms to undermine the slave market.[51] Western North Carolina's James Gwyn and his brother-in-law, Rufus Lenoir, observed this phenomenon firsthand after Rufus's brother, William, committed suicide in May 1861. In executing his estate, they looked to the slave market to resolve his debts. But, Gwyn noted, the national rupture had rendered slave sales an uncertain prospect at best. He harbored no doubts about slavery's future; indeed, he told Lenoir that he would happily receive his own portion of the estate in the form of enslaved people—especially young ones. Gwyn knew, however, that others weighed the threat of war more heavily than he did in valuing human property and admitted that prices would depend "entirely upon whether this horrible war is to be waged against us in reality & how long."[52]

In the spring and summer of 1861, the war's nature, trajectory, and implications for slavery remained ambiguous. While still a civilian, Ulysses S. Grant warned his slaveholding father-in-law that by disrupting the global cotton economy, the impending war would "reduce the value of negroes so much that they will never be worth fighting over again."[53] Prices diverged markedly, however, as slaveholders gauged the relative danger facing them. In Texas, for example, far from any prospective fighting, many buyers appeared utterly unfazed by larger political and economic developments. On the whole, however, purchasers proved scarce in mid-1861.[54] In North Carolina, a would-be seller complained to his congressman that "negroes will bring nothing" and sold only at what he termed a "sacrifice."[55] An Alabama auctioneer similarly bewailed "sacrifices" when no one would give more than $975 for a man who recently would have brought hundreds more.[56]

Figure 2.3 "A Slave Auction at the South." The auction depicted in this image purportedly took place in Charleston during the summer of 1861. From *Harper's Weekly*, Vol. 5, No. 237, July 13, 1861. Library of Congress, LC-DIG-ds-10813.

Low prices hammered slave traders in cities like the new Confederate capital of Richmond. Davis, Deupree & Co. asked the city council for relief from the taxes levied on auctioneers, arguing "that they ceased to do business in June 1861." The council denied them on the grounds that they had not planned to stop trading but "were induced to stop it, because from the condition of the country it had ceased to be profitable." E. H. Stokes sought a similar indulgence later in the summer, but the Commonwealth eventually taxed him on $60,000 in sales.[57] Dickinson, Hill, & Co. reported $133,175 in sales (the firm likely suffered a bit from Charles B. Hill's death that fall), Hector Davis $138,700—steep declines from the millions they had reported only a year earlier—while Silas Omohundro operated in 1861 at a net loss.[58] Would-be sellers, meanwhile, continued to pelt them with letters asking whether the enslaved would sell for "any price," reflecting the desperate lack of demand.[59]

Nowhere did the war's effects manifest themselves more dramatically than in New Orleans. The war transformed the city, in one observer's words, into "a great military encampment," filled with "the sound of marshal music, and the tread of marching troops"—a din that obscured the relative silence of its slave markets.[60] While he enthusiastically endorsed the Confederate cause, Henry F. Peterson acknowledged its adverse effect on his business. In late April, he advertised a gang of "Carolina and Virginia Negroes," but reported privately that he sold very few of them—and those at low prices.[61] As in Richmond, anemic demand shielded some enslaved people (at least temporarily) from sale. On May 11, 1861, seventeen men and women offered by the Orleans Parish sheriff went unsold when no bidder would give even two-thirds of the prices sought.[62] Tom likewise evaded sale when his enslaver, though desperate for cash, despaired of raising it by selling him.[63] C. F. Hatcher—who simultaneously offered thousands of acres of land in exchange for enslaved people—even petitioned the state legislature for relief.[64]

Given its tropical climate, its cholera and yellow fever epidemics, and the growing cycles of cotton and sugar, New Orleans's slave market had always been particularly seasonal. More than two-thirds of its annual slave transactions usually occurred by the end of the spring, with fully 80 percent of imported slaves sold in that period. Only 15 percent took place during the heart of the summer.[65] Unsurprisingly, therefore, June 1861 found the city's business "completely at a stand still," in one merchant's words. Even in the conflict's absence, a periodical pointed out, the city would naturally be "winding ... up the business season."[66]

This diagnosis overlooked the fact that as the Cotton Kingdom's chief entrepôt, New Orleans experienced the collapse of the Rebel staple crop economy extraordinarily acutely. The war soon scotched whatever hopes New Orleanians harbored that secession would resolve their financial crisis and allow the city to resume its financial and commercial preeminence. Within a few weeks of its onset, one newspaper wailed that the Civil War had banished "all thoughts of trade and commerce."[67] By June, the city's merchants lacked sufficient cotton to compose even a single respectable shipment. The sugar market likewise remained, in one factor's words, "very much depressed."[68] This crippled the city's commerce in all goods—including slaves. As a visiting enslaver moaned to his wife, "Business is in a more depressed condition just now than I ever saw it in my life."[69]

The US blockade of the city exacerbated this reality. The same geographic position that made New Orleans the Cotton Kingdom's natural port also rendered it a bottleneck easily stoppered.[70] Even a "threatened Blockade," Moses Greenwood complained, "put a stop to all sales of Cotton."[71] Merchants, planters, and, eventually, the Confederate government exacerbated the blockade's influence by further constraining cotton exports to protect themselves financially and to encourage foreign intervention.[72] As a result, New Orleans's cotton receipts declined by nearly 98 percent.[73] This collapse, combined with Louisiana banks' tightening of credit, a raft of unreliable currency, and a general climate of uncertainty, led one gloomy factor to inform a client, "Credit & every thing is at a stand, & will be until the war is at an end."[74] "King Cotton," one newspaper mourned, "has abdicated for the nonce."[75]

The rest of the Cotton Kingdom likewise suffered the effects of the credit crunch and blockade.[76] Natchez enslaver and banker Stephen Duncan feared that even a Confederate victory would bring the "utter devastation & ruin of all the property & property holders of the South."[77] By the end of 1861, this seemed to have come to pass; the editors of the *Natchez Daily Courier* watched a wagon full of cotton trundle across the city's Cotton Square and lamented seeing "*only* one solitary load traversing our streets" given that in a normal year "there should have been at least one hundred."[78] An Alabama slaveholder, meanwhile, complained that cotton could not be sold "untill the blockade is broken up."[79] Until that happened, a Texan observed, the prices offered for enslaved persons would remain "flat" because "unless" Southerners could "raise cotton ... we have no use for" them.[80] That being the case, in early 1862, Alabama's Sydenham Moore complained that enslaved people continued to be valued too highly. He feared being "subjugated" less than the reality that it would "be impossible to make any thing" at his plantation "this year." Under those circumstances, he resented receiving enslaved people in an estate division given that their high nominal prices prevented his obtaining other assets that he considered more immediately valuable.[81]

Under the weight of these pressures, the slave trade ground almost to a halt during the sweltering summer of 1861. In New Orleans, economists Jonathan Pritchett and Charles Calomiris have found, enslavers sold only sixty people in June and forty-six in July. The city's conveyance records show that the decline continued into the fall: thirty-three people sold in August, twenty-nine in September, and just over forty per month in October and November—a decline of fully two-thirds from the previous year.[82] Some of the transactions that did occur reflected the slaveholding republic's own grandiose expectations. The Southern Pacific Railroad Company, for example, sought to purchase or hire up to one thousand enslaved laborers and offered long-term securities in payment.[83] Others reflected specific individual needs. A De Soto Parish enslaver purchased Edward, a thirty-eight-year-old carpenter. Simeon

Toby sought a woman for housework, John R. Elliott hands for a sawmill. The auction house of McCerren & Landry sold John so that his enslaver could flee the city. The owner of a steamboat, meanwhile, sold a group of enslaved workers after the blockade trapped his craft in the city.[84]

By the winter of 1861, the staple crop economy—the Charybdis that had for decades drawn enslaved people inexorably to the Deep South—had subsided to a trickle. Slave traders increasingly avoided New Orleans and its environs. Letters to and from that city largely disappeared from Dickinson, Hill & Co.'s correspondence, and though Dickinson visited in early 1862, he offered no comment on its slave market.[85] Likewise, Silas Omohundro sold people to Mississippi-bound traders in the fall of 1861, but none to those heading to Louisiana, a clientele he had often served in the past.[86] While Virginia's John Toler and Elijah Brittingham did sell people in New Orleans, their colleagues in the trade complained endlessly of the hard times they faced.[87] A Louisiana planter overseeing an estate division, for his part, refused to bring an enslaved person to the Crescent City, believing he could only be sold there at "a ruinous sacrifice."[88] The financial crisis, blockade, and faltering cotton economy thus accelerated seasonal swings in the slave trade, damaging Confederate slave commerce during the Civil War's first year.

The early months of 1862 suggested that though dire, these injuries would not prove mortal. Indeed, in New Orleans and elsewhere, the trade began to show signs of revival. Would-be sellers like Achille Chiapella, president of the Union Insurance Company, eagerly anticipated the return of the Deep South's "cotton and sugar planters" to markets like New Orleans.[89] By December 1861, traders had also begun returning, and while few operated on their antebellum scale, they showed there was still money to be made in human trafficking.[90] From forty people sold in New Orleans in both October and November 1861, the number of recorded transactions in the city rose to seventy-one in December, more than ninety in January, and 143 in March 1862. These figures matched and, in some cases, exceeded those of the secession winter, though prices remained well below their historic highs.[91] Although anemic demand still forestalled some transactions—the largest sheriff's sale of slaves during this period fizzled when no one offered anything resembling the enslaved people's appraised values—contemporary observers nevertheless found the city's slave market active.[92]

No one exemplified the resurgence of New Orleans's slave trade more than Joseph Bruin. Having begun as an itinerant trader in northern Virginia (where he bought and sold people from families up to and including the

Washingtons), Bruin boasted a quarter-century of experience in slave dealing.[93] As was his custom, in late 1861 and early 1862 he touted groups of between thirty and fifty enslaved people for sale, some of whom allegedly arrived as late as April 18.[94] A New Orleans lawyer noted that by the spring of 1862, Bruin was "the only one who has had a large stock of negroes on hand."[95] From September 1861 onward, Bruin sold at least forty people—and possibly many more—in the city.[96]

Among Bruin's clients that winter was Charles Gayarré, an enslaver and historian who approached the slave market seeking to address yet another burgeoning Confederate problem: inflation. Though the war was less than a year old, the CSA was already struggling to pay for it. As a result, the national and state governments had begun printing money in vast quantities to cover their mounting debts. Inflation swiftly reached 12 percent per month and the Rebel currency depreciated accordingly.[97] Confederate officials might pronounce it "as good as gold," but Gayarré observed that those "replete" with paper money manifested a "most frantic desire" to translate it into real property. Real estate had surged in response to this impulse, and Gayarré wondered whether enslaved property might follow. Hearing rumors of high prices in Virginia, he pestered Confederate official and former journalist J. D. B. De Bow for advice.[98] De Bow replied that the $10,000 Gayarré hoped to invest would easily purchase "15 to 20 prime negroes of both sexes," but he cautioned against doing so. "For my part," De Bow stated, "it is the only property now that I would not touch with a long stick at any price"—not, he quickly added, because "I doubt our eventual success," but because the prospect of a prolonged conflict left him wary of investing in enslaved property.[99]

Gayarré evidently found the potential profits more compelling than De Bow's concerns, for he purchased seven people from Bruin in February 1862.[100] In New Orleans and elsewhere, many joined him in seeking enslaved people in the winter of 1861 and spring of 1862. De Bow's own brother-in-law, perhaps ignoring similar warnings from his relation, frequented New Orleans slave sales in search of bargains.[101] An Alabamian even hounded Confederate Vice President Alexander Stephens for information on the slave market, wondering whether he could "lay" out money "to great advantage in Richmond or any part of Virginia for negroes?"[102] Hector Davis's accounts suggest that he certainly could. Davis's sales had cratered during the summer and fall of 1861. Between May and December, he sold only twenty-six people on his own account—the equivalent of a single bad prewar month. In 1862, however, his business rebounded. He sold as many people in January and

February 1862 (seventy) as he had during those same months in 1861.[103] The resurgence reflected in Davis's books and New Orleans's conveyance records demonstrate that by the late winter and early spring of 1862, the slave market had stabilized. So long as slave trading centers remained securely within the Confederacy, the buyers and sellers who met there trusted that the enslaved would remain property and thus continued doing business. For all the chaos enveloping the Confederacy that spring, slave dealing survived.

In early 1862, military disasters surpassed economic collapse as Confederates' foremost concern. In the eastern theater, Union forces pushed Confederates out of northern Virginia, drove deep into the fertile Shenandoah Valley, and established footholds on the coasts of North and South Carolina. The 100,000-man Army of the Potomac slogged up the Virginia Peninsula and, by May's end, sat encamped within sight of Richmond. The Rebel position in the Mississippi Valley was, if anything, worse. US armies under Grant and Don Carlos Buell, accompanied by fleets of gunboats, captured Forts Henry and Donelson and swarmed up the Tennessee and Cumberland Rivers. By mid-April they had taken Nashville, repulsed a Confederate counterattack at Shiloh, and reached Mississippi and Alabama. Another combined arms expedition moved down the Mississippi River, securing Confederate strongholds as it went. Still another force, commanded by General Benjamin Butler and Admiral David Farragut, advanced upriver against New Orleans. On April 24, Farragut's vessels breached a boom blocking the Mississippi, sped past Forts St. Philip and Jackson, and, the following morning, floated on the city's levee with their guns trained on the South's largest slave market.[104]

These invasions had immediate and profound effects on the slave trade, a reality General Butler later recalled in testimony before the American Freedmen's Inquiry Commission, a quasi-governmental body assessing enslaved people's transition to freedom. Butler would eventually spend eight months in Louisiana. Slavery remained legal for that entire period, as it would in Tennessee and in occupied parts of Virginia's Tidewater. The US military even sporadically supported enslavers' efforts to maintain the institution. And yet Butler oversaw a period during which, by his estimate, "eight out of every ten of the negroes of Louisiana" made themselves functionally "free." This was because Union officials gradually limited slaveholders' access to the government support and police powers that had long upheld slavery. Without these reinforcements, enslavers' remaining authority, Butler judged, "did not amount to a great deal." Unable to retain people as property, enslavers all but ceased to buy and sell them. Thus, by the time Butler left New Orleans, he bragged, "slave property, as a marketable commodity, had gone out entirely in Louisiana." Had he desired to do so, Butler could have bought "the best negroes in Louisiana for $250," an 83 percent discount from their antebellum prices.[105]

Though a gifted self-promoter, Butler actually undersold the Union army's devastating effects on the slave trade in New Orleans and other occupied cities. Where it held sway, the Federal regime was a halfway house between the United States and the Confederacy, military rule and civil authority, a slave society and one based on free labor. As historian Rashauna Johnson points out, it is at such intersections that "the state creates itself," with "officials, residents, and migrants contend[ing] over which people are fit to become part of the body politic (and in what capacity) as well as who should be excluded." The domestic slave trade had long played a central role in this process, affirming African Americans' exclusion and threatening abduction and sale even for those legally free.[106]

The US presence flipped this reality on its head. Even where slavery remained legal, Union soldiers intentionally and unintentionally undercut its laws and limited enslavers' ability to enforce them. Merging with and abetting bondspeople's pursuit of freedom, US forces made slave transactions increasingly difficult to execute. They offered enslaved people a refuge from their captivity—an inconsistent one, to be sure, but a refuge nonetheless. For enslavers, this meant the possibility of the total, uncompensated loss of their enslaved property and the erasure of the future returns they could expect to receive from them. This prospect cast doubt on the future of the institution of slavery and brought the slave market crashing down. By the summer of 1862, in cities where traders had once sold thousands of people annually for hundreds (even thousands) of dollars apiece, US occupation and enslaved resistance had diminished this traffic to the sale of a mere handful of people for pennies on the dollar. Enslaved people and the irregular application of American military might thus eradicated significant parts of the Confederate slave trade, accomplishing in a few months what a year of economic turmoil had not.[107]

In occupied cities from Norfolk to Natchez, Nashville to New Orleans, two realities struck at the heart of slave commerce in those locales. First, US forces and policies placed significant legal and administrative hurdles in the way of anyone trying to buy and sell people, making it exceedingly difficult to engage in slave commerce even where buyers were forthcoming. The lack of purchasers stemmed from the second prong of the Federals' assault on slave commerce: their subversion of the slaveholding state. The Union army undercut municipal and state police powers, hindering the legal and extralegal mechanisms that governed enslaved life and punished transgressions against the white power structure. It also injected a countervailing force against the superior power that enslavers had long enjoyed over their bondsmen and women. Federal invasions thus empowered enslaved people's freedom-seeking and made slave property so fundamentally risky a proposition that investment in it disappeared.

Much as they had in Alexandria, US forces fanning out from beachheads in northern Virginia and at Fort Monroe on the Virginia Peninsula demolished slave trading centers as they went.[108] For people like Emma Bolt, their arrival could hardly have been timelier. "Thank God," she rejoiced, "that yankees come." Her entire family had fallen into the hands of William W. Hall, a fixture of Norfolk's trade. He had sold several of her siblings during the preceding winter and intended to sell Bolt on what proved to be the Monday following the Federals' arrival. Instead, he decamped from the city, taking one of her brothers with him.[109] White residents of Norfolk and nearby Portsmouth desperately sold people off up until those cities' fall—"hundreds of mothers and children," one formerly enslaved woman recalled.[110] Union occupation quickly ended large-scale sales in both cities. A journalist visiting Norfolk just weeks after its capture found "no sales of negroes... lately," while in Portsmouth, those awaiting sale had fallen "in line and followed the Union army."[111] By the end of 1862, a visiting abolitionist reported, Norfolk's former slave jail no longer "resound[ed] with the groans of the suffering slave" but sheltered fugitives and served as a base of operations for those aiding their emergence from bondage.[112]

Similar scenes unfolded in slave markets located in the western theater. Josh Miles remembered his enslaver selling people in Nashville to fund his flight from Union forces, while Smith Austin recalled being compelled to labor there until, as he put it, "'long come more of de war"—by which he presumably meant the Union army. His enslaver then sold several people and used the money to remove others to places of safety.[113] This enslaver's fears were borne out, for after the Federals took Nashville in February 1862, the Union military slowly eradicated its trade in slaves. Admittedly, this process was neither immediate nor consistent. As late as August, slave trader Henry Haynes kept at least thirty-four people in his "Sale House." Those he retained,

THE "UNCONGENIAL AIR OF FREEDOM" 63

however, reflected the slave trade's increasingly liminal status. Haynes labeled a young woman named Ellis "sold and deliver[ed]," but she was the only one described thus. Most of the other inhabitants had been confined not for sale but for alleged crimes or to prevent their flight. Still others suffered from an array of maladies that rendered them, in Haynes's opinion, "worthless."[114]

This diagnosis aside, Military Governor Andrew Johnson willingly would have allowed Haynes to continue his profession as an extension of loyal Tennesseans' property rights. As 1862 progressed, however, the tumult

Figure 2.4 Josh Miles. As his enslaver drove him from Virginia to Texas, Miles watched him traffic in people along the way. Library of Congress, LC-USZ62-125271.

enveloping the state—economic chaos, the impossibility of parsing enslavers' shifting loyalties, and the military's demand for labor—dissuaded enslavers from investing in humanity. Even as Haynes recorded the denizens of his slave pen, for example, US soldiers prevented three slave catchers from returning to bondage men who had fled from an allegedly loyal enslaver, securing the fugitives' liberty and inverting the "law and order" (as one enslaved woman termed it) on which slaveholders depended by arresting their pursuers. Under the collective weight of repeated reprises of this scene, Johnson's administration eventually "cleaned out the slave pens & the workhouses of all negroes." Before long, a single silver plaque marking a trader's office was the only physical evidence of the city's slave-trafficking past.[115]

This did not mean instant liberty for those confined in the city's slave jails. Johnson himself testified that white Tennesseans ensnared many of those released from Nashville pens and smuggled them south for sale. Others the Union army conscripted as laborers. Some joined voluntarily. John McCline, for example, responded to a Michigan soldier's promise that if he would "Come on . . . and go with us . . . we will set you free" by going "off with the Yankees." In other cases, Union soldiers acted without African Americans' consent. Armed soldiers broke open at least one jail, with the enslaved people held therein "carried off by the army." If the balance of power had not shifted entirely in favor of the enslaved, however, it had moved decidedly away from their enslavers. A Union general declared that in middle Tennessee, "Slavery is dead; that is the first thing." He acknowledged that there were locals who would gladly have revived slavery and the traffic in people, but he credited their elimination to the fact that even these were "cowed by the force of the Gov't."[116]

Two hundred miles to the southwest, the even larger Memphis market—home, by the 1850s, to a dozen slave dealing firms—survived until US forces' arrival in June.[117] As elsewhere, secession and the war's early months disrupted but did not destroy the slave trade. A formerly enslaved man recalled arriving in the city with forty or fifty others during the secession winter, while a visitor found one hundred enslaved people in a trader's jail only weeks before Fort Sumter.[118] Even as Union soldiers closed in, Memphis area enslavers hoped their emancipationist impact would be muted. A newspaper claimed that people sold in the city for $1,100 to $1,300. That being the case, Union policies did "not seem to have much effect upon the prices of darkies." As a result, an enslaved man recalled, those awaiting sale filled "big warehouses." A three- or four-year-old Nancy Gardner lost her parents and siblings as Memphis slavers scattered them to buyers in Mississippi and Alabama.[119] Some Confederates allowed their imaginations to run wild. In the emerging, independent Confederacy, one seller argued only weeks before Memphis's surrender, "cotton will, after a while, regain its power." Though he left the thought unspoken, he must have assumed the slave trade would do the same.[120]

When Union forces captured the city, however, enslavers quickly realized they could no longer deal in human property. A Confederate soldier encountered one fleeing slaveholder intent on "running his negroes south, converting them into cotton, and eventually into gold."[121] Slavery's legal status remained ambiguous, and the city's jails still menaced alleged runaways. But change was afoot. By August, Memphis's Union-backed government had converted Nathan Bedford Forrest's former offices into a municipal jail, embodying the shifting application of state authority.[122] The conquering William T. Sherman later described the change succinctly: "The moment a negro cannot be bought and sold, or when he can run off without danger of recapture, the question is settled."[123]

As spring turned to summer in 1862, New Orleans became the largest market to succumb to the pressures of occupation. Its experiences are instructive as to how this process unfolded. First by accelerating the cotton economy's collapse, then by promulgating policies that targeted disloyal citizens and empowered people of color, military authorities severely impaired slave traders' ability to do business. As US soldiers collided with the slaveholding society of the Lower Mississippi Valley, meanwhile, their presence abetted enslaved peoples' efforts to win free from the plantation complex, abrading the institution significantly. In the end, Union occupation rendered slave property deeply uncertain in and around New Orleans, all but foreclosing individuals' willingness to acquire or invest in it.

The Union advance up the Mississippi compounded the economic crisis that had plagued New Orleans and its environs for more than a year. With what remained of the city's cotton markets stalling, the currency collapsing, and evacuating Confederates destroying anything of value, the slave market also ground to a halt.[124] Even sheriff's auctions ceased with the imposition of martial law in April.[125] The city's crippled economy presented Butler with conflicting challenges when he arrived in the city. Tasked with restoring order, ensuring New Orleanians' loyalty, and reinvigorating the city's economy, his objectives incentivized reestablishing the region's cash crop economy and restraining enslaved peoples' freedom-seeking. Butler was also, however, engaged in an active war. This brought his soldiers into continual contact with enslaved people and made these men and women his natural allies. Their thousands of bids for liberty, abetted by the destabilizing effects of military occupation, terminally undercut slave property and the slave trade in New Orleans.

Given New Orleans's—and cotton's—importance to America's economy, reestablishing its trade with the outside world was of signal importance to occupying Union forces.[126] Lincoln himself reportedly "regard[ed] the renewal of commerce at New Orleans... as a most effective means of bringing this unhappy civil strife to an end, and restoring the authority of the Federal Government."[127] The city badly needed such a renewal. Exports of 1.8 million cotton bales from its port in 1860–1861 declined to only 22,000 in 1862–1863, while sugar exports plummeted to 5 percent of their antebellum total.[128] One Union soldier considered the city under a "continual sabbath," another "desolate beyond description."[129] A British traveler, after seeing "neither a bale of cotton, a hogshead of sugar, a bushel of corn, a packet of merchandise, or a man at work," concluded that "there was neither business nor pleasure going on in New Orleans."[130]

Butler insisted that restoring New Orleans to its status as "a city of the first class" required its inhabitants' "attending to their usual avocations and endeavoring to live quietly under the laws of the Union." In return for their cooperation, Butler promised to uphold their property rights in man, a stance slaveholders applauded. As one Jefferson Parish enslaver assured him, "by returning the negroe to his owner" Butler could be "in peaceful possession of Louisiana in less than a month."[131] The Union high command hoped leaving slavery unmolested would entice the loyal back into the fold, ease the occupation of the city, and direct profits from its trade into Federal coffers.[132]

This policy proved easier to describe than to implement. Union governance spawned what Butler's eventual successor Nathaniel P. Banks would describe as "an immense military Government" with charge over "every form of civil administration, the assessment of taxes, fines, punishments, charities, trade, regulation of churches, confiscation of estates, and the working of plantations."[133] As US authorities reached into each of these arenas, their actions undercut slavery and, explicitly or implicitly, the slave trade.[134] Many of these came in response to Louisianians' uncertain loyalties. Butler's General Orders No. 41, for example, required citizens to swear loyalty oaths to engage in basic commercial functions, including having "money paid them" or "property... delivered to them."[135] This regulation directly impeded slave traders' businesses. As one New Orleanian complained, it rendered all "auction sales null and void, unless the auctioneer has taken the oath of allegiance."[136] Most of the city's traders would have failed any loyalty test spectacularly; Peterson, Bruin, Hatcher, and Walter Campbell, at least, contributed materially to the Rebel cause.[137] Additional policies further hindered slave commerce, banning the removal of people of color from the city by boat without a pass and limiting enslavers' ability to sell enslaved people both within and away from New Orleans.[138] Enslavers indubitably evaded many of these measures, as when Rose Herera's enslaver (who had purchased her in 1861) kidnapped her children and smuggled them to Cuba in early 1863.[139] But these edicts' existence added hurdles to the purchase and sale of people.

Butler and his subordinates also stripped away the state powers upon which enslavers relied. General Orders No. 41's loyalty mandate, for example, required judges, sheriffs, and notaries to affirm their allegiance to the United States to retain their positions. Having allies in these positions had long enhanced slaveholders' efforts to hold people in slavery and been central aspects of slave commerce. Judges endorsed enslavers' professed property rights and the county and parish courts they oversaw conducted perhaps half of all slave sales, resolving debts and dissolving estates.[140] Sheriffs, aided and abetted by slave patrols, militia, and (prior to secession) US agents, secured slaveholders' human property.[141] In New Orleans, every slave transaction had to be notarized, with notaries' stalls on Exchange Alley conveniently located for those buying and selling people.[142] Lacking support from these entities, traders and slaveholders found human trafficking an increasingly difficult proposition.

The United States also attacked the slaveholding state's police powers. In August 1862, Butler barred slave patrols from pursuing runaways into the city and interposed his authority between fugitives and their pursuers.[143] He also limited arrests on behalf of enslavers of dubious loyalty, curtailed their access to carceral facilities, released enslaved people held therein, and abrogated laws that had previously mandated their sale to recoup the costs of their confinement. Butler justified his decisions in pragmatic terms, arguing that enslaved people lacked the "commercial value" necessary to offset these costs. As one newspaper sardonically replied, "it is pretty clear the General don't think slaves are first-class collaterals just now," though it failed to acknowledge the ways in which his actions had contributed to this reality.[144] Butler also banned the sale of children born to enslaved women in the state penitentiary.[145] Such gestures were hardly empty. According to one report, well into 1862, New Orleans held "many men" who made "their living by arresting negroes," while "the jails, and old-time slave-pens of the city . . . were full of these victims." Butler's regulations did not completely eradicate such practices, but they did much to "empty the jails and hell-holes of the city of their hundreds of victims."[146]

The military also offered formerly enslaved people unprecedented legal protection. Even if their treatment did not always equal that enjoyed by their white counterparts, it far outstripped anything that existed under slavery. When, for example, a policeman informed a Rebel who had stolen an American flag from a Black woman that "the word of a negro was worth something," the thief retorted, "yes now that you people have come here."[147] The Federal regime allowed former bondspeople to defend themselves in provost courts, subjecting enslavers to an authority hostile to their claims to human property.[148] One such opportunity permitted free woman of color Mart Bailie to seek the release of her child from a man who claimed him as a slave.[149] In another instance, a provost court blocked the sale of the child of a free Black man on the logic that "when Louisiana went out of the Union she took her black laws with her."[150] It is little wonder, then, that Rachel Jenkins, sold to New Orleans more than a decade earlier, dated her freedom to the moment that "Gen. Butler took possession of this city."[151] Even when unevenly enforced, US policies cumulatively undercut slaveholders' access to state support, thereby striking at the commodification of human beings.

Occasionally, Union officials acted directly against the slave trade. The clearest example occurred when an enslaver kidnapped and attempted to sell Jeff, a barber hiring his time to US forces. When the man in question refused to reveal Jeff's whereabouts, Butler reportedly intervened personally, imprisoning him until he confessed to whom he had sold Jeff. Armed with this information, Butler went after all involved in the process, jailing Jeff's purchaser "for buying a free man" and, upon learning that Thomas Foster had confined Jeff in his slave pen and facilitated the sale, summoning the trader before him. Butler browbeat Foster, informing "him that the business of slave-pen keeping was obsolete in New Orleans, and warn[ing] him against attempting to continue it." He then employed Jeff to trim his own thinning hair.[152]

That Foster lingered in New Orleans at all was remarkable, for many of his fellow slave dealers left in the weeks surrounding the Federals' arrival. They did so even though slavery remained legal, suggesting that they understood better than anyone except the enslaved themselves what Union occupation ultimately meant.[153] Gardner Smith & Co., long one of the city's primary dealers in slaves, dissolved on July 1, 1862.[154] Others retreated into the surviving Confederacy. R. H. Elam fled to Tennessee, Charles Hatcher to Mobile, and Thomas Matthews, embracing a longstanding Southwestern tradition, to Texas.[155] Walter Campbell fled first to his country residence in St. Helena Parish, then to Mississippi. The Union army confiscated his New Orleans slave pen and used it to hold captive Confederates, to the delight of the local Black population. Upon seeing Rebels installed therein, one formerly enslaved person exclaimed, "Got in dar ye-self . . . Use' to put us dar! Got dar ye-self now. De Lord's comin.'"[156]

In the agricultural districts outside New Orleans, Union forces' attitudes evolved more unevenly. Initially, Butler aided purportedly loyal enslavers in keeping people in slavery and maintaining plantation discipline. Official policies excluded enslaved people not working for the Union war effort from occupied territory, exposing them to recapture and abuse by enslavers.[157] Robert Harrison, Robert Morgan, and Joe Lewis fled New Orleans's gas works, only to have US forces send them back into bondage.[158] When a band of refugees from a sugar plantation turned their "cane knives and clubs" against policemen trying to arrest them, Federal soldiers sided with the police.[159] Such actions dovetailed with slaveholders' ongoing efforts to secure the slave regime: increased slave patrols, crackdowns on enslaved mobility, and enforced bans on illicit interactions with slaves.[160]

Few had more experience than Butler in navigating the contradictory impulses of Federal policies toward the enslaved. A year earlier, while stationed at Fort Monroe in Virginia, he had responded to refugees arriving at the fort by implementing the "contraband of war" policy, securing their removal from bondage but resting it on the logic of enslaved people's property status. In New Orleans, their persistent pursuit of liberty again tested Butler. Even more than in Virginia, however, tangled questions of loyalty shaped US forces' interactions with enslaved people even as soldiers' presence offered the enslaved an ally against their enslavers and the slaveholding state.[161]

African Americans began rallying to Union forces before they even set foot on Louisiana soil, convincing one officer that while conservative policies might delay emancipation, they "cannot long prevent a revolution."[162] As they ascended the Mississippi, US soldiers and sailors were "enthusiastically cheered by the negro's," who "were glad the old flag had come back," and sure "their masters wouldn[']t *dare* to use them so bad."[163] As soon as New Orleans fell, one freedman recalled, "slaves were running into the Union line from all around our neighborhood."[164] And when US forces retained "one absconding negro," a Mississippian complained, they created "a temptation to others to abscond."[165] Indeed, shortly after Union troops contained the aforementioned refugees from the cane fields, a second large group arrived in the city.[166] Alexander Pugh bemoaned a "perfect stampede" of people from his upriver property; another group purloined a skiff from William Minor and headed for freedom.[167] Fugitive populations in and around New Orleans could easily double overnight.[168] "Still they come," marveled one officer after recording the arrival of almost 2,000 enslaved people in his lines.[169] Thus, when a family member complained to Moses Greenwood about a similar loss of a person, he replied only that they had suffered an increasingly "ordinary misfortune."[170]

As US forces thrust deeper into the plantation kingdom, such "misfortunes" multiplied.[171] The Union high command hoped to keep African Americans "as far as possible, upon plantations" in order "to have the sugar crop made and preserved, for the owners that are loyal, and for the United States when the owners are disloyal."[172] But the enslaved, Butler complained, fled "Loyal and disloyal masters . . . alike." He worried that indiscriminately accepting refugees would effectively endorse the "actual confiscation of all property," but knew that turning them away would only strengthen the enemy.[173] Many of his subordinates found these distinctions academic.[174] After Union forces passed through his St. Martin Parish holdings, William Palfrey groused that they had "no regard to private property." Having anticipated their particular distaste for keeping people as property, Palfrey had forced his human chattels to a distant refuge.[175]

Lack of similar foresight cost others dearly. Thirty-three miles outside New Orleans, US troops "induced" sixty-six people (whom the proprietor optimistically appraised at $66,000) "to escape by promising the protection of the federal authorities."[176] A Maine regiment told others "that they were free— that everything on the plantation belonged to them and that they could do with it whatever they pleased."[177] Butler increasingly saw this as an inevitable consequence of the conflict, observing to the French consul in New Orleans that enslaved flight was only "natural when their master had set them the example of rebellion against constituted authorities."[178] Another general found it "a singular request" when Mississippi enslavers sought "assistance from an authority they had repudiated" in retaining people in bondage. He theoretically affirmed their right to hold people in bondage but refused to secure it "by the employment of force."[179]

Tensions nevertheless lingered between the army's efforts to restore the Union and its effects on slavery.[180] Though the US government promised fair pay, protection from arbitrary punishment, and care for the freedpeople, reality often involved coerced work on the very plantations they hoped to escape. Paramilitaries reminiscent of slave patrols roamed some regions, with pro-slavery civilian authorities persisting in others. As late as April 1863, an officer found the "civil police . . . called in by planters to arrest their laborers, & the jails . . . used for their 'safe keeping.'"[181] Accordingly, a Treasury Department official noted, "the negro has no confidence in [planters], and constantly fears a renewal of his bonds . . . when Southern slaveholders say a free negro will not work, the statement is partially true. He will not work for them."[182] Against these pressures, formerly enslaved people leveraged their skills in cultivating sugar and an ever-expanding array of Union anti-slavery policies, including a congressional ban on Union soldiers' enforcement of the state's slave code and enrollment in the United States Colored Troops.[183]

The result, in Nathaniel Banks's words, was that "masters had rights in law . . . which they could not execute. The negroes enjoyed a freedom which they could not justify in law, except as a consequence of the war."[184] When, for example, Guy, Peter, and Fred fled from the Weeks family in southwestern Louisiana, the overseer sent to recapture them counted on using all the state mechanisms that had long empowered slaveholders, including the ability to hold the fugitives in local jails as he transported them through the state. A Weeks family member worried, however, that even if he managed to recover the three men, he would find none of the available facilities "very secure" in the present climate. Without a stable "place of confinement," it became "very difficult to keep" fugitives from bondage even "after they are caught."[185] Seeing enslavers deprived of state support and energized by the presence of Union soldiers, a St. James Parish planter claimed late in 1862, "negroes beleive [sic] they are free." "The institution of slavery," he feared, "if not destroyed, has been demoralized"; even active Federal support would be insufficient to "remedy the damage for a long time."[186] Another enslaver considered things still more dire: "It seems this is an end to black slavery & our section is lost to us for ever."[187]

Taken as a whole, enslaved people's ambitions for freedom, aided and abetted by Union soldiers' intervention, had, by 1864, inaugurated what Banks termed a "Revolution" in the relationship between bondspeople and their former enslavers.[188] Despite US efforts to maintain the plantation economy and its nominal protection of slaveholding Unionists, enslavers had lost the bulk of the protections they had once enjoyed and enslaved people had been invigorated in facing down their former captors. Enslaved property thus became a highly uncertain investment, one potentially on the verge of extinction. As one planter bluntly informed Banks, thanks to the US army's presence in Louisiana, "Our slaves have been rendered valueless."[189]

That being the case, it is little wonder that the trade in slaves evaporated in occupied New Orleans. From ninety in April 1862, the number of slave transactions recorded fell by more than half in May. June saw only twenty-one; by July, officials noted merely six.[190] Some of those recorded stemmed directly from the conflict. One family fleeing the city sought to exchange urban workers for agricultural laborers, another to dispose of four "choice and valuable slaves at a bargain."[191] Other transactions were legally mandated, including a handful of estate divisions that occurred despite the faltering market.[192] Others attached enslaved people to exchanges of real estate and other goods.[193] In some cases, African Americans exploited the diminished market to secure their families' legal freedom. Olivette, for example, was sold on the condition she be emancipated; another New Orleanian purchased a woman named Susan on behalf of his free wife.[194] For others, chaos obviated the need to use the slave market entirely. A free man of color named Emperor Williams, who had saved for years to purchase his enslaved wife, abandoned this plan in favor of her simply leaving her enslaver.[195]

As the slave trade collapsed, Union soldiers, abolitionists, and the enslaved themselves celebrated its demise. Former trading spaces became tourist destinations from which visitors reported on the transformation. One soldier in the 20th Iowa, for example, found a former slave mart occupied by a commissary officer. He "derived much pleasure now in knowing that this foul blot upon our national escutcheon had at length been washed away forever."[196] Instead of reporting "fearful scenes of the slave marts," one journalist highlighted their "present desertion."[197] The contrast between the city's slave trading past and the onset of freedom struck a member of the 32nd Massachusetts powerfully when he visited Thomas Foster's former jail. "The slave pen," he discovered, "is now a recruiting office for the Corps d'Afrique."[198]

By 1863, only trace elements of New Orleans's once massive slave trade survived.[199] Conveyance records show only twenty-nine people sold that year, the last in late July.[200] To be sure, some sales may have continued unrecorded and unendorsed by the city government. While municipal records describe no such event, in April, *The Liberator* complained that the Union high command had tacitly endorsed a "public sale of slaves" in the city.[201] At the very least, this report stirred Banks to symbolic action. In late 1863, he ordered an officer to remove the remaining signage from slave traders' former premises. "The events of the past year," he argued, "make it impossible that such business should be continued hereafter."[202]

Union occupation also destroyed the slave trade in New Orleans's upriver counterpart, Natchez, where slave traders had sold people worth more than $2 million annually as recently as 1860.[203] Even though Union advances into northern Mississippi had cut off much of the city's remaining slave traffic, advertisements for the sale of people appeared in its newspapers until the end of May 1863—just weeks prior to the Union army's arrival.[204] Indeed, Henry Scales, enslaved only a dozen miles from the city, lost his mother to the slave trade in mid-May.[205] Half a year later, four thousand freedpeople reportedly lived in the city, with members of the newly recruited 6th USCI dismantling the city's slave pens to construct their barracks. Some of these men had once been sold within those very walls and, as they worked, they shared "many a thrilling reminiscence . . . of the cruelty of traders, of sad partings of husband and wife, of inhuman fathers selling their own children, and a thousand other incidents."[206]

Slaveholding states that remained in the United States likewise saw their trades in enslaved people shaped by conflict between the corrosive power of the Union army and the institution of slavery. Marylanders, for example, continued to buy and sell people during the war's early days. These included Agnes, who underwent sale at the hands of the Tayloe family in October 1861.[207] The presence of Federal troops, however (as George Smith's enslaver foresaw), eroded the viability of the institution. A month after Agnes's sale, Massachusetts soldier Charles Brewster watched Maryland fugitives enter Union lines near Washington, DC. They came in such numbers that it was obvious "this war is playing the Dickens with slavery and if it last much longer will clear our Countrys name of the vile stain and enable us to live in peace hereafter." One enslaved Marylander toured the camps seeking to raise money to purchase himself for $800. "I guess," Brewster surmised, "his master sees that there is not much help for slavery and want to get his money for him before there is no more slavery." Union soldiers instead "told him he was a fool not to take 'leg bail' and save his money."[208] Marylanders also retained some access to slave markets south of the Potomac. As Congress prepared to enact emancipation in Washington in the spring of 1862, Washingtonians reportedly sold off people enslaved in the city. One resident of the district believed that her counterparts might have dispatched as many as two thousand to slave markets in "Maryland Kentucky & Virginia," though she believed that most were destined for the CSA, where they might yet bring "good prices."[209]

Kentucky and Maryland remained, nevertheless, viable markets, ones that could have offered enslavers more of a return than the few hundred dollars Congress provided in compensation for their human property. Neither loyal slave market, however, offered anything resembling antebellum prices. Indeed, when Congress set standard rates for compensated emancipation in Washington, they consulted Baltimore slave broker Bernard Campbell, brother and partner of New Orleans's Walter Campbell. Events in Campbell's own jail evinced the changes afoot. In June 1862, more than sixty enslaved men and women whom enslavers had confined to prevent their flight rose up. "Declaring," as one account recorded, "that the time had come for them to go free," they refused to be locked in for the night and attacked Campbell and the police officers sent to restrain them. Only when the officers discharged their weapons did the uprising falter. Maryland enslavers could still call upon state backing to retain people in bondage, but its strength was on the wane.[210]

Residents of Kentucky and Missouri likewise continued to buy and sell people. As Mattie Jackson, in danger of being sold from the latter to the former, recalled, many loyal slaveholders believed that "as they pretended to take no part in the rebellion . . . they would be allowed to keep" the people they enslaved "without interference."[211] Many of the Union soldiers traversing these states left the institution unscathed. At the outset of 1862, one Kentuckian argued that prices for laborers remained the same as in the previous year. In other cases, however, these forces created the necessary friction to allow enslaved people to slip their bonds, devastating slave commerce. Watching people bought and sold rankled a growing number of soldiers. Members of the 3rd Minnesota, disgusted by the sight of a slave auction, asked permission to break it up. "50 of my men," an officer recalled, "would have whipped 500 slave traders if I had given them a chance." As soldiers collided with civilians, they injected uncertainty into the slave market. Prices dropped, in some cases to between $200 and $500 per person. Because state authorities still actively protected enslaved property, however, sales of human property continued along the border.[212]

Illicit sales also continued in Union-occupied parts of the Confederacy. Nashville's chief of police, for one, complained that enslavers easily could pose as loyal citizens, obtain enslaved people, and "run" them "South."[213] Caroline Dodson suffered precisely this fate. In 1862, her enslaver sold her to a slave trader who, in turn, sneaked her across Union lines and dealt her to broker Robert Clarke in Confederate-held Atlanta.[214] Near Norfolk, meanwhile, a subset of Union soldiers actively subverted their occupation's broader impact. The 99th New York earned notoriety for selling people back to enslavers, who then carried them south. A newspaper correspondent accused the regiment's commanding officer of turning a blind eye to his men's cooperation with slave catchers, while the Superintendent of Contrabands at Fort Monroe reported that the regiment had sold hundreds of people back to their owners for $20 or $50 apiece.[215] A local farmer took this as precedent and offered members of the 178th Pennsylvania $1,500 (roughly the antebellum price for one prime enslaved man) to smuggle five people out of their refuges.[216] As a result, a free man in Norfolk mourned that even behind Federal lines "Human life ... is most terably insecure ... for the Colored people."[217] For all that Union occupation blotted out large-scale slave commerce, then, enslavers' persistent efforts—and the survival of safe havens for purchasers—made its total eradication difficult.

Taken as a whole, however, the Union victories of early 1862 and the subsequent occupations of major slave trading centers leached slave commerce from some of the cities in which it had once been most firmly entrenched. Thus it was that in November 1863, not long before Banks removed New Orleans's remaining slave trading placards, a *New York Times* correspondent stumbled upon an advertisement for a slave sale and decided to attend this increasingly rare event. "Seeing a man, woman, or child put on the auction block ... for sale," he mused, "seemed almost as incredible ... as a glimpse at an Indian suttee, the burning of a witch, the orgies of the King of Dahomey, or any other horror that one has read and thought about." Tellingly, this relic of a passing world was canceled before a single person could ascend the auction block. Thanks to US occupation, the correspondent rejoiced, "slave auctions are done within Louisiana." "What is the use of the auction block," he wondered, "where there is nothing to sell, or rather where there are no buyers?" Who, he asked rhetorically, would buy an enslaved person who could easily leave if his or her enslaver were to "lay one finger upon them?"[218] A rump slave trade might survive, the *Chicago Tribune* similarly supposed, but given the changes wrought on the institution by the war, its practitioners "may as well give it up."[219] As a Treasury agent and educational director in New Orleans reported in October 1864, the few former traders remaining in the city were to be found "gliding about like ghosts, and wasting away daily in the uncongenial air of freedom."[220]

In late 1864, as a Louisiana convention grappled over the state's new constitution, they struggled to determine slavery's place in the emerging order. Alfred C. Hills, a delegate from Orleans Parish, argued that the institution had been irreparably damaged by the war. His evidence came in the form of the disappearing market for enslaved people. Emancipating some African Americans, he declared, had destroyed the market for all. With the assumption of bondage cast into doubt and state support for that status suspended, enslavers' power over their chattels had eroded beyond repair—particularly after Banks had suspended the provisions of Louisiana's constitution pertaining to slavery in January 1864.[221] As a result, Hills rejoiced, "the auction-block has disappeared in the light of the new civilization that has dawned upon us; the slave marts, where human beings were crowded together like cattle, thank God! is no more among us." These had been abolished, "first by the great law of necessity, and secondly by the proclamation of military power." Those who doubted this, he argued, should try selling a person in Federally occupied Louisiana—for, "under the present laws of the State the man he has attempted by force to take to the auction-block stands his equal." The powers that had eradicated the slave trade had effectively "overthrown slavery in this State forevermore."[222]

In the end, out of necessity and through military power, the United States had demolished the laws and state powers undergirding slavery and degraded slaveholders' confidence in enslaved property sufficiently to prevent them from buying and selling people. From the Confederacy's northern marches to the Lower Mississippi Valley, in regions dominated by Federal forces even the most credulous slaveholders could see little future for the institution. Who would buy when the balance of power between master and slave had been fundamentally and irrevocably altered, when the future of human property looked so impossibly bleak? As Hills astutely recognized, the combination of "the great law of necessity"—the economic realities of the war—and of "the proclamation of military power" together overthrew slave commerce in these areas.

That doing so required both is instructive. The hardships of war—financial chaos, blockade, and embargo—greatly diminished the slave trade during the secession crisis and first year of the war. Cut off from world markets and enveloped by financial uncertainty, slave trading lost its economic impetus. And yet the trade survived. Whether driven by necessity or by speculative instincts, slave dealers and their clients bought and sold enslaved men and women until Union forces appeared on their horizons. What ultimately prevented their continuing to do so was the raw force the army brought to bear against the legal structures supporting slavery and the shifting of state power toward the enslaved—a shift enslaved people fully exploited. Whenever and wherever US forces displaced Confederate authorities, they replaced state actors unequivocally committed to human bondage with men whose attitudes ranged from ambivalence to active hostility toward slavery. As a result, as Union army and naval expeditions captured slave trading centers—Alexandria, Norfolk, Nashville, Memphis, Natchez, and, most importantly, New Orleans—these entrepôts vanished. Without the active support of the slaveholding state, slave trading and, with it, slave property withered.

Where the Confederate government held sway, however, the slave trade's fate was considerably more ambiguous. The Alexandria slave pen the 1st Michigan liberated during the war's opening days was only one of the city's two major slave trading facilities. The other belonged to Joseph Bruin, who used it to hold people destined for sale in New Orleans. Though both Alexandria and New Orleans fell to Union forces during the war's first year, however, Bruin did not abandon the slave trade. He returned to Virginia in the summer of 1862, where he explored new options on the Confederacy's northern frontier. Though his unyielding disloyalty earned him a stint in Washington, DC's Old Capitol Prison, upon his release, Bruin made his way to Richmond. Within weeks of his arrival, he resumed buying and selling people—including Lavinia, Moses, and Osborn in the first of many sales he would make within the surviving Confederacy.[223] As long as he was safe in the Confederate interior, Bruin could practice the business he had long pursued. How long he would be able to deal in humanity only time and the course of the war would tell.

3

"Old Abe Is Not Feared in This Region"

The Revival of Confederate Slave Commerce

On November 30, 1862, Sarah, Maria, and Griffin made their escape from the Selma, Alabama mansion owned by Washington M. Smith, melting away into the night and out of the historical record. Why they chose this moment to flee remains as opaque as their fate. Perhaps they took advantage of a favorable stretch of good weather. Maybe they found unlikely aid in central Alabama, for, as Thomas Ruffin had claimed regarding Ned more than two years earlier, Smith suggested that "some person" had "enticed them away." He also claimed that he had given the three "no cause for their absconding," though his other bondspeople could certainly have supplied ample reason for fleeing his grasp. The enslaver's respectable veneer—he was president of both the Bank of Selma and the Selma Insurance and Trust Co. and a member of the state legislature—masked overpowering avarice. During the summer of 1860, Smith had purchased a girl of twelve named Redoshi, smuggled from Africa to Alabama aboard the slave ship *Clotilda*. He renamed her Sally Smith, forced her into marriage with fellow *Clotilda* survivor Billy, and made them labor on his Bogue Chitto property in Alabama's Black Belt. Unlike others whom Smith enslaved, however, Maria, Sarah, and Griffin had not yet had time to form even these coerced familial or communal ties, bonds that often restrained would-be fugitives, for they had only "very recently" arrived from Virginia. Smith had bought twenty-year-old Sarah and eighteen-year-old Maria in Richmond during the summer's waning days from John D. Ragland, a specialist in the Virginia-to-Alabama slave trade, and while the records of Griffin's sale have vanished, Smith likely acquired him around the same time.[1]

Redoshi arrived in Alabama in 1860 as both a desired commodity and a living embodiment of white Southerners' hubris over the untouchability of slavery in the United States.[2] In September 1862, Maria, Sarah, and Griffin followed for similar reasons: a combination of Smith's insatiable desire for enslaved laborers and Confederates' surprising sanguinity during that period. Throughout that summer, Smith's family had battled an array of health problems. These were severe enough that he resigned a position with the Confederate government—surely a wrench for a man who reportedly called on Confederates to "scratch the Yankees' eyes out with our finger nails" if doing so would help win independence. Smith believed his ailing wife would be "suited" by enslaved people who could relieve the strain he considered her to be under and thereby alleviate the "anxiety" he felt about her. Though suffering himself from headaches, and though he labeled it an "ugly job" (not, presumably, for the same reasons Maria, Sarah, and Griffin would have done so), he set out across the CSA in pursuit of human property.[3]

Smith's quest took him through a Confederacy in transition. Rebels had spent much of 1862 in headlong retreat. The year's first six months had cost the aspiring nation western Virginia, Kentucky, central Tennessee, New Orleans, and control of all of the Mississippi River except a stretch between Vicksburg and Port Hudson. Union squadrons blockaded ports from Wilmington to Galveston and landed forces along the coast from Virginia to Georgia; in North Carolina and Virginia, these expeditions penetrated almost to the fall line. Even in distant New Mexico, Union troopers had repelled a Confederate invasion. Closer to Smith's home, moreover, Union raiders had ravaged Alabama towns along the Tennessee River.[4] If Confederates wanted to know "the worst, let it be bad as it may," as the *Atlanta Southern Confederacy* put it that spring, the first half of 1862 had supplied a considerable stockpile of bleak news.[5]

Smith's expedition, however, took him through the extensive Confederate territories as yet untouched by the fighting. Central and southern Alabama, eastern Mississippi, virtually all of Georgia and South Carolina, the vast majority of North Carolina and Virginia, and much of the trans-Mississippi West remained securely in Confederate hands and housed a people bent on seeing the war through. Selma alone contained a major Confederate arsenal, a large iron foundry (which Smith had helped incorporate), and factories producing an array of other war materiel that traveled via a web of rail connections to the rest of the CSA.[6] Smith himself had contributed to the Confederacy's ongoing war effort, helping to outfit a company of the 44th Alabama Infantry, which promptly named itself in his honor.[7]

By the time Smith left Selma, moreover, Confederate prospects had brightened considerably. In Virginia, Thomas J. "Stonewall" Jackson's

Shenandoah Valley command routed three Union detachments in the late spring, menacing Washington, Baltimore, and the critical Baltimore & Ohio Railroad. Hastening to Richmond on the heels of these victories, Jackson arrived just as the newly promoted Robert E. Lee launched a massive assault against the Army of the Potomac, which sat astride the Chickahominy River only miles from the Rebel capital. In the battles soon known collectively as the Seven Days, Confederates drove the Federals away from Richmond and hemmed them into a fortified camp on the banks of the James. "From a bold and threatening attitude," Confederate ordinance chief Josiah Gorgas rejoiced, the Union military position had "been reduced to one which is characterized as safe," a reality that "indicates the nature of our success."[8] Lee's forces then pivoted north, won a shattering victory at Second Bull Run, and invaded Maryland, capturing more than 12,000 Union soldiers and hundreds of fugitive bondspeople along the way.[9] Confederate forces likewise rebounded in the western theater, driving deep into Kentucky and shifting the seat of war hundreds of miles northward.[10]

Ironically, the CSA's successes complicated Smith's tour of its surviving slave markets by driving up the prices demanded for the enslaved. In Charleston, the people on offer were "inferior and high" in price, the latter driven by jubilant Confederates' hot pursuit of human property. Having decided to try his luck in Wilmington, North Carolina instead, Smith found prices "high and going up every day." He contemplated attending a sale of one hundred people in a nearby town, but feared he would find none who met his wife's requirements. Compounding his frustrations, a friend who had promised to help him navigate Wilmington's marts never materialized. As other Confederates celebrated their triumphs, Smith groused over the "toil privation and expense" he expended in pursuit of human property. A chance encounter on the road, however, offered him a reprieve. Somewhere between Alabama and North Carolina, Smith had shared a railroad car with Ragland, whom he knew by reputation "as a trader in Mobile." Ragland offered Smith his services should his search take him to Richmond. Souring on North Carolina, Smith took the Wilmington & Weldon Railroad to the Rebel capital, where he purchased Maria and Sarah from Ragland for $3,050 (and likely Griffin from another seller). Finally satisfied, Smith retraced his steps to Alabama, carrying them into bondage in the heart of the Rebellion—at least, until they made their bid for liberty two months later.[11]

Smith's odyssey from Alabama to Charleston to North Carolina to Richmond and back reveals that while Confederates might have lost major slave trading centers like New Orleans, Natchez, Nashville, and Norfolk to Union occupation, slave commerce survived—and even flourished—wherever the Confederacy could protect it. From the summer of 1862 to the summer of 1863, a wave of military successes boosted buyers' confidence in the eventual success of the slaveholders' republic and, therefore, the institution of slavery's long-term prospects. If the eradication of slave markets along the Mississippi and along the Atlantic seaboard revealed the damage possible when an anti-slavery regime supplanted the slaveholders' state, the endurance of slave trading centers throughout the Confederate interior, whether major urban entrepôts or county courthouses, offers a necessary corollary. As Vincent Brown has written in the context of another conflict, where the enslaved and enslavers remained "under armed guard, within the firing range of a fortress or in the wake of a warship, coercion created stable markets," even in humanity.[12] As long as the slaveholding state held sway, as long as distance combined with Confederate military might to protect the institution and the state apparatuses that maintained it, the slave trade endured. When Confederate fortunes ascended, moreover, it rebounded. Despite cracks in the Rebel foundation—Union military success, the threat of emancipation, inflationary pressures, and deteriorating infrastructure—Confederates bought enslaved individuals in slave markets from the Mississippi to the Rappahannock. Doing so in this, the heyday of the Confederate endeavor, represented a tangible vote of confidence in the slaveholders' republic.

Not long before Maria, Sarah, and Griffin departed Richmond for Selma, Frank arrived in the Confederate capital bedraggled, wounded, and handcuffed. Weeks earlier, he had fled Richmond, aiming for Union lines near Fredericksburg. He might have succeeded had not Confederate advances following the Seven Days battles put the Army of Northern Virginia astride his escape route. Confederate soldiers recaptured him and offered him for sale at Milford on the Richmond, Fredericksburg & Potomac Railroad. There, John H. King purchased Frank, hoping to sell him somewhere further behind Confederate lines. Frank launched multiple escape attempts as the pair moved south. The first came before they had even left Caroline County and forced King to pay for his recovery. In the second, Frank surprised King and threw him from a moving train, earning a temporary reprieve before King eventually caught up, shot and wounded him, and finally dragged him to Richmond, the Confederacy's largest remaining slave trading center.[13]

82   AN UNHOLY TRAFFIC

Already a massive commercial, industrial, and slaving hub, Richmond had only grown during the conflict. As the Confederate capital, a leading manufacturing center, and a haven for those fleeing the war zones around the Commonwealth, its population and economy had surged.[14] Richmond thus presented King with an opportunity, but also with two potential problems. One was unique to his specific circumstances. If he offered Frank for sale in the city, word might reach his former enslavers, exposing King to charges of theft and fraud. The second confronted all those looking to sell enslaved people that summer. Only weeks earlier, Union forces had been poised to capture Richmond and had been repulsed only through some of the war's most desperate and bloodiest fighting to date. After such convulsions, what would be the state of its slave market?

King's greed eventually overcame his discretion, leading him to sell Frank in Richmond. Soon thereafter, he was apprehended in Danville, Virginia. If anyone had asked Frank, his scarred body could have attested to King's true crimes. From the slaveholding state's vantage, however, King's transgressions—including fraud and theft—were against not Frank but his former enslavers, and their magnitude depended on the value that Frank might command. Determining this was a surprisingly difficult task. "I don't know," one witness testified, "how the neighbourhood of the Yankees would have affected the price of negroes." Other witnesses indicated what a difference this made. In threatened Caroline County, King bought Frank for a paltry $100. In sheltered Richmond, he sold him for thirteen times that amount, with Frank's subsequent buyer hoping to obtain still more in the Rebel interior.[15] The initial witness's uncertainty points to a broader tension that emerged in the summer of 1862 and persisted for the remainder of the conflict. With Union and Confederate armies clashing throughout the slaveholders' republic, could enslavers offering women and men like Frank for sale find buyers for them? As Frank's experience shows, the answer depended upon where, when, and to whom that question was posed and would be shaped by both the broader course of the Rebel fortunes and how Confederates interpreted their triumphs and catastrophes.

Even during the Confederate setbacks of early 1862, reports of a robust slave trade seeped out from protected regions in the interior. These offered Confederates assurance of the vitality of their cause. In January, an observer in southern Georgia reassured readers that despite the myriad crises unfolding, there remained "a higher estimate placed upon negroes now than ten years ago," which convinced him "that Old Abe is not feared in this region."[16] A Mississippian likewise found prices "about as high as in good times," while a North Carolina newspaper reported receiving more than fifty inquiries for two enslaved people advertised for sale in its pages. The editors took this to mean that "notwithstanding" recent Union victories at Forts Henry and Donelson, "the people of the South seem to have great confidence in the 'institution.'"[17] Though Northern periodicals derided these high prices as reflecting inflation more than Rebel enthusiasm, Confederates nevertheless interpreted the health of the slave trade as embodying that of their nation.[18]

As the experience of the Mississippi Valley demonstrates, the approach of US forces could degrade confidence even in the CSA's most robust slave markets. In early 1862, Richmond seemed likely to follow the pattern established in cities like New Orleans and Natchez. In March and April, more than 120,000 Union soldiers disembarked at Fort Monroe, aiming to storm up the peninsula between the York and James Rivers and seize the city.[19] Among them was the 3rd Wisconsin Infantry's William Wallace. Just before leaving for the Peninsula, Wallace made a pilgrimage to Charlestown, Virginia, the site of John Brown's martyrdom, and collected splinters from Brown's jail cell. Bearing these relics, he invaded Virginia's Tidewater, one of what a Connecticut officer labeled "six hundred thousand John Browns" the United States had unleashed upon the Confederacy.[20] Much as the slain Brown had hoped, their presence accelerated the African American exodus begun a year earlier at Fort Monroe.[21] Joining a "virtual stampede" (in one soldier's words) to US lines, some men and women fled quite literally wearing the chains in which their enslavers hoped to send them south.[22] Even as that army inched up the Peninsula, a force of 35,000 men under Irvin McDowell advanced on Richmond from the north, menacing slaveholders from another direction and providing a refuge for those who, like Frank, dared seek them out.[23]

Before these invasions ran waves of panic. A denizen of Culpeper clearly identified the connection between military events and emancipation. "Had our army not fallen back from Manassas," she argued, "we would not have suffered such losses" in enslaved people.[24] Confederate officers were hardly more optimistic. General Daniel Harvey Hill, stationed near Richmond, urged his wife in North Carolina to invest in land and to avoid acquiring people. Believing "we will be conquered in three months, probably sooner," he hoped a victorious Union would not confiscate real estate, though "Negro & Bank property they certainly will."[25] In practice, they had already begun to do so; even as Lee defended Richmond, his family lost multiple enslaved people to Union naval forces.[26] It was not, therefore, without reason that a Union general rejoiced to his daughter, "There will soon be no slaves in Virginia. They are either leaving their masters, or their masters are leaving them."[27]

Throughout exposed regions, enslavers scrambled to preserve their human property. One slaveholding woman urged the immediate removal of her family's bondspeople but complained, "there is hardly a place in Va where they might not make their escape if they desired it." The men, at least, she recommended, "had better be carried and placed somewhere in the interior of the South," though she acknowledged that "even that might prove unsafe."[28] John Armistead Selden heeded this advice. In May 1862 he evacuated Westover, one of Virginia's oldest and most prominent plantations. Before him he drove seventeen young enslaved men, women, and children whom he hoped would form the core of an estate rebuilt once the danger passed. If leaving depressed Selden, it landed doubly on them; those whom he left at Westover "wept bitterly" at being separated from their sons, daughters, and loved ones. Even this retreat, however, could not wholly insulate Selden from the war's effects. Three men—James, Anderson, and Horton—fled for Union lines while en route to Richmond.[29]

Panicked enslavers like Selden turned to urban slave markets to protect their human property, thereby forestalling the liberation of extraordinary numbers of enslaved people. "Our place," Hector Davis reported in March, "is crowded with negroes from the exposed portion of the state." Military reverses meant there was "little demand" for them, but Davis promised to do what he could and hoped "that our prospects will brighten soon."[30] Among these men and women might have been the family of Culpeper's Spencer Brown, whom Brown reported had been "sold from him" early in the conflict.[31] Edmund Ruffin Jr., son of the famous secessionist, sold twenty-four people in June 1862 and contemplated selling still more.[32] Such a punishment was not enough for some slaveholders. One soldier urged his brother to keep an enslaved woman from the Yankees even if doing so required him to "drown her in the James River."[33]

Even as Richmond's slave market filled up in March and April 1862, the approach of Union forces significantly depressed demand. Just before the Peninsula campaign, A. J. Rux considered Richmond the liveliest market in the Confederacy—the only one, he believed, with "something doing in the way of trade." Indeed, it would "be time and money saved," he claimed, to reverse the slave trade's normal trajectory and bring people from traditional selling grounds like Alabama to Virginia for sale. The Yankees' approach, however, impeded such a strategy. Returning from North Carolina in April, J. Wimbush Young, another trader, "found it rather a slim chance to buy any negroes at Fair Price."[34] For all his hopes that the market would rebound, Hector Davis watched his sales drop precipitously during the Peninsula Campaign. After selling forty-five people during the brief revival of the winter of 1861–1862, his sales declined to twenty-one in March and to a mere handful of individuals in the months of April, May, and June.[35] This still left him ahead of Silas Omohundro, who sold only two people between April and June.[36] The slave trade did not end. N. M. Lee, for example, spent $150 transporting a group of enslaved people to Tennessee in May. But Union successes had considerably reduced it.[37]

Richmond's experience typified that of the Confederacy's major slave markets in 1862. In Charleston, Benjamin Holmes spent months "kept in the slave mart, ready to be examined" ahead of sales that never came off. Charleston's antebellum traffic had rivaled that of Richmond, and like the Confederate capital, the cradle of secession spent much of 1862 beset by Union naval and ground forces. As in Richmond, commerce in slaves continued. Charlestonians might be on the verge of removing the bells from their famed churches to prevent their becoming Union trophies, but they continued filling the city's slave pens. When the Confederacy's fortunes waned, transactions slowed—hence Holmes's lengthy stay. A literate man, he exacted concessions from his jailer by reading him the news. Because his captivity extended into the autumn, among the items he read aloud was Lincoln's Emancipation Proclamation, a development that sparked rejoicing and an impromptu prayer meeting among those confined for sale.[38]

Rejoice they might, but Union decrees alone could not liberate the men and women subjected to Charleston's slave market. Holmes's enslaver eventually sold him to Chattanooga, one of the hundreds of people Charlestonians dispersed in sales large and small.[39] In April 1862, the auction firm of Wilbur & Son sold fifteen people for nearly $12,000; another enslaver dealt thirty more in June.[40] That month, particularly, saw the prices offered for enslaved people surge. South Carolina Unionist James Petigru noted "the high price of negroes" in the city, attributing this to a desire to obtain tangible property in the face of mounting inflation. That Confederates considered the enslaved viable investments, however, demonstrates their confidence that any reversals they suffered would be temporary.[41]

Savannah's slave market likewise remained active. In March 1859, the city had earned infamy as the host of one of the largest slave auctions in American history: the 440 people sold by Pierce Butler and slave trader Joseph Bryan in the event widely known as "the Weeping Time."[42] Into 1862, Bryan continued advertising for enslaved people from his offices near the city's waterfront, joined by Blount & Dawson, the Meinhard brothers, Alexander Bryan, John A. Stevenson, and many others.[43] These slave brokers and their customers believed in the success of the Rebel cause and the perpetuity of slavery. Stevenson, a relative newcomer to Savannah's slave trading scene, recalled after the war that during the conflict he did not look "forward to anything but trade" because he was "confident that the Negro would still be a slave."[44]

As a result, Savannah's markets operated so vigorously that by early 1862, one Confederate buyer found people in short supply. "I have been all over the City," he informed his wife, "to every house where negroes were kept for sale," but failed to find a woman for purchase.[45] When its marts refilled—including with refugees from the threatened Sea Islands—would-be purchasers took advantage of the opportunity they provided. In the late summer, Henry Wilink, a shipbuilder who contracted with the Confederate navy, undertook the first of at least twenty-five purchases he would make during the

Figure 3.1 William C. Dawson, of the Savannah slave trading firm Blount & Dawson, with his family. Rahn, Dawson, Willet Papers. Courtesy of the Georgia Historical Society.

Figure 3.2 "Auctions and Negro Sales, Whitehall Street." Atlanta's slave markets, one of which is depicted here, flourished during the Civil War. Library of Congress, LC-DIG-cwpb-03350.

conflict.[46] The presence of several brokers in the city created competition, a reality exemplified when an enslaved woman solicited multiple estimates of her monetary value from Blount & Dawson and trader George Wylly as part of her efforts at self-purchase.[47]

As they had in Richmond and Charleston, US army and navy expeditions against Savannah injected uncertainty into its slave market. As one enslaver complained in June 1862, "negroes in districts threatened by invasion" varied enormously in price and in marketability.[48] Cities in the Rebel interior, however, like the boomtown of Atlanta, did not face such problems. Sitting astride a major railroad junction, Atlanta quickly became a major hub for Confederate logistics and manufacturing (one periodical labeled it the "most vital point in rebeldom").[49] This vitality extended to the trade in the enslaved. In January 1862, auctioneers executed a sale of fifty people in the city. The prices obtained resembled those that had prevailed before the war, though inflation helped counteract the downward pressures applied by the conflict. Nevertheless, one newspaper declared, this proved that "confidence in the 'institution' is unimpaired."[50] As sale followed sale into the summer, the press lauded the "high prices" attainable.[51] Merchant Samuel Richards chose this moment to purchase Sally, the first enslaved person he had ever acquired. "I expect the *Yankees* would say," he crowed, "that this was the worst possible investment under existing circumstances seeing that their Congress has declared the slaves of all *rebels* to be free!" He thought otherwise and, with his friends and relations, continued buying people throughout that summer.[52]

On June 21, 1862, L. D. Merrimon of Greenwood, South Carolina, inquired of E. H. Stokes regarding the state of Richmond's slave market. Merrimon wanted to buy "about 8 or 10 negros," and asked Stokes about the current prices and whether there were "many in the market."[53] Whether Stokes responded or not is uncertain, but he could have been forgiven for overlooking Merrimon's query. By late June, the Army of the Potomac had breached Confederate defenses on the Peninsula and, after the indecisive Battle of Seven Pines, sat encamped almost within sight of Stokes's office.[54] War and survival dominated every aspect of life. In theory, business continued. One observer noted "a number of shops open" but acknowledged, "one sees very little of the usual traffic." Other enterprises had been converted to hospitals filled with wounded from battles on the Peninsula and the approaches to the city. Nevertheless, the city remained defiant. "There is not a shadow of fear depicted on the countenance [of] anyone," the same commentator boasted. "Nothing can be seen but a grim determination."[55]

Slave traders, however, fed off exuberance, not grim determination. As a result, while scouring Virginia's Southside for human property, J. Wimbush Young found people reluctant to sell to him. "The great excitement round and about Richmond," he reported, convinced most would-be sellers they would not get what they considered a fair price for their human property in the beleaguered city. The slave trade slackened considerably in Richmond, though it did not disappear. Young eventually sent several people to Stokes for sale, asking him to "do the best you can" in the hopes that "we can make money on them."[56] A King George County, Virginia slaveholder, meanwhile, sent seven people there, in part to prevent them from joining others who had slipped away to Union lines. These included Sallie and her two children, Sydney, Milford, Magnus, and Jinny, whom their enslaver appraised at a combined $5,800—below the market's antebellum peak, but still relatively robust.[57] Such prices translated into opportunity for those willing to chance buying during the depression, including an Alabamian who came to Richmond in June looking for purchases at discounted prices.[58]

Military events shaped slave trading behavior throughout the Confederacy, with enslavers reading them with an eye to their personal affairs. In central Georgia, Mickleberry Driver for several years had hired a woman named Joe from his deceased grandfather's estate. Driver had exploited her sexually in the past and believed himself to be the father of at least one of her children. When his grandfather died, Driver hoped to use slave commerce to bring Joe under his control and, in doing so, to keep their relationship out of the public eye. To that end, he enlisted another Georgian to act as his proxy in either hiring Joe or purchasing her outright. In uncertain times, executors frequently hired enslaved people to avoid being called to account for low sale prices and any resulting harm to the estate. In the middle of 1862, however, Driver worried that Joe and the children might be sold to someone—particularly, he suggested, if military events indicated that "times seems to be getting any better"—and thus moved to secure them for himself.[59]

Joe's fate and Driver's ambitions—like those of enslaved people, enslavers, and traders throughout the South—depended on whether the times would, in fact, get better for the CSA. Stonewall Jackson's Shenandoah Valley victories offered enslavers some encouragement. But all knew that the fight for Richmond would be far more critical. In late May—when, Confederate clerk John B. Jones lamented, "the blackness of midnight brooded over our cause"—the Confederate government laid plans to evacuate the capital.[60] Former slave trader Jeremiah Morton likewise believed the city might be lost. "I am distressed," he wrote a relative, "at the prospects before us," which he blamed on "the want of 'brains' in our government" that left "our cause . . . imperiled by utter imbecility."[61] With anticipation brewing for the impending battle, some Confederates projected bravado. "It is said," one

Richmonder noted, "that a great battle will certainly come off this week." "The <u>utmost confidence</u>," he relayed to J. D. B. De Bow, "<u>prevails</u> here."[62]

The Seven Days battles ultimately more than repaid that confidence. On the afternoon of June 26, sounds of heavy firing to the north could be heard in Richmond as Robert E. Lee opened an offensive aimed at smashing the Army of the Potomac. In a week-long series of bloody clashes, Lee and his men forced McClellan's army to conduct a fighting retreat to Harrison's Landing, well down the James River. Though their efforts to destroy segments of the army failed, Confederates remained jubilant. "The serpent has been killed," Jones rejoiced, "though its tail," lurking in the city's environs, "still exhibits some spasmodic motions."[63] The battles thoroughly reversed the conflict's course. Union morale, ascendant in the first half of 1862, collapsed. Confederate armies seized the initiative. Many Rebels found in Lee a vessel for the capacious faith they maintained in the Confederate endeavor.[64] Jones spoke for many when he proclaimed, "What genius! What audacity in Lee!" and assigned these traits preemptive credit for the CSA's eventual success.[65]

Richmond's slave markets boomed almost as soon as the Army of the Potomac withdrew. Only a week after Malvern Hill, the final clash of the Seven Days battles, the Nalle family of Orange County, Virginia sold Dick through Dickinson, Hill & Co.[66] John Armistead Selden returned to a Westover "entirely ruined" and promptly sold the few people lingering there (thirty-six had escaped). These included Jarratt, Mary, and their seven children, along with two elderly men. While the older people brought only modest returns, the children—especially the teenage and preteen girls—fetched a combined $2,100 in a market where, one Virginia soldier proclaimed, "negroes are now bringing a fine price."[67]

As these sales took place, Confederates continued amassing victories. In central Virginia, Jackson won a string of battles culminating in Second Bull Run, where the timely arrival of Lee's reinforcements shattered attacking Union forces and drove them into the fortifications ringing Washington.[68] Lee then turned north, seeking a signal victory on Union soil that would preserve the strategic initiative, strengthen anti-war Democrats in the fall elections, and perhaps even win the Confederacy international backing.[69] A bloody clash along Antietam Creek forced Lee to retreat and empowered Lincoln to issue the preliminary Emancipation Proclamation. Confederates, however, remained ambivalent about Antietam's impact. Despite their withdrawal, a CSA official labeled the battle "a substantial <u>victory</u> in every way," one that little dampened the enthusiasm that had accumulated during the preceding months.[70]

Confederate forces also rebounded in the western theater. In Tennessee, the eponymous Rebel army recohered after defeats at Shiloh and the critical Mississippi railroad junction of Corinth. Slipping across Alabama, it linked up with other Confederates and drove north through Tennessee into Kentucky. This force won several victories, including a small but costly battle at Richmond, Kentucky, and threatened Louisville before being repulsed at Perryville in October. While this campaign failed to draw Kentucky into the Confederate ranks, it dramatically shifted the battle lines of the theater and provided welcome news in a region where the Rebels had experienced little but reverses.[71]

The triumphs of the summer and early autumn of 1862 left many Confederates jubilant. Recovering in September from a severe wound received before Richmond, J. Johnston Pettigrew, a general hailing from one of North Carolina's largest slaveholding families, hoped that "the defeats experienced by the Yankees . . . will doubtless compel them to withdraw all their good troops from the south."[72] Union forces might have overrun Pettigrew's home in eastern North Carolina, but the run of Confederate triumphs that summer and fall dwarfed what he and many others perceived as localized setbacks.[73] Likewise, in early autumn, Josiah Gorgas argued that the preceding months had presented an unbroken string of successes. The only question remaining was, "Will the fruits of our victories be peace?"[74]

While Confederates awaited an answer, many collected premiums on their resurgence through the slave trade. If New Orleans embodied the dangers of the war for slave commerce, Richmond—pivoting from terror to triumph—demonstrated its possibilities. One merchant rejoiced that in the absence of "immediate danger that Richmond will be taken by the federals . . . there is a proportionate feeling of security in our commercial community," a sentiment in which its slave traders shared.[75] Virtually as soon as Union armies had withdrawn from the city, buyers and sellers returned. A friend wrote Ellen Mordecai asking her to purchase a cook for her. Mordecai referred her to Benjamin Davis, "one in the trade [who] would know such as are or may be offered for sale."[76] Those offered for sale comprised a multitude. W. C. Corsan, an Englishman touring the CSA, encountered "a lot of twenty-one slaves" aboard a train bound for Richmond. Acquired only that day "for 25,000 dollars—a good price, everybody said," their captor was rushing them to the city to sell them again.[77] Once sold, enslaved people likewise flowed back out of the city. In a counterpart to Corsan's encounter, recently paroled Confederate colonel Randal McGavock traveled south from Richmond in a box car "filled with negroes," most of whom were "children purchased in Richmond at very high prices—for an investment."[78]

The opportunities for such investments were extensive. Upon arriving in Richmond, Corsan found that "sales of negroes go on at auction, just as usual." Buyers flocking to these sales ensured that "high prices for" the enslaved, "as indeed all other 'property,' are obtained."[79] This demand revitalized many of the city's slave trading operations. Hector Davis sold seventeen people on his own account in July, thirty-two in August, ninety-four in September, and more than 130 in October. Given that Davis also did business with traders including John B. Davis, Jones & Slater, John Fraser, R. H. Davis, and David McDaniel and let E. H. Stokes use his jail, his records reflect significant activity in the slave trade—a reality borne out by Silas Omohundro's tripling sales in July and August.[80]

Some of this demand originated locally as Richmond-area enslavers sought to replace laborers who had fled with the withdrawing Union army. Simultaneously, however, Richmond's slave dealers also supplied buyers from far and wide through an enduring long-distance trade. A North Carolina soldier reported that a relative "had bin in Richmond for two months buying negroes" at prices "as high as he ever saw them at any time." Only a shortage of money prevented him from making even more purchases.[81] Officers jostled side-by-side with civilians in the city's slave marts. William Tunstel, for example, reported that a Confederate captain had purchased his brother McLeroy around this time.[82] Even Confederate heroes patronized Richmond's slave dealers. General Stephen Dodson Ramseur, recovering from wounds received at Malvern Hill, visited "several negro sale establishments" seeking an enslaved man for his brother. In an act as cynical as it was indicative of his deep confidence in the CSA's prospects, he hoped to leverage rumors of a Union advance into southern Virginia into a lower purchase price. Some evidence suggests, meanwhile, that Stonewall Jackson may have sold a man named Harvey during this period.[83]

Confederate congressmen and governors likewise kept tabs on the slave market. In September, Representative Robert Bridgers wrote to North Carolina Governor Henry Toole Clark informing him that slaves in Richmond were "selling higher here than ever known before," which he attributed to the fact that "the news continues good from the army." If Clark followed Bridgers's urging and sent Lewis and an unnamed woman and child to Richmond, they might have joined Moses on the auction block, whom Jones & Slater sold in October for $1,100.[84] Confederates bought and sold so many people in Richmond that it replaced New Orleans as the commercial benchmark. Paul Semmes, a Georgia officer and large-scale enslaver, used it as a byword in discussing the state of the slave market with his wife. "You recollect," he reminded her in October 1862, "how very high [slave prices] were in Richmond when you were there & priced them."[85]

Confederates riding high in the fall of 1862 also used the slave market's vitality to rebut the Emancipation Proclamation, a measure that theoretically threatened the institution of slavery. In mid-October, shortly after Lincoln released the preliminary Proclamation, the *Richmond Whig* rejoiced "that confidence is yet felt in this kind of property, notwithstanding Uncle Abraham's proclamation."[86] A Macon, Georgia paper reported that even a "confirmed runaway" brought $1,700, derisively postscripting, "send this to Lincoln and ask for titles."[87] Slave commerce and the Confederacy reinforced one another in these reports. Detailing sales in both Richmond and Abbeville, South Carolina, the *Augusta Chronicle* concluded "that the faith of our people is strong in the future of the new republic."[88] A South Carolina newspaper spelled it out yet more explicitly. The high prices offered for the enslaved demonstrated that "every day the war continues strengthens the confidence of the people in the ability of the Confederate States to ultimately secure their independence, and with it the permanency of the institution of slavery."[89]

Confederates' private sentiments matched their public bluster. Anticipating the *Whig*'s specific language, Rebel official Thomas Pollock asked his father to send Tom to Richmond for sale, for he "would bring $1,500 here now, Lincoln's proclamation to the contrary notwithstanding."[90] Edmund Ruffin, meanwhile, recorded in his diary that "The *nominal* market prices now" offered for the enslaved "are higher than before the war, or at any previous time." While he confessed to the page that inflation bore most of the responsibility for this increase, Ruffin nevertheless believed that the threat of emancipation had done nothing to depress them. "It is certain," he argued, "that no sudden shock or notable repression, was given to the current prices of slaves by either the general confiscation & emancipation acts of the Northern Congress, or the recent emancipation proclamation of Lincoln. And," he concluded, "I do not believe that these measures (on paper, & of the threatened future,) have had the least effect on the market price of slaves."[91] Confederates thus understood the slave trade as a proxy for their rebellion's fortunes. High prices offered for enslaved people reflected a likelihood of success. Declining prices could indicate (but were not always read as suggesting) the prospect of defeat.

In late 1862, Confederate War Department official Robert Garlick Hill Kean took to his diary to evaluate the state of the Confederacy. Despite the losses suffered early in that year, Confederates still maintained consistent authority over a sizeable territory, one laid out "in the shape of a boot, of which middle Virginia, North Carolina, South Carolina, and Georgia to the Gulf is the leg and Alabama and part of Mississippi the foot." "Besides this," Kean added, remained "the Trans-Mississippi."[92] All throughout this boot, the Confederate slave trade flourished. Paul Semmes wrote to his wife that should she need to sell, "negroes bring <u>large</u> prices <u>throughout</u> nearly all of the cotton states & sell readily."[93] In Greensboro, North Carolina, meanwhile, a diarist recorded shortly after Antietam that "Prices of negroes are enormous," with young men bringing as much as $2,000. Such prices ensured that untold thousands of men and women like Anderson and Priscilla, sold by a Petersburg slave dealer to Greensboro, Alabama in late 1862, would continue in bondage in the resurgent Confederacy.[94]

In Charleston, Wilbur & Son carried out an escalating spate of "spirited" auctions in which they sold thirty-nine, fifty-five, even seventy-three people.[95] Buyers in that city included G. V. Ancker, who regularly dealt with Hector Davis, and many western North Carolinians acquiring in exposed Charleston people for use in their mountain refuges.[96] As in Richmond, the city's markets pulsed in rhythm with the Confederacy's broader fortunes. One South Carolina soldier observed after the Seven Days battles, "Negroes &c, Confederate bonds & cotton have all jumped up tremendously in Charleston since the Great fight."[97] Shortly thereafter, Wilbur & Son offered twenty-five more people for sale, with John S. Riggs putting five others on the block.[98] Such activity—and the "high prices . . . obtained"—the *Charleston Mercury* noted, "show[ed] what great confidence there is existing in this species of property."[99] Sales continued apace during the late fall and winter. A February 1863 advertisement touted the sale of forty "rice field negroes," while a diarist reported "considerable activity in the selling [of] negroes."[100] These included "Old Phillis," Venus and her three children, and Martha (also a mother of three). With trade robust, auctioneer Alonzo White even sold Martha despite her "defective eyes" and Venus despite her being "unsound."[101]

Much the same was true in Atlanta. In September 1862, a resident of nearby Powder Springs sold a woman and three children for $3,000, a

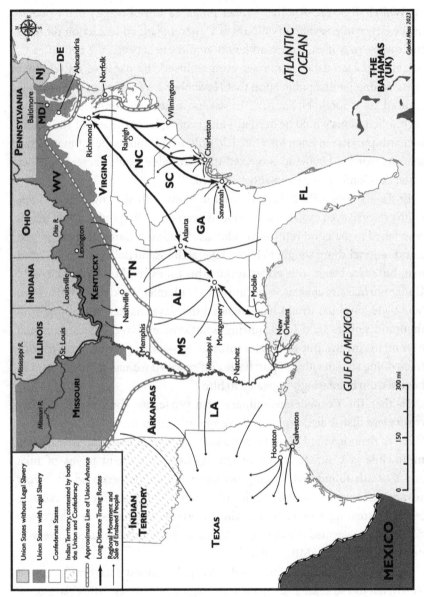

Figure 3.3 The domestic slave trade, summer 1862. Mossmaps.

then-considerable price.[102] In October, Solomon Cohen offered seventy-five enslaved people for sale in the city. Not to be outdone, Robert Clarke soon proclaimed that he would put up for sale 150 bondspeople from his pen on Whitehall Street. Another broker prepared to sell twenty-eight people in the city, while Savannah's Blount & Dawson planned to auction off fifty-three more in Millen, a railroad junction midway between the two cities.[103] Atlanta's boisterous slave market even suffused the pages of its religious press. In one Baptist publication that November, no fewer than three slavers courted its readers' business.[104] Enslavers' continued confidence ensured such solicitations would be heeded—and profitable. At the end of 1862, Sam Richards purchased Ellen for $1,225. Within a few months, he estimated that she was worth $2,000 and projected that her value would increase further when the Confederacy inevitably prevailed.[105]

Enslavers approached these revived markets with shifting expectations. High prices swayed even those previously averse to selling and exposed sellers who failed to get good returns to ridicule.[106] A South Carolinian encamped near Fredericksburg sought to invest several thousand dollars in an enslaved man but feared that with prices surging his funds might be insufficient.[107] Under normal circumstances, meanwhile, Nathaniel Watkins, a soldier from Southside Virginia, would have avoided the slave market. Already several thousand dollars in debt, acquiring additional enslaved laborers seemed beyond his means. But with prices ascending—and appearing likely to continue doing so—the idea of purchasing an enslaved woman named Lucy and her children increasingly appealed to him.[108]

Neither the Confederate military resurgence nor the slave trade's recovery was distributed evenly. A drive against Union-occupied Baton Rouge failed to dislodge the US contingents garrisoning Louisiana. In Mississippi, meanwhile, a Confederate campaign against the railroad towns of Iuka and Corinth foundered, leaving northern Mississippi exposed.[109] Forces advancing toward Vicksburg under Ulysses S. Grant soon filled the vacancy left by retreating Confederates. Though eventually halted at Chickasaw Bayou, they swarmed the city's environs and constantly menaced slavery in northern and central Mississippi.[110]

In threatened portions of the Confederacy, the domestic slave trade revived slowly, if it did so at all. Paul Semmes, though sanguine regarding slave commerce both in Richmond and elsewhere in the Cotton South, conceded that in "districts overrun by the Yankees, or adjoining ones," such a resurgence was conspicuously absent. "But," he consoled himself, "in all others, or nearly all they sell well."[111] William Smedes, who had recently imported dozens of enslaved people to a plantation on Vicksburg's outskirts, agreed that "negroes have no market value" in beset regions.[112] Yet even this represented something of an exaggeration. The survival of slave markets elsewhere in the CSA ensured even the most vulnerable enslaved people would still bring modest prices when offered for sale. In Tibbee, Mississippi, just south of the battlefields at Corinth and Iuka, enslaved people brought nearly $2,000. On the edge of the Mississippi Delta, meanwhile, Louisiana soldier Edwin Fay expressed a desire to acquire people, demonstrating his ongoing confidence in slavery despite his proximity to one of the conflict's epicenters.[113]

Even in and around soon-to-be-besieged Vicksburg, Confederates bought people as property. These included an unnamed woman from Kentucky. Ensnared in an estate battle, she fell into the hands of a commission merchant who, despite a verbal agreement not to sell her more than four miles from her home, succumbed to the temptation of high Confederate prices. Purchased by a Vicksburg resident, she remained there until the city fell to the Federals.[114] As late as the spring of 1863, a Confederate in Hinds County to the east of the city, purchased an enslaved man on the grounds that he could "see no chance for the Yankees to get Vicksburg unless they flank it by way of Yazzoo City."[115] In May 1863, when US soldiers under Sherman occupied Jackson as part of the Vicksburg campaign, they encountered "Yankee Tom." Presumably nicknamed for his ardor for the freedom Union advances promised, he claimed to be the son of a Confederate general who, irrespective of this fact, had tried to sell him for $2,000 only a week before the city's fall.[116]

Admittedly, even some Confederates found these purchases perplexing. Upon seeing an enslaved woman sold in Vicksburg in September 1862, a visitor to the city queried the purchaser "if he did not think it impolitic to buy slaves now?" The buyer responded that so long as one chose the correct enslaved people—specifically, young women and children whom he considered less likely to flee—"there is no danger."[117] Rebel soldiers in the vicinity, meanwhile, directly linked the ability to purchase and sell people and the cause for which they fought. Even as a Louisiana soldier stationed at Vicksburg laid plans to sell a woman named Manda, he reminded his wife that in addition to fighting for "my liberty," he also served to protect "our Negroes and country."[118]

Early in January 1863, a hearse trundled through Richmond's increasingly crowded streets. After nearly two decades of large-scale slave dealing, Hector Davis had passed away at the age of forty-seven.[119] His colleagues on the board of the Traders' Bank of Virginia—mostly comprised of fellow slave dealers—mourned him as "honest, faithful, and true . . . and, as an individual, of kind disposition and urbane manners."[120] None of the (at least) 158 people whom Davis had sold in the preceding month received space to dispute this characterization. Davis had passed at the pinnacle of Confederate slave commerce. In the first half of 1862, his sales had dipped to (in some cases) one or two people per month. By year's end, he was selling more than a hundred people—for more than $100,000—monthly. Indeed, Davis's December 1862 sales were the highest monthly total he had tallied in nearly three years.[121]

Davis's accounts, moreover, reveal a frenzied traffic that bound the slaveholders' republic together. In late December, Davis sold five people to W. H. Gwin, a former St. Louis trader who had relocated to Richmond during the war.[122] John R. Sedgwick, a North Carolina-based dealer, purchased five more and continued buying people as he returned home.[123] Atlanta's Solomon Cohen bought a dozen people in two transactions. Locals also took advantage of the resurgent market. As the year closed, Richmond businessman A. W. Nolting obtained eight people for nearly $8,000. Davis's financial records, moreover, revealed Richmond's expansive yet interconnected commerce in slaves. In the last week of December, just before his death, Davis paid drafts on behalf of Dickinson, Hill & Co., Pulliam & Co., Samuel Fondren, Thomas Otey, the displaced Joseph Bruin, Reuben Ragland (of nearby Petersburg), and E. H. Stokes.[124] Stokes simultaneously affirmed the trade's vigor, informing a would-be client that he could expect to find the "market active & demand good."[125]

The prices attained astonished even the staunchest Confederates. In the Shenandoah Valley, Margaret Junkin Preston, Stonewall Jackson's sister-in-law and the wife of one of his staff officers, found "the price of negroes . . . enormous," with even "a not at all 'likely' woman of 40 and her two babies selling for $3000."[126] A Confederate chaplain from Gloucester County sold eight enslaved people, "most of them small," for $9,000, "quite a high price."[127] A Richmonder, meanwhile, anticipated that with prices rising, a woman named Bridget and her children (a two-year-old and a one-month-old) would bring $2,000, though he thought he could squeeze more from her sale by dividing the family.[128] If a visiting Rebel's estimates were accurate, this seller asked too little, given that he saw people sold for fully $3,000 that January.[129]

Inflation accounted for much of this ascent in nominal prices. By the winter of 1862–1863, the prices of some goods in the Confederacy had ascended to as much as seven times their prewar value. This did little, however, to dissuade Rebels of their belief that the slave market's briskness augured well for their prospects.[130] Instead, they chose to view climbing prices offered for the enslaved as the result of their virtually unbroken military successes in the latter half of 1862. Their ensuing rosy assessments of the future thus fueled rebounding demand. Many agreed with George Barnsley, a medical student in Virginia, who planned to sell a man named Moses at the war's conclusion under the assumption that "after peace . . . negroes will be high." Barnsley believed that peace might arrive as soon as the autumn of 1863, especially if European powers intervened to bring the Federals to heel.[131] A North Carolina newspaper commenting on the high prices obtained in a recent auction likewise concluded that Rebel confidence supplied "the readiness with the people to invest money in this species of property."[132]

This confidence led Confederates to take calculated approaches to the slave market. An exchange between Alabama cavalryman Nimrod Long and his wife, Queen, about the prospective sale of Ellen underscores their careful appraisals of the benefits of selling people. Having rented Ellen to another enslaver in 1862, Queen offered to let the hirer purchase her outright at the beginning of 1863. Nimrod, however, feared that the prospective purchaser would exploit price fluctuations like those seen in 1862 to extract Ellen from them at a bargain price. Only Long's faith in the Confederacy gave him confidence. As 1862 closed and 1863 dawned, Confederates had scored a shattering triumph at Fredericksburg and what they initially considered a victory at Stones River in Tennessee; with campaigning largely ended for the winter, Long believed the CSA's prospects were steady. Indeed, so confident was he in the Confederacy's ultimate victory that Long recommended against selling Ellen at all, advocating that the family retain her as an investment in their future.[133]

Long could afford to delay in selling Ellen because the slave trade in his native Alabama remained almost completely intact at the outset of 1863, with slave dealers frequenting trading centers like Mobile and Montgomery and linking them with the ongoing local trade that permeated the state's smaller towns and cities. The owners of two large Mobile "negro marts," with the combined capacity to hold hundreds of people, advertised in an 1863 travel guide rife with auctioneers and slave dealers. One newspaper in that city even rejoiced that by driving enslaved people from other regions to its markets, the war had broadened access to enslaved property.[134] Montgomery likewise retained numerous traders who catered to a clientele that included Varina Davis, First Lady of the Confederacy.[135] Smaller Alabama towns also saw ongoing transactions in enslaved people; in late 1862, for example, an enslaver sold Margaret and Ellen in Loachapoka in the eastern part of the state.[136] Buyers like William Battle helped drive this demand. Responding to the upward trend in prices, he acquired five "young and likely" boys and girls despite having no immediate use for them.[137] So deeply did the language of the slave trade—and the optimism of 1862–1863—permeate the state that an Alabama soldier joked with his eleven-year-old sister that "she must be getting rich to be buying negroes."[138]

Alabama's slave markets maintained particularly strong connections to Richmond-based traders throughout 1863. A. J. Rux, Robert Booth, and J. Wimbush Young frequented the state until the year's end, with Young and Rux establishing their "headquarters" at Uniontown on its western edge.[139] Jeremiah Morton exploited his longstanding connections with the Yellowhammer State to sell people from his exposed property in the Virginia Piedmont to Mobile and Montgomery. Like Washington Smith, Morton availed himself of the services of John Ragland, who bragged in September 1863 that he had recently sold thirty of Morton's captives for $3,000 apiece. This was "more," he crowed, "than I have sold any of my own men for and higher than they are selling in Georgia or Tennessee."[140] Ragland's chosen comparison was telling. That occupied Mississippi and Louisiana no longer offered reasonable points of comparison revealed how Federal incursions had constricted the interstate slave trade. That he had others at hand, however, attested to its ongoing vigor.

Morton and Ragland defended their part in the continued slave trade in the language of paternalism. But the people they sold saw things otherwise, and taking advantage of a rare chance to communicate to Morton via an intermediary, protested their sale. Contradicting Ragland's assertions that they were happy with their lot, they reproached Morton for giving them to a slave trader rather than ensuring their wellbeing himself. "They disliked," an agent communicated, "being put in Raglands hands for sale worse than being sold." The enslaved touted their past fidelity and excoriated Morton for removing the last shreds of their autonomy. If he were committed to selling them, these men and women put to him, "you should not have herded them like horses & mules to a trader, but done it yourself and given them a chance" to make more favorable arrangements. But much as the trade between Virginia and Alabama survived, so did the profit motive's determinative power.[141]

Georgia-bound traders, the "Georgia men" who had long haunted enslaved people's collective subconscious, also proliferated in 1863. Virginia's Kate Drumgoold lost her mother to one such buyer and spent the remainder of the war watching the southern horizon in the hope that she might return.[142] When Confederates overran antislavery congressman Thaddeus Stevens's ironworks during the Gettysburg campaign, they kidnapped Jane Lyles and her children, carried them to Richmond, and sold her to Savannah.[143] Robert Dixon experienced a similar fate when Rebel forces in the Shenandoah Valley gave him over to a Georgia dealer.[144] Samuel Clement recalled that a Georgia-based trader—one of "so many" who attended his family's sale—led the bidding for his brother, Thomas, and withdrew only upon discovering scarring on Thomas's abdomen that might have reduced his market value.[145]

Other Georgians were less easily deterred. Hinton Graves, operating Long Cane outside of Rome, dealt several people in the early spring of 1863. Even as he subsequently prepared for a buying expedition to Raleigh, North Carolina, he sold a woman and her children to Tennessee and made plans to sell John and Gabe as well. As manager of his brother Charles's affairs, moreover, Graves laid plans to invest in enslaved people, whose high prices and likely appreciation made them a tempting speculation in the face of mounting inflation.[146] Other Georgians pursued similar opportunities in Richmond, while Floridians came north to Georgia slave markets in search of higher prices for people they hoped to sell.[147]

Such demand occasionally produced enormous sales. Across two auctions, one in April and one in June 1863, Savannah broker George Wylly sold more than 170 men, women, and children.[148] Another sale dispersed ninety more people for nearly $115,000.[149] Atlanta's slave traders aspired to similar levels of infamy. In late 1862 and early 1863, Robert Clarke sold fifty-six enslaved people carried from eastern North Carolina.[150] In September 1863, Crawford, Frazer, & Co. offered a staggering one hundred enslaved people for sale from a "stock" that they bragged was "replenished almost daily by Experienced Buyers throughout the Confederacy."[151] As the war lengthened, a host of other slave merchants thrived in Atlanta, some of whom emerged amid the conflict: Mayer, Jacobe, & Co., W. H. Henderson, S. H. Griffin, Levi and Solomon Cohen, and more.[152] The net result was that Atlanta's traffic rose to the point that in 1863, a newspaper declared the city "almost up to Richmond as a negro mart."[153]

Georgia traders, however, enjoyed a symbiotic relationship with their Richmond counterparts. Well into 1863, E. H. Stokes funneled tens of thousands of dollars into the state. In addition to buying people from Hector Davis, Solomon Cohen expended considerable efforts on Hill, Dickinson & Co.'s behalf (the firm changed its name in January 1863 following an internal restructuring). In February 1863, he purchased fifteen people for the firm, including three women with young children; he also distributed its capital to partners in other markets. In total, Hill, Dickinson & Co. gave Cohen some $222,000; he promptly bought and sold enough people to cover all but $29,000.[154] Savannah's Meinhard brothers, meanwhile, advertised in late 1862 their receipt of "a fine lot of Virginia negroes."[155]

Charleston's slave markets remained similarly active during the CSA's 1863 renaissance. Though one would-be seller found the city "awfully gloomy," with "nearly all the stores . . . closed," the slave trade continued apace. John Berkley Grimball found buyers there for forty-eight people in the spring of 1863.[156] Two months later, the Allston family offered sixty-five captives for sale, while three members of the Rhett family purchased 107 more for a whopping $128,400.[157] With the market so active and people bringing "such prices," one South Carolina woman marveled that anyone would not seize the opportunity to sell.[158]

Like all the Confederacy's slave marts, Charleston's ebbed and flowed with the wider fortunes of the slaveholders' republic. In the summer of 1863, with the CSA ascendant, British officer Arthur Fremantle found an auction involving fifteen men, three women, and three children over before he could even observe it. "They had been so quick about it," Fremantle complained, "that the whole affair was over before I arrived, although I was only ten minutes late."[159] In late June, as Confederates surged into Pennsylvania, a South Carolinian rejoiced in the high prices he believed an enslaved man would bring in the city.[160] The buyers who frequented these auctions had ties across the Confederacy. Hill, Dickinson & Co., for example, poured at least $40,000 into the city's slave trade via partners like Ziba Oakes.[161] Slave commerce also flourished in the city's hinterlands. In York, South Carolina, a soldier noted that high prices pervaded, while the brother of Charleston's Catholic bishop watched enslaved people sell in Augusta, Georgia for "pretty good prices," adding that they had been "bought principally by speculators."[162] Still another Carolinian reported an abundance of traders in his neighborhood, who, having already bought significant numbers of people, nevertheless sought more and were "giving very high prices."[163]

North Carolina comprised a significant part of both Richmond's and Charleston's slave dealing territory. Union invasions pressured coastal enslavers to sell, while in the Piedmont and mountains, speculators sought out opportunities—a tension that provided ample opportunity for traffickers. Elijah Brittingham, for one, relocated from Virginia's occupied Eastern Shore to exploit this reality.[164] Likewise, the autumn of 1863 found Richmond's Solomon Davis gearing up for "a raid on the old north state."[165] North Carolina offered traders like Davis a productive hunting ground. In Wilmington, for example, one slave seller reported seeing "sails of negroes Every day . . . and from 1750 to 2000 dollars was the market price."[166] North Carolina buyers and sellers also benefited from access to both the Richmond and Charleston markets and could choose whichever was most secure and offered the highest prices at a given moment.[167] As a result, in early 1863, western North Carolina's James Gwyn found "many negro buyers in this part of the country." He lamented that while he had already sold some people successfully, he had done so "too soon & at too low a price." This included Polly, whom Gwyn accused of theft, and for whom he had received $1,250. Had he waited, Gwyn believed, he could have sold her for fully 50 percent more.[168]

The sale of John, Joe, and Ann illustrates the interlocking outlets and opportunities the wartime slave trade offered Carolinians. These three siblings had been enslaved near New Bern at the mouth of the Neuse River and, if permitted to remain there, would almost certainly have gained their freedom. Instead, their enslaver sold them through Richmond to R. H. Penland, an inhabitant of North Carolina's western mountains, who purchased them to augment his own modest holdings.[169] They soon escaped, but many coastal Carolina slaves followed them into the Richmond slave market, which reaffirmed their enslavement even as liberty beckoned. William Pettigrew, for example, saw a group of one hundred captives bound for Richmond, many of whom eventually "sold . . . at high prices," and applauded a neighbor who turned nineteen people into $15,000 for having "acted like a prudent man."[170]

Slave markets facilitated both the prudence of Pettigrew's neighbors and the exuberance of Confederates whom the events of 1862–1863 convinced that independence was inevitable. Few stated the latter sentiment more clearly than Mississippi's Jeremiah Gage. In early 1863, Gage, then stationed at Goldsboro, North Carolina, argued to relatives at home that

"Negro trading... could be made a profitable business now." He envisioned a business, however, that differed markedly in structure from the antebellum slave trade. Instead of purchasing enslaved people in Virginia and North Carolina for sale in the Mississippi Valley, he argued that Mississippians should send them to Richmond, where he had seen "a very ordinary field negro woman... sell for 1200 dollars" and "field hands from 2000 to 2900." The axis of this new trade was defined not by the cotton economy, but by faith in the Rebel project. Higher prices prevailed in Richmond than in the Cotton South because "the people in these parts have greater confidence in our Government, and our final success than they have in Mississippi."[171]

Sheltered enslavers' "greater confidence" restructured the slave trade during the Civil War. While people still moved from the Upper South to the Lower South, a parallel traffic emerged that reversed this flow, reorienting it around Confederate strongholds as much as around staple crop production. As Gage noted, this made cities like Richmond the lodestones of the Rebel slave trade. Linked to the surviving CSA by rail and road and sheltered by the Confederacy's armies, they provided safe harbors and high prices for Confederates looking to sell and potential bonanzas for those looking to buy. As a result, Cotton Kingdom Confederates began moving people against the grain of the antebellum slave trade. While watching the auction of fifty-seven people in Montgomery, Virginia émigré John M. Sutherlin mused that he could have bought them there and resold them in Richmond for a $20,000 profit. To that end, he invited a family agent to come south and purchase people. The agent in question made two trips to Alabama and a third to Mississippi. He brought back at least five people for sale, but often found Lower South markets so picked over that he struggled to purchase more than a single enslaved man. Silas Omohundro, meanwhile, traveled to Georgia to fill a similar request from Sutherlin's brother William.[172] If these buyers struggled, it was in part because residents of the Deep South sent people north on their own. One Alabama family, for example, offered up Lucinda on the grounds that "Negroes are selling very high in Richmond now."[173]

The confidence espoused by Rebels like Gage brought tragedy for enslaved families. In May 1863, as Confederates celebrated the rout of the Army of the Potomac at Chancellorsville, Meria sprinted into the bedroom of the Barringers, who enslaved her in Raleigh, North Carolina. She lived apart from her husband, Manuel, but had long hoped the Barringers would acquire him. On the morning of May 10, she learned that enslavers' avarice had foiled her plans. Manuel's enslaver had recently visited Richmond, where the high prices that Gage and so many others had noted dazzled him. He thus rushed all the people on whom he could lay hands to the city, including Manuel. Instead of joining Meria in Raleigh, Manuel could not even stop there to see her as he was taken north for sale. Meria's "unearthly groans" of protest proved unavailing.[174] In central Virginia's Charlotte County, meanwhile, Rachel married Robert, who belonged to a neighboring slaveholder. For a year, they enjoyed what wedded bliss slavery permitted before her enslaver separated them by selling her to a Rebel officer for $2,500.[175]

Even enslavers skeptical about the Confederacy's prospects could do irreparable damage to enslaved families. Henry King Burgwyn, a young North Carolina officer, wrote to his father in January 1863 that if US forces advanced into the central part of the state (something he considered plausible), "I would not give you 25 cts on the dollar for all your produce negroes &c." A month later, however, with the threat diminished, he urged his father to purchase people. "Even though you should have to pay a pretty high price for negroes," he argued, "you will gain by it, provided always that you save them from the Yankees."[176] Meanwhile, in Virginia's Clarke County, traversed dozens of times by contending armies, a slaveholder sold Malinda and her three children, Carter, John, and Eliza, on very specific terms. Both purchaser and seller conceded that "the holding of slave property is uncertain on account of the war now existing." They agreed, therefore, to determine a fair price "according to their value" at the war's conclusion.[177]

Riding high after Chancellorsville, the Army of Northern Virginia surged once more across the Potomac, seeking to inflict a devastating, politically salient defeat on Union forces. At Gettysburg, the Army of the Potomac turned them back, forcing Lee's depleted Rebels to return to Virginia. Simultaneously, forces under Grant and Sherman won a series of victories at Jackson, Champion Hill, and the Big Black River, besieged Vicksburg, and, on July 4, captured the Confederate stronghold.[178] For all their military significance, these setbacks diminished enslavers' desire for enslaved property only modestly. A Virginian successfully sold twenty-one people in Montgomery three days after Gettysburg while a resident of Petersburg demanded $1,500 for a twelve-year-old girl named Minerva—a price she considered reasonable given that "servants have advanced so much in value."[179]

Varying reports from these far-flung fields of battle diluted their impacts and cushioned the blows they might otherwise have dealt enslavers' spirits. One Louisianian conceded that Vicksburg's fall would devastate slavery in the surrounding regions. But he saw Gettysburg as a successful counterweight.

"I do not think," he wrote, "that we have any good grounds to despair of [the] Ultimate success of our cause" even though "our part of the country" might "suffer terribly."[180] A resident of Hinds County, Mississippi, meanwhile, regrouped his holdings in Alabama. He had lost many people before, during, and after Vicksburg but had "bought more than I lost," even at the cost of "2500 for men & 2000 for women."[181] A Mississippi soldier retreating from Gettysburg instructed his family to send enslaved people to Alabama or Georgia, where he believed they could "sell them for a good price."[182] James Henry Hammond's son took advantage of similar sales, purchasing Milly in Lynchburg, Virginia in the weeks following Gettysburg and Vicksburg.[183]

Even many of those discouraged by these battles, as well as by subsequent defeats in central Tennessee, considered these setbacks only temporary. As one soldier encouraged his mother, "I think this is the darkest hour we have ever had, tho the darkest hour is just before day."[184] Well after Union forces had bulled through Tennessee, an official found that many Confederates retained "a lingering hope that by some hocus-pocus things will get back to the old state" and were therefore disinclined to completely abandon slave property.[185] Even glimmers of hope could illuminate the signing of bills of sale. Several Tennesseans bought people in the summer of 1863 only to have Union advances force them to Alabama with their acquired chattels.[186] E. H. Stokes purchased Daniel for $2,250 during the Army of Northern Virginia's withdrawal; another trader even argued that the moment was actually a favorable one. "Opportunities," he wrote to Stokes, "are beginning to present themselves in a way that I can make some purchases."[187] In a similar vein, Davis, Deupree & Co., which had been shuttered by the secession crisis in 1861, reformed in the late summer of 1863, citing "the former popularity of the firm" and the "fresh start" that "the times allow."[188]

In August 1863, a Mississippian crossed the Mississippi River bound for Texas, only to find the trans-Mississippi in chaos. The Union army and navy patrolled most of the river's length, with expeditionary forces ascending its tributaries. As a result, Confederate soldiers, governments, and citizens on the west bank of the river were (as this traveler put it in a letter to the *Houston Tri-Weekly Telegraph*) "cut off pretty much from communication with the seat of government, and reliable intelligence from our armies." Rumors and uncertainty pervaded western Louisiana, Arkansas, and Texas following Gettysburg and Vicksburg, as did economic turmoil. Inflation combined with shortages in key goods to produce considerable hardship, which the Confederate public blamed on speculators, "merchants and government agents." These, through hoarding, price gouging, and sheer incompetence, were "destroying the country" and "weakening" Confederates' "faith in the final result of things." Though, the paper conceded, if you asked these merchants, among whom they included the "auctioneer" or "negro trader," "they will wonder you cannot see they are the very mainstays of the Confederacy."[189]

Nevertheless, the *Tri-Weekly Telegraph* cheered, there was little reason to despair. "Our information from the other side of the river," incomplete though it might be, "is that the people were never more determined than at the present moment." "The fall of Vicksburg," it continued, "has not depressed but made the people more resolute." "Are we to give up the precious boon of liberty," it queried its readers, "because we have been once or twice unsuccessful?" Hoping for foreign intervention, certain to a degree bordering on the absolute that God remained on their side, Confederates would do their "whole duty," thereby "showing to the world that we are indeed what we profess to be, a nation determined to be free."[190]

From their nadir in the spring of 1862, Confederates' hopes had rebounded dramatically, paralleled and reinforced by a revived slave trade. This commerce linked cities like Richmond, the epicenter of the Rebel cause, with surviving (and thriving) Confederate hubs: Charleston, Atlanta, Savannah, Montgomery, Mobile, and innumerable smaller markets dotting the CSA's interior. With confidence in their ultimate victory restored, enslavers in all these cities bought and sold freely, driving slave commerce in some cases within hailing distance of its prewar volume. As a barometer of Confederate faith, an avatar of Confederate exuberance, and a means of securing their independence and confronting emancipation, the slave trade had, in fact, become precisely what the *Tri-Weekly Telegraph* derided slave traders for believing it to be: a "mainstay" of the Rebel endeavor.

4

"Negroes Will Bear Fabulous Prices"

Inflation, Speculation, and the Confederate Future

In August 1863, Virginia's Francis Smith sent his father-in-law a plan to strengthen the family's finances during the war and to profit following a Rebel victory. Smith was among the Confederates undeterred by Gettysburg and Vicksburg. Indeed, he radiated optimism regarding the Confederacy's future and affirmed his faith through his preferred acquisitions. For those "sure that the Confederacy would succeed," he argued, enslaved people represented "the only perfectly safe investment." Smith, moreover, saw opportunity in the relatively low real prices human property commanded that summer, trusting that the rebellion's success would reinvigorate the slave economy and bring renewed wealth and status to those holding people in bondage. With victory accomplished, "money . . . invested in negroes" during the war would pay slavery's acolytes "a handsome percentage." That the Confederacy might fail was utterly anathema to his thoughts. As Smith put it, "that idea does not enter my brain except in argument." "Even if it did," he concluded, "the prize is well worth the risk."[1]

Battlefield losses were not the only obstacles confronting Confederates in the latter half of 1863. The military situation remained ambiguous, but their unfolding economic catastrophe was undeniable. Most significantly, hyperinflation disrupted business and impeded nearly every aspect of Confederate economic life.[2] In the meantime, US policy makers, Union soldiers, and the enslaved themselves took additional steps against the institution of slavery. As a result, the threat of uncompensated emancipation mounted. Nevertheless, Confederates continued—as they had from the war's beginning—to invest in enslaved property. In doing so, they made calculated choices rooted simultaneously in their evaluation of the available investment options, in their unshakeable belief in Confederate independence, and in their lofty expectations for slavery's future.

Three fundamental realities shaped the host of wartime slave purchases and sales that enslavers undertook purely in the pursuit of economic gain. First, they demonstrated powerful continuity. For generations, enslaved property had been white Southerners' investment of choice. As South Carolina industrialist William Gregg noted in 1863, white Southerners were "a peculiar people. . . . Our capital consists mainly in lands and negroes, and the habits of our wealthy people for generations have kept them in one channel; that of producing cotton, tobacco and rice, the surplus products to be invested in land and negroes."[3] The high prices they willingly paid for human property into and beyond that year indicate that Rebels believed this would not change. Rather, they hoped that their independent slaveholding republic would enable them to perpetuate this practice.[4]

Second, the Confederacy's unfolding economic collapse perversely and specifically incentivized slave commerce by making enslaved people appear to be relatively safe repositories of value. The Confederacy lacked sufficient specie to make hard currency a viable investment option, and while some preferred other nodes of the slave economy (land or cotton), many considered the enslaved the most promising investment.[5] With inflation wracking the CSA, enslaved property outshone Rebel bonds, notes, or paper currency. Some buyers speculated wildly. Others bought people in rearguard actions aimed at preserving their wealth. With their economy a shambles, Confederates sought financial stability in the slave market as much as anywhere else in the slaveholders' republic.

Finally, many Confederates for much of the war considered their victory inevitable. They manifested this faith in fever dreams regarding the prices of enslaved property in the postbellum marketplace. Slave prices had ascended steadily throughout the 1850s, accelerating in the latter half of the decade despite escalating moral, economic, and political attacks on slavery.[6] In 1860, an independent South would have been the world's fourth richest nation, with a white per capita income significantly outpacing the North's.[7] If adequately defended, white Southerners believed, slavery could easily endure for a century or more, particularly given the increasing flexibility the institution manifested.[8] With King Cotton restored, the enslaved people on whose backs his throne rested would soar in value. Declining real prices during the war were only a temporary setback. After its conclusion, people would be worth more than ever before.[9] Confederates looking to buy people during the Civil War thus looked past the conflict's immediate effects and emphasized enslaved peoples' long-term value.

An independent Confederate States of America was central to this vision because of the long investment horizon required for enslaved assets. Slaveholders valued the people they held captive for their present productive capacity as well as for what they expected to extract from them in the future. When purchasing women, they weighed equally the labor they would perform and the children they might bear. When buying children, they anticipated the work they would force from them in the ensuing years, even decades.[10] In the words of one scholar, slaveholders were, fundamentally, "speculator[s]" who hoped "to endow [their] progeny for generations to come" through the "capital accumulation" represented in the growing numbers of people they enslaved.[11] The returns from slave ownership, therefore, were long-term and intergenerational.[12] With assumptions of victory foreshortening their perspectives, enslavers targeted not just slaves, but specifically women and children, for acquisition, expecting their labor in the fields and the birthing bed to vindicate their speculations.

As the Civil War entered its third and fourth years, its progress ground away at slave commerce. Economic chaos hindered enslavers' abilities to buy and sell, while expanding emancipation rendered enslaved property ever more uncertain. These realities prevented or dissuaded many Confederates from acquiring enslaved people. Their effects, however, were neither universally distributed nor chronologically consistent. Despite the uneven course of the conflict, Confederates continued to pursue enslaved people as an investment, making calculated bets on the enduring value of enslaved property securely defended by a victorious slaveholder's republic. In doing so, they both responded to wartime crises and revealed their expectations for the Confederate future.

In March 1864, John R. Sutton, a lawyer from King and Queen County, Virginia, mailed $9,000 to Richmond. The resolution of a long-running legal dispute had left him temporarily flush, but he knew that holding cash that spring was a bad idea. Not only were the Armies of the Potomac and Northern Virginia bracing for a spring campaign that might well traverse his property, but the value of the Confederacy's fiat currency was fluctuating wildly. Prudence dictated translating paper money into property. To that end, Sutton asked Hill, Dickinson, & Co. to "lay out" as much of the funds as possible "in negroes." Three years of war had diminished their real prices, but, Sutton believed, this only meant that "negroes will not be any cheaper" and therefore "it will be well to invest all in them."[13] The value stored in these men and women would shield him from inflation and would appreciate dramatically following Confederate victory.

From the secession crisis forward, financial uncertainty had shaped the Confederacy's trade in slaves. Building on the initial credit crunch sparked by secession, blockades and embargoes swiftly ruined the Rebel staple crop economy.[14] Nevertheless, as Georgia's comptroller general evaluated the state of enslaved property at the end of the war's first year, he argued that "the decrease in the value of slaves" was really "very small indeed." Prices had declined perhaps 10 percent from their 1860 peak, which he attributed to circumstantial rather than structural factors. An antebellum price bubble, "the fact that our Ports have been blockaded by the enemy," and the resulting disruption of the cotton market were primarily to blame. Even at these reduced prices, however, enslaved people remained more valuable than they had been as recently as 1857.[15] All in all, Georgia's leading financial officer concluded, enslaved property had held up relatively well.

As the war lengthened, however, problems that had simmered during the war's early days began to boil over. Though many Rebels initially considered their predominantly agricultural economy an advantage, escalating demands for manpower, materiel, and money swiftly rendered it a decided hindrance.[16] Beginning in April 1862, widespread conscription drew much of the remaining white male population into the military. Agricultural productivity—particularly on the smaller farms that fed the Confederacy—plummeted. The fledgling nation's inability to maintain its transportation infrastructure inhibited the distribution of food and other goods. While some areas remained well-fed and well-stocked, therefore, others (particularly cities swollen by refugees) experienced serious hunger pangs.[17] Collectively, these changes heightened the war's social and economic distortion and impinged upon the market for slaves.

Inflation proved still more significant. Reluctant and ineffective taxation forced the Confederate government to borrow heavily to finance the war and, when loans dried up, to print vast quantities of money to cover its expenses. Across the war's first three years, the Confederacy raised almost 60 percent of its funds solely through treasury notes and other paper.[18] Individual states also churned out new notes; Louisiana alone produced nearly $8 million in paper currency.[19] The net result was an almost inconceivable level of inflation. In 1861, it averaged 12 percent monthly, an alarming figure, but one the citizens of a revolutionary republic could tolerate so long as the conflict proved brief. As the war stretched on, inflation produced terrible economic pressures. A price index of two dozen goods rose by 10 percent monthly for fully three years, and even more quickly in the Confederacy's overcrowded and undersupplied cities.[20] As early as October 1862, therefore, even Treasury Secretary Christopher Memminger feared that the swelling "quantity of money in circulation" would ultimately "produce depreciation and final disaster."[21]

Combining with the economic dislocation of secession and war, inflation forced Confederates to reevaluate their strategies for preserving their wealth.[22] Almost immediately, this shaped transactions involving enslaved people. In 1861, for example, a Shepherdstown, Virginia woman sold a twenty-four-year-old man for $700—well below his antebellum market value—because she received payment in money she trusted.[23] A. J. Rux, meanwhile, complained of having to take "dead old field paper" for enslaved people and refused what he described as "all the notes" in Mississippi for one woman.[24]

By the spring of 1862, Confederates increasingly recognized their vulnerability to inflation. As one Richmond mercantile firm complained that April, "We have before us now no scope for the profitable use of money."[25] North Carolina brothers Walter and Rufus Lenoir likewise realized the war's "gigantic proportions" meant that "prices, in paper currency at least, must necessarily advance, and will doubtless continue to advance till the close of the war."[26] Seeking to use his money profitably, South Carolina's Alfred Mulligan worked to "invest what money I may have ... for money goes very fast when not turned to good interest."[27] "Money comes in so fast that we hardly know how to dispose of it to advantage," Sam Richards concurred from Atlanta.[28] To Franklin County, North Carolina's Alfred Bell, inflation seemed both an opportunity and a curse. He advised his father, "Now is the time to make money but don't keep it for fear of it being of no value."[29]

Rather than keeping money on hand, many invested it in the enslaved. Though the war's first year drove down the real prices slaves commanded, it left intact long-term confidence in their value. As Confederates hunted out safe harbors for their depreciating currency, the enslaved presented an ideal combination of present value and long-term appreciation. Those persons most concerned about inflation's impact eagerly purchased slaves. Walter Lenoir preferred buying "some negroes at ... half the former highest prices" rather than risk "keeping ... much paper money."[30] Alfred Mulligan pushed his wife to acquire slaves and cotton, while Sam Richards bought enslaved people alongside Confederate bonds and real estate.[31] Alfred Bell's wife, Mary, meanwhile, purchased enslaved property for the family whenever possible across the next two years.[32]

So many decided to invest in enslaved people that they influenced the market for them. James Petigru attributed Charleston's robust slave market in the summer of 1862 to the fact that "people are glad to get off paper money for anything that has intrinsic value, even if worth very little."[33] That same summer, an Arkansan encouraged his wife to purchase a person if given the chance to do so. With all available assets a "big risk," he believed that human property offered the most lucrative potential reward.[34] A Texan was willing to buy people even "at a big price" rather than keep "Confederate money laying idle."[35] Not all such efforts were successful, as those holding the enslaved often retained them rather than take Rebel currency for their most valuable property. They sometimes refused to sell even when menaced by US forces. When a buyer approached future Mississippi governor William Sharkey about an enslaved girl, Sharkey turned him down. "Bad property as negroes may be," he argued, "they are still better than the money."[36]

Rebels more enthusiastic than Sharkey raced to spend Confederate money on the antebellum South's—and, presumably, an independent Confederacy's—most valuable form of property. During the Seven Days battles, an Alabamian asked E. H. Stokes to "invest" for him in "some ten or fifteen" enslaved people. Two months later, a South Carolinian asked him to buy him six or eight others. Richmond's Henry Easley gave Stokes $5,000 to invest in slaves; presumably pleased with the result, he doled out another $3,000 six months later.[37] Others considered enslaved property so solid that they exchanged other forms of property for it. An acquaintance of Albemarle County, Virginia's Micajah Woods reportedly spent $210,000 made in the cotton trade on slaves.[38] A Tennessean similarly swapped cotton for people, several North Carolinians traded industrial facilities for them, and a Texan land.[39] For those certain of Rebel victory, the future returns available from human property far outshone alternative investments.

Even as the Union victories of 1862 severely undercut Confederate confidence, they created unique opportunities for those willing to perform their faith in the Rebel cause through speculations in enslaved property. Advancing Federals drove before them a wave of refugees who often sold enslaved people rather than allow them to fall into US hands. This created market surpluses and depressed prices. Professional slave dealers bewailed the resulting declines, but other Confederates exploited this opportunity.[40]

Observing the exodus from coastal North Carolina, a Williamston doctor informed E. H. Stokes that with adequate funding, he "could have invested $10.000 in negroes near the Yankee lines at fair prices & good profits" and invited him to join in a future venture.[41] Walter Lenoir, watching the crisis unfold from a camp near Kinston, North Carolina, argued that the enslaved would be an excellent "long investment," particularly given they could be purchased cheaply "near the points where they are in the greatest present danger, & remov[ed] . . . to the mountains," where they would be secure.[42] Nearly a year later, Henry King Burgwyn urged his father to "send some reliable agent down near the Yankee lines & buy some negroes there," as he "might get them very cheap."[43]

This behavior was not restricted to coastal North Carolina. Jesse Kirkland, a Mississippian stationed in Fairfax County, Virginia, encountered a man willing to sell him an entire enslaved family if Kirkland could smuggle them out from behind Union lines. The opportunistic Kirkland hoped this would be merely his first chance to acquire enslaved people; before the war concluded, he "intend[ed] buying a good many."[44] While defending the approaches to Charleston in 1862, General Nathan "Shanks" Evans purchased an enslaved family carried from the Sea Islands "cheap for cash." With Lowcountry planters fleeing the region, he declared to his wife, "now is the time to invest what little money we have in negroes."[45] The ongoing Lowcountry collapse provided speculators with extensive opportunities. In the summer of 1863, an Upcountry South Carolina newspaper rejoiced that thanks to Union coastal incursions, local "negro marts are crowded with plantation negroes."[46] As late as 1864, in occupied Arkansas, a man willing to pay a premium for enslaved people enticed a Methodist minister to smuggle them through US lines for sale.[47] The progress of Union arms thus had contradictory effects on the slave trade. While US armies disrupted the institution wherever they marched, they fed slave markets behind Confederate lines, with the increasing supply of human property available holding down the real prices asked for them. This process created ideal conditions for the Rebels most emotionally and politically invested in the Confederacy to stake their financial hopes on the future of the slaveholders' republic.

Late in 1862, Edmund Ruffin took stock of the war's effects on enslaved property. After losing significant parts of his own workforce during the Peninsula Campaign, he was no stranger to the conflict's deleterious potential. Having sold at least twenty-nine people whom he recaptured—some to markets as far away as Texas—he understood the slave trade equally well.[48]

His long career as a plantation pundit, moreover, led him to pontificate on the institution's trajectory. In June of that year, his prognosis was negative. The real prices offered for slaves, he estimated, had fallen between 25 and 50 percent as Union forces closed in on Richmond. But by October, he saw the slave market rebounding. Where prices had declined due to military losses and the economic woes that Ruffin labeled a "want of employment & profit of labor," by the fall slave prices had "rallied, & latterly have been increasing." Some of this increase, he knew, stemmed from inflation. He argued, however, that much of it lay in the value Confederates placed on human property as an investment. "The present prices for slaves," he contended, "are higher than any available employment can return a profit upon now." The fact that prices had not declined following direct threats by the United States against enslaved property—the Confiscation Acts and the preliminary Emancipation Proclamation—showed slaveholders' confidence in the Confederacy's ultimate triumph and enslaved people's ongoing value as a speculative commodity.[49]

Throughout 1863, Confederates derided emancipationist policies by pointing to the vitality of the slave trade. Yet the high nominal slave prices they considered evidence of the Confederacy's strength also pointed to the rot metastasizing in its finances.[50] By the end of 1862, the Confederate financial collapse had become a full-fledged crisis.[51] Failed reform legislation, the raging conflict, and shipments of specie abroad to pay for war materiel further depressed the value of Confederate money.[52] Five times as many Confederate notes circulated as had the previous winter and the prices demanded for necessities outpaced even this increase in the money supply.[53] The strain began to tell on many Confederates. South Carolina's William Ravenel found it clear "that our 'circulation' is too much inflated," while John Sutherlin informed his brother that though he remained "hopefull that Congress will do something to release our currency from the dredfull doom that is apparently awaiting it," he considered it "plain to the mind of every practical man that Something must be done and that speeday too or our country will be ruined."[54]

The Confederate Congress tried to staunch the bleeding in October 1862 and March 1863 with laws aimed at restraining the money supply. The Confederacy's inability to otherwise fund a lengthening war, however, ensured that the printing presses rolled on, depreciating the currency still more with every turn.[55] By early 1863, some merchants refused to accept paper money altogether, including for the enslaved.[56] Near Knoxville, a Confederate soldier noted that while people could be purchased cheaply there, "it would take gold to get them."[57] Distrust of the currency reached critical levels. Ravenel found that "the condition of our currency is now causing more apprehension than any other danger to which we are exposed," while Walter Lenoir complained, "but for our ruined currency, our independence might safely be considered as an accomplished fact." "Alas!" he lamented, "the currency."[58] Even an enslaved blacksmith declared himself "mighty oneasy" about receiving payment in Confederate notes.[59] Inflation skewed all commodity prices. Ravenel found that "land & houses, negroes, stocks &c. have gone up to double or treble their former prices," while an 1863 Confederate textbook asking its students to calculate the average price of 125 people sold was soon laughably outdated (the correct answer was a paltry $601).[60] In paper currency, slave prices fluctuated to the degree that a trader who sold people in September 1863 for more than $2,750 apiece—fully double their prewar prices—could complain of "a very dull time."[61]

The tumultuous economic climate enhanced enslaved people's appeal as investments. In March 1863, the French consul in Charleston reported slave prices (and those of select other commodities) tripling as the denizens of that city rapidly offloaded depreciating paper.[62] Those holding the enslaved either sold them dearly or retained them in the belief that whatever money they received in return could not provide equal value. One Virginian acknowledged that while slaves "are selling very high now . . . so is everything else and they are priced really comparatively low." An equally significant obstacle to selling was the fact that "we could not invest the money to a greater advantage in anything else, and to hold the money would be ruinous to us."[63] Another enslaver declined to sell the people he owned, arguing, "if we gain our independence they will be very good property for they will bring a big price."[64] Even North Carolina Treasurer Jonathan Worth, who had a fiduciary duty to "sustain the credit of Confederate currency," advised a friend not to sell people on the grounds that "negroes" were "far better property than the currency or stocks of the Confederate Government."[65] While some took issue with such an unpatriotic calculus (a South Carolina newspaper complained that because the values of slave property and the Confederate currency depended equally on a Rebel victory, they should command the same degree of investment), Confederates' rush to purchase people revealed considerably more popular faith in human property than in government paper.[66]

Confederates might store little trust in the competence and credit of their government (congressional elections in 1863, for example, proved a bloodbath for incumbents), but they reposed much in the slave system it defended.[67] One slave trader who abetted this belief urged his clients, "Now is the Time to Strike!" and offered to exchange "negroes and land for Confederate money" via a slave trade that he labeled "reviving."[68] An Alabamian embraced a similar ethos, informing his father, "I intend to keep my last dollar invested in tobacco, cotton & Negroes" rather than the "folly" Confederate bonds represented.[69] John Sutherlin tried to invest more than $100,000 in an Alabama plantation and sixty-five people, but was frustrated by a creditor who refused to take paper currency in return.[70] Anticipating a fall in bond prices after Gettysburg and Vicksburg, another Confederate instructed his wife to "dispose" of their bonds and invest the proceeds in an enslaved person. Both nominally depended on the success of the slaveholders' republic, but, as this instance shows, Rebels consistently preferred enslaved people to Confederate money.[71]

Rebels living at a remove from US invasions turned currency into enslaved property particularly zealously. Nowhere was this truer than in Texas, where speculators exploited an influx of refugees from Missouri and the Lower Mississippi Valley who brought with them tens of thousands of enslaved people. While some enslavers purchased land or hired their forced laborers to industrial concerns, feeding, clothing, and otherwise supporting them proved difficult.[72] Texans took advantage of this disruption to purchase people at discount prices. As one Texan informed his wife, the "Missourians" then flooding the state "have no money," and valued "their Negroes *low* and [my] lands *high*."[73] A resident of McLennan County indulged his "mania for buying negroes" until the war's final months.[74] Others pursued enslaved people beyond the state's borders. On his way to Virginia, Arthur Fremantle encountered "an old man from Matagorda, buying slaves cheap in Louisiana"; a Texan, meanwhile, reported that multiple acquaintances had gone to Arkansas to buy enslaved workers for sale in Texas.[75] Fueled by such actions, Houston's slave market embarked on a boom that continued through the war's end. By September 1863, the city's leading trading firm reported that it could not "keep Negroes in stock."[76]

Largely sheltered from Union incursions, Texans expressed far greater confidence in the enslaved than in any other investment, and prices remained remarkably stable there.[77] A formerly enslaved man recalled being bought early in the war by a buyer emboldened by assurances that removing to Texas would protect his investment.[78] As the war progressed, enslaved people's worth relative to other investments only increased. In 1863, a Texan cavalryman urged his wife to acquire real property, as "all pay ... better than Confederate money." The enslaved, though "awful high" at the present, would hold their value while also laboring for the family.[79] Another called on family members to liquidate other property in favor of investing in "Sheep ... good mares or [N]egroes."[80] With so many speculating in human property, it should come as no surprise that one Texan found the state in 1863 "full of negro buyers"—to the detriment of his own purchasing efforts.[81] One of these buyers, Frederick A. Rice, may well have bought dozens of people in April of that year.[82]

Kit Hall of Grimes County found the potential returns from slave property tempting enough to kill for them. In the fall of 1863, he met two slave traders traveling to Houston. From them he bought one person for cash and several more on credit. When the duo tried to collect, Hall lured them to a remote patch of woods and shot them both. Upon returning home, he began building lodgings for his doubly ill-gotten laborers. His newfound wealth was immediately conspicuous. A neighbor found it "magical and wonderful" and speculated that he had either "visited the valley of Diamonds we read of in the Arabian nights, or ... found Aladin's [sic] lamp." Locals were unsurprised, however, when a posse arrived, identified some of the traders' possessions, and took both Hall and the enslaved into custody.[83]

Wherever Rebels considered themselves safe, they exploited distortions in the slave market. Residents of Florida's interior actively pursued enslaved people in 1862 and 1863 as US raids drove many from the coast.[84] Slaveholders (and aspiring enslavers) in western North Carolina likewise seized opportunities created by the Union's coastal incursions to either hire or purchase enslaved laborers outright.[85] Mary Bell persistently sought to buy an enslaved woman named Martha. Though averse to making "big speculations by myself," Bell determined that the flood of people into the backcountry meant "it would be advisable to buy negroes at this time."[86]

Speculators like Bell sought human property amid an ever-deteriorating economy. While Confederates were ambivalent as to Gettysburg's and Vicksburg's strategic impact, at a minimum, these defeats augured a prolonged war. This expectation, as well as scarcities in key commodities, accelerated inflation in the latter half of 1863. Prices in the eastern Confederacy tripled that year, doubling between June and December alone.[87] The costs of food, clothing, farm equipment, and more soared. Bacon increased nearly tenfold, salt by a factor of twenty-five, and coffee as much as forty times over.[88] As one Richmonder bleakly observed in September 1863, "the crash has got to come." For many, it already had.[89]

The prices of enslaved people rose alongside the prices of other commodities, and while few Confederates truly trusted the high nominal prices attached to them, captive laborers nevertheless remained an appealing investment compared to the available alternatives. As the *Raleigh Semi-Weekly Standard* put it, their prices reflected "not so much the value of the negro as the want of value in the currency."[90] The *Richmond Examiner*, meanwhile, marveled, "at no time of the year have we seen such a plethora of Money," which encouraged "investment in Real Estate, Negroes, Tobacco, Government Securities, Stocks—in fact anything that admits of an exchange."[91] All real assets were better than paper, but enslavers packed much of their "plethora of Money" into human capital as an economic life raft amid the deluge. As a result, one Virginian noted in the fall of 1863, "Negroes are very high." In practical terms, this meant that a man named Tom, whom his family hoped to sell, "would bring at least $3000 if not $4000."[92]

Formerly enslaved people vividly recalled the mad rush to invest in them even decades later. Joanna Draper, once held in Mississippi, said that her enslaver regularly "exchange[d his] money for people," while Virginia's Peter Barber remembered a buyer handing over a mix of Confederate and Union currency for him.[93] Jack Lucas noted that his seller only reluctantly took Confederate money for him, while Moses Mitchel reported his seller would receive only "new issue" Confederate currency (the most valuable possible form of paper money) and a mite of gold in payment.[94] These memories reveal the eagerness with which Rebels exchanged increasingly suspect notes for enslaved people.

Ironically, even the Confederate Congress's efforts to stave off the currency's collapse funneled money into the enslaved. Its October 1862, March 1863, and February 1864 acts sought to rein in inflation by offering Rebels the chance to purchase higher-yielding Confederate bonds and cutting the value of older currencies relative to newly issued notes.[95] By discouraging Confederates from holding older money, however, these laws precipitated a rush to spend, increasing inflation.[96] With the downward spiral unchecked, many Confederates spent depreciating money on human property. Trying to stay ahead of the 1863 Act, for example, Edwin Fay urged his father-in-law to purchase a person with soon-to-be-devalued currency.[97] Later in that year, with yet another contraction on the horizon, Alfred Bell encouraged Mary to do the same.[98] As their fellow North Carolinian Paul

Cameron warned a friend who was weighing selling people, "you are to be paid in Confederate bonds. Have you not enough of that sort of stock?"[99]

The Confederacy made its final bid to tame inflation through February 1864's Currency Reform Act. It aggressively taxed notes not exchanged for newly issued currency, used to pay taxes, or swapped for long-term bonds to impose order on Confederate money. The Act briefly stabilized bond prices and slowed the rate of currency issuance, but in the process it outraged the Confederate populace, who considered it tantamount to repudiation.[100] A Georgian declared it "equivalent to robbing the public creditors of one half of what is due to them," adding, "my faith in Confederate honor and honesty is at an end."[101] A disgusted Floridian spat, "I want no Confed. money—I have had a gorge of that trash."[102] Confederates were deeply aware of the bleak fiscal histories of revolutionary republics, including the United States under the Articles of Confederation. As a result, one South Carolinian warned, "real estate & negroes ... should be held by all, who are not compelled by debts to sell, because when peace comes they will have some value."[103]

In the ensuing months, the Currency Reform Act actually increased inflation. Rather than restoring monetary order, "the effect of the currency bill has been to enhance the price of all articles," William Ravenel wailed.[104] Its effects on the slave market were ambiguous. Uncertainty, fears of deflation, and a persistent shortage of the new currency forestalled many transactions.[105] Lewis C. Robards, a notorious Kentucky slaver who had relocated to Lynchburg, Virginia during the war, saw his business plummet. He had sold roughly twenty people in each of the five months preceding the Act's passage but dealt only seven in the subsequent month.[106] The disordered currency had much to do with this. Richmond's leading slave traders explicitly refused older currencies, cutting themselves off from the funds available to many would-be purchasers.[107] Hill, Dickinson & Co. reported sales of more than $1.2 million in the first quarter of 1864 but a mere $152,000 in the second, suggesting that, as one Richmonder noted that April, "the sales of negroes have all but stopped" because "the people have not the new issue."[108]

Even this crunch, however, created opportunity for those with the means to purchase. As sales slowed, one Virginian reflected, this meant that "Negros are veary cheep at this time owing to the Curancy as money is veary scarce."[109] Purchasers included E. H. Stokes's nephew, who bought Anthony in February 1864, and G. V. Ancker, who bought Dave, Robert, and Jack in Columbia, South Carolina.[110] Even a bolstered currency, however, could be translated only with difficulty into any property of real value—much less into highly desirable human property. Indeed, when Richmond trader S. M. Bowman purchased Eliza and Margaret—whom he described as "little girls"—he distinctly remembered fully two years later having paid for them in gold.[111] Shortly after the act's passage, a Virginian congratulated his brother on having "funded your Confederate 'scrip' in negro property," while a South Carolina trading firm played on Rebels' continued trepidations by claiming to represent their "Last Chance" to "invest your money" in enslaved property.[112]

Even as inflation encouraged enslavers to acquire human property as a hedge against depreciating currency, it prompted Confederate debtors to sell people. The enslaved had always suffered the consequences of slaveholders' addiction to credit, whether passively as collateral or actively as liquid assets.[113] That the idiom of being "drunk up"—sold to pay for extravagances or degeneracies—pervaded enslaved people's vocabulary suggests both the frequency of this practice and the vehemence of their resentment of it.[114] In the antebellum period, such sales were generally reactive, with courts forcing indebted enslavers to yield slave property. During the war, however, soaring nominal slave prices combined with legislative moratoria and stay laws (which limited creditors' ability to collect debts during times of crisis) to strengthen debtors' hands. Confederates thus moved proactively in attacking their obligations, seeing a chance to gain financial independence by selling the enslaved and paying down their debts in depreciated currency.[115]

Even Confederate generals like Clement Evans pursued this logic. Encamped along the Rapidan River in December 1863, Evans looked ahead to the conflict's conclusion. He felt trepidation not for the Confederacy's ultimate fate, but over his own financial position. "If I could only relieve myself of every pecuniary obligation," he mused, "I should at the close of the war be a happy man." With this in mind, he and his wife Allie weighed multiple options, including selling their enslaved property. She negotiated the sale of some of the family's real estate, a transaction that hinged on the prospective purchaser converting an enslaved person into cash. If it fell through, she planned to sell a man named Charlie to address the couple's debts. Though Clement worried that any cash she raised might not be accepted (particularly with the Currency Reform Act looming), he nevertheless argued self-interestedly, "I believe it is the conscientious duty of all citizens to receive the currency in payment of debts." Human chattels represented enslavers' surest means of obtaining currency.[116]

From the war's outset, Rebels rich and poor moved to obviate their debts by trading in people—a fact freedpeople like Lee Pierce bitterly remembered long after the war.[117] A member of South Carolina's Middleton family reportedly sold men and women worth $20,000 for that purpose. A poorer North Carolina soldier urged his wife to sell Lias to pay a smaller obligation.[118] As inflation accelerated, the temptation to sell increased.[119] In April 1863, a South Carolina woman bemoaned missing a chance to dispose of Easter and Hester while slave traders were offering high prices.[120] Another Carolinian succeeded where she failed. Hoping to reduce his prewar debts and acquire better land, he offered Hagar for sale at the price of $2,000.[121] Houston County, Georgia's Antoinette Moore, meanwhile, strove to offload two enslaved people tied to her late husband's estate as they "can now be sold for a very high Cash price & . . . by their sale the debts of her said trust can be cancelled."[122]

A combination of enslaved resistance, ineptitude, and the broader economic collapse thwarted a number of Confederates' attempts to execute such transactions. Frank, for example, fled a Mississippi enslaver while the latter awaited a higher price that would enable him to resolve his debts.[123] In other cases, fears of indebtedness obstructed purchases. One Virginian worried that buying an enslaved person would mean incurring a debt that would have to be repaid in good money at the war's end.[124] A pair of South Carolinians preparing to go into business using enslaved people to farm and labor on railroads, meanwhile, separated their enslaved property from their shared assets. With each "individually bound for all indebtedness," one partner argued, "it would be madness to witness the loss of the property when it can be so easily (as far as the negroes are concerned) converted." Other property they might risk, but the enslaved had to be preserved.[125] Nevertheless, for many Rebels, the wartime slave trade offered a chance to exploit one of the few favorable financial circumstances created by inflation.

As these Carolinians' precautions show, not all the Rebels who sold enslaved people to meet debt obligations did so voluntarily. This reality ensnared several members of Kate Drumgoold's family. One member of the House family—among whom the ten Drumgoold sisters were dispersed—died in debt during the conflict. The remaining Houses sold Frances and Annie Drumgoold to offset the debts that he had accrued during a dissolute life, offloading them quite literally "to pay off his drink."[126] Others fought to protect (or gain) enslaved property during estate settlements.[127] An Alabama family struggled to pay off a deceased member's liabilities without selling people. "It will be more beneficial," they argued, "to sell the real estate than to sell the slaves" given what the latter would likely command after the war. When real estate proved insufficient to cover the debts in question, however, only a slave sale could make up the shortfall.[128] Virginia's Charles Bruce moved in January 1864 to purchase four people in an estate sale, perhaps looking to offload Confederate currency ahead of the Reform Act.[129] A more optimistic soldier took advantage of a respite in the fighting to advise his family in purchasing an enslaved family made available through an estate sale.[130] Though stay laws and moratoria on actions against debtors sometimes forestalled court-mandated sales, they could not protect bondspeople from their enslavers as the war lengthened.

By the spring of 1864, the collapse in Confederate currency had converged with a worsening military situation. Rebel forces had rebounded from Vicksburg by defeating the Union Army of the Cumberland at Chickamauga in September 1863, after which they besieged the retreating Federals in Chattanooga. By year's end, however, their situation had worsened. A reinforced and rejuvenated Federal force broke the Confederate leaguer and drove toward Atlanta. In May 1864, the Army of the Potomac, directed by Ulysses S. Grant, embarked on what would become known as the Overland Campaign. In a series of massive clashes—the Wilderness, Spotsylvania, the North Anna Crossing, Cold Harbor, and more—Grant drove Lee from the Rappahannock into defensive works around Petersburg, Virginia. These six weeks of fighting, however, failed to destroy the Army of Northern Virginia and cost the Army of the Potomac more than 60,000 casualties.[131]

While the fighting took nearly as high a toll on the Confederacy, many Rebels remained buoyant. As one Georgian put it in late 1863, "The Confederacy is truly passing through a dark and gloomy period & I fear is destined to see a darker day," though, he added, "I will never despair of the final result . . . we will succeed though it may be at the extreme of all that we hold near and dear to us."[132] Despite their losses and the territory ceded, they not only retained their overall confidence in Lee's ability to prevail but also believed a political settlement might well be imminent. They knew the horrific losses Grant's forces had suffered and believed that disappointed and disaffected Americans might consider the cost too high.[133] If a candidate favoring peace defeated Abraham Lincoln in that fall's presidential election, he might well concede Confederate independence. As War Department clerk John Jones wrote in his diary in August 1864, despite the ongoing siege of Petersburg, "Everything depends upon the result of the Presidential

124   AN UNHOLY TRAFFIC

election in the United States. We rely some little upon the success of the peace party."[134]

Banking on the Democrats' success, Confederates continued to buy people as the armies clashed. In Augusta, Georgia, a North Carolina enslaver purchased Jim, Tom, and Albert. Another Carolinian purchased Bob in Columbia, South Carolina.[135] Enslavers sent Jordan, Waller, and Bob Johnson out of Petersburg during the siege, while a Virginian dispatched Henry from the Shenandoah Valley to the mountains of North Carolina.[136] A subset of Confederates trusted more in Northern Copperheads' victory than they did in Confederate money. From the Petersburg trenches, a North Carolinian urged his wife to hoard enslaved people as the family divided an estate, for he wanted "as little . . . in money as possible."[137] William McFall, a South Carolinian likewise fighting before Richmond, asked his family in October 1864 not to sell enslaved people in an estate division, considering them "better property than [the] Confederate bonds" that they might receive in exchange.[138]

Rebels seeking an economic safe harbor traded all manner of assets for enslaved people. A South Carolinian offered up grinding mills and a sawmill

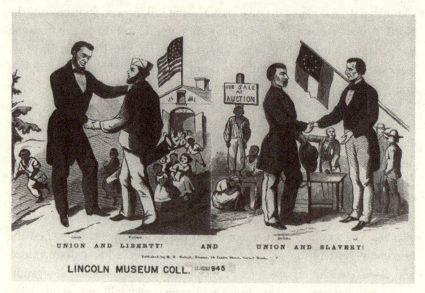

Figure 4.1 "Union and Liberty! And Union and Slavery!" As this cartoon suggests, victory by a Democratic candidate in the presidential election of 1864 might well have preserved the slave trade by conceding Confederate independence. M. W. Siebert, 1864. Library of Congress, LC-USZ62-945.

for people; a North Carolinian offered lands on the Cape Fear River for "young negroes at a fair price" and rejected proffered Rebel money.[139] Even in Georgia, where Sherman's forces were advancing toward Atlanta, enslavers sought to turn real property into human property. One Georgian offered his plantation for Confederate money or enslaved people, both of which could be removed from the invaders' path.[140] A resident of Baldwin County, on the other hand, dealt another Georgian a person for two hundred acres of land. The former divested himself of at-risk property, the latter gained a potentially worthwhile and portable investment.[141]

Not all Confederates considered enslaved people the optimal form of wealth, particularly given the prospect of emancipation. Offered the chance to expand his already immense holdings, Paul Cameron—North Carolina's largest antebellum slaveholder—refused to "add any thing to my cares and unprofitabilities," concluding, "I have about as much as I can stagger along with."[142] Some skeptics preferred cotton, others land, and a few Confederate bonds.[143] Others sought to diversify their holdings. Even those who desired different forms of property, however, used the slave trade to protect themselves, their ambitions, and their futures. In early 1864, one soldier planned to sell a person if he could get a good farm in return, believing, "In a revolution like this, landed property is far safer than any other."[144] Additional Confederates, chastened by Black resistance, traded people for assets that could not escape. After the better part of his labor force fled to the Yankees, South Carolina's John Berkley Grimball sold the more than forty people who remained (his son labeled them "a risky & dead (at present) capital") and put the returns in Confederate securities.[145] His fellow Carolinian Augustin Taveau, fearing "how uncertain everything is," likewise exchanged people for Confederate bonds.[146] Rebel enslavers varied considerably in their preferred wartime investment, but slave commerce enabled the measures that those not sanguine about the state of human property took to protect themselves.

Whether driven by ambition or as a hedge against inflation, fears of debt or a desire to diversify, enslavers throughout the Confederacy sought enslaved property as the Civil War's outcome hung in the balance. As the real prices offered for the enslaved dropped and as inflation mounted, Black bodies increasingly seemed to be the safest property available in the slaveholders' republic. The ebb and flow of the conflict encouraged many to purchase, particularly those in areas that they considered safe from emancipation. The downward spiral of the Rebel currency, meanwhile, drove others to place bets on the property that had built the South and that slaveholders had gone to war to preserve. The wartime slave trade thus provided them, deep into the conflict, with a means of insulating themselves against the Confederacy's financial birth pangs and of buying into a slaveholding future.

Several years after the conflict, a Mississippi jurist retroactively described wartime purchases of enslaved people as "a mere wager on the result of the war."[147] Into the summer of 1864, with major Union offensives stalled before Richmond and Atlanta and with Lincoln's re-election in jeopardy, Confederates anticipated that they would win that wager, secure their independence, and establish a slaveholding republic. Some rested their faith on battlefield victories, others on an unshakeable hatred for Union invaders, a sense of divine favor and civilizational destiny, or an inability to contemplate their world without slaveholding.[148] Shifting goalposts, information deficits, and selective myopia about the state of affairs shaped still others' willingness to buy.[149] However they conjured them, through the summer of 1864, Confederates retained expansive hopes for their final victory and the slaveholding nation it would secure.[150] Their emerging nationalism was neither total nor monolithic, especially as the war strained the slave society's fabric to its breaking point. Nevertheless, the endurance of the wartime slave trade and Rebels' continued appetite for acquiring people as property reveal a widespread, fervent belief in the Confederacy's eventual success.[151]

Nothing demonstrated this absolute faith more clearly than the emphasis Confederates placed on the youth and future value of those whom they purchased. Enslavers had long coveted enslaved people based on the years of income and childbearing they could expect to appropriate from them.[152] With the war disrupting the Southern staple crop economy, many enslavers looked past the immediate returns their human property offered and focused on what they would provide in the years to come. Confederates understood all too well that a US victory likely meant slavery's eventual extinction. Acquiring assets whose value lay in forthcoming agricultural or reproductive labor thus reveals implicit assumptions that widespread emancipation would never come to pass. Optimistic Confederates acquired enslaved property during the war intending to profit from its appreciation in the boundless slaveholding future their triumph would secure.[153]

Fortified by these expectations, many enslavers scrutinized enslaved people with an eye to their postwar values. When, for example, Union forces threatened Charles Pettigrew's property on North Carolina's Albemarle

Sound, he did little to arrest the impending flight of the people he enslaved. Appalled by Charles's apathy, his brother William reminded him what was at stake. Already, "negro men command in Richmond," he informed Charles, "sixteen hundred doll[ar]s, & women fifteen hundred," making their escape an immediate and significant loss. It paled, however, in comparison with the postbellum implications of their flight. "Within a year or two after the close of the war," William speculated, "negro men will command four thousand doll[ar]s." "I lay these facts before you," he concluded, "as an evidence of the large sum at stake."[154] Preserving or acquiring enslaved property in the present would lay a firm foundation for a slaveholding future.

Other Rebels similarly weighed postbellum slavery's prospects against their present trials. As Walter Lenoir argued in April 1862, the prices that the enslaved commanded were then "depreciated in value," by "political considerations & the peculiar character of the war waged by our powerful & unprincipled foe." But, he asserted, the enslaved "after the war must almost necessarily rise again in price," and it would be well to acquire them in the present.[155] After interrogating his wife about the health of an enslaved woman whom he hoped to purchase as a speculation, a Georgian rejoiced that "Negroes are rising continually." He expected prices to eventually exceed $4,000 or even $5,000.[156] A Floridian rejected a neighbor's efforts to pry away his enslaved property because "the impression prevails that after the war they will command fabulous prices." Edwin Fay likewise heard rumors that "negroes will bear fabulous prices" at the war's conclusion, which inspired him "to buy now while they are low."[157]

For much of the Civil War, battlefield events did little to dissuade these Confederates of their eventual success. Even setbacks appeared to be (in historian Gary Gallagher's words) "no more than temporary obstacles on the path to independence."[158] As a result, though prices fluctuated, men like North Carolina's Paul Cameron sought to hold enslaved property. Already the owner of more people than anyone else in the state, Cameron had little need for additional captive workers. He articulated to others, however, the logic for retaining those they held and, implicitly, for acquiring more. In September 1863, for example, he wrote to George Mordecai, "If we succeed in the great struggle the increased value of all this sort of property if then sold will more than pay off."[159]

Even amid the grinding combat of the Overland and Atlanta campaigns, enslavers fantasized about the prices the enslaved might yet command. Some understood this to be a gamble. A soldier fighting in Louisiana in the summer of 1864, for example, conceded that it was possible that "Twelve months from now the negro might not be worth a cent." But in purchasing one, "the risk would be very little, compared to the gain should we come out all right."[160] For others, the fog of war obscured the risks involved. As they maneuvered toward Atlanta, for example, high Union casualties belied the steady progress Sherman's forces were making. This led Alex Spence, an Arkansan fighting before the city, to report, "It takes a pile over here to buy a negro. They are worth 4,000 to 6,000 dollars." Despite directly experiencing US pressure and observing this astronomical price, Spence nevertheless "wish[ed] to buy much." Encouraging news from disparate parts of the Confederacy, true or rumored, whetted Confederates' appetites. For Spence, advances in the trans-Mississippi and a belief that his home state would soon be cleansed of "the presence of the hated foe" made purchasing an enslaved person a tempting prospect, even in beset Atlanta.[161]

This optimism also shaped the specific enslaved people whom Rebels targeted. Slaveholders had long valued women for their childbearing prospects and children based on their promise as laborers and reproducers.[162] Because the conflict so thoroughly disrupted the slave economy, these demographics almost certainly could not produce returns commensurate with their wartime purchase prices. With slavery secured by Confederate victory, however, their reproductive labor and years of work would allow them to appreciate considerably in the long peace to follow. The fact that many Confederates specifically sought out such speculative opportunities proves their faith in the future prosperity of their slaveholding nation.

Edwin Fay's dogged pursuit of enslaved women clearly illustrates this line of thinking. Beginning in 1862, Fay pressed his wife Sarah to acquire people, demands he initially made alongside directions to chastise their enslaved woman Cynthia for failing to conceive a child. For refusing to increase his holdings, Fay threatened to "whip her [Cynthia] almost to death." His insistence that she reproduce and his desire to possess enslaved people both stemmed from a belief that their postwar values would more than double, rising as high as $3,000. He thus fixated on controlling Black women's fertility. "I bought her to breed," he fumed, "and she shall or I won't own her long." Simultaneously, Fay pursued Black women in the form of "two likely negro girls" whom he ordered his wife to acquire in the hopes that they "in all probability would increase before many years." On still another occasion, Fay complained that his father had wasted money buying a woman beyond her childbearing years rather than a fifteen-year-old girl whose prospective children would underpin his family's future.[163]

From the Civil War's beginning, others shared Fay's desire to obtain enslaved women's and children's bodies. A Mississippian voiced their collective logic with shocking candor. Writing amid the secession crisis, during which the relative prices for enslaved women and children equaled and even outpaced those of prime enslaved men, he moved to acquire the husband of a woman whom he enslaved. Drawing a direct comparison between slaveholding and livestock husbandry, he claimed that uniting the two "would be productive property as it is not easy for hens to lay eggs & have chicks without a 'Cock.'" Buying him thus "would be profitable in the way of negro increase."[164] A slave trader, meanwhile, expressed a willingness to pay what Virginia's Kate Drumgoold recalled as "the largest sum offered . . . for a girl as I was," perhaps the largest "that was ever offered for anyone." Drumgoold's age (about eight), sex, and likely fertility (she was one of ten sisters) surely shaped this offer, enticing the dealer with a lifetime of potential production and reproduction. Her enslaver eventually rejected this offer, a choice likely influenced by his own perceptions of Drumgoold's future worth. In doing so he spared her—by the narrowest of margins—from the wartime slave market.[165]

Across the Confederacy, however, untold numbers of women and children entered that market, where buyers fixated on the future acquired them. In late 1862, a Texan gave $2,000 for Agnes and her child. That he paid in specie demonstrates the value he placed on the pair.[166] Another Texan sought out either "No. 1 negro women, 18 or 20 years old or young boys from 10 to 14."[167] In early 1863, a North Carolinian sold a forty-year-old man named Henry for $1,200, a sum he planned to translate into "a young woman or 2 small negroes."[168] His fellow Carolinian, Henry King Burgwyn, considered buying enslaved people a "capital plan," as he (like Fay and Pettigrew) expected their prices to rise as high as $4,000 after the conflict. He particularly desired "boys & girls from 15 to 20 years old" and urged his father to "take care to have a majority of girls" as "the increase in number of your negroes by this means would repay the difference in the amount of available labor." Indeed, in their last communication before his death in the Gettysburg campaign, Burgwyn told his father to purchase a girl "of from 13 to 14 years old," whom he considered "the best investment" available.[169] Confederate upon Confederate joined them in this pursuit, believing, as Virginia's William Jones argued in 1863, that "If this war is ever ended fairly, women and children are the property to put money in. I think that first class men and women will bring $5000 then."[170]

Other Confederates preferred enslaved children to women, anticipating that they would pay off as they matured in an independent Confederacy. Wash Wilson remembered that when an enslaver purchased him and his family at the war's outset, he was puzzled by the buyer's eagerness given the possibility of emancipation. But the purchaser had no such fears. As Wilson recalled, "Marse Bill say we's a likely bunch of chillen . . . so guess he take de resk."[171] Similarly, a young Georgian's guardian argued in favor of investing the boy's inheritance in enslaved people because "the negroes are mostly young and will be in their prime when [he] becomes of age."[172] In an independent Confederacy, a young man could hardly hope for a better start. A South Carolinian overseeing an estate division agreed, stating, "land & negroes are the best kind of property to leave to children."[173] In April 1864, mere weeks before the Battle of the Wilderness, an Alabamian looked to the future when bemoaning the impending sale of an enslaved family. They would, he noted, "in a few years be valuable—most of them being small children yet."[174]

Slave traders' wartime correspondence and advertisements reveal a similar demand for enslaved children, indicating that those who most eagerly sought out slave property amid the war looked to the future when acquiring it. A Roanoke, Virginia trader demanded "tolerably likely girls" in the spring of 1862, specifically targeting those "13 years old." A South Carolinian investigated the possibility of acquiring children aged from eight to fourteen. In both communiqués, the traders in question sought people whose peak values would arrive after the war's presumed end.[175] This trend continued through 1863. Early that year, a South Carolina firm sought to purchase "fifty likely young negroes" and offered to exchange a woman with four young children for other (presumably older) people.[176] Meanwhile, in December, Hill, Dickinson & Co. reported that though prices for most enslaved people had declined, they remained "more steady especially for young negroes."[177] The purchase of enslaved children was an explicit bet on the Confederacy's ultimate triumph and a gamble on the future it would secure—one that numerous Confederates were more than willing to make.

On July 3, 1863, Edward Porter Alexander commanded the artillery barrage preceding the Pickett-Pettigrew assault at Gettysburg—"a grand & exciting moment," he later recalled, with the CSA's massed guns "roaring in the very joy of battle." Within minutes, however, Alexander realized the charge was doomed. "I thought it madness," he remembered. Alexander rejected, however, the idea that Gettysburg represented "the crisis of the war." In importance, it fell far short of Grant's stymied advance against Petersburg in June 1864, an outcome that saved Richmond and boosted the Confederacy's hopes for a negotiated peace.[178] Alexander's contemporary actions backed his postwar editorializing. Mere weeks after Gettysburg, he contemplated purchasing an enslaved woman and her child whom he considered a "fine speculation at $2000." Though Alexander ultimately declined to purchase this young woman, he was deterred more by personal whims than by concern for the Confederacy's fate.[179]

Some Confederates remained sanguine far longer. A Virginian, for example, paid $5,500 for Richard in September 1864. "When I bought," he later complained, "we had not heard that Atlanta had fallen." This setback, however, only slightly cooled his ardor; he immediately laid plans for acquiring more enslaved people in the year to come.[180] As 1864 closed, an unnamed Alabamian traveled to Columbus, Georgia, where he paid over $13,000 in Confederate currency for Jerry and Miner—a decision that shocked his peers. Central to his actions was a relentless focus on what he termed "the bright side" of the war, embodied in his resolution to "never give in to the idea that the South would, or could, be conquered." When pressed, he urged questioners to "Wait till you get to the bridge before you cross the river."[181] Though more optimistic than many Confederates at that late juncture, his confidence underscored the tenacity with which slaveholders adhered to their belief in the Confederacy's invincibility and the inevitable establishment of the slaveholders' republic. His choice to express this faith, moreover, through the acquisition of the same property for which Rebels had gone to war demonstrated the powerful linkages between the war's outcome and the future of enslaved property.

The Civil War caused remarkable economic upheaval in the Confederacy. Between devastating Union invasions, the strangling effects of the blockade, self-inflicted export embargoes, and the failures of Rebel financial policies, the economic infrastructure on which the domestic slave trade depended cracked and crumbled. The trade nevertheless continued despite—and frequently because of—these obstacles. Because enslaved property represented a reservoir of future value, Confederates fervently pursued it throughout the war as an antidote to inflation and to other, more individualized forms of economic turmoil.

The expectations with which Confederates acquired slaves also demonstrate their abiding certainty of victory deep into the war. They lacked faith in many things: their political leadership, their currency, even the long-vaunted fidelity of the people they enslaved. For much of the war, however, their belief in the ultimate triumph of the Confederate nation remained unshaken. Having gone to war to preserve slavery's future by securing its political power, social stability, and potential for expansion and growth, Confederates' faith in the institution of slavery remained similarly unwavering. They proved their faith through works—a series of slave transactions that underscored simultaneously the depth and longevity of Confederates' expectations for victory and independence and, by extension, the perpetuity of their slave society. With the South made safe for slavery, the value of enslaved property would resume its antebellum rise, and enslaved assets would continue to appreciate through their agricultural, mechanical, and reproductive labors. Wartime dealing in slaves, therefore, cohered perfectly with the broader Confederate endeavor and allowed Confederates to acquire shares in the slaveholding future for which they fought.

5

"Liable to Be Sold at Any Moment"

State-Making, Continuity, and the Slave Trade

On May 3, 1863, Sandy, Jerry, and Bryant escaped from Buena Vista Furnace, an iron-producing facility on the South River near Lexington, Virginia. Only "recently purchased" in Richmond by forge owner Samuel F. Jordan, they fled through a landscape remade to feed Rebel furnaces (Jordan himself held 12,000 acres to support his operations). They skirted fields in which enslaved laborers raised provisions for forge workers, transited forests from which Black lumbermen harvested charcoal, and moved up the gorge known locally as "Iron Valley," pitted by the slave-worked mines and furnaces that residents called "iron plantations."[1]

One hundred miles from Buena Vista, on the very day these men fled, the Army of Northern Virginia cracked the Army of the Potomac's lines at Chancellorsville, completing Robert E. Lee's most dazzling victory.[2] In fleeing, however, Jerry, Sandy, and Bryant scored a small victory of their own, one that resonated in critical ways far from the front lines. By evading the work forced upon them, they struck a blow at the Confederate war effort, to which their sale had made them unwilling accomplices. Pig iron forged in the Blue Ridge and Allegheny Mountains flowed overwhelmingly to Richmond's Tredegar Ironworks, a massive foundry and rolling mill complex and one of the largest industrial operations in the Confederacy, and exited as naval guns, railroad ties, iron plating, gun carriages, shot and shell, and myriad other parts of the vast Rebel accoutrement. Tredegar's owners had offered its services to the Confederacy at the inception of the slaveholders' republic and the firm received significant backing from the Confederate government. This included direct financial support and priority in obtaining the raw materials required to do what was in a literal sense some of the CSA's dirtiest work. These encompassed coal, iron, and labor, the last an increasingly scarce resource as Confederates conscripted men into the lengthening conflict.[3]

At both ends of their ironmongering, Samuel Jordan and Tredegar's Joseph R. Anderson deployed the slave trade to arm the Confederacy. In addition to the hundreds of enslaved men and women they hired from individual enslavers (a practice they had long pursued on a smaller scale), their agents frequented Richmond's slave market. There, in early 1863, Jordan purchased Sandy, Jerry, and Bryant as well as Bartie, Peter, Platter, Johnson, and Jordon. In Rockbridge County, closer to the forge's operations, he bought Martha and her four-year old son Eli.[4] Tredegar, larger than Buena Vista and located mere blocks from Shockoe Bottom, acquired even more people. This included seasoned blacksmiths like John, Wallis, and Dick and laborers like Coleman, Randall, Harvey, and Colbert. Tredegar also bought John's family, perhaps to ensure his good behavior and to forestall the flight of someone they considered a valuable asset.[5] In all, between 1862 and 1865, its agents purchased at least nineteen men, women, and children outright and may well have bought many more. Held by firms deeply committed to the Confederate cause and central to the Rebel war effort, their forced labor helped build the insurgent nation that fought for their continued captivity.

Confederates went to war hoping to deliver from the United States the nascent nation they believed the slaveholding South to already be, a country-in-the-making with a shared culture, united in its opposition to political, economic, religious, and cultural threats from the United States.[6] The experience of conflict, however, swiftly revealed that in building a nation, ideological and cultural unity were necessary but insufficient components, especially given the Confederacy's severe deficits in the sinews of war: manpower, manufacturing, infrastructure, and agricultural production.[7] As the conflict expanded, it taxed the new nation's modest resources. In response, its central government took on an expanding, aggressive, even revolutionary cast. The Rebel state backed industries to arm and equip its forces. It exacted provender, fodder, and livestock from its citizenry. It conscripted vast numbers of men into its armed forces and put thousands more to work on critical infrastructure projects.[8]

In all these efforts, the Confederacy depended on enslaved labor. Enslaved people grew food; toiled in mines, mills, and factories; laid and repaired railroads; built fortifications; and performed innumerable other tasks essential to the Confederate war effort.[9] That Rebels used enslaved people in these capacities is unsurprising, for enslavers had long wedded slave labor to the state making process. Slaveholders, meanwhile, were eminently comfortable in expanding the power of the central state when doing so protected the peculiar institution.[10] White Southerners also deployed the enslaved extensively in the region's burgeoning industries.[11] As a result, the ideological roots for a modern, state-directed slave economy had sunk deeply in the antebellum South.[12]

As the war demanded more of companies and individuals, Confederates used the surviving commerce in people to exploit the enslaved as a reservoir of capital, a labor force, and real assets. War-spawned conditions thus dovetailed with their pre-existing intellectual and economic equipage. As Raimondo Luraghi has argued, "war is the hardest test to which a given society is subjected." As a result, "every society meets" this test "in a way that is directly linked to its social, moral, ethical—in other words, its cultural—scale of values."[13] The rendering of people into movable property was the antebellum South's dominant cultural and economic idiom. In decisions so immediate they were all but unthinking, Confederates channeled their impulses to engage in slave commerce into everything from outfitting soldiers to confronting strained gender roles.[14] Wartime slave commerce's utility made its practice widespread, creating innumerable instances of what historian Edward Ayers has termed "deep contingency." Sweeping, determinative forces—the movement of armies, the advent of emancipation, the sucking mire of the Confederate economy—collided with and were mediated by individuals' "culture and ideology" and uniquely "personal or local motivations." As they commingled with overarching impulses, individual circumstances, relationships, and interactions fed into a massive traffic in humanity as Confederates turned it to purposes as diverse as their experiences of the conflict.[15]

Whatever way the conflict pressed them, Confederates shared a commitment to perpetuating the existing slaveholding order. Doing so required them to continue practices that had long governed the lives and experiences of the enslaved and exposed them to sale for what passed in enslavers' minds as mundane reasons. Throughout the war, courts and individuals sold people to settle debts, divide estates, and punish trespasses against the racial order. Where the slaveholders' republic maintained its authority, it ensured that its citizens would sell people to meet the dictates of a system constructed on human property. This meant that even when enslavers disdained slavery as an investment, the accrued momentum of centuries of slaveholding and its enduring legal architecture moved courts, government agents, and citizens to sentence enslaved people to separation and sale until forced to do otherwise.

The universe of reasons for which Confederates bought and sold people underscores slave commerce's centrality to Rebel society. The slave trade enhanced their ability to do virtually everything the war demanded of them, whether individually or collectively: produce materiel, weather shortages, pay debts, and navigate the innumerable stresses the war placed upon the slaveholding state and upon enslaving households. It also enforced continuity amid a conflict radically reshaping the lives of enslaved and enslaver alike. This made slave commerce both a mundane reflection of slavery's persistence and a punishing reminder of the world for which Rebels fought.

Confederates had gone to war to preserve a society based on slave agriculture, but the lengthening conflict and the corrosion of their economy forced them to retool for a modern war.[16] This was a tall order, given their significant disadvantages in core resources. Loyal states produced four times the wheat, twenty times the iron, and thirty-two times the firearms that their rebellious counterparts did. When the war began, the Confederacy had only enough gunpowder to provide each soldier with thirty rounds of ammunition—less than one sixth the recommended supply—and, with the populous and economically diversified Border States remaining in the Union, largely lacked the facilities needed to close these gaps.[17] At the war's outset, Rebel ordinance chief Josiah Gorgas recalled, "we were not making a gun, a pistol nor a sabre, no shot nor shell." Arming and equipping the Confederate forces required factories and immense amounts of raw materials, as did replacing consumer goods no longer arriving from abroad and maintaining the CSA's infrastructure. Feeding armies larger than all but their largest cities as well as the residents of urban areas swollen with refugees, meanwhile, demanded that Confederates convert vast acreages of cotton and other cash crops to foodstuffs.[18]

Reviewing the situation in 1864, however, Gorgas saw profound changes. "We now make," he bragged, all sorts of weapons and munitions "in quantities to meet the demands of our large armies," via "large arsenals . . . at Richmond, Fayetteville, Augusta, Charleston, Columbus, Macon, Atlanta and Selma," "a superb powder mill," "lead smelting works," "a cannon foundry," and more.[19] The Rebel state compelled much of this evolution by funding (or acquiring outright) existing industrial facilities, nurturing nascent ones, and actively stimulating food production.[20] Doing so, Gorgas noted, demanded "incessant toil and attention," much of which Confederates exacted from enslaved laborers.[21] Several factors centered the enslaved in the Rebel war effort. Even as the conflict demanded escalating levels of production and infrastructure maintenance, the military absorbed more and more of the CSA's white manpower. The Confederacy's labor demands also allowed enslavers to employ workers idled by the dismal cotton economy or displaced by Union invasions.[22] Finally, the conflict accelerated longstanding trends toward working enslaved people in industrial facilities, from iron foundries like Tredegar to coal mines and other extractive endeavors.

As a result, enslaved workers became critical cogs in the Confederacy's war-making machine. In Georgia, hundreds toiled in arsenals, powder works, mines, and mills as well as in textile and shoe factories.[23] In neighboring Alabama, more than three hundred enslaved people labored at the Selma Naval Works alone, some of whom overseers worked nearly to death for the Confederate cause.[24] Another sixty bored tunnels through the Sauta Cave, seeking saltpeter for the Rebel Ordnance Bureau. The Shelby Iron Company's coal mining was "done entirely, or nearly so, with negro labor."[25] Confederates, in short, compelled Black labor on an immense scale. By 1864, the Niter and Mining Bureau alone deployed 4,301 enslaved or free people of color, with untold thousands more toiling in other departments or on Rebel fortifications.[26]

Confederates impressed or hired the majority of these workers, as Southern industrialists long had. The high prices demanded for enslaved laborers prevented most antebellum industrial or infrastructure projects from purchasing people, while the abundance of enslaved workers in the Upper South (where most such efforts were located) obviated the need to do so.[27] Many industrial leaders pursued a similar course during the conflict. In the spring of 1862, for example, Joseph Anderson wrote one enslaver that the firm would happily take "all the negro men you have for hire" at "the highest market price" to work "our furnaces [or] our coal pits."[28] Even late in the war, of the 303 enslaved people worked by the Shelby Iron Company, the company only owned twenty-one outright. The rest it rented from twenty-nine different slaveholders.[29] The Gorgas Mining and Manufacturing Company, meanwhile, contracted for enslaved laborers into 1865.[30]

The pressures of war reshaped the Confederate hiring market much as they did that for the purchase and sale of enslaved people. After enduring a downturn caused by the financial crunch and uncertainty of secession, enslavers often enjoyed high demand for rented laborers thanks to the needs of the Confederate government and of refugees inhabiting Confederate cities. As J. D. B. De Bow noted in late 1861, "Negroes hire well" in Richmond thanks to the "increase of population" in the city.[31] The prolonged conflict, however, applied uneven and often contradictory pressures on the hiring market. Moments of Confederate peril encouraged some enslavers to rent out people because doing so allowed them to retain long-term control over them while mitigating the short-term risk of holding them. During the Union advances of 1862, therefore, one Confederate soldier in Tidewater Virginia urged his parents, "If you want to save negro property save it now—hire them if you can to [the] Government."[32] Such moments, however, led other enslavers to withdraw people from the hiring market so that they could exercise complete control over them. Crises also discouraged would-be hirers from laying out cash even to rent laborers in the short term. In a threatened Richmond in the spring of 1862, Hector Davis found "no one is disposed to hire." Even though a flood of enslaved refugees sent from the rest of the Commonwealth had driven rental prices down, many Confederates feared embracing even this modest financial exposure.[33]

As Confederate fortunes rebounded in 1862 and 1863, so did the demand for rented laborers. Both the course of the conflict and the inflation plaguing the CSA shaped the prices demanded for them. In 1861, a Petersburg auctioneering concern had rented people out for between $40 and $140 for the year. By 1863, the lowest rate for which they hired out an enslaved person had climbed to $150.[34] On January 1—the day on which enslavers typically struck hiring agreements for the ensuing year—of that year, one Virginia enslaver found that while prices in his immediate vicinity were high, "unheard of" figures could be obtained in Richmond.[35] A Virginian who had taken advantage of the aforementioned "unheard of" prices swiftly regretted hiring an enslaved blacksmith to Tredegar for $400. Had he waited six months, he believed, he could have charged 50 percent more.[36]

As prices fluctuated in both the hiring and sale markets, and as enslaved resistance and Union soldiers threatened the stability of human property, the relative benefit of hiring and purchasing people converged in enslavers' minds. Hiring or selling people became interchangeable, options to be pursued alternately as opportunities opened and closed.[37] Nimrod Long, for example, struggled to sell Ellen because a would-be purchaser hemmed and hawed over whether to hire or purchase her outright. It soon became clear the man in question was trying to time the market. If slave prices ascended, Long believed, he would purchase her; if they fell, he would rent her for the year instead.[38] Similarly, in late 1863, a Confederate suggested selling Tom instead of renting him. The price of his hire would be similar to an installment payment on his sale, while selling him would also mitigate the risk of his flight.[39]

Tom's case indicates the degree to which the prospect of emancipation made many Confederates ambivalent about hiring or purchasing enslaved people. As Lexington, Kentucky's Francis Peter put it in November 1863, "It is rather significant that at the present writing it is considered nearly if not quite as cheap to buy negroes as to hire them." This was due in part to the surging costs of feeding and clothing hired workers (a cost traditionally borne by the hirer), but also to the "undoubted fact that we are much nearer emancipation now, than even last year." "Everything," Peter concluded, "is tending to decrease the value of the negro as a servant."[40] The threat of emancipation remained less salient in the CSA, but Confederate hiring markets reflected similar considerations, dictated primarily by the perceived trajectory of the war. In early 1864, for example, these markets again filled with laborers, fueled in part by the fact that (as one Virginian put it), "people are very gloomy & despondent & the worst apprehensions are indulged in regard to the coming campaign" and in part by the impending Currency Reform Act.[41]

As Confederates mobilized for war, therefore, they benefited from the ability to hire as well as to purchase enslaved laborers. In many cases, however, the exigencies of the conflict specifically incentivized people to buy rather than rent workers. As Union forces carved through the South, many enslavers leased people only reluctantly—if they did so at all—to industries or infrastructure projects that might be overrun, from which the enslaved might escape, or from which they themselves might be cut off. As one railroad superintendent complained, when Sherman's army approached, "Most of the negro mechanics" were "taken away by their owners." Tredegar's operators faced similar problems when US forces menaced the outlying forges supplying them with pig iron.[42] Enslavers also contended with the Confederate government, which frequently impressed enslaved laborers.[43] Under these pressures, many Confederate industries bought people outright to ensure stable workforces and continued operations. Ironworks in Atlanta and in Shelby, Alabama, joined Buena Vista, Tredegar, and more in acquiring men skilled in forging, casting, and producing munitions. One Alabama industrialist, meanwhile, urged his wife at the beginning of 1864 to see that he got "as many mules as possible & negro men" so that he could run his furnace in the coming months.[44]

The slave trade permitted these works to acquire and retain skilled laborers and to mobilize labor for exceptionally dangerous projects. Among the more than two dozen people Savannah's Henry Wilink acquired during the war was George, a thirty-year-old carpenter, whom he likely put to work building ships for the Rebel navy.[45] The proprietors of Virginia's Buffalo Forge purchased two enslaved men in 1863 to meet one of the CSA's regular requisitions. Rather than sending their own highly trained workers to the Confederate works, they sent the two purchased men as placeholders, only to sell them when their stint working for the Confederacy ended.[46] Enslavers also purchased people to work in coal mines, important but notoriously dangerous operations. Among these was Joe, who fled Virginia's Midlothian Coal Mines shortly after the company bought him in early 1864.[47]

Facing reluctant enslavers, increasing competition, and mounting Black resistance, some military contractors begged the Rebel government to aid them directly in buying enslaved workers. William Phineas Browne sought $75,000 from the Confederate navy to purchase laborers for his Alabama coal mine. The operator of a Selma foundry similarly struggled to hire workers and requested that the government buy people on his behalf.[48] Well-connected Rebels, meanwhile, exploited this sort of demand. Charleston's George Trenholm—a financier, politician, and blockade runner—purchased many people amid the conflict, a number of whom he turned over to a local saltpeter works where their labor would profit him while advancing the Confederate cause.[49]

The slave trade also enhanced the Confederacy's ability to maintain its infrastructure. Saltworks, sources of a commodity critical to Confederate food production and storage, regularly acquired enslaved people to supply the Confederate military and populace.[50] Amos and Alfred, once enslaved near New Bern, fled soon after the Washington Company Salt Works in southwest Virginia bought them. Virgil, Edward, and Wilson, all bought in Richmond in the fall of 1863, likewise escaped the Virginia Salt Works.[51] Virginia's Henrico County, meanwhile, authorized its salt commissioner to buy two people to help supply its denizens.[52]

Railroads spent hundreds of thousands of dollars on human property in their constant struggle against war-induced entropy. At least sixteen people fled the Piedmont Railroad after it purchased them from exposed regions of Virginia and North Carolina.[53] The Virginia Central Railroad purchased at least thirty-five people. The Charlotte & South Carolina Railroad bought forty, the Mobile & Ohio at least sixty (and possibly hundreds more). The Raleigh & Gaston line appropriated $125,000 for enslaved laborers in 1861 alone.[54] Even during the war's final six months, the North Carolina Railroad bought twenty-eight people.[55] Little wonder, then, that what an Atlanta newspaper called the city's "greatest negro sale" occurred when a railroad purchased thirty-five people in one fell swoop.[56]

The enduring commerce in slaves also helped enslavers and industrial facilities enforce labor discipline, an important role given Southerners' latent fears of what they considered the deleterious effects of factory work and urban life on the enslaved.[57] When the war thrust thousands of enslaved people into these settings, slaveholders deployed the threat of sale to maintain their authority. A Norfolk, Virginia enslaver, for example, asked Dickinson, Hill & Co. to sell a man who had become "too much annoyance in a city" and who, he deemed, required chastisement through a return to plantation labor.[58]

Finally, the domestic slave trade allowed Confederate war industries to adapt as setbacks obviated their need for enslaved labor, turning them from buyers into sellers. After the fall of Atlanta, Georgia's Flint River Factory sought to shed thirty-five people.[59] The Etowah Manufacturing and Mining Company likewise offered fifteen laborers for sale after the Federals' passage forced their closure.[60] Though buyers were by this point scarce, slave commerce gave these firms at least a chance to minimize their losses amid the Rebel collapse. These operations had exemplified the Confederacy's effort to produce a slaveholding state through the commodification and exploitation of the enslaved. Such was the Confederate commitment to that reality that even its death throes occurred through slave commerce.

As the Civil War took on an increasingly existential cast, the state not only took command of the Confederate economy but escalated its demands on individual enslavers.[61] Besides backing war industries, the Confederate government conscripted much of its white male population, while authorities at all levels of government encouraged, cajoled, and coerced their citizens into providing the food and other materials required to keep armies in the field and the nation's bodies and souls together.[62] Already pressed by enemies and economic crises, these enslavers used slave commerce to help them meet these demands.

Few Confederate requests taxed the Rebel citizenry more than did its demand for soldiers. The Confederacy had begun conscripting men between the ages of eighteen and thirty-five in April 1862, a range that the Confederate Congress gradually but inexorably expanded. The men forced into service in the spring and summer of 1862 were generally older, poorer, and more encumbered by family responsibilities than had been those who volunteered in 1861. Most accepted their military obligations, though many did so grudgingly.[63] These included Abner Dawson Ford, who joined a Virginia artillery unit following the 1862 Conscription Act.[64] By January 1863, after nearly a year of hard campaigning, the thirty-three-year-old farmer and father fretted over his family's financial situation. Desperate to escape military service, he begged his wife Mary Jane to exploit a loophole in the Conscription Act and pay a substitute to replace him in the army.

The Fords, however, possessed modest means: only $4,400 in personal property, most of which rested in the bodies of the people they enslaved, Elviry and her three small children.[65] Under most other circumstances, they would have served as the foundation of the Fords' future wealth. But Abner Ford was willing to risk them to escape the army. "You must," he urged Mary Jane, "raise the money some way if you have to sell the negroes I want to get home very badly." He hoped Elviry might fetch $3,000 in Richmond but was willing to take less so long as she brought enough to bring him home. Only her untimely death prevented the Fords from sacrificing her to buy Abner's freedom.[66]

Whether to avoid danger or to tend to their families and livelihoods, perhaps 70,000 Confederates succeeded where Ford failed. Substitute seekers often held human property but lacked significant personal wealth. Substitutes themselves, meanwhile, were often destitute. Replacing a slaveholder in the military offered a means of acquiring an enslaved person, a property that only a few years earlier had been virtually unattainable and that was certainly more compelling than depreciating cash.[67] In the months following the passage of the Conscription Act, for example, a Mississippian dangled "a likely negro boy and five hundred dollars" to anyone who would take his place in the army. Virginia's William House, meanwhile, staved off service by selling Kate Drumgoold's mother, using her (Kate remembered) "to keep the rich man from going to the field of battle."[68] North Carolina's William T. Nelson likewise offered his father-in-law a number of people whom he could sell to pay someone to "get me out of this war."[69] An embittered South Carolinian in the process of divorcing her husband sued him over the loss of her enslaved woman, whom he had sold to procure a substitute.[70]

Substitute-seeking Confederates sometimes sold the enslaved for cash, but as it became an increasingly "hard job" (as one North Carolinian put it) to hire substitutes, slaveholders offered them directly for relief.[71] As a Texan reported, would-be replacements "wont talk about Confederate money."[72] In the Lone Star State, where one observer found "the substitute mania [was] running high," multiple men thus tried to swap enslaved people directly for replacement soldiers. When, for example, one prospective substitute declined $5,000 in cash, a Texan countered with $4,000 and an enslaved woman.[73] Rusk County's Charles Scott, meanwhile, took another Texan's place in the army in exchange for a teenaged girl named Charlotte.[74]

Because enslaved men, women, and children often represented a family's most valuable assets, enslavers surrendered them only reluctantly, even when confronting the dangers of military service. An Alabama soldier repeatedly asked his brother to raise the money necessary for a substitute but cautioned him to sell their human property only as a last resort; whatever money was required to persuade a potential replacement "could not be better invested than in negro property."[75] If these transactions were a financial wrench for enslavers, enslaved people felt them exponentially more. Georgia's Angeline Lester, for example, long recalled that her enslaver had sold her, her mother, and her sister to procure for himself a substitute.[76] The bitter irony of being sold to sustain a war fought to extend their bondage scarcely dissipated across long decades tainted by the loss of loved ones.

Confederate conscription policies also created perverse incentives for slave commerce. For the wealthiest planters, the so-called Twenty Negro Law, a measure aimed at keeping sufficient white men at home to deter slave rebellions, provided a potential means of escaping service. In Alabama, a slaveholder with nineteen bondspeople advertised for a twentieth whom he might purchase to avoid the army. Though he found no willing sellers, he eventually received a reprieve through the reproductive labor of one of his enslaved women.[77] With the stakes thus elevated for those close to the line, Sam Watkins recalled, "Negro property suddenly became very valuable, and there was raised the howl of 'rich man's war, poor man's fight.'"[78] Enslavers who could not escape service used the slave market to mitigate the resulting loss of direct oversight on their human property. As one slaveholder said to justify selling John, a carpenter and a blacksmith, "I was afraid he might give me some trouble as I am in the army and could not see to him."[79] Other enslavers sold entire estates due to their inability to manage them while away.[80] As the war thus blinkered the panopticon under which the enslaved had long labored, enslavers who felt their control lessening sold people rather than see their grasp loosened.

Among the hundreds of thousands of men who embraced rather than resisted the Confederacy's call were many who used the ongoing trade in slaves to facilitate their service, equipping themselves for battle and projecting the experience of mastery into the ranks.[81] Early in the war, a

Figure 5.1 Angeline Lester. Lester's enslaver sold her family to acquire a substitute during the war. Library of Congress, WPA Slave Narrative Project, https://www.loc.gov/item/mesnp120062/.

South Carolinian offered two enslaved people as collateral when acquiring clothes—possibly his uniform.[82] From the trenches at Petersburg, Thomas Martin implored his mother to trade a person to get him a horse.[83] Others sought enslaved people to serve them in camp—to cook, clean, and otherwise cushion the hardships of soldiering. While most Confederates either brought one of the people they already enslaved or hired someone to carry out these functions, at times competition for slave labor was so fierce that soldiers purchased people instead. An Arkansan, for example, sought to buy an enslaved man to serve him in camp, while Robert Turner, campaigning in Virginia, searched for an enslaved cook.[84] This dependence on bonded laborers sometimes created a specific market for camp servants. In December 1862, for example, Charleston slave dealer John S. Riggs offered an enslaved man who would "most admirably suit an officer in camp," having been "for several months engaged in that capacity."[85]

Even as the slave trade abetted the CSA's warmaking efforts, Confederates used it to cope with that same state's failings. Foremost among these were widespread food shortages. Several aspects of the conflict converged to restrict the Confederacy's food supply. The military absorbed thousands of white laborers even as thousands of enslaved workers fled. Battling armies erased entire crops, while massed soldiers and cities swollen with refugees clamored for food. The Confederate government tried impressing provisions but did so ineffectively, inflicting hardships on those subjected to impressment, stirring widespread resentment, and earning blame for accelerating inflation without solving the problem at hand. Compounded by inflation, occupation, and a deteriorating transportation network, these factors created widespread shortfalls throughout the Confederacy.[86]

Where possible, Confederates used slave commerce to displace this burden onto the enslaved. The Confederacy's industrializing efforts encouraged the purchase of people, but the agricultural sector's failings often incentivized their sale. In the spring of 1863, an enslaved man entered Union lines in Virginia and, as fugitives often did, relayed intelligence to Federal officers—specifically, that Richmonders were "hard up for enny thing to eat." Perhaps because of this, he had been scheduled for sale the day prior to his flight.[87] Such sales were exceedingly common in the wartime South. Unable to feed the human property they already possessed and afraid of the unrest hunger would produce, Confederates turned to the slave market for relief, selling some people in order to enable them to feed and consolidate their hold over those they retained.[88] By 1864, one South Carolinian reported that her neighbors were "selling negroes all the time to furnish support for the rest." Another Lowcountry planter followed this course to rectify a "scarcity of food."[89] A desperate Kentuckian who had driven enslaved people southward alongside Confederates retreating from Perryville exchanged them—including a man named Peter—for a farm in Georgia.[90] A North Carolinian sold Amy both because he considered her a "bad girl" and because he sought money to "live on as a matter of necessity."[91]

Some enslavers exploited these shortages through the slave trade. South Carolina's George Walton Williams bought more than one hundred men and women from exposed portions of the state and put them to work raising food for sale in urban markets.[92] More often, however, enslavers fought food shortages through the sale of enslaved laborers, particularly as the prolonged conflict began to pinch. When, in the summer of 1863, many of those enslaved on the Ball family's South Carolina holdings refused to work until they received food and clothing, Eliza Ball recommended the family "sell out" in response.[93] Another Carolinian contemplated selling Tom because feeding and clothing him was "costing... very much more than he is worth."[94] In Georgia, a relative urged the refugee Lila Chunn to sell "that abominable Martha to bear expenses" and Ann because "you've been supporting her instead of her you."[95] A Floridian followed through on these threats, trading an enslaved man for livestock; South Carolina's John Bratton—who, in late 1863, had advised against selling human property—in 1865 encouraged his family to sell or "trade them off for land, something that can't eat or run away."[96] So prevalent were such sales, a Petersburg woman marveled at the end of 1864, that a previously unimaginable reality had occurred: a time had arrived when "'masters would run from their slaves, not slaves from their masters.'"[97]

Food shortages were merely the most prominent manifestation of the Confederacy's broader economic crisis and, as was ever the case in the slave South, enslaved people bore the brunt of their enslavers' financial woes.[98] Selling slaves provided an economic safety valve, a means through which enslavers could insulate themselves from the full effects of various crises that the war spawned. They might be reluctant to sacrifice their most valuable assets, but as the slaveholders' world tottered, human property cushioned them against its total failure. A Black clergyman from Savannah perceived this most clearly. "Since the war began," he noted, "white men have [been] obliged often to raise money suddenly, and slave property being especially insecure we were liable to be sold at any moment."[99]

Vicksburg enslaver William Smedes's negotiations with South Carolina banker William Johnson exemplified this willingness to exploit the enslaved as protection against economic catastrophe. Smedes had bought more than seventy men and women from Johnson just before the war to cultivate his Mississippi cotton lands. This plan went immediately awry. Fully one-third of the enslaved succumbed to disease upon arriving in Mississippi. A series of floods consumed successive crops. By the end of 1862, US forces menaced his immediate vicinity. The enslaved, Smedes conceded, knew "as well as you or I all about" Lincoln's preliminary Emancipation Proclamation "& they consider that they will be free as soon as the Federals come." To forestall their escape and to recoup his losses, Smedes proposed trading the fifty survivors of his experiment back to Johnson. If Johnson declined, Smedes intended to sell them at whatever "sacrifice" was required. Even as the conflict offered enslaved people new opportunities and new hope, the continuing slave trade enabled enslavers to deflect wartime hardships onto them, people who had already labored and (in many cases) died on their behalf.[100]

Countless Confederates joined Smedes in sacrificing the enslaved on the altar of financial survival. In late 1862, an economizing refugee from northern Virginia planned to sell Mira and Nancy Ellen in Richmond. They would enter the brutal and uncertain confines of that city's slave market; his wife would merely "have to learn to live with fewer servants than we have heretofore been accustomed to."[101] Alexander Taliaferro likewise begged Dickinson, Hill & Co. to get the best prices possible for people he hoped to sell given that Union advances had rendered his family "refugees."[102] A few months later, James Harvey Campbell and his wife looked to a family whom they enslaved to stave off destitution. "If you are pushed," Campbell informed his wife, "we will have to sell Fanny and her two children. That is the only way I can see how you can manage to live."[103] In 1863, an Alabama woman managing a deceased relative's estate worked to sell an enslaved family whom she considered "a hindrance and expense." Rather than abandoning slavery, however, she hoped to purchase "others more suitable" to the exigencies of war.[104] As late as 1865, a Georgia family reduced to living in a cabin strove to shed an enslaved family, while neighbors gossiped that a member of Lynchburg's Brockenbrough family had sold an enslaved woman in order to "meet expenses."[105]

Many of the war's stresses, including those exacerbated by the Confederate state's failings, fell particularly heavily on Confederate women—who, in turn, pushed off what they could onto the enslaved through the slave trade. On larger farms and plantations, white women traditionally controlled domestic spaces and were responsible for providing food, clothing, and rudimentary healthcare to both their own families and the enslaved. This, historian Thavolia Glymph points out, made the home a primary site of struggle between enslaver and enslaved, in which contest enslaving women drew upon the support of their male relatives and their community.[106] As Confederate men swarmed into military service, women at home assumed broadened duties in running farms and plantations. A Georgia soldier succinctly summed up this transition to his wife, informing her, "you must be the man and the woman both now."[107]

Confederate women faced formidable obstacles in performing these dual roles. Besides food and labor shortages, they confronted mounting enslaved resistance.[108] Seizing the opportunities the war provided, Glymph notes, enslaved women "targeted the planter household, the scene of 'so much devilment,' for destruction, desecration, occupation, and transformation." Early in the war, a Georgia woman claimed that "None but the slaveholder can know the tender affection that there is between owner and slave." She and her counterparts soon learned otherwise. A northern Virginia woman spat that the people she enslaved had become "treacherous. . . . We cannot trust any these days," while Louisiana's Kate Stone found that with slavery crumbling, "Negroes will not even pretend to work and are very impudent." Struggling to control the men and women from whom she demanded obeisance, Stone concluded, "the life we are leading is now a miserable, frightened one."[109]

The slave trade helped many of these women shore up fragments of order against the ruin of the slave system. Responding to his wife's complaints about a mutinous group of enslaved people, Georgia's Robert Thach raged that he would "teach them how to disobey my orders so flatly" by "sell[ing] the last one of them just as soon as I can get them to Atlanta."[110] Eastern North Carolina's Susan Popes followed through on a similar threat, selling several people to a trader after they ran for Federal lines.[111] Sale also helped enslaving women confront people they considered insurrectionary. A Floridian urged his wife to have neighbors intimidate a man named Dane, whom he considered a threat to his family and to labor discipline. Should this fail, he argued, "you had better have him sold or he will be hung."[112] Other enslavers pursued sales simply to minimize the demands placed on their wives. Abner Ford, foiled by Elviry's death in his attempt to hire a substitute, pushed his wife to sell her orphaned children. Unable to manage them from the front, Ford hoped his wife would simply "sell the negroes out of your way."[113]

Other Confederate women pursued relief from the additional labor the war demanded of them through slave commerce. Knoxville, Tennessee's J. J. Craig, already possessed of half a dozen people, found his wife "deviled to death" by their increasing refusal to work. In response, he sought to purchase an older woman whom he considered unlikely to escape and helpful in "relieving our domestic troubles."[114] From Savannah to Richmond, Rebels visited slave markets seeking enslaved women who could perform domestic labor for their wives.[115] Fluctuating prices made such wartime purchases particularly enticing. A South Carolina soldier, who had previously encouraged his wife to hire an enslaved woman to ease her own labor, pushed her to purchase one outright when prices reached a level he considered a bargain.[116] With the war empowering the enslaved and granting women unprecedented responsibility over them, the domestic slave trade helped offset these war-driven changes.

Whether for punishment or profit, increasingly autonomous women also broadened their direct engagement in slave trafficking. White women had long been intimately involved in slave commerce, but the removal of white men from the scene gave them greater scope for action. While some women reflexively deferred to male relatives, others actively involved themselves in slave commerce.[117] Few did so as avidly as western North Carolina's Mary Bell. Responding to her husband's request to help manage the family's investments, by November 1862 Bell had begun pursuing enslaved people, arguing that "it would be advisable to buy negroes at this time," though, she disclaimed—perhaps in a nod to traditional gender roles—"I am not a judge of such things." For the remainder of the war, however, she did precisely that. After disposing of a woman whom she considered troublesome, she acquired a carpenter dispatched from South Carolina. She later executed what she labeled a "big nigger trade" that satisfied her greatly. By the end of 1864, Bell had even begun instructing her husband regarding the purchase of the enslaved for both speculative purposes and immediate needs.[118]

Other women joined her in trading slaves during the war's latter years. Mary Pope recalled that the Southampton County woman who enslaved her had been moderately kind until the war came "and Massa went away." After his departure, Pope's enslaver first drove her harder than ever producing cloth for sale and then, as emancipation loomed, threatened to sell Pope and her children, driving her to escape.[119] North Carolina's Baldy Capehart deferred extensively to his wife, Meeta, in dealing with enslaved people he suspected of theft. While he recommended their sale, he left the matter up to her discretion; "You must do as you think best in all things," he wrote her, assuring her that "I shall be satisfied with your judgment."[120] Similarly, Margaret Glen, wife of longtime North Carolina slave dealer Tyre Glen, took the initiative to sell Robert, whom she believed had defied her authority by stealing wheat and flour.[121] Slaveholding women, by war's end, engaged widely in slave commerce to control the enslaved, acquire needed help, and mitigate the conflict's social and economic fallout.

As the Confederacy's ability to protect its people deteriorated, Confederates used slave commerce to adapt to this reality. Those fleeing Union invasions often protected their enslaved property by selling a portion of it. When South Carolina's Grimball family sold forty-eight people in early 1863, William Grimball lauded the transaction for enabling the family to "enjoy [a] quiet life" at their inland refuge. His mother Meta agreed. A neighbor who had likewise sold out, she reported, felt "quite relieved" at having shed his obligations and enslaved assets.[122] Retreating from his own massive Lowcountry holdings, Robert Allston sold Sango and his family and used the money to purchase a North Carolina farm where he could keep his other laborers away from marauding Yankees and raise the supplies needed to maintain them.[123] Others joined Allston in leveraging enslaved people to facilitate their flight. A Craven County, North Carolina slaveholder promised an enslaved child to whomever would help him refugee his other chattels; a Georgian offered up a woman and four children to finance his escape.[124] However the war pressed enslavers, the slave trade could provide a means of deflecting its impact.

Increased mobility within the slaveholding South embodied the CSA's degrading capacities. Rebels moving to and from the front, US forces piercing Confederate territory, refugees seeking safety, Union prisoners of war escaping Confederate prison camps, and enslaved people pursuing liberty demonstrated that neither polities nor enslavers exercised total control over those they claimed to rule.[125] While this chaos offered the enslaved opportunities to flee, it also deprived them of even the meager protections antebellum Southern laws had once provided and thereby exposed them to a host of unscrupulous men and women willing to profit from their vulnerable status.[126]

African Americans, enslaved or free, thus transited the wartime South at considerable peril. A few days after one of Kiziah Love's brothers departed on an errand, the mule he had been riding returned without him. Love guessed that he had "run off or was stole and sold." Both were plausible outcomes, and in the absence of firm information, they had similar impacts on the family he left behind.[127] Linton Stephens, brother of the Confederate vice president, believed John had suffered a similar fate. Though he thought John had run away, he attributed his flight to the actions of a white man and believed that "he has been or will be sold by his seducer in all probability."[128] Instead of ameliorating this chaos, agents of the state regularly contributed to it. Edmund Ruffin Jr. believed that Confederate soldiers evacuating his property had stolen a man named Israel. A Richmond detective, meanwhile, kidnapped and sold Jim to pay a debt.[129] Even free people of color, nominally defended by the law, vanished easily into the wartime slave trade.[130] A soldier near Petersburg sold a free family whom he had abducted from behind Union lines; Confederate authorities eventually arrested a member of the 6th South Carolina for selling a free person.[131] Even as the dislocation of war created unprecedented opportunities for the enslaved to seize their liberty, it camouflaged illegal slave sales and masked the retrograde motion they injected into the Civil War.

Shifting borders and fluctuating loyalties also sparked commerce in the enslaved. Whether in the Border States, in Unionist enclaves, or in absentia, both the CSA and the USA challenged the loyalties of men and women whom they considered insufficiently devoted to their cause. The Confederacy swiftly passed legislation enabling the confiscation and sale of property belonging to those it deemed internal enemies.[132] This property often included enslaved people, who became casualties of their enslavers' insufficient Confederate nationalism. When a Charleston receiver claimed the property of Christopher Meyers, the fate of his bondsman George Washington was left to the discernment of the presiding judge.[133] A Virginia court seized Armistead, Hannah, and eight other people and, in "an expensive and hazardous enterprise," arranged their extraction from occupied Loudoun County to Richmond for sale.[134] Those enslaved by prominent men or on famous estates particularly drew Confederates' attention. A Tennessee receiver detained and sold several people belonging to Andrew Johnson—a fact Johnson exploited rhetorically for his own political benefit.[135] People enslaved at Monticello likewise faced sale when Uriah Levy's connections to the US Navy rendered his property forfeit. Locals bought several of the estate's enslaved inhabitants. The Confederacy scattered others abroad.[136] Confiscations continued throughout the CSA until the war's end; Hill, Dickinson & Co. sold Anne and her three children (and two additional children) in one such transaction in January 1865.[137]

Questions of loyalty also hastened the sale of enslaved people as Southerners, fearing for their lives or livelihoods under an unfriendly government, sought ready cash or to make their escape. Questioning by US officials undermined Louisville's Alexander Jeffrey's ability to conduct business. He met the shortfall by selling his human property.[138] Well to the south, the Northern-born husband of a Corpus Christi, Texas resident urged her to flee the Confederacy with him. He planned to sell three enslaved women to finance their escape.[139] Others sold people to dodge confiscations. In a gambit that failed spectacularly, Confederate general Gideon Pillow reportedly dealt away several captives to a Unionist neighbor, hoping through this token transfer to avoid their confiscation by advancing Federals.[140]

Loyalty and slave trading remained entwined even after Appomattox. When Southerners sought compensation from the United States for property losses during the war, their participation in slave commerce became a litmus test. Slave dealing, Southern Claims Commission officials argued, ignored the government's emancipatory edicts. An 1864 slave transaction thus demonstrated one claimant's "utter disregard of the authority of the Union."[141] Perhaps fearing similar repercussions, former slave dealers seeking postbellum pardons uniformly obscured their past occupations.[142] The ties between slave trading and national allegiance demonstrated the knife's edge on which the enslaved lived during the Civil War. On questions abstracted from their own lives hung the fates of countless Black men, women, and children.

Slave trading thus supported rapid wartime industrialization, allowed Confederates to mitigate the war's other material hardships, enabled them to confront shifting gender roles, and reflected enslavers' attachment to the slaveholders' republic. Institutionally through government-backed industry or individually in innumerable ways, Confederates fed a vicious loop that ensnared captive laborers and forced them to help create and perpetuate the state and social order that held them in bondage. The domestic slave trade, supported by the Confederacy and pursued by its citizens, therefore proved both central to the future for which Confederates fought and an active means through which they pursued that future.

In February 1863, court officials in Caldwell County, North Carolina paraded Elsy, Judy, and their children before the handful of men who had braved the mountain winter to conduct business before the court. Ascending a makeshift auction block, these families continued a journey inaugurated in 1861 by William Lenoir's suicide. After two years of legal wrangling over his estate, his surviving brothers had decided to exploit rising slave prices to pay off its debts. While hundreds of miles away thousands of soldiers faced off along the Rappahannock, Stones River, and other lines of battle, in western North

Carolina, the Lenoirs' sale proceeded unimpeded. It ultimately netted them $3,100, though Judy's son Sid and Elsy's son Mose remained unsold. This all but guaranteed the families would be insuperably rent, divided not only by enslavers' avarice but by the laws governing the ownership of human property and the ongoing power of the slaveholding state.[143]

The effort to birth an independent slaveholding republic sparked massive social and economic changes. Yet at the heart of these labor pains rested a conservative enterprise. Fundamentally, white Southerners went to war to preserve enslavers' near-total authority over their human property and the backing the slaveholding state offered.[144] As a result, they devoted considerable efforts to maintaining the legal and social structures that had long sustained slavery even in the midst of their revolutionary project; indeed, to the degree that they understood their efforts as radical, it was in reforming and strengthening slavery for the future.[145] Wherever unhindered by military events, sheriffs, judges, and various Confederate officials dealt and facilitated the sale of enormous numbers of enslaved people. They auctioned people to settle estates, resolve debts, and punish enslaved and free Black people for activities deemed criminal. As they performed these tasks, they continued in the roles that had long made them functionally the largest slave dealers in the South.[146] Individual enslavers, meanwhile, likewise sought continuity amid the conflict and performed this stability by dealing in people for reasons virtually indistinguishable from those pursued before the war. For all the changes the war wrought on slave trafficking, then, Confederates' efforts to establish and maintain a slaveholding republic resulted in tragic continuities in the purchase and sale of people.

The legal codes governing slavery regularly, as Frederick Douglass put it, delivered bondspeople into "the hands of strangers," assigning them values and dividing and selling them accordingly. "A single word from the white men," he remembered, "was enough—against all our wishes, prayers, and entreaties—to sunder for ever the dearest friends, dearest kindred, and strongest ties known to human beings."[147] Such transactions' legal and fiscal precision treated lives and relationships capriciously. One formerly enslaved woman recalled her enslaver's heirs partitioning her community by drawing their names from a hat.[148] The Civil War undermined the state authority that allowed some Confederates to engage in such practices, but where the Confederacy held sway, the legal mechanisms underpinning slavery ground on. The conflict altered them, to be sure. The widespread imposition of stay laws and martial law, for example, blocked some sales of enslaved people intended to settle debts. The passage of the armies disrupted the functioning of courts and police mechanisms. But in secure pockets throughout the CSA, legally mandated sales persisted; indeed, the survival of the Confederacy and its constituent states all but demanded that they do so.

As in Elsy's, Judy's, and their families' cases, court-arranged sales took place throughout the wartime South. Many followed enslavers' deaths, an omnipresent menace amid a conflict that claimed hundreds of thousands of lives. When North Carolina's Julia Gwyn recorded a neighbor's death at Gettysburg, she reflected that she could not predict "what will become of his negroes now" and paused (albeit briefly) to bemoan their probable sale.[149] Daniel, enslaved in collapsing eastern North Carolina, fled to escape this fate after hearing rumors that his enslaver had perished.[150] Another enslaver hoped to arrange matters following the death of his brother so that the family's enslaved people would not go to someone who would "sell them like cattle."[151]

Given the turmoil pervading the slave market, enslavers often resented legally required sales. These mandated the sale of slaves at whatever prices then prevailed, figures that ranged during the war from $44 to $5,000.[152] One slaveholder complained that selling forty people belonging to his recently deceased aunt in early 1862 was "a sacrifice" given that "negroes is rated very low."[153] Even Richard H. Dickinson could salvage only modest prices for people sold from his father's estate in early 1862.[154] Others reveled in the bargains available. All but rubbing his hands with glee, a slave trader planned to attend three Alabama auctions deriving from debt or death in November 1863 at which more than two hundred people would face sale.[155] When a Mississippi partnership failed a year later, eighty-three people mounted the block to "settle the business" of the firm.[156] As late as 1864 in Union-occupied Missouri, a slaveholder's death resulted in the sale of dozens of people.[157]

Such transactions devastated countless families. Katie Rowe's Arkansas enslaver died mid-war, after which she watched the property's overseer casually sell her community, one by one, to passing traders.[158] Even those who awaited their enslavers' deaths hopefully could find themselves disappointed amid the conflict. When a Lynchburg, Virginia slaveholder died in 1862, he emancipated the sixty people he enslaved in his will. Scheming family members, however, broke the will and put these unfortunates up for sale.[159] Enslavers displayed a remarkable capacity for excusing their complicity in these sales. When claimants dissolved an estate in South Carolina, one family member used the law to shield himself from any culpability in the resulting division. "I hate to see the negroes sold," he complained, "but cannot help them." All he could muster in their favor was an impotent hope that they would not fall into the hands of a notoriously abusive local family.[160] The law and the market thus continued to exercise extraordinary influence over the lives of the enslaved even amid the dawn of freedom.

Indeed, state agents within the Confederacy used slave commerce to augment their powers over the enslaved. For generations, Southern states had rendered numerous transgressions punishable by sale beyond their borders, with other statutes bolstering the racial order by selling free people of color into slavery.[161] Where the Confederacy held sway such laws remained applicable, as demonstrated in the actions of the Richmond Hustings Court. During the secession crisis, it sentenced Lewis to sale for striking a white man, with his assessed value ($400) to be remanded to his enslaver from the proceeds. Almost simultaneously, it sold Frank Banks (a free man of color) for stabbing an enslaved man. Slaveholders ensnared free people for trivial offenses: Richard Thompson for having stolen "two pair of pantaloons, one coat, two pair of drawers, four shirts and collars, all of the aggregate value of thirty dollars," Joseph Gray for stealing a watch, Sarah Edmondson a dress. Even as Confederates made the enslaved repositories for their Confederate money, the Court sentenced William Ross to sale for stealing Rebel scrip.[162] Where the slaveholding state remained vital, it exercised its punitive powers through the ongoing commodification of African Americans.

Even as Confederate state mechanisms fought to preserve normalcy in the legal realm, individual slaveholders pursued their own understandings of continuity through slave commerce. They used slave commerce to meet perceived needs, alleviate discomfort, address what they considered essential aspects of mastery, and maintain the standards of living to which they had grown accustomed. As the war swirled around them, slaveholders continued to define and purchase people according to specific utilitarian functions and in reference to their own conceptions of need. Encamped in March 1863 above a bend in the Arkansas River, for example, Texas's Elijah Petty dreamed about possible futures for his family and watched for opportunities to actualize them. Five months earlier, he had encouraged his wife to invest in enslaved property. As the prospects for doing so grew more and more promising, he fantasized about what this could mean for the Pettys. An acquired bondswoman would be not only a valuable asset but would also relieve his family from menial tasks and facilitate their social ascent. "The negro will," Petty believed, "keep my darling daughter out of the kitchen" and "enable her the better to pursue with assiduity her studies and the accomplishment of her mind."[163] Acquiring an enslaved laborer at wartime prices would thus accomplish goals that transcended the war: leisure, social advancement, and the sense of mastery that stemmed from the subordination of another.

Confederates' motivations for such purchases were expansive. Some sought laborers to build out their operations. North Carolina's David Schenck rejoiced at acquiring an enslaved man in the autumn of 1862. "I have long desired," he recorded, "to have just such a servant to carry on a little farm and take care of things when I am away. So I feel about as proud of this acquisition as any I ever made."[164] Still others sought workers for their homes. A Richmond resident reported that the city's slave traders did a robust business in "city wants, especially ... cooks &c."[165] Enslaved nurses and wetnurses were also in high demand. Edward Porter Alexander articulated a willingness to "sell & buy often" to find a woman who met his requirements.[166] They did so without any discernible reference to the conflict, save (as a Texan who purchased a valet put it) for an underlying belief that "slavery is popular and will be likely to continue for many years yet."[167] As late as January 1865, North Carolina's Margaret Cronly tried to purchase a seamstress for as much as $10,000, while Stonewall Jackson's one-time cartographer Jedediah Hotchkiss acquired William for half that sum.[168] Continuities between antebellum and wartime life, then, dovetailed with a belief in slavery's permanence to encourage the purchase of enslaved people.

As enslavers dealt people away on whims—one because "they are not such negroes as" he "desire[d]," another because he possessed "more of this class of servants than needed"—they imagined themselves as benevolent paternalists who sought the best for the Black members of their extended households.[169] This already-cracked façade gaped as tensions between enslaved people's desires and enslavers' financial wellbeing escalated. Though flattering themselves that they cared about the families and feelings of those whom they held in bondage, slaveholders regularly refused to abide either the financial losses or the loss of mastery required to meet their chattels' most fundamental desires.

When John Berkley Grimball prepared to sell the people he enslaved who had not escaped to Union lines, he discussed the prospect with some of the community's elders, implying to them that they had "options." Nelly argued against Grimball's plans, while Alfred begged to remain with his family. They did so to no avail. Blaming "the stringent circumstances which at this moment govern my action" for providing "reasons in favor of selling [that] were strong enough to determine me," Grimball shattered these families in spite of their fidelity. It was, he claimed, a "sickening business," but insufficiently so to either deter him or prevent his complaining that Nelly and Alfred represented "hindrances" to the "large prices" he hoped to extract from them.[170]

Time and again, Confederates prioritized their pocketbooks over the desires of the enslaved. A Mississippi family hoped to swap Sally and her daughter Catharine for a woman named America. As they negotiated, a third party threatened to purchase America and take her to Texas. Though she informed her would-be purchasers that she would rather go to Texas than be owned by anyone save them, her enslavers sold America to the highest bidder.[171] Members of Virginia's Cabell family expressed a desire to preserve an enslaved family. "Freely would I loose my right hand," one intoned, "to save them all from the horrible uncertainty of a public auction." Another added that "each servant that is secured for the future is a source of devout thankfulness to me." In the end, however, the family delegated their chattels' fate to an intermediary accountable only to the family's finances.[172]

Even when enslavers took enslaved people's desires under consideration, they took action through slave commerce. A Florida general hoping to reunite families that his mother had sundered sought to acquire Thomas, the son of Alice, whom he enslaved. To do so, he offered up another person in Thomas's place.[173] Alabama's F. E. Duggar, meanwhile, used slave commerce to coerce Jim into acting in Duggar's own interests. Duggar planned to sell Jim paternalistically by encouraging him to "find a master he likes." In a scarcely veiled threat, however, he informed Jim that he didn't "wish to sell him at public auction" and even positioned himself as willing to make a sacrifice by taking slightly less than market value in a transaction Jim favored. Duggar, however, required at least $4,500 from Jim's preferred enslaver, a reality that severely limited the options available to the beleaguered man.[174]

Other enslavers used the market to gain leverage over the people they held captive. A member of Louisiana's Stubbs family resolved to purchase John rather than risk his fleeing and taking with him his wife, Molly, whom they enslaved.[175] Another Louisianan promised to purchase an enslaved woman's children at the war's conclusion, hoping this would ensure her fidelity during the conflict.[176] An Alabama family sold Amy to the family enslaving Frank, whom she hoped to marry. They structured the transaction, however, to maintain their authority over the pair.[177] Enslaved people's status as commodities shaded even seemingly favorable transactions. Florida's James Barrow attempted to purchase an unnamed woman whom Riley wished to marry, but at the last minute, the seller cut off negotiations and sold her to a higher bidder.[178] When men and women held by Virginia's Carrington family faced division, an enslaved woman named Dublin urged Eliza Carrington to get her brothers to purchase them so that they could remain together but could not compel her to do so.[179]

Other enslavers tried to leverage enslaved family bonds into purchases favorable to them. Virginia's Charles Meriwether worked to sell Mat to Sterling Neblett (who, in addition to having close financial ties to Richmond's slave traders, enslaved Mat's children and grandchildren). When Neblett persistently offered less than Meriwether sought, Meriwether used larger offers received for Mat's brother, Ben, to wheedle a few more dollars from him.[180] A Shenandoah Valley slaveholder, meanwhile, highlighted family ties to cajole another slaveholding family into purchasing a woman and child he had acquired at an estate sale.[181] And when the Simms family sold Wyatt in Albemarle County, they offered a $500 discount to sell him nearby "in consideration of his family" even as they warned a potential buyer that they "intend[ed] to take him to another market soon" to avoid "sacrificing too much on the negro."[182]

Slaveholding families sometimes worked at cross purposes in their efforts to retain the loyalty of their enslaved people, with some members acting punitively, others paternalistically. As the Rebel army massed along the Rappahannock ahead of Chancellorsville, General Dorsey Pender learned that a man whom his brother enslaved had fled and been recaptured. Pender hoped to acquire him for the sake of the man's wife, whom he already held. But before Pender could make an offer, his brother sent the man to the Richmond market. Pender conceded the depravity in this, writing to his wife, "This separating man and wife is a most cruel thing and almost enough to make one an abolitionist." His solution, however, was to try to purchase the man in question himself, not to reconsider his role in conducting a war to maintain his right to do so.[183]

Amid the Civil War, then, significant elements of antebellum slave commerce persisted largely unchanged. Legal entities continued to mandate the sale of people, even as individual enslavers used the slave trade much as they always had: to meet their self-defined needs, to indulge their lifestyles, and to project paternalism. But wartime slave sales, like their antebellum counterparts, revealed paternalism's stark limits. Thus, even as war and emancipation profoundly altered the fledgling nation they hoped to inhabit, enslavers' participation in the slave market acted as a practical, ideological, and commercial bridge between the world they had long inhabited and that for which they now fought.

On a frigid day in January 1865, William Henry Terrill penned a critical missive to his profligate son George from a perch in Virginia's Allegheny Mountains. Despite deepening shortages of food and money, George recently had purchased an enslaved woman, a decision the elder Terrill believed lacked "rational economy and a politic foresight." George would have to feed and clothe his newest acquisition and pay the taxes Confederate and state governments levied on enslaved property. William planned to avoid these same issues by selling a woman named Elizabeth and her children as soon as the weather permitted travel and by actively avoiding the receipt of enslaved people left to him by his deceased sister (who, he argued, would "starve" if "thrown upon me"). A week later, however, Terrill contradicted himself, deploring George's decision to sell two people (at least, at the prices he obtained) even while urging him to sell another woman at a state-backed auction. However ambivalently, Terrill trusted slave commerce and, implicitly, the state that supported it, to raise money, alleviate the strains of war, and dictate domestic relations.[184]

The Terrills' correspondence underscores the varied forces shaping slave commerce late in the war. The tumult that enveloped the Confederate economy created unique incentives for slave trading, whether by industrial concerns securing their labor forces or, as in William Terrill's case, by individuals selling enslaved people as provisions ran short. Such sales reflected the deep contingencies the war injected into the lives of the people caught in the slave trade's undertow. George Terrill's acquisition of an unnamed woman likewise shows how slaveholders used the wartime slave trade to not only translate money into enslaved property, but also to pursue a lifestyle predicated on dominion. A remade Confederate economy, thousands of individual crises, and the continuities Confederates sought thus incubated transactions involving thousands of enslaved people even as freedom dawned.

6

Sold "Far Out of the Way of Lincoln"

Emancipation and Counterrevolutionary Slave Commerce

Under the cover of night on June 10 and 11, 1864, an exhausted John Powell stumbled through the woods of northeastern Mississippi. That morning, he had marched into battle as a private in the 59th United States Colored Infantry. By the time night fell, he was in the hands of Confederate slavers, being driven inexorably south. As the eighteen-year-old Powell trudged through the darkness, he likely recalled his childhood removal from Virginia to Memphis, in the environs of which he, like most of the other members of the 59th USCI, had been enslaved. Union occupation of the city had left the institution there impotent and when the Union began recruiting Black men to its cause, Powell joined up. He thereby completed what he surely considered an irrevocable movement out of bondage. He may not have enlisted willingly. As one of his officers recalled, "recruits were collected from plantations and from camps," with men whom enslavers considered property "appropriated as such . . . and confiscated as a 'military necessity.'"[1] Nevertheless, through his service Powell simultaneously fought against the institution of slavery, laid a claim on the United States, and became a tangible symbol of the war's emancipatory potential.

His experiences that June day, however, imperiled this revolutionary moment. Two weeks earlier, the 59th had joined a Union detachment advancing from Memphis into northern Mississippi. Its mission was to shield the supply and communication lines of William T. Sherman's Atlanta-bound forces from Rebel raiders, most notably former slave trader Nathan Bedford Forrest. The expedition was troubled from the beginning. For days, US soldiers struggled through pouring rain and along muddy roads. When the rain ceased, the sweltering June sun replaced it. On June 10, Forrest caught the exhausted Union column unawares at Brices Cross Roads, where, after several hours of intense fighting, the Union contingent collapsed. The 59th and 55th USCI fought a desperate rearguard action, but Forrest's troopers eventually overran them. As the Confederates hunted stragglers into the night, they murdered many in cold blood, a cruel irony given that the two regiments had gone into battle wearing badges emblazoned "Remember Fort Pillow." The Rebels also captured a number of Black soldiers, among them John Powell.[2]

As he moved south in the hands of Forrest's men, Powell's fate hung in the balance, for Confederates' treatment of captured USCTs varied dramatically. African American captives' mere existence raised thorny legal and ideological questions for a nation founded on the principle of their subordination. According them official POW status and exchanging them for captured Rebels conceded men recently raised from servitude an unacceptable level of equality. "We must sacrifice every thing," James Henry Hammond sputtered, "rather than do it." Black prisoners thus faced an array of potential outcomes. Some Confederates executed, considering them enslaved people in rebellion. Far more performed forced labor on Confederate fortifications and infrastructure projects, working alongside the men sold and hired there to sustain the Rebel state. Thousands lingered in prison camps. An unknown number Confederates gave over to enslavers who claimed them as their property. Still others fell victim to the Confederate slave trade.[3]

John Powell fell into this final category. After Brices Cross Roads, he disappeared from the official record; Union officials labeled him "missing in action June 10, 1864," with "no record of capture." This was because the Confederates who carried him away from the battle chose to combine profit and punishment. Withdrawing to Kosciusko in central Mississippi, where the slaveholders' republic still held sway, Powell's captors sold him to sawmill operator Joe Taylor for $5,000. Taylor put him to work cutting lumber in a steam mill, the output of which fed the Confederate war machine. For the rest of the war, Powell would again be enslaved, the persisting slave trade having erased the freedom he had attained through the war. The Confederates who sold him, meanwhile, found in slave commerce a means to keep (albeit temporarily) emancipation's effects, so effectively embodied in Powell's person, at bay.[4]

John Powell's sale reveals the ties and tensions between emancipation and wartime slave commerce. As enslaved people circulated rumors of coming liberation, fled to Union lines, and even enlisted in the US Army and Navy, they sparked thousands of conflicts with panicked enslavers.[5] Like Powell, many paid for their freedom-seeking through sale. There was little inherently new about this. Enslaved flight had long bedeviled the peculiar institution, escalating into a full-blown crisis in the 1850s with the passage of the Fugitive Slave Act.[6] The slave trade was a longstanding and potent weapon in the arsenal of cruelties with which enslavers confronted the restive people they held captive.[7] When, for example, Harriet Jacobs's enslaver sought leverage over her, he threatened to sell her children, leaving her "rooted to the spot" with horror.[8] Calculated or capricious, punitive slave sales effectively suppressed resistance, from idling to flight to outright rebellion. As George Johnson, once enslaved near Harpers Ferry, recalled, "If a man did any thing out of the way, he was in more danger of being sold than of being whipped."[9]

The Civil War offered enslaved people unprecedented incentives and opportunities to act "out of the way." The influx of white men into the Rebel military, widespread food shortages, the insertion of the Confederacy into relationships between enslaver and enslaved, and Union military threats frayed slaveholders' grip on their chattels, and the enslaved exploited the resulting openings.[10] From labor slowdowns to physical confrontations, the millions of men and women held in bondage probed the limits of their confinement or rejected it outright in what Paul Cameron bemoaned as "a Revolution" against the institution.[11] Enslaved people's efforts forced the US government to keep pace. Fugitives made soldiers and authorities reconsider their obligations to the men, women, and children arriving in their lines, rendered abstract property rights confoundingly concrete, demonstrated their utility and devotion to the United States, and staked unprecedented claims on the nation for rights and, eventually, citizenship.[12]

Enslaved people's journeys toward liberation, however, were neither linear nor safe.[13] US agents' responses to them ranged from charity to neglect to outright cruelty, with the Union's overarching emphasis on victory excusing widespread disdain and disregard for people of color.[14] Meanwhile, beyond the reach of what historians Greg Downs and Kate Masur term "the stockade state"—Union armies, garrisons, and their immediate environs—emancipation's practical effects were more muted.[15] A Mississippi enslaver conceded that the "danger of the whole negro population of the South becoming greatly demoralized" increased as the war lengthened, but noted that this effect predominated "wherever [the Union] army goes."[16] Wartime emancipation, in short, was dependent on the exercise of Union power and shot through with ambiguities.

Refugees from slavery also remained dangerously close to a state whose raison d'etre was their continued commodification and captivity. Outside

US lines, Rebel guerrillas, raiders, and armies harassed freedpeople and endeavored to return them to bondage, while in the Confederate interior, the slaveholding state protected slavery and the commerce in humanity that allowed the institution to function.[17] The CSA did so fairly successfully; the overwhelming majority—some 80 to 85 percent—of those enslaved at the war's outset remained so at its end, with liberations heavily concentrated in the Border States, Mississippi Valley, and Atlantic seaboard.[18] Even in these liminal spaces, slaveholders fortified themselves against emancipation's cascading effects through the slave trade, a vascular network linking them to the still-beating heart of the slaveholders' republic.

Such transactions placed significant hurdles in African Americans' path to freedom and thereby profoundly shaped its onset. With Union forces advancing and the political climate clearing, liberty seemed more attainable than ever. Against these threats enslavers deployed the slave trade. Those who strove most boldly for freedom suffered punitive sales. In some cases, sheriffs, home guard units, guerrilla bands, or Rebel armies effectively served as what one scholar has called "slavery's sword and shield" by returning fugitives to bondage and facilitating their sale.[19] In others, enslavers preemptively sold for fear of escape, using the Confederate interior as a slave jail writ large. As external and internal frictions undermined slaveholders' dominion, even the most trivial infractions against the racial order could result in a trip to the auction block. Where African Americans made their stands against the slaveholders' republic, as soldiers or laborers in Union employ, the slave trade offered enslavers a means of reasserting control through renewed commodification. Against the revolution that men like Powell had inaugurated, then, enslavers fought an effective counterrevolution through their continued ability to buy, sell, and hold people in slavery.

In December 1861, just eight months into the Civil War, three men slipped away from the Nalle family's property in Orange County, Virginia. Crossing the hills known as Jack's and Quarles Mountains, Dick, Daniel, and George struck east toward the snarled second-growth forest that would soon gain infamy as "the Wilderness." Patrollers captured Daniel and George within a day of their escape, but Dick evaded them and eventually reached Fredericksburg. As he searched for a means to continue northward toward US lines, a passerby identified him as a fugitive. Dick tried to escape, but either because he fled or because he fought against capture, a slave catcher shot him through the thigh. This vigilante delivered him to the local sheriff, who jailed him for a month while the Nalles deliberated his fate.[20]

Dick's, Daniel's, and George's flight illustrates the defense-in-depth enslavers deployed against their chattels well into the Civil War, layers of protection Walter Johnson has termed the South's "carceral landscape."[21] Backing slaveholders against the limits of their own oversight, slave codes criminalized Black mobility and sought to deny enslaved people information about the world outside the plantation sphere. Slave patrols culled away potential allies and harassed those who slipped enslavers' bonds. Slaveholders also used printed and oral communications to head off fugitives, while private slave hunters, community-organized vigilantism, and state-supported slave catching threw their weight behind enslavers in their struggle against the enslaved.[22]

When this trio fled, the Confederacy was young and vital. Its borders extended almost to the Potomac, with Rebel soldiers occasionally glimpsing the Capitol from their foremost positions in northern Virginia.[23] If Dick, Daniel, and George moved too soon, however, their enslavers correctly gauged the prevailing winds. The Nalles knew that in August 1861 the US Congress had passed the First Confiscation Act, affirming Union forces' ability to withhold fugitives from bondage. They also likely saw that where the United States held sway it effectively negated slave patrols and other state agents of violence.[24] The Nalles, like many on the emerging Rebel frontier, saw harbingers of a world in which they would lack the absolute, state-backed authority that Confederates had rebelled to preserve. Rather than risk this, they used slave commerce to reassert their mastery. George's and Daniel's quick return to bondage may have obviated the Nalles' desire to punish them. The family, however, decided to make an example out of Dick, who had fled the furthest and cost the most to recapture. They did so by handing him over to Dickinson, Hill & Co. Thanks to the slowdown in the trade caused by the military setbacks of early 1862, Dick lingered in the firm's jail for more than half a year. Eventually, however, they found a buyer for him amid the resurgence following the Seven Days battles, and Dick vanished into the Rebel interior, far from the freedom he had sought.[25]

In subsequent years, similar transactions imposed direct consequences on men and women seeking liberty. Such sales publicly punished those who fell short and, enslavers hoped, inoculated captives remaining behind against the spreading contagion of liberty. They also offset enslavers' financial losses.[26]

The surviving slave trade thus existed symbiotically with the slaveholders' republic. The CSA's armies preserved the state and markets for enslaved property, while the slave trade circulated power to the Confederacy's extremities and linked enslavers to the surviving state. The Confederacy preserved the slave trade even as the slave trade bolstered individual enslavers and their slaveholding nation against the threat of emancipation.

The further an enslaved person lived from a Union beachhead, the greater the slaveholding state's power over them. Jack, Venus, Glasgow, and Frank confronted this reality in the spring of 1862 after North Carolina's William Pettigrew forced them inland from the Albemarle Sound. Hired out to abusive Piedmont enslavers, they quickly grew restive. Tensions came to a head when Jack and a pregnant Venus prevented an overseer from harming an enslaved girl. A disgusted Venus stormed away from the confrontation and declared that "she was going to the Yankees." The overseer responded by severely beating both of them (he later confessed that "if he had had a gun he would have killed some of them"). He struck Venus with a chair, causing her to miscarry. Glasgow faced a whipping for accusations of theft, leading him to threaten "he would not be long to anney body in a few days," while Frank repeatedly challenged Pettigrew's control over him.[27]

With removal to the interior having failed to quell their desire to escape, Pettigrew called upon the resources of the slaveholding state. For Jack's and Glasgow's "impudent & threatening language" and their threats "to run away & to go to the Yankees," Pettigrew placed them in solitary confinement in a county jail on a starvation diet. He hoped this would forestall their "contaminat[ing] others" with "any evil plans they may have in contimplation." Should they escape, he asked an associate to circulate their descriptions, offer a reward, and mobilize local slave patrols. Frank, moreover, was to be sold outside of North Carolina "to prevent, as far as possible, his ever returning."[28]

Slaveholders, befuddled by the enslaved and hampered by the fog of war, did not always deter or recapture fugitives. But where individuals failed, in many cases the state succeeded.[29] Sheriffs and slave patrols apprehended, detained, and advertised runaways, selling those who went unclaimed after a predetermined period.[30] As a Randolph County, North Carolina jailer put it after capturing Hence midway through the war, he could and would "be disposed of as the law directs."[31] Likewise, when yet another Dick escaped from yet another Orange County holding, state and local authorities caught him, confined him in Richmond, and assisted in his sale.[32]

In parts of the CSA, these defenses remained robust deep into the war. In January 1865, the sheriff of Virginia's Albemarle County upheld slavery's laws by jailing Mary for six months then selling her.[33] Mere days before Grant finally excavated the Army of Northern Virginia from its Petersburg fortifications, a soldier petitioned Lee's headquarters for permission to visit Richmond "to identify a negro of mine captured from [the] enemy" before the state could sell the person in question.[34] Wherever Confederate armies and the geography of war shielded them, local authorities continued governing enslaved life and mobility and, combined with the punitive slave commerce this protection enabled, fought to check enslaved resistance.

These measures rendered enslaved property relatively secure in the interior. Katie Rowe, enslaved in southwestern Arkansas, recalled watching many coffles pass carrying men and women away from the collapsing Mississippi Valley. So far were they from the liberating Federals that slave dealers ceased to restrain their chattels physically given they "didn't have no place dey could run to anyway."[35] A Mississippi soldier hoped to take advantage of this reality in the wake of Vicksburg's fall, urging his mother to send their human property into "the Interior states" via the slave trade.[36]

Even in Union-occupied areas, echoes of the slaveholding state survived and ensnared people through slave commerce. Evolving US emancipation policies, their tenuous legal bases in executive and legislative war powers, and the corrosive effects of occupation meant that freedom arrived unevenly. In the Border States and occupied regions, therefore, slavery long retained its legal sanction—a fact that enabled slave sales, punitive or otherwise, to continue. In 1863, for example, a group of fugitives from slavery captured in Kentucky escaped sale only when Lincoln himself intervened.[37] The insertion of the United States between enslavers and enslaved greatly diminished the prices obtained for captive laborers. In a Maryland town just outside Washington, DC, for example, thirteen people brought less than a thousand dollars in the spring of 1863.[38]

But in jurisdictions across the slaveholding South's upper reaches, authorities continued to apprehend, jail, and sell the enslaved.[39] After William fled northwestern Virginia, Maryland authorities captured and jailed him. Ignoring the emerging national boundaries, his enslaver sought to recover him before a local court could sell him, reflecting the solidarity that enslavers expected from the slaveholding state.[40] Indeed, during the war, Kentucky accelerated the pace at which it sold fugitives from bondage. Its antebellum statute required jailers to wait six months before selling in order

SOLD "FAR OUT OF THE WAY OF LINCOLN" 167

to permit enslavers to reclaim escapees. In 1863, responding to an influx of men and women fleeing their captivity, the state reduced this to one month, resulting in a flood of sales that continued throughout the conflict.[41]

US soldiers occasionally facilitated slave commerce in ways that exceeded the ambiguities in official policies. In May 1862, a Confederate soldier gleefully reported that Federals on Virginia's Eastern Shore were "selling the

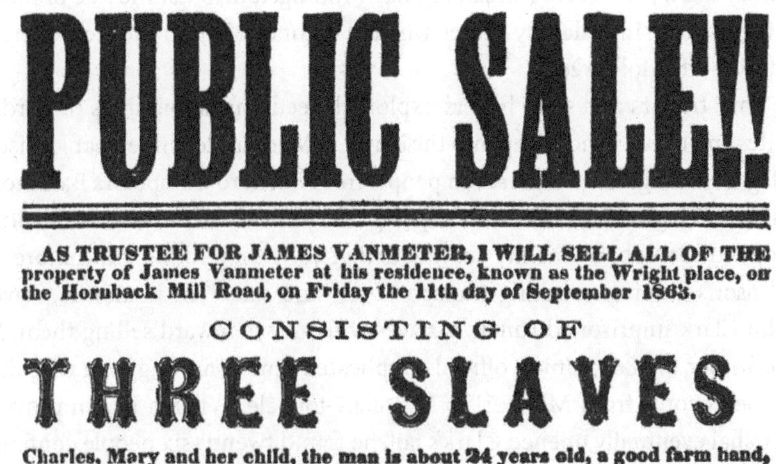

PUBLIC SALE!!

AS TRUSTEE FOR JAMES VANMETER, I WILL SELL ALL OF THE property of James Vanmeter at his residence, known as the Wright place, on the Hornback Mill Road, on Friday the 11th day of September 1863.

CONSISTING OF

THREE SLAVES

Charles, Mary and her child, the man is about 24 years old, a good farm hand, the woman is an excellent cook and washer.

HORSES, MULES, CATTLE, SHEEP, HOGS

AND CROP. CORN IN THE FIELDS,

OATS, WHEAT, TOBACCO

Kitchen Furniture, &c., Farm Implements of every kind. Terms of Sale, a credit of 4 months will be given on all sums of $10, and over carrying interest from day of sale. The purchaser to execute Notes with good security.

Winchester August 24th 1863.   JAS. H. G. BUSH, Trustee.

1863: Auction sale of slaves along with livestock and personal property.
© Pioneer Historical Society

Figure 6.1 "Notice of Slave Sale." This advertisement, likely placed in Kentucky, demonstrates that slave sales continued there well into 1863. Schomburg Center, New York Public Library.

negroes back to their masters" and intimated to his wife, "you know how they will fare after having run off and sold back to their original owners."[42] In Lexington, Kentucky, a diarist reported that enslavers and speculators were bribing Union soldiers to hand enslaved people over to them.[43] Unscrupulous officials and contractors along the Mississippi and the Ohio Rivers exploited vulnerable African Americans for a quick profit, with one superintendent of contrabands even using his position to traffic an enslaved boy back to his enslavers.[44] Layered within the Union army's liberating potential was a profiteering streak regularly indulged through the sale of Black refugees back into slavery—after which a second sale into the Confederate interior often followed.

Slave traders and slave buyers exploited freedom's ambiguities in border states and borderlands deep into the conflict. Marylander Greenleaf Johnson allegedly smuggled at least seven people from Bernard Campbell's Baltimore jail into Virginia for sale in the spring of 1863. When Federal authorities emptied Campbell's facility for good that July, they found nine more of Johnson's captives awaiting transportation and sale.[45] In Louisville, slaver John Clark imprisoned runaway slaves with an eye toward selling them. In the winter of 1863, Union officials implicated him in a smuggling ring that carried people from Missouri to Kentucky for sale. When a Union provost marshal eventually opened Clark's jail, he found twenty-six people confined there—the barest portion of the estimated two thousand people sold illicitly between the two states. Kentuckians also sold people who had escaped thence from the Confederacy. Among them was Amy Moore, who, with her family, fled bondage in Alabama and reached Louisville in the summer of 1863. A city watchman arrested and incarcerated them (possibly in Clark's facility), after which city authorities sneaked them through US lines and sold them.[46]

If authorities within the United States treated those fleeing bondage inconsistently, the Confederacy did not. At virtually every opportunity, Confederates—soldiers and sailors, raiders and guerillas, and civilians of all kinds—imposed enslavement on African Americans who had attained freedom and used slave commerce to return them to their purported former status. Such efforts brought easy profits, extended the reach of the slaveholding state, and embodied the impulses underpinning the Confederacy. On the march and occupying territory, Rebel armies provided slaveholders with a first line of defense against Federal predations and a last recourse against enslaved flight.[47] They were not, admittedly, universally salubrious for the slaveholding order. Their insatiable demand for labor and appropriation of enslaved workers, for example, undermined enslavers' control.[48] Military encampments swarmed with camp servants, teamsters, and laborers, offering anonymity to fugitives and, ironically, regularly bringing them within hailing distance of Union lines.[49] As one Richmonder watching camp servants pass through the city scoffed, "There is ... sixteen thousand dollars' worth of negro property which can go off on its own legs to the Yankees whenever it pleases."[50] William Fisher demonstrated the veracity of this prophecy. A stonecutter from near Harpers Ferry, the Confederate military conscripted him in 1861 first to remove machinery from that city's US arsenal then to work on Richmond's fortifications. He fled in November but was caught and jailed, after which slave trader N. M. Lee bought him, carried him to Richmond, and sold him again to a southbound trader. Fisher ultimately escaped and arrived in Washington, DC in December, securing his freedom and depriving both his enslaver and the Confederacy of a valuable asset.[51]

While the Confederacy compensated some enslavers for the loss of enslaved laborers due to military demands, sale offered a surer means of ensuring their continued dominance.[52] A Lynchburg slaveholder, weary of sacrificing an enslaved man to Confederate requisitions, declared that he would rather sell him than risk losing him "when I cannot control him."[53] Others found enslaved workers returning from government projects "demoralized," a euphemism that described their restiveness after having briefly left their place of confinement. In practical terms, one South Carolinian reported, this meant that the people her family enslaved had become "hard to manage." Given that since their return "they all seem waiting for freedom and utter idleness," she hoped her family would sell them and purchase others who might prove more tractable.[54]

The Confederacy nevertheless depended on its military to protect slavery. Before Virginia had even completed its secession, Fredericksburg slaveholders prevailed upon Confederate cavalry to pursue fugitives for them.[55] The 12th Texas Dragoons, meanwhile, took custody of a fugitive named Stephen, standing in for impotent civilian authorities in northern Arkansas and southern Missouri.[56] In Virginia's King George County, Rebel pickets captured Moses "on the Potomac signaling to Yankee tugs," after which his enslaver sold him.[57] A South Carolinian demanded and received a cavalry detachment to arrest "a stampede" by his captive workers. In 1864, a Georgian requested that Confederate pickets "watch very close" and arrest Big Al, Zack, Tilman, and Aleck on their flight to the Federals.[58] Others served as unofficial slave catchers, including a Mississippi soldier who volunteered to help capture runaways and "crushed their freedom in the bud."[59]

Even when the demands of war prevented Confederate soldiers from supporting individual enslavers, the slave market allowed them to protect slavery more broadly. When in 1864 Confederate cavalry captured "a large number of negroes" near King and Queen Courthouse, Virginia, the captives followed a legally dictated track toward sale.[60] In other cases, soldiers speculated on their own behalf, selling people for easy cash under the cover of wartime chaos. In the war's first months, for example, a northern Virginia Unionist watched Confederates plot to take a free Black man "south and sell him."[61] Following Harpers Ferry's 1862 surrender, meanwhile, Confederates captured hundreds of fugitives who had taken refuge with the Union garrison and sent at least two train cars full of people to Richmond for sale.[62]

Fugitives who reached Union refuges remained vulnerable to the slave state and to speculating soldiers. Confederates could drag freedmen on Union-operated plantations, intended to serve as nurseries for the new birth of freedom, back into bondage with frightening rapidity. Along the Mississippi, for example, Union soldiers held only what Sherman called a "long, weak line," that could be "broken at any point by a guerrilla band of 100 with perfect impunity."[63] When one guerrilla did just this, his unit "captur[ed] all the negroes we could find"—1,340 in all. Another raid netted hundreds more, whom partisans hoped to sell in Texas.[64] Mingo, a man enslaved in Mississippi, experienced a similar fate. Though US cavalry had liberated him from the plantation upon which he labored, he knew how tenuous his freedom truly was. As he moved north, seeking refuge within Federal lines, a company of Confederate raiders captured him and sold him to a planter from Thibodaux Parish, Louisiana.[65] In Missouri, guerrillas stormed a steamboat, captured its Black passengers, and sold them into renewed slavery.[66] Confederate officers occasionally issued orders protecting captives from indiscriminate sale, but they did so to protect enslavers' property rights rather than the enslaved.[67] Indeed, some Rebel citizens encouraged the extraction of people from Union hands. In January 1865, for example, Richmond's W. B. Cook offered dual rewards for Hampton Johnson's capture: $500 if taken within Confederate lines, $1,000 if brought from behind Federal works.[68]

When operating on US territory, Confederates carried the project of the slaveholding state with them. They treated the African Americans they encountered as fugitives and subjected them to commodification and sale. Nowhere was this clearer than during the Gettysburg Campaign, when Confederates kidnapped hundreds of people and sent many of them to slave markets in Richmond and elsewhere for reduction to bondage.[69] Abductions began before the Army of Northern Virginia left the Confederacy. A North Carolina soldier, writing from the Shenandoah Valley's head, affirmed that the army had rounded up "many hundred slaves." He intended to profit from this effort. Though he personally believed "negroes are worth nothing at all," he nevertheless "expect[ed] to make purchases in that line for Southern exportation."[70]

Once in Pennsylvania, Confederates captured and sold people of color as part of a broader effort to reassert the slaveholding society's control over African American lives. Their victims included Eliza Alesworth and her children, who had escaped to the state in 1862. The receding Confederate tide swept them into the jail of a Richmond slave trader.[71] One combatant carried ten free people all the way from York, Pennsylvania to Charlotte, North Carolina for sale.[72] It would have been surprising had they done otherwise, for, as historian Allen Guelzo has argued, "to have left Pennsylvania's blacks in undisturbed freedom would have been tantamount to denying the validity of the whole Confederate enterprise."[73]

Other Confederate incursions begat similar efforts. In October 1861, Rebel raiders in Missouri captured a free Black man named Isaac who had dedicated himself to helping others become free and carried him to New Orleans for sale.[74] Under the cover of Confederates' 1862 invasion of Kentucky, Lexington slave trader George Ferguson purchased Prince, Lize, their children, and Larkin, whom he hurried southward alongside the retreating Rebels.[75] When Confederates again raided Pennsylvania in 1864, they captured Union teamster James Hamilton in Maryland and a woman and three children near Greencastle and sold them upon returning to Virginia.[76] Rebels' conflation of race and slavery exposed all Blacks inhabiting free spaces to capture, commodification, and enslavement by the agents of the slaveholders' republic. So long as that republic could project power, its forces did all that they could to reduce them to the slaves they believed them to be.

United States Colored Troops' defiance of the slaveholding state rendered them vulnerable to the slave market. When four Black soldiers captured near Gloucester Point arrived in Richmond's Libby Prison, an apoplectic crowd demanded their execution. Their captors, a fellow prisoner recalled, gave them the choice of being hanged or being sold.[77] This choice recurred implicitly or explicitly wherever soldiers of color fell into Rebel hands. Confederate soldier John S. Wise reported seeing a captured Black soldier elect sale under these circumstances, while John H. Butler of the 23rd USCI dodged death after the Crater through sale to a Charles County, Virginia slaveholder.[78] Rebels also used the slave trade to intimidate those considering donning a blue uniform and to retaliate against those who made such a choice. Francis Cook may have suffered this fate when her enslaver sold her from Tennessee to Richmond following her husband's enlistment.[79] As one Union officer reported, "The policy of selling families or the threatening so to do seems to have been adopted to deter enlistments," and was effective in doing so into 1864.[80]

Confederates even viewed African American soldiers who remained beyond their control through the lens of the slave market, rhetorically reducing them to slavery despite their combatant status. After engaging a Black unit, one Texan declared, "We killed in our front about a million dollars worth of Negroes at current prices."[81] Another soldier wrote sardonically that putting Black soldiers in the field would make cavalry service popular given the "opportunities for" capturing and "speculating in 'human flesh' as the Abolitionists say."[82] Financial considerations may have shaped the treatment USCTs received. "A negro at $5,000," in one newspaper's words, "is too valuable to be shot."[83] This reality reportedly drew "a number of Richmond negro traders" to one battlefield, the slave merchants "being anxious to get the first pick of the" Black prisoners taken there.[84]

Confederates applied the laws of slavery equally vigorously on the high seas. William Tillman faced Charleston's slave market after Rebel privateers commandeered the *S. J. Waring*, but struck back, setting upon his sleeping captors with a hatchet and liberating the vessel. Instead of his being sold for a like sum, the US government awarded him $6,000 for securing the ship.[85] When Confederates captured the *Star of the West* (famous for having tried to resupply Fort Sumter during the secession crisis), they allegedly sold off three Black crew members.[86] Others abducted Dorsey from a steamboat and sold him in the months following South Carolina's secession.[87] On land or at sea, Confederates paralleled their war for slavery by using the slave trade to reinforce connections between race and enslavement.

When Dick, Daniel, and George struck out for freedom in the autumn of 1861, they faced long odds for success. The soldiers and citizenry of the newly founded slaveholders' republic supplemented slave patrols, vigilantes, and enslavers' longstanding carceral mechanisms. Behind all of these lay the ongoing trade in slaves, a commerce that helped them fight advancing emancipation. Through the slave trade, Confederates re-baptized those who had sought or tasted freedom into the slaveholding order, performing their commodification and stamping them as property. As Confederates confronted the greatest threat American slavery had yet seen, they traded people to bolster the institution against the surging challenge and to contain the freedom impulses of those whom they sought to retain in bondage.

That Confederates would use slave commerce to confront the revolution inaugurated by the enslaved was abundantly clear even from the war's earliest days. The methodology they would employ emerged clearly in the travails of Martin, a young man enslaved in Fredericksburg, Virginia. In May 1861, before the Civil War had even begun in earnest—indeed, before Virginia had officially seceded from the United States—he sensed liberty on the wind. The twenty-two-year-old gardener and house servant reportedly held the newly inaugurated Lincoln "in great favor" and, inspired by his understanding of the president's anti-slavery sentiments, aggressively contested his bondage. His enslaver, John R. Taylor, soon found that Martin required "a tighter rein than I can keep upon him." Martin correctly interpreted freedom's first portents but moved too soon, for Taylor had also discerned the implications of secession and war. Much as Thomas Ruffin had done a year earlier, and as thousands of Confederates would do in the years to come, Taylor turned to the slave trade, asking Dickinson, Hill & Co. to sell Martin. To ensure that this sale would be truly counterrevolutionary, he demanded that the firm sell him to a buyer from Alabama or Louisiana, which would "put him far out of the way of Lincoln."[88]

Martin's escalating resistance and Taylor's retributive use of the slave trade reflected anxieties enslavers had nursed through the long antebellum years.[89] Behind their paeans to paternal affection between enslaver and enslaved flowed a deep current of fear.[90] The war and the opportunities it presented the enslaved raised these tensions to a level previously reached only during suspected slave revolts.[91] As the conflict progressed and the flood of refugees to the Federals mounted, so did Confederates' fears. North Carolina's Catherine Edmondston, for example, recoiled upon learning that an enslaved man lodging overnight at her home had been extracted only recently from Union lines. Still worse, he remained unbowed and "expressed the intention of joining them 'when they were ready for him.' Pleasant news," she fumed, when "he was at that moment 'cheek by jowl' with your own servants." Such freedom ambitions she considered nothing less than a "moral pestilence."[92]

Confederates met this "pestilence" with an array of brutalities. Georgia's Charles Colcock Jones Jr. called for the execution of runaways, arguing that "our entire social system will be upset if the supremacy of the law of servitude and the ownership of such property be not vigorously asserted."[93] As invading Union armies counterbalanced enslavers' power, however, physical punishments cowed the enslaved less and less. A whipping might even encourage rather than discourage flight. Capital punishment destroyed as yet valuable enslaved property. The domestic slave trade provided enslavers with a middle way by offering a severe punishment, an example to those contemplating escape, and ready cash in exchange for increasingly troublesome captives.

Striving to keep emancipation's contaminating effects at bay, enslavers sold recaptured fugitives with abandon. The Woods family's treatment of Henry typified their course of action. Henry fled Albemarle County, Virginia in June 1863, likely stowing aboard the Virginia Central Railroad then following the Valley Turnpike north toward US lines at the mouth of the Shenandoah Valley. Unfortunately, the Gettysburg-bound Army of Northern Virginia cut across his escape route. Henry was captured in New Market, Virginia, escaped, and was caught again. He would never, however, return to Albemarle County. On that point the family patriarch was emphatic. "I had no idea," John Woods informed his soldier son Micajah, "of permitting him to come home" as "the moral effect" of doing so "on the balance of my negroes will be very pernicious." For his part, Micajah viewed the question pecuniarily. "What," he inquired of his father as he retreated from Gettysburg, "is 'importing & exporting stock' selling for, now?" Both found their answers in Richmond's slave market. By selling Henry south, they quarantined the rest of their captives from his influence, compensated the family for his loss, and leavened the transaction with spite, for John explicitly had him sold "where he will have but little chance to get to the Yankees."[94]

Throughout the CSA, enslavers centered slave markets in their efforts to inoculate their enslaved property from the lure of emancipation—a strategy the enslaved clearly recognized. Marauding Rebels apprehended a group of fugitives near Vicksburg and prepared to execute Stephen Jordon as their ringleader. As Jordon recalled, "I was the educated one; I was the one that had planned all this devilment . . . and I was to be killed as an example to all the rest." At the last minute, his jailer sold him to a Texas-bound migrant, where he spent the remainder of the war.[95] William Johnson fled northern Virginia after learning that Rebel soldiers planned to take him behind the lines to "be kept safe or sold." Henry Dilworth and Jim Johnson escaped in the Shenandoah Valley "to avoid being sold to Richmond."[96] Amos Williams, a fifty-year-old man enslaved in Virginia's Warren County, meanwhile, fled because his master aspired to "sell us all if he could" and had already sent many people south.[97]

Confederates nevertheless continued pursuing punitive sales. A Mississippian plotted to sell Tom and another fugitive for fear they would soon "be gone again," taking with them the rest of the people he enslaved.[98] Bondsmen and women indeed laid such plans but ran huge risks in doing so. Enslavers whipped, chained, and sold Sam and Thomas in Charleston for securing boats to rescue other Lowcountry slaves.[99] A Gloucester County, Virginia slaveholder hoped to find his recaptured slaves in a Richmond jail "so that they might be sold at once."[100] A few months later, one of his neighbors carried seven people to Richmond after learning they planned to abscond.[101] A Southampton County, Virginia family extracted Dick from Union lines and dispatched him immediately to E. H. Stokes, in one fell swoop punishing him and recouping some of their potential loss.[102]

Even where individual slaveholders risked retaining enslaved people who had once escaped, slaveholding communities often coerced their sale. Such pressure drove a Fauquier County, Virginia enslaver to give her agent carte blanche in handling two enslaved women who had gone with the Federals in the spring of 1862. Upon recapturing them, she found them "very much enraged" at their fate and worried they "would do mischief if they remained here." Her "only wish" was "never to see them again"—a sentiment her community reinforced.[103] Residents of Virginia's Southampton County, perhaps recalling Nat Turner's Rebellion, explicitly demanded the sale of people who had sought the Yankees for fear they would corrupt those who had not.[104] Slaveholding communities thus used the slave trade to excise those they considered tainted by emancipation.

By making precarious enslavers' hold on their human property, the Civil War also reduced their standards in evaluating perceived threats and lowered the bar for selling provocateurs. Many who never reached Union forces—even many who never attempted to do so—faced sale. The Manigaults of Georgia, for example, sold Jack Savage after he hid in the rice swamps for nearly a year. They could have recovered their investment by selling him to a neighbor but refused to do so, fearing that a local sale would not prevent "the corruption that such a Negro would effect on his former companions."[105] In North Carolina, meanwhile, Henry King Burgwyn, generally an enthusiastic speculator in slaves, urged his uncle to sell Ben, whom he considered "a dangerous negro" and a threat to "corrupt a plantation."[106]

As enslavers pursued such sales to offset the war's emancipatory effects, buyers' postures varied. People offered after flight could be bargains or they might prove incendiaries in waiting. In an echo of the terror that inspired antebellum bans on the importation of enslaved people convicted of crimes or suspected of involvement in slave uprisings, many slaveholders grew wary of purchasing potentially dangerous influences.[107] As William Sutherlin worked to acquire enslaved property, for example, concerns over the riskiness of the people available for purchase impeded his aspirations. Silas Omohundro informed him in January 1863 that the only enslaved people available were refugees from North Carolina and that he could not vouch for "anything about their caracters [sic]."[108] Shortly beforehand, another Virginian likewise complained that the slave market was populated by none "but those who have been with the Yankees" who might well "corrupt the whole neighborhood of servants."[109]

Others found fugitives (real or potential) a tempting speculation. Clement Evans, noticing a Black man captured in the wake of First Bull Run, salivated over how much this "likely" man would bring in a distant slave market.[110] Two years later, when Hanover County officials jailed Albert, a fugitive from Richmond's fortifications, a slaveholder not only risked purchasing him, but leveraged his runaway status into a discounted price.[111] For those optimistic about their ability to resist emancipation, and particularly for those nestled in the bosom of the slaveholders' republic, sales of recaptured and vulnerable enslaved people presented a golden opportunity.

The experiences of those retaken and sold reveals how contingent freedom remained for enslaved people during the Civil War. US forces seemingly promised security, but through the slave trade enslavers exploited openings in US policies to evade or overrun weak local authorities. Enslavers claiming allegiance to the United States, for example, slipped through gaps in confiscatory legislation, claimed fugitives from slavery, and sold them before anyone was the wiser. Near New Bern, North Carolina, Nicholas Bray promised to swear a loyalty oath in exchange for a permit to extract Harriet and her sister from Federal lines. He successfully obtained her sister, but Harriet evaded both him and the slave market.[112] Enslaved people who had fled the property of S. L. Burritt, a judge and Federal collaborator, went to similar lengths but with less success. Burritt leveraged aid that he had rendered the Union into permission to regain them, after which he reportedly carried them to Richmond, sold them, and invested the proceeds in land.[113]

Throughout the war, enslavers remained acutely aware of how much enslaved people's flight cost them and defined their loss in terms of the slave market. When Union soldiers passed through John Dickinson's property in May 1862, he noted the flight of five people worth, "according to the price of negroes, about $4000."[114] Joseph Acklen (who married Isaac Franklin's widow and thus oversaw much of the trader's fortune) complained in August 1862 of the loss of eight hundred people whose value, he cried, would "foot up two millions."[115] Such constant attention to market value occasionally worked at cross purposes with slaveholders' efforts to control the enslaved. In 1862, a resident of Gloucester County, Virginia sold a recaptured fugitive without whipping him, fearing that scars would diminish his price. A neighbor exploded at this violation of the communal solidarity he considered essential to slave discipline, fuming that future runaways "ought to be hung or shot & paid for," rather than sold. "It would be economy to do it," he argued, for "it might prevent thousands from going off."[116]

As panicked enslavers worried about their hold over their human chattels, they executed sales at the slightest suspicion that enslaved people might slip beyond their control. In the fluctuating wartime slave market, such transactions might mean accepting a financial loss in absolute terms. Measured alongside the possibility of losing all to the Yankees, however, for many slaveholders the choice was a clear one. A mere two weeks before most of John Berkley Grimball's bondspeople bolted, his son William encouraged his father to cash out. Rather than risk losing them (not to mention feeding and clothing people whose produce he could not sell), William warned his father that "unless you sell you will loose a great deal even if negroes should be high after the war."[117] Similarly, after Edmund Ruffin arrested the flight of much of his enslaved workforce through sale, he complained of the "pecuniary loss" he had sustained—though, he conceded, keeping them would also be costly given their declining productivity and continued threat of escape.

Ruffin had enacted the sale in question during the summer of 1862 when, to prevent them from following family members who had escaped during the Peninsula Campaign, he sold twenty-nine enslaved people in Petersburg. He blamed this transaction entirely on its victims. "Nearly all had shown," he complained, "whether of those who had gone, or those who had remained, almost perfect disregard of their family ties," not to mention the bonds "between the master & his family & the slaves." Selling them, in his mind, merely continued a process they had already initiated, which, an Alabamian in proximate circumstances argued, absolved him "from all complaint on their part and from all conscientious scruples on [his] own."[118] These enslavers justified their actions in paternalist terms, arguing that their captives had violated the code of reciprocity they imagined existed between them. But the eagerness and rapidity with which they sold undermined their aggrieved tone and declarations of paternal affection and displayed an understanding that enslaved people resented their station and would abandon it at the first opportunity.[119]

Throughout the CSA, slaveholders used the slave trade to confront the enemy within, banishing people whose flight threatened the institution. Slave commerce allowed them to confine these transgressors in the Confederate interior, where the laws and police powers of slavery could check them. The persisting value with which they imbued these men and women, moreover, allowed Rebels who considered themselves safe to speculate in enslaved property and those on the front lines to recoup losses they might otherwise suffer. Slave commerce could neither hold emancipation at bay nor entirely offset enslaved people's exodus. But at an individual level, it permitted slaveholders to counter the revolution unleashed by the war and lent them a potent weapon to wield against their bondspeople's aspirations.

By March 1862, Charles Pettigrew's world was among the many that this revolution had begun dismantling. While the North Carolinian still maintained a tenuous hold on the men, women, and children he enslaved, Union forces' advances had them (as one of his neighbors put it) "disapated [sic] with the thought of freedom," displayed through work stoppages, impertinence, and flight. Matters came to a head when local whites, afraid this "dissipation" prefigured an armed uprising, stormed his property to suppress what they considered a nascent slave revolt. Fearing for their lives, Pettigrew reported, his captive laborers demanded that he protect them, "rush[ing] round their master, [and] beg[ging] him 'never to leave them again.'" He knew, however, that this was only an act. With freedom at hand, "any . . . injudicious treatment" on his part could "send a few to the Yankees & then the spell w[ould] be broken."[120]

Pettigrew still possessed one powerful deterrent. As the enslaved knew all too well, if they ended the plantation charade too early, before the balance of power in the region had swung in their favor, he could invoke his preferred response to enslaved resistance: "to sell the ringleaders." Having watched many of Pettigrew's neighbors carry people to Richmond for sale or sell them locally, they knew this was a threat to be taken seriously. With enslavers watching for the slightest rebellion against their authority, the smallest misstep on the part of the enslaved could lead to their dispatch away from family, community, and nascent liberty.[121]

Captives contesting their bondage had always risked the slave trade, but the crisis of the Civil War made enslavers increasingly wary over slippages in their control. Unsettled by visions of a Saint Domingue-style uprising, unmoored by a string of insurrection scares in 1860 and 1861, and unnerved by enslaved people's demonstrations of the lengths to which they would go for freedom, enslavers cracked down.[122] As a result, many captives faced sale for the barest pushback against the slave regime. During the secession crisis, a Virginian reported the sale of several people, including "One... found with a pistol & powder," others who "were not obedient & run about at night," and another whom he simply labeled "a villain."[123] These sales thus removed potential insurgents from enslaved communities and punished transgressors against the racial order.

Flight provoked the bulk of punitive transactions, to the point that a Louisiana enslaver refused to guarantee Farris against "his habit to runaway" during his sale.[124] But enslaved people did not have to actually depart to trigger panicked sales. Fear that they might flee, particularly as Union soldiers approached, sparked a wave of slave commerce. Cushing Biggs Hassell, a merchant and clergyman living only a few miles inland from the Pettigrews, recorded in his diary in June 1862 that "negroes" were "running away almost every night & going to the Yankees." He and his neighbors used slave commerce prophylactically against those whom they feared might go next. One sold Tom and Henry, considering it "advisable" to do so before they "went to the Yankees." Hassell helped another, a woman who had already lost "about 3500 dollars worth" of human property, sell those who remained.[125] These men and women had not yet crossed the plantations' Rubicon (or, in this case, Roanoke River). But as slavery crumbled, enslavers struck first, anticipating flight, heading off financial losses, and strengthening the institution by making public examples of those who threatened it.

Preemptively selling enslaved people prevented the financial losses that slaveholders would suffer should their captive workers make good on their escape, a particular consideration given that fugitives tended to be the prime field hands and "No. 1" women who brought the highest prices in interior markets. As Gloucester County, Virginia's Colin Clarke complained, when US forces arrived, "our negros would all go off, who are valuable." Only those he considered "worthless . . . would remain."[126] Stealing a march on the would-be fugitives, "a good many" of Clarke's neighbors (a Richmond paper noted) were heeding "the experience of others" and selling off people.[127] Clarke considered this a viable option into 1864, instructing his son to "keep an eye on the few servants I have & if you suspect them of wishing to get to the enemy, to sell them & invest the money in any way you please."[128]

Preemptive sales occurred all along the Confederate perimeter as US soldiers arrived. A Spotsylvania enslaver sold away Aaron Carter's mother as the contending armies neared.[129] A Virginia artilleryman, meanwhile, lauded his brother who "sold 5 or 6 of his negroes for fear they would run away."[130] Pitt County, North Carolina's Bryan Grimes managed to sell ten people in early 1863; those he failed to sell, however, were effectively "now free" thanks to the presence of Union forces.[131] An Alabama planter sold off his holdings and captives before fleeing further inland. A South Carolina planter did the same with twenty-five people he feared losing.[132] Failing to offload enslaved people who subsequently fled could inspire a sort of nonseller's remorse. As one Virginian lamented, "It would have been better to have dispensed with the hands . . . valuable as they are," than to lose them to the Federals.[133]

In 1864 and 1865, with Union armies carving the remnants of the slaveholders' republic into ever-smaller portions, enslavers used the slave trade to keep enslaved people away from the liberators and to tap into the slaveholding state's waning power. As Grant moved south, Joseph Treague (living on what would shortly be the Wilderness battlefield) sold Benjamin Frazier and four small children to the Shenandoah Valley.[134] Another enslaver sold Malinda out of the wreck of Confederate Tennessee during the last year of the war.[135] With Sherman's forces burning their way through Georgia, a soldier in the 147th Pennsylvania opened a slave jail holding a reported three hundred enslaved people intended for sale ahead of their arrival.[136] As parts of the Confederacy evaporated, so did enslavers' ability to use the slave trade to preempt losses to the Federals, to punish people who dreamed of liberty, and to preserve their slave society. Sales in the war's latter months, however, reveal the tenacity with which they clung to this vision and the ways slave commerce helped them to tighten their grasp on it.

The impact of enslaved flight was obvious, immediate, and clear. But amid the miasmas of fear and rumor pervading the wartime South, anxious Rebels reacted strongly to smaller contestations of bondage. Physical violence, for example, a reality endemic in the wartime South, both stemmed from threats of sale and resulted in it. A woman recently sold in Atlanta poisoned her enslavers and ran for the advancing Federals, while Sam attacked his captor with an axe and received a trip to the auction block for his troubles. A Virginia woman, meanwhile, turned her axe on herself, cutting off several fingers to diminish her value—perhaps fearing the sexual abuse that might follow her sale.[137]

Enslaved people had always used sickness (feigned or real), theft, and mobility to contest the terms of their bondage.[138] Under the pressures of war, however, enslavers jumped to sell in response to these mild forms of resistance. Catharine, enslaved in Mississippi, suffered from a recurring illness that her enslavers tried to "whip . . . out of her." When this failed, sale loomed. As one put it, "I would rather sell a negro than be always whipping them."[139] Harry's hard drinking led to high doctors' bills and made him "too independent . . . to manage," leading his enslavers to try to offload him.[140] North Carolina's James Gwyn sold Lark for "speculation," likely in purloined goods sold to collaborators in the broader community.[141] Similar concerns about mobility led a North Carolinian to sell a woman and child who stole foodstuffs. Even the self-styled paternalist and colonization advocate John Hartwell Cocke sold Richard to prevent him from moving freely about the countryside.[142]

As slaveholders comprehended the precarity of their control, remarkably trivial behaviors took on apocalyptic casts. When, for example, Frank Smith broke a valuable, ivory-handled knife, his widowed captor sold him. She probably would not have done so, he later mused, save for the fact that she "was gitten worried over the war."[143] Slaveholders sold people for giving them "trouble," for being an "unmitigated rascal," for "getting above himself," or failing to "come square up to the exact line of duty."[144] In a particularly heartrending case, an enslaver sold a woman away from her three-month-old child apparently because she became "insolent and displease[d]" him.[145] While the slave system's erosion offered the enslaved opportunities to pursue their liberties, it also triggered enslavers to sell at the slightest sign of trouble.

These included thought crimes on the part of the enslaved. Moses's enslaver sold him for acquiring "ideas very prevalent in this part of the country since war began"; Wyatt's threatened to do the same because he had become "to much a man of his own head."[146] Slaveholders punished a New Orleans woman for becoming literate by cutting off several of her fingers and then selling her away from the city.[147] Those who revealed pro-Union sentiments faced particularly quick retribution. Mattie Jackson's Missouri enslaver gave her mother to a slave trader for displaying a picture of Abraham Lincoln, while William Pettigrew's overseer demanded Virgil's sale after he gloated that soon "there would be <u>no more slavery & he was glad</u> of it."[148] Mandy similarly taunted Louisiana's Bond family that "the Yankees will come here," rejoicing in the prospective pillaging of the captors she loathed. They promptly sold her, with her enslaver reveling, "I feel as though an incubus had been removed from my presence."[149]

Rebels' efforts to shore up the crumbling institution through sale could, however, accelerate its erosion. Enslaved people who caught wind of slaveholders' plans often fled, risking the uncertainties of life among the Federals rather than acceding to sale. As a member of North Carolina's Kenan family bluntly stated, "many of the negroes have taken alarm believing they were to be sold," which rumors were "well calculated to drive them away."[150] Indeed, the three original "contrabands" whose flight to Fort Monroe in May 1861 inaugurated the United States' emancipationist policies may have sought that refuge to avoid the slave market.[151] As the war ground on, uncounted others imitated their gambit. Jefferson Lovelace made his way into Union lines near Wickliffe, Kentucky in early 1862. When asked what had prompted him to flee, he responded simply, "Sellin' South, boss." The United States, however, betrayed his trust and returned him.[152] Scheduled for sale in Caroline County, Virginia in 1863, Spencer broke for freedom but was stopped short and arrested. His enslaver grew "apprehensive [Spencer] would escape" again and had Hill, Dickinson & Co. sell him. Joe and William, enslaved alongside Spencer, successfully reached Union lines.[153] In coastal South Carolina, Rose had been legally freed by her enslaver, but his relations conspired to sell her and her children. Taking advantage of Federal forces' proximity, they escaped to the safety of their lines. After Charleston slave traders appraised William Summerson and his wife for sale, meanwhile, the pair smuggled themselves to a Union gunboat concealed in barrels.[154]

Even once ensnared by the slave trade, enslaved people fought to extricate themselves from its jaws. In Floyd County, Georgia, a slave trader's acquisitions seized their freedom, while in 1864 a woman belonging to Richmond's Solomon Davis slipped her bonds.[155] Bill, Daniel, Richmond, and Henry made their escape from Robert Clarke's Atlanta pen.[156] Advertisements for people who fled virtually immediately after their sales proliferated. John escaped Richmond only two days after trader Robert

H. Davis acquired him. Plummer departed within three weeks, fourteen-year-old Millie within days.[157] A Florida enslaver, meanwhile, bought Anna and her four children, but they escaped the night before the seller was to hand them over.[158]

As droves of people fled to avoid sale, slaveholders adapted their methods. Where possible, they prepared sales in secret, concealing their plans from their victims. When Archer Anderson urged his mother-in-law to sell the people she enslaved in Virginia's exposed Southampton County and retreat to South Carolina, he warned her not to let them "catch the slightest hint that you are discussing this matter" with slave dealers. If word leaked out, it would spark the very flights she hoped to forestall.[159] Another enslaver used family members as bait to ensnare an enslaved woman so that she could be sold.[160] In some cases, the prospect of resistance was sufficient to forestall a sale. An Alabamian, for example, declined to sell Isaac, fearing that if he did so the others he held in bondage would make their collective escape.[161]

The sales that enslavers pursued during the Civil War point to critical tensions within antebellum slavery. Supported by a scaffold of laws, police mechanisms, and enabling ideologies, slavery as an economic and social system could appear unassailably strong. For much of the Civil War, large portions of this superstructure survived. Simultaneously, however, enslavers' willingness to sell people at the least challenge to the slaveholding order reveals enslavers' endemic fear that any weakness could prove fatal. Rifts within the institution gave the enslaved room to maneuver, while the proximity of US forces provided them with unprecedented leverage. Such fissures, however, also encouraged enslavers to use slave commerce to lock down the institution. The last pulses of the trade in humanity, long slavery's lifeblood, thus oxygenated its death throes.

As enslavers scrambled, US soldiers and ships erased ever more slave markets from the Confederate landscape. August saw Union ships seize control of Mobile Bay. In September 1864, Sherman's forces took Atlanta, destroying both the city and the slave trade it had incubated during the war. A Union soldier specifically marked the city's "negro marts" as kindling for the fires that swept Atlanta as US forces departed. "Our negro property," Sam Richards wailed, "has all vanished into air." Two years earlier, Richards had scorned warnings that such property might prove uncertain. Now he could only mourn, "How I wish I had the value of our city lots and negroes in gold at this juncture."[162] As Sherman's forces closed in on Savannah (destroying smaller slave markets as they went), the traders Blount & Dawson and

Alexander Bryan tried to preserve some of the value that Richards mourned and fled, driving coffles before them. Bryan may have escaped, but the people Blount & Dawson enslaved attacked their captors and vanished.[163] With Columbia, South Carolina next in Sherman's sights, observers commented on the enduring (if deflating) state of the slave market. One man, watching dolls raffled off for hundreds of depreciated dollars at a charitable bazaar, quipped that for the same prices, one could just as easily buy enslaved children.[164]

A diminishing number of Confederates nevertheless shrugged off the impact of such setbacks. One soldier recited the full litany of Rebel defeats but minimized them as the loss of "a few outposts at Mobile, the desolated village of Atlanta, & the possession of the unimportant city of Savannah." Even in light of these events, he remained "as bright as I have ever been" about the CSA's prospects, concluding, "I feel about as sure of success as I have ever done."[165] Some Rebels espoused an overtly religious belief in the Confederacy. A surgeon stationed in South Carolina assured his wife, "I believe, and will" continue "to believe, until proven to the contrary, that if we persevere that God will crown us with victory. Our cause is a righteous cause, and God has promised that he will never forsake the righteous."[166] Still others, like former Virginia governor John Letcher, placed their faith in the survival of Confederate strongholds. "While Richmond is safe," Letcher assured a constituent, "the State is safe, and with the State safe, the Confederacy is safe."[167]

Such flickers of optimism encouraged some Confederates to retain or seek out human property. In December 1864, one South Carolinian denounced his father's efforts to sell the people the family enslaved as "a very bad plan." He advocated instead for keeping their enslaved property from the Yankees, thereby providing a foundation for rebuilding the family's wealth after the war. Poor though the Confederacy's outlook might be, he maintained, "we are a long way off from selling negroes yet."[168] Eastern North Carolina's Michael Cronly took things a step further, exploiting "the confusion and upsettings of war [that] had thrown numbers of them upon the market" to buy people in late 1864. "The ultimate success of the South," he "believ[ed] firmly," would vindicate such purchases.[169] Given that during the last three months of 1864, Hill, Dickinson & Co. sold enslaved people worth more than $1 million (with Lee & Bowman adding nearly $380,000 more), Cronly was clearly not the only purchaser in the market. Even with prices inflated to several thousand dollars a person, these totals represented the sale of several hundred people.[170]

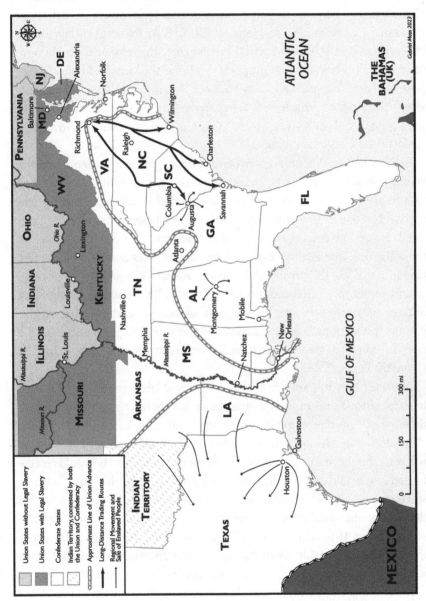

Figure 6.2 The domestic slave trade, autumn 1864. Mossmaps.

Die-hards like these provided counterparts for discouraged Rebels looking to sell in the wake of the CSA's multiplying defeats. Shortly after Philip Sheridan's Union troopers bested Jubal Early's Confederates at Fisher's Hill, a nearby Shenandoah Valley enslaver found purchasers in Richmond for Francis, Eliza Anna, and Margaret Ellen.[171] As the siege of Petersburg ground on, Eliza Harrison advised her daughter that enslaved people were "certainly most troublesome property" and that she "would do well to dispose of them." By year's end, the younger Harrison had followed this advice.[172] Around the same time, a King George County slaveholder worked to sell a woman and child, using buyers in the Confederate interior as insurance against Petersburg's capitulation.[173]

In the war's latter months, enslavers expressed a deep ambivalence over the viability of enslaved property. The relative convergence in the prices required to hire or purchase an enslaved person reflected this fact. As these prices approached one another, the disposal of enslaved laborers became a complicated choice. The costs of feeding and clothing enslaved people mounted in the collapsing Confederacy even as Confederate taxes on enslaved laborers climbed, making the prospect of renting laborers less and less appealing. Hirers, under those circumstances, shouldered all the costs of slaveholding but attained none of the long-term benefits of slave ownership.[174] "I Cant give you any instructions," a South Carolina soldier wrote his father regarding the fate of a woman named Judy. "Either Sell or hire out," he encouraged him, as "[you] think best."[175]

In some cases, this ambivalence gave enslaved laborers additional leeway in shaping the terms of their employment; in others, enslavers simply sold them away.[176] As one Virginia woman suggested to her husband in late 1864, "Why don't you sell one of the servants who is either bringing in nothing, or will run off at the first opportunity?" Even the modest return he would receive by doing so would outpace that obtained by hiring him or her out.[177] Others still feared incurring the total loss of the value of enslaved property. Worried that Richmond would fall in December 1864, one woman demanded that her son sell rather than rent out an enslaved woman to "secure her in the event that the City should fall." With the capital's fate uncertain, she argued, "I do not think she will ever benefit us any and would like to dispose of her."[178]

Even at this late date, some enslavers still viewed the enslaved as viable alternatives to the free-falling Confederate currency. A Virginian offered Rebel money for a person late in 1864, though he acknowledged that both were a "grate risk" given "the condition that our country is in at the preasant."[179] Mary Bell "would not take $3000 . . . in Confederate money" for one man she enslaved, while an Alabamian complained that his wife held more paper money than was wise and yet not enough to purchase an enslaved woman.[180] Ambivalence toward acquiring people grew increasingly widespread. A Virginia woman groused in 1865 that she desired to sell her human property but that the collapsing currency left her with "no way of investing the proceeds."[181] A soldier hoped to do the same, but only if the funds obtained could be immediately invested in land. "I don't want money now," he warned, "unless it is gold or silver."[182] A Confederate congressman expressed relief that a friend had divested himself of his chattels, while a South Carolinian urged his wife to exchange their Confederate money for any property except captive laborers. "Anything," he concluded, "is as good as Confederate money at this time or negroes."[183]

In December 1864, as Sherman advanced on Savannah, Georgia cavalryman Lavender Ray conceded the likelihood of emancipation and urged his father to sell as many as half of the people they enslaved before it could take place. "Negro property," he argued, was "the most uncertain and expensive of any," given the probability the war would "result in the emancipation of slaves, if not immediate . . . gradual." Paradoxically, however, Ray advocated investing the resulting funds through the purchase of new enslaved people, preferably individuals untainted by Confederate impressment or by proximity to freedom. He grounded this assessment in an ongoing hope in Confederate victory. He admitted in February 1865 that the Confederacy's prospects appeared "gloomy enough" but continued to "hope and think we will yet be independent" on the strength of the Confederate armies remaining in the field.[184] Like Ray, Confederates held these ideas in tension. Slave commerce, which remained extant so long as the war's outcome hung in the balance, offered them a crucial way of doing so, combining a means of offsetting the threat of emancipation with investment in their hopes for victory.

As the winter of 1864–1865 crept over the Virginia Tidewater, Mary Pope settled into "the Ropewalk," a Norfolk contraband camp. She was cold, tired, and hungry. Accommodations were spare, provisions sparse, and she and her children (Rachel, Betsey, Albert, and Amos) had not yet acclimated to life in this freedmen's colony. Perhaps cognizant of the conditions they would find, the family had long lingered in slavery in nearby Southampton County. But in late 1864, they and six others suspected that their enslaver, a woman also bearing the surname Pope, "was going to send us to Richmond." This was no idle threat. Mrs. Pope and her neighbors had gradually sold off the better part of the slave community the Popes inhabited. These included Mary's husband, Joe Dardin, whom enslavers traded during the war's first year after the Union presence at Fort Monroe made his visits to Mary and their children an unacceptable risk.[185]

Mary Pope fled in response to the combined weight of Dardin's sale, the proximity of Union forces, and the ongoing threat of the slave trade. That it took such a combination, even for a woman living perhaps a day's walk from US lines, underscores enslavers' persistent power, the contingency of emancipation, and the tragedy injected into freedom's onset by the wartime slave trade. Enslavers like Pope's deployed slave commerce to raise cash and to combat resistance as slavery came under strain; with crises emerging on every side, even Joe Dardin's brief sojourns with his family seemed an existential threat to the system of slavery writ large. By selling Joe, the Popes punished him for his meager liberties. But in doing so, they unwittingly encouraged Mary and her children to seek freedom, steeling them against the risks of flight and of life in a contraband camp, for fear of suffering the same. The dispatch of one man into the heart of the Confederacy thus helped spark his family's liberation. By the time Mary arrived at the Ropewalk, liberty seemed all but inevitable for her and her children. They entered into that liberty, however, deprived of their husband and father. The wartime slave trade had thus struck a blow against the wholeness they had hoped for in freedom, one that redounded through Black lives and families for generations after Appomattox.[186]

7

"Broke ... All Up"

The Ends and Afterlives of the Wartime Slave Trade

In April 1865, the political, social, and military currents running against the Confederacy breached the levees that had long constrained them. On the first of that month Petersburg fell, sending Lee's army into its final retreat, dislodging the Rebel government from Richmond, and provoking Robert Lumpkin's desperate bid to remove his coffle from the city. Just over a week later, the Army of Northern Virginia stacked arms at Appomattox Courthouse. Confederate forces in North Carolina, Alabama, and the trans-Mississippi would surrender in the ensuing weeks, but Lee's agreement with Grant marked the effective end of the bid for an independent slaveholding nation. What precisely would follow remained uncertain.[1]

Less than a month after these events, Harriet Jacobs traveled in a party of abolitionists to Richmond to render material and spiritual aid to the people emerging from slavery. Like many postbellum tourists, the group visited the Confederate capitol and the prisons where Union soldiers had been held before descending into Shockoe Bottom. There, the haunts of Richmond's slave dealers shocked even activists hardened by years of work amid slavery's ruins. Though Union soldiers had opened the pens weeks earlier, the miasma of cruelty accrued over their decades of use had not yet dissipated. "The very air," Quaker abolitionist Julia Wilbur recalled, "was heavy with quiet. We could not breathe freely."

Eventually, they reached the entrance to the infamous Devil's Half Acre. The fifty people whom Lumpkin had tried to stow aboard the last train departing the city were long gone, but the jailer himself remained. Jumping to his feet at the group's arrival, Lumpkin eagerly squired them around his premises. In contrast to Nathaniel B. Hill, who openly boasted of Hill, Dickinson & Co.'s thousands of slave sales (a "hard, hateful man," Wilbur furiously recorded), Lumpkin was obsequious. He assured them that he had treated those he incarcerated kindly, pointing out where (he claimed) they had feasted, sung, even danced. He also described his own enslaved family and summoned his son John for their inspection. "He seemed to think," Wilbur marveled, this "would be a recommendation in our eyes." Most incredibly, Lumpkin claimed to have never bought or sold anybody and expressed his happiness at the liberation of the enslaved.[2]

As this scene unfolded, a crowd gathered in Lumpkin's yard, including many African-American observers curious to see the inside of the jail from the vantage of freedom. His distortions enraged several watchers—among them a young man who had lost a brother to Lumpkin—at which point Jacobs joined the fray.[3] As a child, Jacobs had watched her grandmother sold and had almost lost her brother to the trade. Her enslaver had menaced her with the sale of her children, and she had seen many people she knew disappear through slave commerce.[4] As a result, Lumpkin's disavowal of his culpability drew forth her fury to the point that "he winced under it." The watching crowd, predominantly men and women whom enslavers until recently could have turned over to Lumpkin on the thinnest of pretexts, saw something revolutionary in this confrontation. They were, Wilbur noted, "delighted to hear us talk to Lumpkins. It was a new era in their existence. Where no one either black or white had dared to say a loud word against Slavery. They now heard the plainest kind of talk to a negro trader's face."[5]

Encapsulated in this moment was the profound change the Civil War wrought. Jacobs, whom Lumpkin might once have sold with the consent of her enslaver and support of the slaveholding state, now confronted him on terms of startling equality. The war had stripped away the privileges that property rights in man conferred on enslavers. While freedpeople, white Southerners, and political leaders on all levels would fight over the bounds of Black civil and political equality for decades to come, something fundamental had shifted. The chattel principle, the reduction of a person to a price, no longer operated. With it dissipated a considerable part of the power enslavers had once wielded.

If Jacobs's verbal assault on Lumpkin embodied the war's transformative effects, however, other visitors to the slave market revealed the incompleteness of the national metamorphosis. Several days later, a woman known only as Mrs. Cooper arrived in Richmond. In 1863 or 1864, N. B. Hill had sold Cooper and her daughter to North Carolina and her son to an unknown location. Cooper eventually escaped from bondage during the war. Her daughter did not. After working in an Alexandria hospital for the remainder of the conflict, Cooper rushed at its conclusion to find her lost children. She came to Hill's offices—surely a nightmarish trek—hoping that he or one of his partners might provide some clue as to where they had sold her children. They uniformly refused her request.[6] Cooper no longer belonged to them, but their records did, and no pleas from formerly enslaved people could prevent them from enacting petty revenge for the loss of their livelihoods and the slave system that relied upon them.

The end of the Civil War thus marked a dramatic break with the past. The war's aftermath brought African Americans, in Eric Foner's poignant phrase, "nothing but freedom." The component elements of that freedom were matters over which formerly enslaved people and their former enslavers fought fiercely. The demise of the slave trade did much to embody the triumphs of the Civil War. No matter how much white Southerners strove to render it otherwise, the commodification and sale of laborers that had underpinned their slave society was no more—a fact freedpeople recognized and in which they rejoiced. As they drew on the power of the United States to reconstruct families, to pursue education, and even to assume their place in the governance of the formerly slaveholding states, they not only worked to heal the wounds inflicted by decades of human trafficking but used slave commerce as a powerful rhetorical weapon in their fight for an ever more capacious freedom.[7]

Even as they did so, however, the afterlives of slave commerce haunted people emerging from slavery. They felt the effects of both the wartime and antebellum traffics keenly, but sales that took place amid the conflict took on a particular resonance for the contrast they offered between hope and tragedy.

INFORMATION WANTED.--My daughter, HANNAH BUTLER, formerly owned by Dr. William White, of Deep Creek, Norfolk county, was sold from the auction house of N. B. Hill, of the city of Richmond, one year ago, since which time I have not heard from her.

Any information in regard to my child will be thankfully received by her distressed mother.
TULA BUTLER,
Norfolk City.

de27—4t*

Figure 7.1 "Information Wanted," *Norfolk Virginian*, December 28, 1865. Tula Butler was one of many women who, like Mrs. Cooper, sought children sold by Richmond slave traders during the war. Boston Athenaeum.

These transactions deprived people of kin on the very verge of freedom and denied them the opportunity to enjoy the fullness of the liberation they pursued. They dispatched others to regions far from their loved ones and communities, forcing them to begin their lives anew at a disadvantage that augmented the racial oppression they already confronted. For those seeking family, those eager to establish themselves economically, those aspiring to rise in the postbellum United States, the legacies of the wartime slave trade played a powerful and often tragic role in shaping freedom's dawning.[8]

Two months after Jacobs's arrival in Richmond, former Virginia slave trader James Hargrove stormed into a Lynchburg general store. Pacing the floorboards, he ranted for several frenzied minutes about having "been robbed of everything." He then produced a revolver and, before anyone could intervene, shot himself in the head. Hargrove's infamously "excitable nature" and propensity for violence (he and Hector Davis had once exchanged gunfire on a Richmond thoroughfare) were not solely responsible for his suicide. His death, observers agreed, stemmed from "the breaking down of the Confederate cause" following Appomattox and the personal financial implications thereof: specifically, the loss of thirty enslaved people purchased only three days before Lee's capitulation.[9] His investment, despair, and death underscore Confederates stubborn efforts (as a Louisiana court put it after the war) "to cling to the desperate fortunes of the Confederacy" until the conflict's final days.[10] No matter how desperate these fortunes grew, no matter how likely emancipation became, they sought enslaved people—and explored avenues for selling them—until the war's complete and total end.

Among those sold during the war's last, frenzied moments was Millie Thompson. Born in Virginia around 1825, she had almost certainly been traded before the war to Augusta, Georgia. For most of the conflict, she lived there alongside her husband Philip and their children Nancy, Cary, and Charles. Whether because of enslavers' diverging evaluations of the CSA's prospects, because Millie brought an irresistibly high price, or because she tried and failed to reach freedom, Thompson's enslaver sold her at the last possible moment during the conflict—"just before the surrender of Lee's army," in the words of a Freedmen's Bureau official who met her after the war. The faltering trade in humanity almost certainly bore Thompson back to Virginia. The war's end found her in Washington, DC, working as a cook and fighting to return to her family, especially after word reached her of illness among her children. After months of pleading and bureaucratic fumbling, she succeeded. By the decade's end, the Thompsons had reunited, healing some of the wounds inflicted by the wartime slave trade.[11]

As Millie Thompson moved north during the Confederacy's fading months, Charles Dice traveled south. A member of the 23rd USCI from Prince George's County, Maryland, Dice had joined his comrades in the ill-fated Crater assault in July 1864. Storming into the gap left by Union engineers' detonation of a mine under the Rebels' Petersburg works, Confederates captured Dice after shooting him in the hip and foot and bayoneting him in the calf. As he recovered from these wounds, Confederate authorities transferred Dice to Robert Lumpkin. Lumpkin sold him to Elijah Brittingham, who picked his way through Southside Virginia and the North Carolina Piedmont—two of the increasingly few regions where the CSA retained control—before finally selling him in Charlotte. Dice labored there until freedom found him in the form of George Stoneman's cavalry. As Stoneman's raiders carved through Appalachia, demonstrating the impotence of the various Confederate and state authorities tasked with stopping them, they scooped up Union prisoners and fugitives from slavery. Dice was both, and rode with the troopers to safety in the Union stronghold in eastern Tennessee.[12]

Others joined Thompson and Dice in the slave market as the trade and Confederacy stumbled toward their twin collapse. A trader sent Julia Johnson from Virginia's Shenandoah County to Richmond's Lee & Bowman, while other Virginia enslavers purchased Jefree, Major, and Ishmael.[13] Enslavers sold Camilla at least twice in the war's waning months. Her final sale brought her into the hands of G. V. Ancker, who had relocated from Charleston to Salisbury, North Carolina in the dwindling Confederate heartland. Whether or not he managed to sell Camilla a third time remains unknown.[14] In Hargrove's hometown of Lynchburg, meanwhile, the executor overseeing an estate sale scheduled for March 1865 sought a postponement until the following autumn, hoping there would be renewed interest in enslaved property at that later date.[15]

Late-war transactions could still attain a surprising scale. Lewis Robards recorded no sales in the fall of 1864 but engaged in a final burst of trading that winter. He sold nine people in December 1864, twenty in January 1865—almost exactly what he had managed a year earlier—and five more in February. These men, women, and children sold for an average price approaching $5,000 per person. Robards even found buyers among the

Confederacy's officer corps. A Colonel Langhorn bought Sandy; a Lieutenant Ireland bought John. Even men personally engaged in the failing Confederate fight, who should have been most aware of its diminishing hopes, felt confident investing in enslaved people in the war's waning months.[16]

What drove these buyers to continue accumulating enslaved property in what was increasingly a lost cause? It was certainly not the laughably inflated prices. As one North Carolina soldier grimly joked, "if negroes were selling for a good price," he could make a fortune selling the bedraggled and filthy men serving alongside him.[17] A Tennessean put things more simply. Despite the cartoonish dollar figures enslaved people brought, he found "Negro slavery of no Value, but much Expense."[18] With the present value attributed to enslaved people low, a diminishing number of Confederates continued looking to the future. South Carolina's Eldred Simkins advocated purchasing people on the straightforward grounds that "if we don't succeed the money won't be worth anything and if we do slaves will be worth . . . 1000 times more than now."[19] On a similar logic, Edwin Fay still sought enslaved women in March 1865 but had no viable medium for purchasing them.[20]

Other transactions reflected Confederates' increasingly dire straits. With their currency all but useless, Rebels bartered goods for people and vice versa. A North Carolinian offered lumber products for one enslaved person, while Texans (who outlasted virtually all Rebels by trading people deep into the summer of 1865) regularly exchanged humans for livestock and other goods.[21] In the ironically named Liberty, Texas, merchant James Madison Hall had dealt in slaves throughout the war for the full gamut of reasons his fellow Confederates had embraced. After selling several people to settle a debt in April 1861, he speculated on a young enslaved woman and two men during the Confederate resurgence of 1862–1863. In February 1863, he sold still another woman after she fled his holdings. Hall closed the war in February 1865 by purchasing an enslaved woman named (remarkably) America and her daughter Claudine for ten bales of cotton.[22]

Through formal sales and ad hoc dealings, Confederates persecuted enslaved people up until the very moment the guns fell silent—and, in some cases, into the silence that followed. In besieged Petersburg, a formerly enslaved woman recalled, auctioneers sold men and women until "just before the shelling."[23] One of Virginia's many slave-dealing Davises victimized Esther Jackson, selling her from Richmond to Staunton, Virginia "a short time before the evacuation" of the Confederate capital. A North Carolinian sold Charlotte away from her children just prior to "the surrender," while Armaci

Adams recalled that her enslavers sold people right up to the Confederacy's end.[24] They found some of their buyers in the Rebel ranks. Cavalrymen from Texas likely purchased John Coates following the Crater and sent him southward from Richmond.[25] En route to Appomattox, Rebel cavalryman Thomas Rosser stumbled upon a group of Georgia soldiers giving gold for enslaved people whom they planned to drive south behind the cover of Lee's retreating army—even though that crumbling force remained only hours ahead of their Union pursuers.[26] Even after the surrender, as eminent a Rebel as Thomas Bocock, speaker of the Confederate House of Representatives, saw his way clear to buy sixteen people.[27]

Such transactions represented Confederates' desperate effort to cling to and manipulate commodified African Americans. Foolish as they may seem, the impulse they represented was real and powerful—not least because as the slave trade slowly, finally vanished, so did the vast wealth that it created. Once white Southerners could no longer buy and sell people, they lost the capital stored in their persons. They could no longer translate them into ready cash or use them as collateral. The war's broader effects on the slave system might be ambiguous; Confederates still hoped to compel African Americans' labor, restrain their movements, and curtail their rights. But at a stroke, the end of the slave trade erased the wealth they represented—a figure estimated at $3 billion before the conflict and a total that Confederates had hoped would grow in their independent future.[28]

White Southerners understood all too well the economic catastrophe sparked by the end of the slave trade. As Georgia's Ella Thomas recorded in her diary, "By the surrender of the Southern army slavery became a thing of the past and we were reduced from a state of affluence to comparative poverty." She herself had lost at least $30,000 in the form of enslaved people given her by her parents upon her wedding. Unable to buy, sell, or otherwise commodify these men and women, that sum evaporated.[29] A Mississippian testifying before a postbellum congressional committee captured the potentially devastating nature of this collapse when he stated that the value lost to him through emancipation exceeded that of the rest of his property combined.[30]

Such losses led some Confederates to bewail having engaged in the wartime slave trade and others to regret failing to have done so. A Texas lawyer sought a postwar patronage appointment to redeem the fact that all his previous earnings had been "prudently (as I thought) invested in slaves," all of which was "now gone by emancipation."[31] Gerard Brandon, a Mississippian

196   AN UNHOLY TRAFFIC

Figure 7.2 John Coates. Taken captive and likely sold during the Civil War, John Coates launched a teaching business after the conflict. National Archives and Records Administration.

who had fled to Texas, mourned not having sold when he could have done so, a course he had rejected because "then I had confidence in the powers & people who have lost us our cause."[32] Small wonder, then, that slaveholders made extraordinary efforts to secure some compensation for their losses, some of which they pursued well into the postbellum period.[33] As John Quincy Adams, once enslaved in Virginia, remembered, his enslavers had been "very wealthy," primarily "off of negroes and land," and had regularly laid hands on enslaved children, "say[ing], 'here is $1,000, or $1,500 or $2,000.'" "How much a negro was worth then," Adams marveled, "and now not worth 25 cents a piece."[34]

As the dust settled after Appomattox, the human toll inflicted by wartime slave commerce slowly became clear. It was embodied in the hundreds (perhaps thousands) of women like Mrs. Cooper who took up their pens or to the roads in search of lost loved ones. It underpinned the wide-ranging claims that freedpeople made upon former slaveholders for rights and upon the government for aid and assistance. It became a critical political rallying cry as formerly enslaved people made their voices heard in the councils of the nation. The end of slave commerce proved a defining—often the defining—aspect of freedom for people emerging from bondage. Their words, actions, and efforts, including reclaiming slave trading sites and invoking slave commerce as a means of claiming rights, emphasized the transformation represented by the end of their commodification. At the same time, its legacies—the ongoing harms it inflicted on their families and psyches—underscored the limitations of that freedom in the postwar South.

Though a precise accounting of wartime slave sales remains elusive, the number of transactions in humanity conducted during the conflict surely numbered in the thousands. Their traumatic effects radiated out to touch innumerable Black families. Historian Michael Johnson estimates that as many as a quarter of all the family separations that took place during the late antebellum period occurred amid the war. The war caused these separations in many ways, including flight, refugeeing, kidnapping, and Confederate impressment, but the wartime slave trade was responsible for a sizable portion of them.[35] As a result, even as formerly enslaved people celebrated the dawn of freedom, they also mourned what they had lost. Jubilation and lamentation blended from the war's beginning. In 1861, for example, fugitives in a camp in Leavenworth, Kansas reconnected with loved ones, sang, danced, and generally rejoiced. Amid the broader celebration, however, a group of mothers gathered around a fire, united by the reality that each of them "yet feared what would become of her child" or by their "mourn[ing] for those who, sold South, where [sic] for life separated from her."[36]

As slavery cracked under the pressures of war, African Americans fought to heal the wounds the slave trade had inflicted upon them. Given the degree to which the trade had enabled the division of Black families, it is unsurprising that one of the primary ways in which they did so was by seeking those lost before and during the conflict. Such searches dovetailed with a widespread understanding that restoring and protecting the integrity of their families was a critical part of freedom, making them both intensely personal and highly political acts.[37] African Americans began their hunts for loved ones well before the guns fell silent. Immediately after New Orleans's fall, a Black woman working as a cook for Treasury Secretary Salmon P. Chase asked him to help in finding her daughters, Charity Stamps and Grace York, whom she believed had been sold through the captured city.[38] A few months later, a boy enslaved near the Crescent City made contact with his mother, from whom he had been sold some years before. Informing her that his master was disloyal, he appealed to her to leverage this fact to secure his freedom.[39] After receiving legal documentation of her freedom in St. Louis in 1863, meanwhile, Mary Armstrong set off for Texas in search of her mother, narrowly avoiding being sold herself as she navigated the wartime South.[40]

Free people of color turned the tumultuous wartime slave market to their advantage, exploiting fluctuating slave prices to win freedom for their family members. Harness maker Nicholas Johnson, who had bought his own liberty before the conflict, acquired his wife and two of their children during the secession crisis "just as slave property was falling." He had bought himself for $1,300 but acquired them for a combined $1,000. A third child, Johnson noted, "cost nothing" after he "stole" his family and fled to Kansas due to the ongoing threat of kidnapping and sale. He "thought freedom was coming," he later told a journalist, but "Mr. Lincoln seemed too slow for me."[41] Albert Brooks, who later served on the grand jury for Jefferson Davis's treason case, purchased his own freedom and that of his wife and two of his children during the conflict.[42] Tennessean Miles Childress bought his son Henry, securing legal title to him as a bulwark against slavery's return.[43] The pursuit of such transactions, however, could backfire amid freedom's uneven unfolding. When Louisa Alexander asked her Missouri enslaver to sell her to her husband, Archer, her efforts enraged him. "He flew at me," she informed Archer, "and said I would never get free only at the point of the Baynot." She consequently asked him to employ his own bayonet to win her liberty. Her attempt and her enslaver's reaction show the continuities slaveholders sought to preserve even as the slave system cracked.[44]

Enslaved people's efforts to win control of their families could reach still more desperate tenors. In September 1862, with Harpers Ferry about to fall to Stonewall Jackson's forces, a terrified Ellen begged a female journalist from

New York to take the extraordinary step of purchasing her. Ellen had fled to save herself and her children from the slave market and sought any avenue that would protect her from being recaptured and sold away. The journalist declined, only to see shortly thereafter Ellen and her progeny among those whom the Confederates were rounding up in the town. Their situation was hopeless, Ellen reported, for her enslaver had made it known that "he was coming to take me," her husband, and her children, "to Richmond jail and sell me down South."[45] That Ellen would seek the security offered by an alternate purchaser underscores the tragedy of the wartime slave trade, which permitted enslavers to seize people on the threshold of freedom and render them back into bondage, devastating Black families just as they had achieved that which for decades they had eagerly pursued.

Alongside these scenes, however, unfolded remarkable family reunions as African Americans exploited the enhanced mobility offered by the conflict to seize what they understood to be one of its foremost promises. When a New England officer interviewed an elderly fugitive in eastern North Carolina, she related the loss of her children, grandchildren, and great-grandchildren to slave commerce—including a last grandchild taken while asleep on her knees and sold near Raleigh. "She seemed wonderfully comforted," the officer reported, "when I told her that we meant to go there by-and-by," exclaiming, "Bress de Lord! I shall see my grandchild again."[46] The threat of loss and the possibility of reunion thus coexisted during the Civil War, each a plausible outcome of the profound uncertainty out of which freedom emerged.

A number of these reunions occurred during the conflict. In December 1861, on South Carolina's Sea Islands, David rushed to embrace his wife Lucinda and son Frank, whom enslavers had sold away nearly a decade earlier.[47] Sold just before the war to a man who planned to "get his thousands for her," Tilly likewise escaped. By late 1862 she had not only married, but also had reunited with her mother.[48] Remarkably, Edward Klinkets traced multiple family members who had been "sold separately" during the conflict and brought them together in Washington, DC.[49] Such reunions did not come easily. A northern Virginia man knowingly risked capture and sale to return to the site of his enslavement and rescue his wife.[50] But people emerging from slavery considered the integrity of their families of inestimable value and went to great lengths to rebuild them. Their successes emphasized the triumphs of the conflict, leading one journalist watching families reunite to muse, "surely war has its sweet as well as its bitter fruits."[51]

Freedom's ambiguities, however, rendered reunions far from certain even in theoretically secure areas. One woman enslaved in the District of Columbia escaped with her children to forestall their sale in the war's first year. She laid plans to return in 1862 to convince her husband to flee as well. Her former enslaver, however, found out about these plans and plotted in turn to have her "arrested and sold" should she return to Washington's environs—an outcome that remained plausible despite the abolition of slavery in the District that April.[52] Sarah Burgess, meanwhile, had been sold in Baltimore at the beginning of the war. When she tried to visit a child from whom sale had parted her, her former enslaver screamed, "you damned bitch, what are you doing here?" and struck her on the head with a revolver.[53]

African Americans' opportunities to reconstruct their families expanded considerably following the Confederate surrender. People newly freed from bondage flooded into former slave markets hoping, like Mrs. Cooper, to trace those sold from the point of sale. A correspondent for the *New York Evangelist* encountered a convoy of formerly enslaved people on the Virginia Peninsula headed for Richmond in search of "lost members of families broken up by that relic of heathen savagery—the slave auction block." A Black delegation meeting with Andrew Johnson likewise reported that large numbers of freedmen were flocking to the city to find lost family members.[54] These included a woman named Bess, who walked all the way from Georgia in search of the mother and brother she had lost to the trade.[55]

Some of these seekers succeeded. Garland White, who entered Richmond with the 28th USCI, encountered many "broken-hearted mothers" in Richmond looking for lost children. Among them was his own. She had persistently sought information on his whereabouts from his one-time enslaver, former congressman and Confederate general Robert Toombs and used the knowledge she acquired to facilitate their serendipitous reunion in the fallen capital. White reported, moreover, that their meeting was one of many that he observed.[56] Among those he watched may have been that of George Teamoh, who found family members from whom he had been sold impoverished but alive in Richmond.[57] Other searchers remained deprived of their loved ones. J. H. Holmes found no evidence in the Devil's Half Acre of his family members' fate, while Lucinda Lowery traced her daughter Caroline from a Nashville slave trader to Robert Clarke's Atlanta jail, at which point the trail went cold.[58]

When enslaved people encountered these dead ends, they turned to new allies they had found during the war. These included private charities, Black communal institutions (especially churches), and, crucially, the US government.[59] African Americans' access to governmental authority, particularly through the Freedmen's Bureau, demonstrated the Civil War's revolutionary impact. Enslavers had long depended on the state to preserve their right to hold human property. In the war's aftermath, however, those once bought and sold with its endorsement harnessed the state's assistance to reconstruct their families. A Quaker friend of the Lancaster family encapsulated this transition clearly when the family sought eight members sold from Goldsboro, North Carolina in 1862, suggesting "perhaps getting the Agents in the freedmen's Bureau in Richmond interested in making the search, will be the most likely way to find them."[60] This aid was not always available from the under-staffed Bureau. Nor was it always willingly given, nor always successful. Indeed, the failures and shortcomings of US state action in rectifying the legacies of slave commerce swiftly augured limitations in the project of Reconstruction.[61] Nevertheless, the fact that people who, less than a decade earlier, the Supreme Court had declared anathema to American citizenship could call upon the aid of the government indicated the dramatic changes afoot.

Formerly enslaved people readily sought this assistance. After Memphis's fall in the summer of 1862, Kitty Young lost her children Dallas and Laura when their enslaver carried them to Columbus, Mississippi. When she asked him for information on her children's current whereabouts, however, he withheld it. Kitty appealed to the Bureau, who determined that the enslaver in question had sold Dallas and Laura to Knoxville, Tennessee in 1863 and pursued further information on them in that city.[62] Freedpeople even accessed the highest echelons of the Bureau's hierarchy. Rachel Jenkins, who had found her sold father, brothers, and sisters with the help of the US Christian Commission, contacted the Bureau's head, General Oliver O. Howard, to find her still-missing mother.[63] Requests for information sometimes passed through the hands of nearly a dozen Bureau officials before reaching local agents for on-the-ground inquiries. When, for example, an Augusta, Georgia teacher sought information about Henry and Peyton Barber, sold in Richmond during the war, the Subassistant Commissioner in that city "took special care" to find them, making announcements in local churches and visiting places like Chimborazo Hospital where the two might have worked.[64]

Sometimes the combined efforts of freedpeople and the Bureau produced reunions. As one operative boasted, "The desire for reunion of families (colored) separated in years past by the vile traffic of the slave trader, is general and often, through medium of this office, successful."[65] Its motivations were not purely benevolent. Agents regularly pursued family reunifications to obviate the Bureau's responsibility for destitute freedpeople and to prevent them from developing what it understood as dependence on the government. Whatever the underlying reasons, however, numerous examples suggest there was much truth to this assertion.[66] After several setbacks, agents located the Barbers and relayed their whereabouts to family.[67] Others pinpointed Dallas and Laura Young's sale to "a bookseller on Gay Street in Knoxville," returned Dallas to his mother, and determined Laura was likely living near Lexington, Kentucky.[68] Another found Esther Jackson near Staunton, but warned her parents, "from personal observation . . . I judge she is not well."[69] After Emma Drumgoold returned to her daughters on a sunny summer day, Kate Drumgoold rejoiced, "I would that the whole world could have seen the joy of a mother and her two girls on that heaven-made day." Bureau agents guided her and her children to a refugee camp outside of Petersburg and then to employment in New York.[70]

All too often, however, the destructive effects of the wartime and antebellum slave trades forestalled efforts to reunite Black families. This proved true even when freedpeople possessed specific information about the sale of friends and relatives. Harmon Baker, newly freed in the Shenandoah Valley, had lost his wife, Eliza, and children Bob, Betty, and Amanda, to sale during the war. He suspected a Major Melton had bought them and was holding them at Chester Courthouse, South Carolina. John De Forest, the nearest Bureau agent, reported back that while Eliza and Bob were there, Betty had perished in the intervening years and Amanda had vanished entirely.[71] Many petitioners learned far less about their families' fates. Agents found "no trace" of George and Shirley, sold in Richmond following the Seven Days battles, nor of George Lee, traded away in the war's first year.[72] Martha Ann Levi (or Lewis), herself sold during the conflict, knew the name of the man who had bought her son Charlie in 1862. The Bureau learned, however, that the name was a common one and that several people bearing it had "bought and sold a good many" people "before & during the late war." The sheer volume of wartime slave commerce thus obscured the boy's fate.[73]

Even when the Bureau located freedpeople who had been sold, it could not always return them. Agents traced Cinderella Gwathmey from Virginia to Texas and issued an order for her return. Turnover in the Bureau hierarchy, however, combined with intransigence on her former enslaver's part (and, perhaps, the thirteen-year-old Cinderella's not-unreasonable reluctance to undertake a transcontinental journey) to forestall a reunion with her mother.[74] Former enslavers regularly and actively obstructed family reunions. In North Carolina, a man named Smithwick fought to keep two enslaved children from their mother, whom he had sold during the conflict. Another ex-Confederate struggled to retain Martha, bought and sold three times between 1861 and 1865. A Mississippian held Austin despite having sold him away prior to Appomattox.[75] For Diana, the cost of liberating herself and her infant from her former enslaver proved to be leaving behind her older children.[76]

As Mrs. Cooper did in seeking her daughter, Bureau agents took the logical (if distasteful) step of soliciting ex-slave traders' assistance in repairing the slave trade's damage. Their inconsistent success in extracting the desired information underscores the flaws embedded within the opportunities of postbellum freedom. Freedpeople and Bureau officials sometimes prevailed, advancing the Civil War's revolutionary ends and mending the fissures the wartime slave trade rent in the Black community. But the victors could rarely compel these former Rebels to aid them. Slave traders had backed secession enthusiastically and thrown their support behind the Confederate war effort. In the war's aftermath, they gave rein to their spite toward those who had overthrown it by thwarting formerly enslaved people's searches for family. In doing so, they perpetuated the cause of the Confederacy. The wartime slave trade and its perpetrators thus continued to hinder the spread of freedom even in the conflict's aftermath.

The longest-lasting Confederate stronghold and slave trading fastness, Virginia became the epicenter of these struggles. Albemarle County's Simon Flemming had lost three children to Hector Davis and urged the Bureau to question R. D. James, Davis's nephew, clerk, and successor in the trade, regarding their location.[77] Bureau officials similarly asked R. H. Dickinson for information regarding Dorsey Jefferson and N. M. Lee about Jeff Dunaway (Lee sold Dunaway in December 1863, making him one of three sons his mother lost that month to the slave trade).[78] Going hat in hand to former slave dealers rankled. An official forced to deal with Staunton, Virginia's James Carson declared him "a bitter rebel," while a formerly enslaved person expressed amid the ruins of Charleston's slave market a sentiment surely shared in Richmond: "I cannot like the man who sells his brother and drinks his blood."[79]

Some traders cooperated with the Bureau. Petersburg's Lew Jones, for example, provided clues that helped Susan Jackson find her children Anderson and Priscilla.[80] More often, however, they compounded the harm done by their sales and refused their assistance. True to his reputation, Carson proved unhelpful. The Bureau arrested him when he ignored a summons, but the fact that Carson suffered any consequences whatsoever for his defiance made him an outlier. James openly refused to help locate Flemming's children, while Dickinson and Lee claimed that fires following Richmond's fall had consumed all their relevant documentation—a claim belied by the fact that abolitionists had obtained several sets of Dickinson, Hill & Co.'s records. That Dickinson himself fought to keep a formerly enslaved girl long after the war's end further suggests that intransigence also played a role.[81] Stonewalled by the brokers themselves, at least one agent sought aid from Fleming, an elderly Black man who likely had worked for slave trading firms.[82] While some inquiries proved successful in spite of the slave traders' obstruction, a Bureau agent conceded that the loss or denial "of the books of the large Slave Marts at Richmond" presented a "great obstacle in the way of prosecuting such enquiries," especially when traders spurned the Bureau's requests.[83]

These men's resistance points to the potency of the slave trade's afterlives even when confronted by national authority. Bureau agents, stretched thin across the South and overwhelmed by the violence and injustice riddling the former Confederacy, had limited resources and even fewer recourses for even symbolically confronting the past evils the wartime slave trade represented even when they genuinely desired to do so.[84] Using state agents to coerce defeated Rebels—even slave brokers—into action also contradicted the immediate postwar impulse to restore civilian authority and republican government.[85] The reluctance of the state to back the war's outcomes with force augured ill for the broader project of Reconstruction. As a North Carolina minister hoping to reunite a mother and child separated by an 1863 sale reported, former Rebels might "have a wholesome fear of Uncle Sam and his agents," but their purported acceptance of the new order was but a charade. "Take the agents away," he warned, "and they will return like the dog to his vomit, to their old ways."[86]

Beyond and often in place of state aid, freedpeople developed their own resources and institutions to find loved ones. Black newspapers and religious periodicals swelled with advertisements for those who had disappeared into the wartime slave trade.[87] Sometimes they were successful across years or even decades. Miranda Plummer, sold just before Lincoln's election, returned to her Maryland home shortly after the war's close.[88] "A chance remark" passed from mouth to mouth helped Anna Wright find her daughter, Anna Freeman, in 1892, twenty-nine years after sale had separated them.[89] Thirty-seven years after Margaret Young's enslaver sold her away from her children in Missouri in 1861, her employers chanced to see an advertisement from her son seeking her. She traveled to Chicago, where they reunited and promptly laid plans to find a daughter and sister lost in slavery.[90]

Far more longings for family, however, remained unrequited. Even though some could pinpoint the precise moment of loss—Emily Williams, for example, knew not just when she had lost her children, Philip, Edward, and Sarah, but who had purchased them—deficits in money, communication technology, and mobility kept families apart even after the onset of legal freedom.[91] Ten years after his 1861 sale, Henry Teasley still sought a brother and friends from whom he had been separated.[92] In 1882, S. M. Hightower reached out for relatives lost in the 1863 division of his enslaver's estate.[93] Nearly three decades after the war, a woman sought her sister, sold from Charleston in 1862.[94] Nancy Gardner recalled that for a similar period after her wartime sale, neither she nor her father knew whether the other was alive or dead.[95] Such sentiments fueled an entirely understandable bitterness. More than half a century after Appomattox, Annie Harris refused to allow white people on her property, blaming them collectively for her sister's sale on the eve of the war.[96]

Reversing the slave trade's effects by restoring and protecting their families' integrity was not the only way in which freedpeople used the end of slave commerce to define their freedom. Formerly enslaved people and abolitionists alike contraposed the horrors of the trade against the benefits of a free labor society, seeing in the demise of the former the advent of the latter. "Abolish slavery," an oft-echoed argument ran, "and school-houses will rise upon the ruins of the slave mart," with cascading societal improvements to follow.[97] As Bayley Wyat, a freedman living near Yorktown, Virginia, similarly argued, the terror of losing loved ones to the slave trade—foremost among slavery's evils—had, thanks to "the overrulin' providence of God," been replaced by the "great blessin'" of freedom.[98]

Freedom's blessings became readily apparent in areas like religious and educational life, where the contrast between the evils of slave commerce and postwar realities manifested itself starkly. Enslavers had long denied enslaved people autonomy over their religious lives, fearing independent meetings might be a source of insurrection.[99] The slave trade backed these restrictive efforts. Benjamin Howard, a Black minister in Maryland, remembered being arrested, imprisoned, and eventually sold during the war for "holding meetings" with his congregants. After the conflict, he rejoiced that such days lay in the past. In the wake of the war, African Americans seized autonomy over their religious institutions and rendered their faith communities central to the work of Reconstruction.[100]

Much the same could be said in education, another right enslavers nearly universally denied those they held captive. Education would become a core part of the mission of Reconstruction. Indeed, it would be that which the Freedmen's Bureau pursued longest and most avidly. Freedpeople saw schools as vehicles for their own uplift, while white reformers understood them as a means of civilizing people emerging from slavery and preparing them for citizenship.[101] The changes afoot were embodied in the conversion of slave traders' rooms into facilities of learning. Mary Lumpkin, Robert Lumpkin's enslaved concubine, helped transform the Devil's Half Acre into a school for freedpeople.[102] In New Orleans, Joseph Bruin's former offices became a school, with other former slave pens in the city possibly serving like purposes.[103] Similar scenes repeated themselves in cities and towns from Savannah (where freedpeople appropriated Alexander Bryan's former slave mart) to Alexandria, Virginia, as former captives and their allies converted places of torment into spaces for the pursuit of knowledge and citizenship.[104]

Beyond the creation of schools, formerly enslaved people read freedom broadly into the transformation of slave trading spaces. An African-American sailor returning to Wilmington, North Carolina noted that for all that the war had devastated the city, "there is still a greater change for the better": the absence of "the Auction Block in Market Square where the traffic in human beings used to be carried on" and the transformation of "Traders Jails . . . into military Guard Houses" in which were confined former Confederates.[105] Walter Campbell's New Orleans facility and Lewis Robards's Lexington jail likewise functioned as holding facilities for Rebels.[106] Solomon Davis's Richmond offices became a hub for the distribution of rations to destitute denizens of the city (doubtless including many once exposed to sale there), while the Freedmen's Bureau made Dickinson, Hill & Co.'s into a storehouse.[107] These facilities' fates, however, also reflected some of the war's ambiguities. Richmond authorities used some abandoned slave jails, for example, to hold itinerant workers ensnared by postwar labor regulations. The Bureau also eventually paid rent on some of the facilities it commandeered and soon returned many to ex-slave brokers.[108] Their transformation thus encapsulated the Civil War's revolutionary potential while also indicating its incomplete nature.

As formerly enslaved people fought to expand the freedom they had won through the war, they invoked the memory and impacts of the slave trade to help make their cases. In some instances, they did so in response to immediate needs. In others, they used the slave trade rhetorically to underscore the legitimacy of their demands or to express frustrations with the pace of freedom's advance. Some formerly enslaved people made highly pragmatic claims, demonstrating the ways in which the slave trade had denied them the family support that underpinned the economic vision of a free labor society.[109] Armstead Smith sought his wife Malinda, whom enslavers sold to Alabama in the fall of 1863, so that they could support each other in their old age. Margaret Downey, traded from Petersburg to Raleigh in 1862 or 1863, redoubled her efforts to rejoin her children so she could care for them during an illness.[110] In North Carolina, meanwhile, a group of freedpeople afflicted by smallpox sought public relief partially on the grounds that "their children" had been "sold from them long ago," depriving them of support in their afflictions.[111] Others exploited the language of property rights, long a compelling line of argument for people of color even in the slaveholding South.[112] Ellen Young fought to regain $200 in property lost due to her wartime sale. The Beals family, sold first to Richmond then to South Carolina during the war, requested Freedmen's Bureau aid on the grounds that having been sold, they confronted freedom "with no earthly possessions except the few ragged clothes they wore" and in utter destitution, despite "their energy and determination to help themselves."[113]

Freedpeople also leveraged the legacies of the slave trade to make broader claims on the US government. During the conflict, they sometimes compared Union recruiting practices to slave trading and demanded relief from this exploitation.[114] After the war, landownership moved to the center, the foremost desire of formerly enslaved people and a tentpole of their conception of freedom.[115] Bayley Wyat, after lauding the Union for its role in ending slave commerce, criticized the United States for having expelled freedpeople from lands they had occupied and worked during the conflict. They deserved access to this property, he argued, not least because enslavers had purchased it with money raised through the slave trade. "Our wives, our childern, our husbands has been sold over and over" to obtain them, he declaimed. "For that reason," he concluded, "we have a divine right to the land."[116]

As they watched enslavers mobilize against Reconstruction, formerly enslaved people critiqued their reactionary programs by invoking the slave trade. Any resurrection of a semblance of slave commerce, one of the foremost evils of the slave system in the eyes of the white North, became an immediate injustice to be confronted. When Richmond authorities forced freedpeople to carry passes and compelled them to labor on public projects, African Americans complained to US officials that "all that is needed to restore Slavery in full is the auction-block as it used to be."[117] In the rural South, planters intimidated freedmen and women by threatening them with sale to Cuba if they left the sites of their captivity. Freedpeople promptly reported these threats to the Freedmen's Bureau and, while local officials struggled to act upon them, they nevertheless ascended to the agency's leadership.[118] When former enslavers refused to relinquish their hold on people they had once enslaved, moreover, freedpeople attacked their practices by invoking the slave trade. One aggrieved community—which included several USCT veterans—complained that if any semblance of slave commerce had survived the conflict, "all our Laber was in vain."[119]

As formerly enslaved people moved into the political realm, they also found the slave trade an effective tool for invoking the emancipatory meaning of the Civil War and depicting the costs associated with the nation's failure to enforce the war's revolutionary results. Its demise was cause for celebration. As one periodical rejoiced, people once held captive had "leaped from the auction block to the tribunal," and swiftly moved from "chattel" to "contraband, freedman, soldier, citizen, voter, counselor, magistrate, representative, senator."[120] But people of color also employed the memory of the slave trade as a warning against what they saw as the insufficiently vigorous prosecution of Reconstruction. A group of Black Virginians warned the "Loyal Citizens" of the United States that even though the war had ended, Andrew Johnson's lenient treatment of former Confederates had left them "entirely at the mercy of these subjugated but unconverted rebels, in everything save the privilege of bringing us, our wives, and little ones, to the auction block."[121] A freedman addressing a Tennessee Republican convention advocated rejecting any political coalition that involved compromise with former buyers and sellers in humanity. He argued that "any man who had ever been a slave dealer ought to have his heart strings cut out," adding that if any of his listeners wanted to do it, "he was ready to lead them."[122] Memories of the slave trade thus shaped the ways in which formerly enslaved people understood and defended their freedom in the political sphere.

Such memories resonated because of the myriad and deeply felt trauma the slave trade had inflicted on the Black community. For individuals, the lingering injuries of slave commerce could be severe, even life-altering. As Charles Jackson informed a journalist following his family's sale during the war's early months, this cataclysmic event "broke me all up" and left him sick to the point of death.[123] Harriet's wartime sale from Georgia to North Carolina debilitated her mentally and physically to the point that she could not work and simply answered "yes" to any question posed to her.[124] If Jackson's losses took him to the point of death, sale to a Texan pushed a Memphis man even further, driving him to a public suicide rather than acquiesce to separation from his family. His death moved his enslaver not at all; rather, irked by the loss of "so much money," he "swore excessively at the mutilated corpse of the death-emancipated mulatto."[125]

African Americans carried physical as well as psychological scars out of the wartime slave trade, both of which conditioned the ground on which they encountered freedom. Like Charles Dice and John Coates, the 7th USCI's Moses Johnson had been wounded and captured before Richmond in 1864. His recovery was impeded by the fact that Confederates shuffled him first from a military prison to a public jail, then into the slave jails of N. M. Lee and E. H. Stokes. These movements—and confinement in the insalubrious conditions inherent in slave facilities—incubated disabilities that followed Johnson for the rest of his life.[126] A slave broker sold George W. Matthews (likewise captured in late 1864) to a Lunenburg County, Virginia slaveholder. When his new enslaver forced him to fight a house fire, Matthews suffered a three-story fall and sustained injuries that plagued him for decades thereafter.[127] Not all the injuries Civil War slave commerce inflicted were this tangible. But for all that the demise of the wartime slave trade provided a firm demarcation between slavery and freedom, the legacies of the former permeated the latter thoroughly.

Three days after the Civil War's end, Charlotte Brown sat with other Virginia freedmen and freedwomen debating the meaning of liberty. Much was uncertain: their legal and political rights, the measures of social equality they would enjoy, their access to the fruits of their labor, the integrity of their families, and more. Yet as they sat together, talking all "quiet an' peaceful," an aged woman began to sing:

> Tain't no mo' sellin' today,
> Tain't no mo' hirin' today,

> Tain't no pullin' off shirts today,
> It's stomp down freedom today.

For all the unknowns facing the formerly enslaved, a few things had been settled entirely by the war. Foremost among these changes was the fact that no more would the slave trade plague them, separating them from loved ones and turning their persons and labor into capital for someone else. Many of the war's other outcomes might remain ephemeral, tainted by the legacies of slave commerce, but with the end of the ability to buy and circulate property in man, something had truly, fundamentally, permanently changed. As Brown recalled, the freedpeople celebrated raucously. "Wasn't no more peace dat Sunday... dat was one glorious time!"[128]

The full glory of the times could, however, be long in coming—if it came at all. In the summer of 1907, four decades after Brown's impromptu celebration, John Johnson, a formerly enslaved man living in Talbot County, Maryland, received a letter postmarked in Madison, Louisiana. Its author named himself as Richard Johnson, which surely shocked John beyond imagining. John had once had a brother by that name, but he had disappeared in the fall of 1864 and his family had presumed him dead (their sister Mary had even named one of her children in his memory). In 1863, Richard had joined the 7th USCI. Like Moses Johnson and George Matthews, he had been captured late in 1864 and sold. Possibly his enslaver, Daniel Lloyd, personally urged this course, a small revenge for the family's loss of control over much of its enslaved labor force. His experiences closely mirrored those of Charles Dice. Hill, Dickinson & Co. sold Johnson to a trader heading to North Carolina, who sold him to a hotelkeeper in Greensboro, one of at least three people the proprietor bought during the conflict.[129]

Johnson remained in Greensboro for a year or so after the Civil War, then moved south, first to South Carolina (where he spent close to a decade), then, at the urging of a labor agent, to Louisiana. As a result, his wartime sale resulted in a life lived apart from his Maryland family. "I have not seen nor heard from either of my parents, since the war," Johnson stated in 1906. "The same is true of my brothers." "We all heard you was dead maney years past," John Johnson affirmed; the first indication that they had received otherwise came in the form of a pension agent trying to substantiate Richard's application for US support. Johnson's mother had applied for a pension several years earlier, believing herself entitled to one as Richard's survivor. Though she passed away in the intervening years, his application raised suspicions in a Pension Bureau ever attentive for fraud, especially from African American applicants. The case, an examiner marveled, "is a very peculiar one and sounds more like a story than history." And yet, he concluded, "one seems forced to believe it."[130]

The wartime domestic slave trade thus lived a series of long afterlives for those whom it had deprived of loved ones. They won their liberty during the Civil War and defined their freedom in large part through the end of slave commerce. Families sought one another out. Educational opportunities, religious instruction, and the ability to build and rebuild communities flourished, fulfilling longstanding African American desires that had been hindered by the threat and realities of slave commerce. And yet the full promises of freedom remained nearly as much promise as reality thanks in no small part to the damages inflicted by wartime slave commerce. For all the Freedmen's Bureau's efforts to aid them in their quest for family members lost in captivity, for all the access they gained to state backing, families remained shattered. Years of commodification only translated exceptionally rarely into recompense or restitution.[131] As the formerly enslaved moved into a republic increasingly structured around a vision of free labor and the sanctity of the nuclear family, they entered on terms shaped to a dramatic degree by slave commerce.[132]

Epilogue

In the century and a half following the Civil War, the Devil's Half Acre slowly faded from the Richmond landscape. Robert Lumpkin died in 1866. A year later, Mary Lumpkin rented his property out to the Richmond Theological School for Freedmen (later Virginia Union University). When, three years later, the school relocated, the property began a long deterioration. Lumpkin's buildings became low-rent tenements before giving way to first an iron foundry, then a railroad. In the mid-twentieth century road construction buried the site, much of which now lies beneath Interstate 95. Large parts of the remainder were quite literally paved over for a parking lot. Today, a retaining wall and a screen of vegetation separate the site of Lumpkin's jail from the thousands of drivers who pass through Richmond daily all but unaware of its presence.[1]

The slow erasure of Lumpkin's jail from the cityscape dovetailed with a broader forgetting of the domestic slave trade and the almost total eradication of its connection to the Civil War. Even in the antebellum period, white Southerners had begun distancing themselves from slave commerce. Rhetorically, they rendered it the sole domain of the "negro trader," an ostracized quasi-Yankee who carried on a regrettable and particularly peculiar part of the institution of slavery. This was, of course, an absurd exercise in mental gymnastics designed to insulate enslavers from criticism for their own involvement in slave commerce. But it presaged an overarching—and often successful—effort to disentangle the practitioners of the slave trade from the institution writ large.[2]

While the innumerable Black families sundered by enslavers and their professional slave dealing accomplices never forgot this connection, it largely disappeared from white Americans' collective memory. The withdrawal of many of the most notorious slave dealers from public life aided this shift. Some, like Hector Davis, Silas Omohundro, William S. Deupree (who blew himself up on a mine while working for the Confederate Torpedo Bureau), and Robert Lumpkin, died either during or shortly after the Civil War.[3] Others, like Richard H. Dickinson and Nathaniel B. Hill, faded into obscurity. Dickinson retired to his rural Virginia farm, where he died in the early 1870s. Hill withdrew into the Virginia countryside, where he ran a mercantile business.[4] Still others laundered their slave trading profits into more savory endeavors. Dickinson's and Hill's junior partner, John B. Davis, for example, ran livery stables in Richmond and became wildly successful in banking and other projects. Davis's brother Henry became US Senator from West Virginia; the *Southern Planter and Farmer* noted in a laudatory profile that in his "zeal and ability," the former slave broker "greatly resembles his brother," and was a "character worthy of emulation" for the "youth of our State." Davis's career as a trader received only scant attention. He had worked, the author of this glowing piece noted, for "that old and well-known firm of Hill, Dickerson & Co., traders of this city" (the misspelling of the firm's name emblematic of the forgetting underway). He did not say in what, specifically, Hill, Dickinson & Co. traded, but noted that "many a farmer who reads this sketch, can bear testimony to the well deserved reputation of this firm."[5] With a wink and a nod, thousands of sales of men and women disappeared from the public eye.

As the nineteenth century gave way to the twentieth, historians also excised slave commerce from the study of American slavery, and the institution of slavery from the study of the Civil War. In recent decades, however, interest in both has rebounded. In Richmond, this took on a particularly tangible form. City officials put forward plans to redevelop Shockoe Bottom, prompting renewed interest in Lumpkin's Jail and an archaeological search for its remains. Carving five to ten feet through asphalt, earth, and the accumulated detritus of the intervening decades, investigators uncovered material evidence from the site—ceramic shards dating to the mid-nineteenth century, glass, a child's doll, and, finally, structural remains of the kitchen that fed the people held in Lumpkin's prison.[6] Visitors who successfully navigate the series of one-way streets, detours, and construction fencing between Lumpkin's property and the rest of Shockoe Bottom can now view the barest traces of the Devil's Half Acre, the minimal yet evocative remains of its horrific past.

Change, however, is in the air. After a long campaign by local activists, in early 2022, the city of Richmond allocated money to be used for the creation of a museum of American slavery near the site, one visible to all those passing on the interstate, and one that if constructed, will tell the history of the nation's enslaving past. The proposed redevelopment of the Lumpkin site is an appropriate companion to the ways in which Americans are reconsidering both

Figure E.1 Site of Lumpkin's jail. Today, the Devil's Half Acre sits between a parking lot and the retaining wall on which runs Interstate 95, but is the site of a proposed museum exploring the history of enslavement. July 12, 2023. Photograph by the author.

the place of slavery in their national life and the costs the Civil War inflicted upon the United States. Historians have revised upward estimates of the war's death toll and have looked beyond the battlefield to include the civilians and enslaved people who perished during the conflict. They have counted the damage the war wrought upon flora, fauna, and the landscape. And they have lengthened the war's chronological bounds, exploring the ways in which the Civil War resounded through the decades in the minds of those who fought in it.[7] Studies of the war's memory, moreover, assess its impact on the nation it produced, from the ways in which it shaped the development of social policies to the human costs of its ideological legacies—as exemplified in cities like Charleston and Charlottesville, where racial violence erupted within a few hundred yards of former slave trading spaces.[8]

Including the thousands of men, women, and children sold during the Civil War in this reevaluation of the conflict's human toll is critical in comprehending the scale of the war's tragedy, the price of advancing the cause of freedom, and the dramatis personae of those who paid that price. It aligns understandings of the War for the Union with Nell Irvin Painter's call for a consideration of the psychological costs slavery inflicted upon those caught up in it. The ongoing "soul murder" she details—the mental and emotional ruin that sale, separation, and commodification left upon those held as chattels—remained in effect throughout the war that produced their liberty, and must be accounted for as part of that war's history.[9] Throughout the Civil War, Confederates preyed upon African Americans physically and emotionally to advance their own causes: to cash in on the conflict, to create the materiel required to fight the war, and to insulate themselves against the negative effects of the forces they had unleashed. They particularly sacrificed those they enslaved to suppress the emergence of Black freedom. For decades thereafter, enslaved people marked these moments, stored them away, and sought to rectify them as best they could. The story of their struggle deserves to be heeded.

In April 1863, Julia Wilbur, Harriet Jacobs, and many others visited an Alexandria, Virginia slave pen that until the onset of war, Joseph Bruin had operated. The facility had a "stylish front" and looked at first glance "like a gentleman's country house." Closer inspection, however, revealed the "dungeons below." Examining these prisons moved them all, but especially Jacobs, deeply. In an effort to use physical artifacts to magnify the significance of such spaces in the war against slavery, Wilbur came away with various instruments of confinement—a staple, a bolt, and a chain once used to bind enslaved people's ankles—and with an impetus to share the stories of those who suffered in that place. "A volume," she believed, "might be written about what I have seen today," though, she acknowledged, "If God has patience, I suppose I must be satisfied to wait."[10] Wilbur never compiled her study of the horrors of the slave trade she encountered during the war. Nor, in the intervening years, has anyone else done so. But with slave trading facilities like those operated by Franklin & Armfield and Robert Lumpkin sitting at the center of reevaluations of slavery's place in American life, the stories of the slave trade, its victims, and the war required to destroy it are now more essential than ever.[11]

Notes

Abbreviations

Archives, Microfilm Collections, and Databases

CHM	Chicago History Museum
DBCAH	Dolph Briscoe Center for American History, University of Texas, Austin
DHCRC	Dickinson, Hill & Co. Records and Correspondence, Digital Collections and Archives, Tufts University
Duke	David M. Rubenstein Rare Book & Manuscript Library, Duke University
Emory	Stuart A. Rose Manuscript, Archives, and Rare Book Library, Emory University
FSSP	Freedmen and Southern Society Project, University of Maryland, College Park
GLC	Gilder Lehrman Collection, Gilder Lehrman Institute of American History, New York
HL	The Huntington Library, San Marino, California
HNOC	Williams Research Center, Historic New Orleans Collection
LC	Library of Congress
LS	Last Seen: Finding Family After Slavery
LVA	Library of Virginia
MHS	Minnesota Historical Society
NARA	National Archives and Records Administration
NCDAH	North Carolina Department of Archives and History
NYHS	New-York Historical Society
OIEAHC	Omohundro Institute for Early American History and Culture
OPCO	Orleans Parish Conveyance Office
OPNA	Orleans Parish Notarial Archives
OR	*Official Records of the War of the Rebellion*
RASP	Records of Antebellum Southern Plantations from the Revolution to the Civil War
RSFB	Race, Slavery, and Free Blacks: Petitions to Southern Legislatures and County Courts, 1775–1867
RSPEGM	Records of Southern Plantations from Emancipation to the Great Migration
SCHS	South Carolina Historical Society

SCL	South Caroliniana Library, University of South Carolina
SHC	Southern Historical Collection, Wilson Library, University of North Carolina at Chapel Hill
SUSC-AAS	Slavery in the United States Collection, 1703–1905, American Antiquarian Society
UGA	Hargrett Rare Book and Manuscript Library, The University of Georgia Libraries
UVA	Albert and Shirley Small Special Collections Library, University of Virginia, Charlottesville, Va.
VHS	Virginia Museum of History and Culture (formerly the Virginia Historical Society)
VS	Valley of the Shadow: Two Communities in the American Civil War, University of Virginia Library

Bureau of Refugees, Freedmen and Abandon Lands

AS	Assistant Superintendent
ASC	Assistant Subcommissioner
DCFOR	Washington, DC and Georgetown Field Office Records
LS	Local Superintendent
NCFOR	North Carolina Field Office Records
SC	Subcommissioner
VAFOR	Virginia Field Office Records

Introduction

1. Charles Carleton Coffin, *Freedom Triumphant: The Fourth Period of the War of the Rebellion* (New York: Harper & Brothers, 1891), 422; Maurie D. McInnis, "Mapping the Slave Trade in Richmond and New Orleans," Buildings & Landscapes, 20, no. 2 (Fall 2013), 105–110; H. Cowles Atwater, *Incidents of a Southern Tour: or The South, As Seen With Northern Eyes* (Boston: J. P. Magee, 1857), 34–35; Maury Brothers to Samuel Mordecai, May 4, 1857, Mordecai Family Papers, SHC. On the evolution of Richmond's slave market, see Frederic Bancroft, *Slave Trading in the Old South* (1931; repr. Columbia: University of South Carolina Press, 1996), 88–119; Michael Tadman, *Speculators and Slaves: Masters, Traders, and Slaves in the Old South* (Madison: University of Wisconsin Press, 1989), 57–64; Robert H. Gudmestad, "The Richmond Slave Market, 1840–1860" (MA thesis, University of Richmond, 1993); Calvin Schermerhorn, *The Business of Slavery and the Rise of American Capitalism* (New Haven, CT: Yale University Press, 2015), 52–56, 126–129, 143–147; Alexandra Finley, "Cash to Corinna: Domestic Labor and Sexual Economy in the 'Fancy Trade,'" *Journal of American History* 104, no. 2 (September 2017): 410–430.

2. "Five Hundred Dollar Reward," *Richmond Daily Dispatch*, February 12, 1865; "Two Hundred Dollars Reward," *Richmond Whig*, January 16, 1865; Deposition of Charles Dice, September 17, 1901; Dice to Pension Office, May 27, 1902, Charles Dice, File 634.433, RG 15: Records of the Department of Veterans Affairs, NARA. On the explosive growth of the Confederate capital, see Emory M. Thomas, *The Confederate State*

of Richmond: A Biography of the Capital (Austin: University of Texas Press, 1971); Midori Takagi, "Rearing Wolves to Our Own Destruction": Slavery in Richmond, Virginia, 1782–1865 (Charlottesville: University Press of Virginia, 1999), 124–144; Stephen V. Ash, Rebel Richmond: Life and Death in the Confederate Capital (Chapel Hill: University of North Carolina Press, 2019); Mary DeCredico, Confederate Citadel: Richmond and Its People at War (Lexington: University Press of Kentucky, 2020).
3. Phoebe Yates Pember, A Southern Woman's Story: Life in Confederate Richmond (Jackson: McCowat-Mercer Press, 1959), 130; Coffin, Freedom Triumphant, 422.
4. Coffin, Freedom Triumphant, 422.
5. Nor did many official records make it onto the trains, resulting in their widespread destruction. Keith S. Bohanon, "Many Valuable Records and Documents Were Lost to History: The Destruction of Confederate Military Records during the Appomattox Campaign," in Petersburg to Appomattox: The End of the War in Virginia, ed. Caroline Janney (Chapel Hill: University of North Carolina Press, 2018), 170–191.
6. William Ira Smith, Map of a Part of the City of Richmond Showing the Burnt Districts (Richmond, VA: Richmond Whig, 1865), LC, https://www.loc.gov/item/99448330 (accessed July 24, 2023). "Letter from Richmond," Christian Recorder, April 22, 1865; R. J. M. Blackett, Thomas Morris Chester, Black Civil War Correspondent (Baton Rouge: Louisiana State University Press, 1989), 288–293, 296–297; Coffin, Freedom Triumphant, 422; Maurie D. McInnis, Slaves Waiting for Sale: Abolitionist Art and the American Slave Trade (Chicago: University of Chicago Press, 2011), 215–216.
7. Coffin, Freedom Triumphant, 422; "Letter from Richmond," Christian Recorder, April 22, 1865. See Leon F. Litwack, Been in the Storm So Long: The Aftermath of Slavery (New York: Knopf, 2010), 167–168; James Oliver Horton and Lois E. Horton, Hard Road to Freedom: The Story of African America (New Brunswick, NJ: Rutgers University Press, 2001), 180; Bruce Levine, The Fall of the House of Dixie: The Civil War and the Social Revolution that Transformed the South (New York: Random House, 2013), 273; David L. Lightner, Slavery and the Commerce Power: How the Struggle Against the Interstate Slave Trade Led to the Civil War (New Haven, CT: Yale University Press, 2006), 178.
8. Jeffrey Kerr-Ritchie, Rebellious Passage: The Creole Revolt and America's Coastal Slave Trade (New York: Cambridge University Press, 2019), 87; Jeff Forret, Slave Against Slave: Plantation Violence in the Old South (Baton Rouge: Louisiana State University Press, 2015), 143; Governor's Message and Annual Reports of the Public Officers of the State, and of the Boards of Directors, Visitors, Superintendents, and Other Agents of Public Institutions or Interests in Virginia (Richmond: Samuel Shepherd, 1849), 5; January 18, 1849, Robert Lumpkin Account Book, Valentine Museum; Charles Emery Stevens, Anthony Burns: A History (Boston: John P. Jewett and Company, 1856), 187–195; Charles H. Corey, A History of the Richmond Theological Seminary, with Reminiscences of Thirty Years' Work Among the Colored People of the South (Richmond, VA: J. W. Randolph Company, 1895), 46–50, 74–78.
9. Writers Program, Works Progress Administration, The Negro in Virginia (New York: Hastings House, 1940), 164; "Slave Days: Extract from the Autobiography of Otis Bigelow," Frederic Bancroft Papers, Columbia University Rare Book and Manuscript Library. On slave traders' social position, see Michael Tadman, "The Reputation of

the Slave Trader in Southern History and the Social Memory of the South," *American Nineteenth Century History* 8, no. 3 (September 2007): 247–271.

10. On Mary Lumpkin, see Phillip Troutman, "'Black' Concubines, 'Yellow' Wives, 'White' Children: Race and Domestic Space in the Slave Trading Households of Robert & Mary Lumpkin and Silas & Corinna Omohundro," unpublished paper presented at the Southern Association of Women Historians, 2003 (accessed via academia.edu, October 8, 2018); Corey, *A History of the Richmond Theological Seminary*, 46–50, 74–78. Other enslavers pursued similar relationships, including Hector Davis, Silas Omohundro, and, reportedly, Richard H. Dickinson. See Alexandra Finley, *An Intimate Economy: Enslaved Women, Work and America's Domestic Slave Trade* (Chapel Hill: University of North Carolina Press, 2020), 37 and "Cash to Corinna," 410–430; Joshua D. Rothman, *Notorious in the Neighborhood: Sex and Families across the Color Line in Virginia, 1787–1861* (Chapel Hill: University of North Carolina Press, 2003), 114; Hank Trent, *The Secret Life of Bacon Tait, A White Slave Trader Married to a Free Woman of Color* (Baton Rouge: Louisiana State University Press, 2017); Edward E. Baptist, "'Cuffy,' Fancy Maids,' and 'One-Eyed Men': Rape, Commodification, and the Domestic Slave Trade in the United States," *American Historical Review* 106, no. 5 (December 2001): 1619–1650.

11. Michael Guasco, *Slaves and Englishmen: Human Bondage in the Early Modern Atlantic World* (Philadelphia: University of Pennsylvania Press, 2014), 195–226; Peter H. Wood, *Black Majority: Negroes in Colonial South Carolina From 1670 Through the Stono Rebellion* (New York: Norton, 1974); Edmund S. Morgan, *American Slavery, American Freedom: The Ordeal of Colonial Virginia* (New York: Norton, 1975); John J. McCusker and Russell R. Menard, *The Economy of British America, 1607–1789* (Chapel Hill: University of North Carolina Press for the Institute for Early American History and Culture, 1984), 134–143, 169–188; Allan Kulikoff, *Tobacco and Slaves: The Development of Southern Cultures in the Chesapeake, 1680–1800* (Chapel Hill: University of North Carolina Press for the OIEAHC, 1986); Robert Fogel, *Without Consent or Contract: The Rise and Fall of American Slavery* (New York: Norton, 1989), 30–31; Kathleen M. Brown, *Good Wives, Nasty Wenches, and Anxious Patriarchs: Gender, Race, and Power in Colonial Virginia* (Chapel Hill: University of North Carolina Press for the OIEAHC, 1996); Ira Berlin, *Many Thousands Gone: The First Two Centuries of Slavery in North America* (Cambridge, MA: The Belknap Press of Harvard University Press, 1998); Philip D. Morgan, *Slave Counterpoint: Black Culture in the Eighteenth-Century Chesapeake & Lowcountry* (Chapel Hill: University of North Carolina Press for the OIEAHC, 1998); Jennifer Morgan, *Laboring Women: Reproduction and Gender in New World Slavery* (Philadelphia: University of Pennsylvania Press, 2004), 69–106, 144–165; Gregory E. O'Malley, *Final Passages: The Intercolonial Slave Trade of British America, 1619–1807* (Chapel Hill: University of North Carolina Press for the OIEAHC, 2014), 171–218, 264–290; Ryan A. Quintana, *Making a Slave State: Political Development in Early South Carolina* (Chapel Hill: University of North Carolina Press, 2018), 15–88.

12. Lorena S. Walsh, *Motives of Honor, Pleasure, and Profit: Plantation Management in the Colonial Chesapeake, 1607–1763* (Chapel Hill: University of North Carolina Press

for the OIEAHC, 2012), 246–247; Steven Deyle, "The Irony of Liberty: Origins of the Domestic Slave Trade," *Journal of the Early Republic* 12, no. 1 (Spring 1992): 37–62 and "'By farr the most profitable trade': Slave Trading in British Colonial North America," *Slavery & Abolition* 10, no. 2 (1989): 107–125.

13. Lewis Cecil Gray, *History of Agriculture in the Southern United States to 1860* (Washington, DC: Carnegie Institution of Washington, 1933), 2 vols., II: 606–609, 673–720, 888–915; Damian Alan Pargas, *The Quarters and the Fields: Slave Families in the Non-Cotton South* (Gainesville: University of Florida Press, 2010), 15–21; Barbara J. Fields, *Slavery and Freedom on the Middle Ground: Maryland During the Nineteenth Century* (New Haven, CT: Yale University Press, 1985), 4–22; Calvin Schermerhorn, *Money over Mastery, Family over Freedom: Slavery in the Antebellum Upper South* (Baltimore: Johns Hopkins University Press, 2011), 4–21; Steven Deyle, "An 'Abominable' New Trade: The Closing of the African Slave Trade and the Changing Patterns of U.S. Political Power, 1808–60," *William and Mary Quarterly* 66, no. 4 (October 2009): 833–850; Sven Beckert, *Empire of Cotton: A Global History* (New York: Knopf, 2014), 29–42, 63–74, 119, 121, 136–165, 180, 206, 248; Gavin Wright, *The Political Economy of the Cotton South: Households, Markets, and Wealth in the Nineteenth Century* (New York: Norton, 1978), 44–55, 114–116, 129–130; James Oakes, *The Ruling Race: A History of American Slaveholders* (New York: Knopf, 1982); John Hebron Moore, *The Emergence of the Cotton Kingdom in the Old Southwest: Mississippi, 1770–1860* (Baton Rouge: Louisiana State University Press, 1988); Adam Rothman, *Slave Country: American Expansion and the Origins of the Deep South* (Cambridge, MA: Harvard University Press, 2005); Joshua D. Rothman, *Flush Times and Fever Dreams: A Story of Capitalism and Slavery in the Age of Jackson* (Athens: University of Georgia Press, 2012); Walter Johnson, *River of Dark Dreams: Slavery and Empire in the Cotton Kingdom* (Cambridge, MA: The Belknap Press of Harvard University Press, 2013); Edward E. Baptist, *The Half Has Never Been Told: Slavery and the Making of American Capitalism* (New York: Basic Books, 2014).
14. Tadman, *Speculators and Slaves*; Walter Johnson, *Soul By Soul: Life Inside the Antebellum Slave Market* (Cambridge MA: Harvard University Press, 1999); Steven Deyle, *Carry Me Back: The Domestic Slave Trade in American Life* (New York: Oxford University Press, 2005); Robert H. Gudmestad, *A Troublesome Commerce: The Transformation of the Interstate Slave Trade* (Baton Rouge: Louisiana State University Press, 2003); Lightner, *Slavery and the Commerce Power*; Schermerhorn, *The Business of Slavery*; Finley, *An Intimate Economy*; Joshua D. Rothman, *The Ledger and the Chain: How Domestic Slave Traders Shaped America* (New York: Basic Books, 2021).
15. Tadman, *Speculators and Slaves*, 169–178; Jonathan Pritchett, "Quantitative Estimates of the United States Interregional Slave Trade, 1820–1860," *Journal of Economic History* 61, no. 2 (June 2001): 467–475.
16. Herbert Gutman, *Slavery and the Numbers Game: A Critique of Time on the Cross* (Urbana: University of Illinois Press, 1975), 124–126.
17. Daina Ramey Berry, *The Price For Their Pound of Flesh: The Value of the Enslaved, from Womb to Grave, in the Building of a Nation* (Boston: Beacon Press, 2017). On reproductive labor, see also Deborah Gray White, *Ar'n't I A Woman? Female Slaves*

in the Plantation South (1986; repr. New York: Norton, 1999)), 62–118; Morgan, Laboring Women; Baptist, The Half Has Never Been Told, 233–244; Deirdre Cooper Owens, Medical Bondage: Race, Gender, and the Origins of American Gynecology (Athens: University of Georgia Press, 2017).

18. James L. Huston, Calculating the Value of the Union: Slavery, Property Rights, and the Economic Origins of the Civil War (Chapel Hill: University of North Carolina Press, 2003), 27–29; Roger Ransom and Richard Sutch, "Capitalists Without Capital: The Burden of Slavery and the Impact of Emancipation," Agricultural History 62, no. 3 (Summer 1988): 133–160; Eugene Genovese, The Political Economy of Slavery: Studies in the Economy and Society of the Slave South (1968; repr. Middletown, CT: Wesleyan University Press, 1989), 33–51; John Ashworth, Slavery, Capitalism, and Politics in the Antebellum Republic. Volume I: Commerce and Compromise, 1820–1850 (New York: Cambridge University Press, 1996), 93–121; Johnson, Soul By Soul, 107–112, 135–161 and River of Dark Dreams, 12–14, 222–228; Bonnie Martin, "Slavery's Invisible Engine: Mortgaging Human Property," Journal of Southern History 76, no. 4 (November 2010): 817–866; Richard Holcombe Kilbourne Jr., Debt, Investment, Slaves: Credit Relations in East Feliciana Parish, Louisiana, 1825–1885 (Tuscaloosa: University of Alabama Press, 1995); Kathryn Boodry, "August Belmont and the World the Slaves Made," in Slavery's Capitalism: A New History of American Economic Development, ed. Sven Beckert and Seth Rockman (Philadelphia: University of Pennsylvania Press, 2016), 163–179; Karen Ryder, "To Realize Money Facilities: Slave Life Insurance, The Slave Trade, and Credit in the Old South," in New Directions in Slavery Studies: Commodification, Community, and Comparison, ed. Jeff Forret and Christine E. Sears (Baton Rouge: Louisiana State University Press, 2015), 53–71; Schermerhorn, The Business of Slavery, 95–123; McInnis, Slaves Waiting for Sale, 87; Sharon Ann Murphy, "The Financialization of Slavery by the First and Second Banks of the United States," Journal of Southern History 87, no. 3 (August 2021): 385–426.

19. William J. Cooper, Jr., Thomas E. Terrill, and Christopher Childers, The American South: A History, 5th Edition (Lanham, MD: Rowman & Littlefield, 2016) (2 vols.), I: 216; Johnson, Soul By Soul, 1–17; Deyle, Carry Me Back, 41–93, 206–244; Baptist, "'Cuffy,' Fancy Maids,' and 'One-Eyed Men,'" 1619–1650. On the benefits of the racial caste system for white Southerners, see George Fredrickson, The Black Image in the White Mind: The Debate on Afro-American Character and Destiny, 1817–1914 (New York: Harper & Row, 1971), 44–96; David Roediger, The Wages of Whiteness: Race and the Making of the American Working Class (London: Verso, 1991). On the ways slavery shaped Southern economic development, see Genovese, The Political Economy of Slavery; Fred Bateman and Thomas Weiss, A Deplorable Scarcity: The Failure of Industrialization in the Slave Economy (Chapel Hill: University of North Carolina Press, 1981), 113–127, 160–163; Harry L. Watson, "Slavery and Development in a Dual Economy: The South and the Market Revolution," in The Market Revolution in America: Social, Political, and Religious Expressions, 1800–1880, ed. Melvyn Stokes and Stephen Conway (Charlottesville: University Press of Virginia, 1996), 43–73; John Majewski, A House Dividing: Economic Development in Pennsylvania and Virginia Before the Civil War (New York: Cambridge University Press, 2000),

especially 141–167; Keri Leigh Merritt, *Masterless Men: Poor Whites and Slavery in the Antebellum South* (New York: Cambridge University Press, 2017).

20. Ulrich B. Phillips, *American Negro Slavery: A Survey of the Supply, Employment, and Control of Negro Labor as Determined by the Plantation Regime* (New York: D. Appleton & Company, 1918); Winfield H. Collins, *The Domestic Slave Trade of the Southern States* (New York: Broadway Publishing Company, 1904); Wendell Stephenson, *Isaac Franklin: Slave Trader and Planter of the Old South* (University: Louisiana State University Press, 1938). A notable exception is Frederic Bancroft, whose 1931 *Slave Trading in the Old South* challenged those inclined to minimize the traffic in slaves. Even Stanley Elkins's vituperative critique of slavery, however, devoted only scant attention to the slave trade. Elkins, *Slavery: A Problem in American Institutional and Intellectual Life* (Chicago: University of Chicago Press, 1968), 40, 211. Eugene Genovese, Robert Fogel, and Stanley Engerman largely downplayed the scale and importance of slave trading, though for different reasons. Genovese, *Roll, Jordan, Roll: The World the Slaves Made* (New York: Vintage Books, 1974); Fogel and Engerman, *Time on the Cross: The Economics of American Negro Slavery* (2 vols.) (Boston: Little, Brown & Co., 1974), I: 44–52, 126–130. Other signal works on slavery during the 1970s, including John Blassingame, *The Slave Community: Plantation Life in the Antebellum South* (New York: Oxford University Press, 1972); Herbert Gutman, *The Black Family in Slavery and Freedom, 1750–1925* (New York: Pantheon Books, 1976); Lawrence Levine, *Black Culture and Black Consciousness: Afro-American Folk Thought From Slavery to Freedom* (New York: Oxford University Press, 1977); and Albert J. Raboteau, *Slave Religion: the "Invisible Institution" in the Antebellum South* (New York: Oxford University Press, 1978) emphasized the strength and resilience of the Black community under the pressures of slavery, relegating the slave trade to the background. See also William Calderhead, "How Extensive Was the Border State Slave Trade?: A New Look," *Civil War History* 18, no. 1 (March 1972): 42–55 and "The Role of the Professional Slave Trader in a Slave Economy: Austin Woolfolk, a Case Study," *Civil War History* 23, no. 3 (September 1977): 195–211; Gutman, *Slavery and the Numbers Game*, 102–118.

21. On slave trading and American political economy, in addition to works already cited, see Rothman, *Slave Country* and Matthew Mason, *Slavery and Politics in the Early American Republic* (Chapel Hill: University of North Carolina Press, 2006), 163–176. On gender and the slave trade, see also Stephanie Jones-Rogers, *They Were Her Property: White Women as Slave Owners in the American South* (New Haven, CT: Yale University Press, 2019). For studies of the slave trade's impact on enslaved communities, see Brenda Stevenson, *Life in Black and White: Family and Community in the Slave South* (New York: Oxford University Press, 1997), 175–204; Lynda J. Morgan, *Emancipation in Virginia's Tobacco Belt, 1850–1870* (Athens: University of Georgia Press, 1992), 35–42; Edward E. Baptist, *Creating an Old South: Middle Florida's Plantation Frontier Before the Civil War* (Chapel Hill: University of North Carolina Press, 2002), 61–88; Richard Follett, *The Sugar Masters: Planters and Slaves in Louisiana's Cane World, 1820–1860* (Baton Rouge: Louisiana State University Press, 2005), 52–65; Schermerhorn, *Money Over Mastery*; Rothman, *Flush Times and Fever Dreams*; Berry, *The Price for Their Pound of Flesh*.

22. Deyle, *Carry Me Back*, 40–62; Tadman, *Speculators and Slaves*, 47–108; Johnson, *Soul By Soul*, 78–116, 135–161 (quote on p. 17); Walter Johnson, "Introduction: The Future Store," in Johnson, *The Chattel Principle*, 1–31; Baptist, *The Half Has Never Been Told*, 171–259.

23. The existing corpus of scholarship on the wartime slave trade consists of Bell Irvin Wiley, *Southern Negroes, 1861–1865* (Baton Rouge: Louisiana State University Press, 1974), 85–98; Robert Leo Mooren, "The Slave Trade and Fugitive Slaves During the Civil War" (MA thesis, University of Wisconsin-Madison, 1949); Jaime Amanda Martinez, "The Slave Market in Civil War Virginia," in *Crucible of the Civil War: Virginia From Secession to Commemoration*, ed. Gary Gallagher, Edward Ayers, and Andrew Torget (Charlottesville: University of Virginia Press, 2006), 106–135.

24. For efforts to quantify elements of the trade, see Donald Sweig, "Reassessing the Human Dimensions of the Interstate Slave Trade," *Prologue* 12 (1980): 4–21; Herman Freudenberger and Jonathan B. Pritchett, "The Domestic United States Slave Trade: New Evidence," *Journal of Interdisciplinary History* 21, no. 3 (Winter 1991): 447–477 and "A Peculiar Sample: The Selection of Slaves for the New Orleans Market," *Journal of Economic History* 52, no. 1 (March 1992): 109–127; Jonathan B. Pritchett, "The Interregional Slave Trade and the Selection of Slaves for the New Orleans Market," *Journal of Interdisciplinary History* 28, no. 1 (Summer 1997): 57–85 and "Quantitative Estimates of the United States Interregional Slave Trade, 1820–1860," 467–475; Charles W. Calomiris and Jonathan Pritchett, "Preserving Slave Families for Profit: Traders' Incentives and Pricing in the New Orleans Slave Market," *Journal of Economic History* 69, no. 4 (December 2009): 986–1011 and "Betting on Secession: Quantifying Political Events Surrounding Slavery and the Civil War," *American Economic Review* 106, no. 1 (January 2016): 1–23; Jonathan Pritchett and Mallorie Smith, "Sequential Sales as a Test of Adverse Selection in the Market for Slaves," *Journal of Economic History* 73, no. 2 (June 2013): 477–497.

25. M. H. Church to S. W. Groesbeck, November 1, 1866, Letters received, A-F, 1866, Assistant Commissioner, Tennessee, 9: 823/1551 RG 105: Records of the Bureau of Refugees, Freedmen, and Abandoned Lands, NARA M999.

26. See, especially, Yael Sternhell, *Routes of War: The World of Movement in the Confederate South* (Cambridge, MA: Harvard University Press, 2012).

27. Joint Select Committee to Inquire into the Condition of Affairs in the Late Insurrectionary States, *Testimony Taken by the Joint Select Committee to Inquire into the Condition of Affairs in the Late Insurrectionary States. Mississippi. Volume XI* (Washington, DC: Government Printing Office, 1872), 508. On the census of 1870, see, among others, J. David Hacker, "New Estimates of Census Coverage in the United States, 1850–1930," *Social Science History* 37, no. 1 (Spring 2013): 71–101; Judith Giesberg, "'A Muster Roll of the American People': The 1870 Census, Voting Rights, and the Postwar South," *Journal of Southern History* 87, no. 1 (February 2021): 35–66. On the unique laws governing slavery in Louisiana, see, among others, Judith Kelleher Schafer, *Slavery, the Civil Law, and the Supreme Court of Louisiana* (Baton Rouge: Louisiana State University Press, 1994).

28. On slavery and capitalism, see among others, Eric Williams, *Capitalism and Slavery* (Chapel Hill: University of North Carolina Press, 1944), particularly pp. 19–29;

Fogel and Engerman, *Time on the Cross*; Wright, *The Political Economy of the Cotton South*; Oakes, *The Ruling Race*; Peter Coclanis, *The Shadow of a Dream: Economic Life and Death in the South Carolina Low Country, 1670-1920* (New York: Oxford University Press, 1989), 59-60; William Dusinberre, *Them Dark Days: Slavery in the American Rice Swamps* (New York: Oxford University Press, 1996), 397-410; Follett, *The Sugar Masters*, 6-8; Seth Rockman, *Scraping By: Wage Labor, Slavery, and Survival in Early Baltimore* (Baltimore: Johns Hopkins University Press, 2009), 6-8, 234-241; Rothman, *Flush Times and Fever Dreams*; Caitlin C. Rosenthal, *Accounting for Slavery: Masters and Management* (Cambridge, MA: Harvard University Press, 2018).

29. Johnson, *River of Dark Dreams*, 13, 246, 282; Baptist, *The Half Has Never Been Told*, 116-121, 138-144.

30. Karl Polanyi, *The Great Transformation* (Boston: Beacon Press, 1944), 63-76, 130-162, 223-236.

31. Lightner, *Slavery and the Commerce Power*, 37-50, 71-89; Brown, *Good Wives, Nasty Wenches, and Anxious Patriarchs*, 107-136; Morgan, *Laboring Women*. On property rights and the American founding, see, among others, Holly Brewer, "Slavery, Sovereignty, and 'Inheritable Blood': Reconsidering John Locke and the Origins of American Slavery," *American Historical Review* 122, no. 4 (October 2017): 1038-1078; James Farr, "Locke, Natural Law, and New World Slavery," *Political Theory* 36, no. 4 (August 2008): 495-522; Patrick Rael, *Eighty-Eight Years: The Long Death of Slavery in the United States, 1777-1865* (Athens: University of Georgia Press, 2015), 33-41, 62-79; James L. Huston, "Property Rights in Slavery and the Coming of the Civil War," *Journal of Southern History* 65, no. 2 (May 1999): 265; Gary B. Nash, *Race and Revolution* (Lanham, MD: Madison House, 1990); Eliga H. Gould, "The Laws of War and Peace: Legitimating Slavery in the Age of the American Revolution," in *State and Citizen: British America and the Early United States*, ed. Peter Onuf and Peter Thompson (Charlottesville: University of Virginia Press, 2013), 52-76;

32. On slave codes and their enforcement mechanisms, see Richard S. Dunn, *Sugar and Slaves: The Rise of the Planter Class in the English West Indies, 1624-1713* (Chapel Hill: University of North Carolina Press for the OIEAHC, 1972), 238-246; Wood, *Black Majority*, 270-326; William M. Wiecek, "The Statutory Law of Slavery and Race in the Thirteen Mainland Colonies of British America," *William and Mary Quarterly* 34, no. 2 (April 1977): 258-280; Philip J. Schwarz, *Twice Condemned: Slaves and the Criminal Laws of Virginia, 1705-1865* (Baton Rouge: Louisiana State University Press, 1988); Alan Watson, *Slave Law in the Americas* (Athens: University of Georgia Press, 1989); Thomas D. Morris, *Southern Slavery and the Law, 1619-1860* (Chapel Hill: University of North Carolina Press, 1996); John Hope Franklin and Loren Schweninger, *Runaway Slaves: Rebels on the Plantation* (New York: Oxford University Press, 1999), 97-123, 149-181; Sally E. Hadden, *Slave Patrols: Law and Violence in Virginia and the Carolinas* (Cambridge, MA: Harvard University Press, 2001); Gautham Rao, "The Federal 'Posse Comitatus' Doctrine: Slavery, Compulsion, and Statecraft in Mid-Nineteenth-Century America," *Law and History Review* 26, no. 1 (Spring 2008): 1-56; Emily Blanck, *Tyrannicide: Forging an American Law of Slavery in Revolutionary South Carolina and Massachusetts* (Athens: University of Georgia

Press, 2014), 115–146; Edward Rugemer, *Slave Law and the Politics of Resistance in the Early Atlantic World* (Cambridge, MA: Harvard University Press, 2018). As Ryan Quintana and others rightly point out, slave laws rarely permitted total hegemony over the enslaved, but were forged in large part in response to enslaved efforts to carve out spaces and liberties. See Quintana, *Making a Slave State*.

33. James W. Ely, Jr., *The Guardian of Every Other Right: A Constitutional History of Property Rights* (New York: Oxford University Press, 2008), 46; Paul Finkelman, "Slavery and the Constitutional Convention: Making a Covenant With Death," in *Beyond Confederation: Origins of the Constitution and American National Identity*, ed. Richard Beeman, Stephen Botein, and Edward C. Carter (Chapel Hill: University of North Carolina Press, 1987), 188–225; Don E. Fehrenbacher, *The Slaveholding Republic: An Account of the United States Government's Relations to Slavery* (New York: Oxford University Press, 2000); David Waldstreicher, *Slavery's Constitution: From Revolution to Ratification* (New York: Hill and Wang, 2009); Matthew Karp, *This Vast Southern Empire: Slaveholders at the Helm of American Foreign Policy* (Cambridge, MA: Harvard University Press, 2016); John A. E. Harris, *The Last Slave Ships: New York and the End of the Middle Passage* (New Haven, CT: Yale University Press, 2020), 183–234. On the Constitution's antislavery potential, see Sean Wilentz, *No Property in Man: Slavery and Antislavery at the Nation's Founding* (Cambridge, MA: Harvard University Press, 2018) and James Oakes, *The Crooked Path to Abolition: Abraham Lincoln and the Antislavery Constitution* (New York: Norton, 2021).

34. Beckert, *Empire of Cotton*, xv, 37–52, 155–174; Rothman, *Slave Country*, 9–45, 103–117, 139–162; Johnson, *River of Dark Dreams*, 18–45; Baptist, *The Half Has Never Been Told*, 16–73; Claudio Saunt, *Unworthy Republic: The Dispossession of Native Americans and the Road to Indian Removal* (New York: Norton, 2020).

35. Albert Burton Moore, *Conscription and Conflict in the Confederacy* (1924; repr. Columbia: University of South Carolina Press, 1996); Ella Lonn, *Desertion During the Civil War* (1928; repr. Lincoln: University of Nebraska Press, 1998); Georgia Lee Tatum, *Disloyalty in the Confederacy* (Chapel Hill: University of North Carolina Press, 1934); Charles H. Wesley, *The Collapse of the Confederacy* (1937; repr. Columbia: University of South Carolina Press, 2001); Steven Hahn, *The Roots of Southern Populism: Yeoman Farmers and the Transformation of the Georgia Upcountry, 1850–1890* (New York: Oxford University Press, 1983); J. William Harris, *Plain Folk and Gentry in a Slave Society: White Liberty and Black Slavery in Augusta's Hinterlands* (Middletown, CT: Wesleyan University Press, 1985); Wayne K. Durrill, *War of Another Kind: A Southern Community in the Great Rebellion* (New York: Oxford University Press, 1990); Armstead Robinson, *Bitter Fruits of Bondage: The Demise of Slavery and the Collapse of the Confederacy, 1861–1865* (Charlottesville: University of Virginia Press, 2005); Stephanie McCurry, *Confederate Reckoning: Power and Politics in the Civil War South* (Cambridge, MA: Harvard University Press, 2012); Levine, *The Fall of the House of Dixie*.

36. James L. Roark, *Masters Without Slaves: Southern Planters in the Civil War and Reconstruction* (New York: Norton, 1977), especially 85–91, 94; Jason Phillips, *Diehard Rebels: The Confederate Culture of Invincibility* (Athens: University of Georgia

Press, 2007); Drew Gilpin Faust, *The Creation of Confederate Nationalism: Ideology and Identity in the Civil War South* (Baton Rouge: Louisiana State University Press, 1988); Gary W. Gallagher, *The Confederate War: How Popular Will, Nationalism, and Military Strategy Could Not Stave Off Defeat* (Cambridge, MA: Harvard University Press, 1997); Stephen V. Ash, *Middle Tennessee Society Transformed, 1860-1870* (Baton Rouge: Louisiana State University Press, 1988), 172; William Blair, *Virginia's Private War: Feeding Body and Soul in the Confederacy, 1861-1865* (New York: Oxford University Press, 1998); Aaron Sheehan-Dean, *Why Confederates Fought: Family and Nation in Civil War Virginia* (Chapel Hill: University of North Carolina Press, 2007); Joseph T. Glatthaar, *General Lee's Army From Victory to Collapse* (New York: Free Press, 2008); Paul Quigley, *Shifting Grounds: Nationalism and the American South, 1848-1865* (New York: Oxford University Press, 2012), 128-213.

37. On Confederate fiscal and monetary policies and inflation see John C. Schwab, "The Finances of the Confederate States," *Political Science Quarterly* 7, no. 1 (March 1892): 38-56 and *The Confederate States of America 1861-1865: A Financial and Industrial History of the South During the Civil War* (New York: Charles Scribner's Sons, 1901); Eugene M. Lerner, "The Monetary and Fiscal Programs of the Confederate Government, 1861-1865," *Journal of Political Economy* 62, no. 6 (December 1954): 506-522 and "Money, Prices, and Wages in the Confederacy, 1861-1865," *Journal of Political Economy*, 63, no. 1 (February 1955): 20-40; Douglas B. Ball, *Financial Failure and Confederate Defeat* (Urbana: University of Illinois Press, 1991); Richard C. K. Burdekin and Mark D. Weidenmier, "Suppressing Asset Price Inflation: The Confederate Experience, 1861-1865," *Economic Inquiry* 41, no. 3 (July 2003): 420-432.

38. On slavery's compatibility with industry, see Robert S. Starobin, *Industrial Slavery in the Old South* (New York: Oxford University Press, 1970); Richard C. Wade, *Slavery in the Cities: The South, 1820-1860* (New York: Oxford University Press, 1967), 33-40; Kathleen Bruce, *Virginia Iron Manufacture in the Slave Era* (New York: The Century Co., 1930); Tom Downey, *Planting a Capitalist South: Masters, Merchants, and Manufacturers in the Southern Interior, 1790-1860* (Baton Rouge: Louisiana State University Press, 2006); Wilma A. Dunaway, *Slavery in the American Mountain South* (New York: Cambridge University Press, 2003), 103-138; James L. Huston, "The Pregnant Economies of the Border South, 1840-1860: Virginia, Kentucky, Tennessee, and the Possibilities of Slave-Labor Expansion," in *The Old South's Modern Worlds: Slavery, Region, and Nation in the Age of Progress*, ed. L. Diane Barnes, Brian Schoen, and Frank Towers (New York: Oxford University Press, 2011), 120-144. On the wartime transformation of the Confederate economy, see Emory M. Thomas, *The Confederacy as a Revolutionary Experience* (Englewood Cliffs, NJ: Prentice Hall, 1971) and "Reckoning With Rebels," in *The Old South in the Crucible of War*, ed. Harry P. Owens and James J. Cooke (Jackson: University Press of Mississippi, 1983) 3-14; Charles W. Ramsdell, *Behind the Lines of the Southern Confederacy* (Baton Rouge: Louisiana State University Press, 1944), especially 70-75; Charles B. Dew, *Ironmaker to the Confederacy: Joseph R. Anderson and the Tredegar Iron Works* (New Haven, CT: Yale University Press, 1966); Mary A. DeCredico,

Patriotism for Profit: Georgia's Urban Entrepreneurs and the Confederate War Effort (Chapel Hill: University of North Carolina Press, 1990), 21–71; Frank E. Vandiver, "The Shelby Iron Company in the Civil War: A Study of a Confederate Industry" (3 pts.), *The Alabama Review*, Vol. I, Nos. 1–3 and *Ploughshares Into Swords: Josiah Gorgas and Confederate Ordnance* (Austin: University of Texas Press, 1952), 55–83, 172–184; Gordon B. McKinney, "Premature Industrialization in Appalachia: The Asheville Armory, 1862–1863," in *The Civil War in Appalachia: Collected Essays*, ed. Kenneth W. Noe and Shannon H. Wilson (Knoxville: University of Tennessee Press, 1997), 227–241; Michael Brem Bonner, *Confederate Political Economy: Creating and Managing a Southern Corporatist Nation* (Baton Rouge: Louisiana State University Press, 2018).

39. Mary Elizabeth Massey, *Ersatz in the Confederacy* (Columbia: University of South Carolina Press, 1952); Paul W. Gates, *Agriculture and the Civil War* (New York: Knopf, 1962); John Solomon Otto, *Southern Agriculture during the Civil War Era, 1860–1880* (Westport, CT: Greenwood Press, 1994); R. Douglas Hurt, *Agriculture and the Confederacy: Policy, Productivity, and Power in the Civil War South* (Chapel Hill: University of North Carolina Press, 2015). See also Robert A. Taylor, *Rebel Storehouse: Florida in the Confederate Economy* (Tuscaloosa: University of Alabama Press, 1995), 44–132; Blair, *Virginia's Private War*; Tim Smith, *Mississippi in the Civil War: The Home Front* (Jackson: University Press of Mississippi, 2010); McCurry, *Confederate Reckoning*, 133–217; Erin Stewart Mauldin, *Unredeemed Land: An Environmental History of the Civil War and Emancipation in the Cotton South* (New York: Oxford University Press, 2018).

40. Foundational work on the history of emancipation comes from the Freedmen and Southern Society Project, particularly Ira Berlin, Barbara Fields, Thavolia Glymph, Joseph P. Reidy, and Leslie S. Rowland, eds., *Freedom: A Documentary History of Emancipation 1861–1867, Series I, Volume I: The Destruction of Slavery* (New York: Cambridge University Press, 1985); Berlin, Steven F. Miller, Reidy, and Rowland, *Freedom: A Documentary History of Emancipation 1861–1867, Series I, Volume II: The Wartime Genesis of Free Labor: The Upper South* (New York: Cambridge University Press, 1993); Ira Berlin, Thavolia Glymph, Steven F. Miller, Joseph P. Reidy, Leslie S. Rowland, Julie Saville, eds., *The Wartime Genesis of Free Labor: The Lower South* (New York: Cambridge University Press, 1990). A distillation of many of the project's key findings can be found in Berlin, Barbara J. Fields, Miller, Reidy, and Rowland, eds., *Slaves No More: Three Essays on Emancipation and the Civil War* (New York: Cambridge University Press, 1992). See also Louis Gerteis, *From Contraband to Freedman: Federal Policy Toward Southern Blacks, 1861–1865* (Westport, CT: Greenwood Press, Inc., 1973); Fields, *Slavery and Freedom on the Middle Ground*; Clarence Mohr, *On the Threshold of Freedom: Masters and Slaves in Civil War Georgia* (Athens: University of Georgia Press, 1986); Thavolia Glymph, "'This Species of Property': Female Slave Contrabands in the Civil War," in *A Woman's War: Southern Women, Civil War, and the Confederate Legacy*, ed. Edward D. C. Campbell Jr. and Kym S. Rice (Charlottesville: University of Virginia Press, 1996); Leslie Schwalm, *A Hard Fight for We: Women's Transition from Slavery to Freedom in South Carolina* (Champaign: University of Illinois Press, 1997); Anthony E. Kaye, *Joining Places: Slave

Neighborhoods in the Old South (Chapel Hill: University of North Carolina Press, 2007); Susan Eva O'Donovan, *Becoming Free in the Cotton South* (Cambridge, MA: Harvard University Press, 2007); James Oakes, *Freedom National: The Destruction of Slavery in the United States, 1861–1865* (New York: Norton, 2012); Glenn David Brasher, *The Peninsula Campaign and the Necessity of Emancipation* (Chapel Hill: University of North Carolina Press, 2012); Jim Downs, *Sick From Freedom: African-American Illness and Suffering During the Civil War and Reconstruction* (New York: Oxford University Press, 2012); Chandra Manning, *Troubled Refuge: Struggling For Freedom in the Civil War* (New York: Knopf, 2016); Amy Murrell Taylor, *Embattled Freedom: Journeys through the Civil War's Contraband Camps* (Chapel Hill: University of North Carolina Press, 2018).

41. For the integration of enslaved people into communities after their sale, see Damian Alan Pargas, *Slavery and Forced Migration in the Antebellum South* (New York: Cambridge University Press, 2015), 173–217.

42. Heather Andrea Williams, *Help Me to Find My People: The African American Search for Family Lost in Slavery* (Chapel Hill: University of North Carolina Press, 2012).

43. On what scholars have termed "the dark turn" in Civil War scholarship, see Stephen Berry, ed., *Weirding the War: Stories from the Civil War's Ragged Edges* (Athens: University of Georgia Press, 2011). J. David Hacker, "A Census-Based Count of the Civil War Dead," *Civil War History* 57, no. 4 (December 2011): 307–348; Drew Gilpin Faust, *This Republic of Suffering: Death and the American Civil War* (New York: Knopf, 2008); Downs, *Sick From Freedom*; Megan Kate Nelson, *Ruin Nation: Destruction and the American Civil War* (Athens: University of Georgia Press, 2012); Mauldin, *Unredeemed Land*; James Marten, *Sing Not War: The Lives of Union and Confederate Veterans in Gilded Age America* (Chapel Hill: University of North Carolina Press, 2011), 245–285; Brian Matthew Jordan, *Marching Home: Union Veterans and Their Unending Civil War* (New York: Liveright Publishing Co., 2014).

44. Brian Matthew Jordan, "The Hour that Lasted Fifty Years: The 107th Ohio and the Human Longitude of Gettysburg," in *Upon the Fields of Battle: Essays on the Military History of America's Civil War*, ed. Andrew S. Bledsoe and Andrew F. Lang (Baton Rouge: Louisiana State University Press, 2018), 265.

45. Nell Irvin Painter, "Soul Murder and Slavery: Toward a Fully Loaded Cost Accounting," in *Southern History Across the Color Line* (Chapel Hill: University of North Carolina Press, 2002), 15–40. On the effort to reconstruct Black families, see Williams, *Help Me to Find My People*. On slavery's afterlives, see Saidiya Hartman, *Lose Your Mother: A Journey Along the Atlantic Slave Route* (New York: Farrar, Straus and Giroux, 2007), 6.

46. Litwack, *Been in the Storm So Long*, xiii; Thavolia Glymph, *Out of the House of Bondage: The Transformation of the Plantation Household* (New York: Cambridge University Press, 2008), 12–17; Baptist, *The Half Has Never Been Told*, xxv, 427 n 4; Jones-Rogers, *They Were Her Property*, xvii–xx. For cautionary voices, see John Blassingame, "Using the Testimony of Ex-Slaves: Approaches and Problems," *Journal of Southern History* 41, no. 4 (November 1975): 473–492; Johnson, *Soul By Soul*, 226 n 24; Ethan J. Kytle and Blain Roberts, *Denmark Vesey's Garden: Slavery and Memory in the Cradle of the Confederacy* (New York: The New Press, 2018), 225–258.

Chapter 1

1. Thomas Ruffin to Dickinson, Hill & Co., June 18, 1860, DHCRC; D. A. Montgomery to Thomas Ruffin, June 14, 1860, Thomas Ruffin Papers, SHC; William Henry Hoyt, ed., *The Papers of Archibald D. Murphey* (Raleigh, NC: E. M. Uzzell & Co., 1914), I: 334–335; "A New Railroad Project," *The Western Democrat*, March 9, 1858; David S. Cecelski, *The Waterman's Song: Slavery and Freedom in Maritime North Carolina* (Chapel Hill: University of North Carolina Press, 2001), 131–152; Viola Müller, *Escape to the City: Fugitive Slaves in the Antebellum Urban South* (Chapel Hill: University of North Carolina Press, 2022).
2. D. A. Montgomery to Thomas Ruffin, June 14, 1860, Ruffin Papers, SHC.
3. J. G. de Roulhac Hamilton, ed., *The Papers of Thomas Ruffin* (Raleigh, NC: Edwards & Broughton Printing Co., 1920), IV: 256; Sally Hadden, "Judging Slavery: Thomas Ruffin and *State v. Mann*," in *Local Matters: Race, Crime, and Justice in the Nineteenth-Century South*, ed. Christopher Waldrep and Donald G. Nieman (Athens: University of Georgia Press, 2011), 1–28, quote on p. 5; Laura F. Edwards, "The Forgotten Legal World of Thomas Ruffin: The Power of Presentism in the History of Slave Law," *North Carolina Law Review* 87, no. 3 (March 2009): 855–900; Eric L. Muller, "Judging Thomas Ruffin and the Hindsight Defense," *North Carolina Law Review* 87, no. 3 (March 2009): 757–798.
4. Thomas Ruffin to Dickinson, Hill & Co., June 18, 1860, DHCRC. Emphasis in original. In 1830, Ruffin similarly demanded that Bridget be sold "a thousand miles" away, and while he relented from this specific demand, he later personally beat her severely. Muller, "Judging Thomas Ruffin," 780–785.
5. Calomiris and Pritchett, "Betting on Secession," 12–16; Phillips, *American Negro Slavery*, 368–377; Gray, *History of Agriculture*, II: 663–667.
6. Dickinson Hill & Co. to "Dear Sir," June 16, 26; July 14, 21, 1860, William A. J. Finney Papers, Duke; "Dickinson, Hill & Co., Auctioneers," *Richmond Daily Dispatch*, July 3, 1860.
7. Robert Colby, "'Observant of the Laws of this Commonwealth': An Enslaved Family Between Forced Migration and Slave Capitalism," *Journal of the Early Republic* 42, no. 3 (Fall 2022): 345–349.
8. James Redpath, *The Roving Editor, or, Talks With Slaves in the Southern States* (New York: A. P. Burdick, 1859), 246–247.
9. Sales by Dickinson Hill & Co. For Judge Thos. Ruffin, Ruffin Papers, SHC. For an example of an enslaved man undercutting Dickinson, Hill & Co.'s efforts to sell him, see R. H. Dickinson & Bro. to "Dear Sir," December 29, 1851, Wyllie Family Papers, VHS.
10. See, for example, Benjamin Chambers to Thomas Ruffin, January 18, March 1, 1822, Ruffin Papers, SHC; Muller, "Judging Thomas Ruffin," 785–791; Hadden, "Judging Slavery," 7–8.
11. Edwards, "The Forgotten Legal World of Thomas Ruffin", 855–900 and "Status without Rights: African Americans and the Tangled History of Law and Governance in the Nineteenth-Century U.S. South," *American Historical Review* 112, no. 2 (April 2007): 365–393.

12. Thomas Ruffin to Dickinson Hill & Co., June 18, 1860, DHCRC.
13. Joseph B. G. Roulhac to Thomas Ruffin, June 15, 1860, Ruffin Papers, SHC.
14. See, for example, Winthrop D. Jordan, *Tumult and Silence at Second Creek: An Inquiry into a Civil War Slave Conspiracy* (Baton Rouge: Louisiana University Press, 1993), 136-148; R. J. M. Blackett, "Dispossessing Massa: Fugitive Slaves and the Politics of Slavery After 1850," *American Nineteenth Century History* 10, no. 2 (June 2009): 119-136.
15. Booker T. Washington, *Up From Slavery: An Autobiography* (New York: Doubleday & Co., 1901), 7-8. Some African Americans even claimed to have met Lincoln on supposed covert visits to the South before the war. Thavolia Glymph, *The Women's Fight: The Civil War's Battles for Home, Freedom, and Nation* (Chapel Hill: University of North Carolina Press, 2020), 288-289 n 57.
16. Pritchett and Calomiris, "Betting on Secession," 1-23.
17. Bancroft, *Slave Trading in the Old South*, 116-117; "City Taxes," *Richmond Times*, July 13, 1865; Charles B. Dew, *The Making of a Racist: A Southerner Reflects on Family, History, and the Slave Trade* (Charlottesville: University of Virginia Press, 2016), 144-145.
18. Reuben Gold Thwaites, *Early Western Travels, 1748-1846*, Vol. III (Cleveland: The Arthur H. Clark Company, 1904), 277. Gray, *History of Agriculture*, II: 673-720, 888-907; Beckert, *Empire of Cotton*, 29-42, 63-74, 101-103, 248. See also Wright, *The Political Economy of the Cotton South*, 44-55, 114-116, 129-130; Oakes, *The Ruling Race*; Moore, *The Emergence of the Cotton Kingdom in the Old Southwest*; Rothman, *Slave Country*; Schoen, *The Fragile Fabric of Union*, Rothman, *Flush Times and Fever Dreams*; Johnson, *River of Dark Dreams*; Baptist, *The Half Has Never Been Told*.
19. Gray, *History of Agriculture*, II: 893, 896-898.
20. Claiborne to Madison, December 1, 1801; Claiborne to Madison, January 23, 1802, in Dunbar Rowland, ed., *Official Letterbooks of W. C. C. Claiborne* (Jackson: State Department of Archives and History, 1917), I: 28, 39.
21. Jed Handelsman Shugerman, "The Louisiana Purchase and South Carolina's Reopening of the Slave Trade in 1803," *Journal of the Early Republic* 22, no. 2 (Summer 2002): 272-290; Rothman, *Slave Country*, 18-35; Deyle, "An 'Abominable' New Trade."
22. Bancroft, *Slave Trading in the Old South*, 312; *Mitchell v. Comyns* in Francois-Xavier Martin, *Orleans Term Reports, of Cases Argued and Determined in the Superior Court of the Territory of Orleans* Vol. I (New Orleans: John Dacqueny, 1811), 135; Bill of Sale, June 20, 1807; May 23, 1809; March 1, 1810; August 26, 1817, Trist Wood Papers #800, SHC; Jean-Pierre Le Glaunec, "Slave Migrations and Slave Control in Spanish and Early American New Orleans," in *Empires of the Imagination: Transatlantic Histories of the Louisiana Purchase*, ed. Peter J. Kastor and François Weil (Charlottesville: University of Virginia Press, 2009), 216-217; John Clark, New Orleans 1718-1812: An Economic History (Baton Rouge: Louisiana State University Press, 1970), 317-318.
23. Charles Ball, *Fifty Years in Chains; or, The Life of an American Slave* (New York: H. Dayton, 1859), 10-14, 29-65. Quote on p. 45.
24. "Lucinda Keys," LS, http://informationwanted.org/items/show/501 (accessed April 24, 2018).

25. Frederick Douglass, *The Life and Times of Frederick Douglass, Written By Himself* (Boston: De Wolfe & Fiske Co., 1892), 46. On "Georgia Men," see also J. W. C. Pennington, *A Narrative of the Life of J. H. Banks, an Escaped Slave, from the Cotton State, Alabama, in America* (Liverpool: M. Rourke, Printer, 1861), 25; Leonard Black, *The Life and Sufferings of Leonard Black, A Fugitive from Slavery* (New Bedford, MA: Press of Benjamin Lindsey, 1847), 22–27.

26. Various entries, James A. Mitchell Account Book, James A. Mitchell Papers, Series F: Duke, Part 3, RASP.

27. George W. Featherstonhaugh, *Excursion Through the Slave States* (London: John Murray, 1844), I: 120–123, 167–169.

28. Rothman, *The Ledger and the Chain*, 71–148.

29. Reebs & Booker to Rice Ballard, April 18, 1833; James R. Franklin to Ballard, April 24, 1833; Check, Yeatman, Woods & Co. to Ballard, April 16, 1833; James R. Franklin to Ballard, October 29, 1833; Isaac Franklin to Rice Ballard, November 5, 6, 7, 1833, Rice C. Ballard Papers, SHC. On Franklin & Armfield, see Stephenson, *Isaac Franklin*, 43; Robert H. Gudmestad, "The Troubled Legacy of Isaac Franklin: The Enterprise of Slave Trading," *Tennessee Historical Quarterly* 62, no. 3 (Fall 2003): 193–217; Baptist, *The Half Has Never Been Told*, 238–259; Schermerhorn, *The Business of Slavery*, 124–168; Rothman, *The Ledger and the Chain*, 149–256. For an example of the firm's agents, see Joshua D. Rothman, "The American Life of Jordan Saunders, Slave Trader," *Journal of Southern History* 88, no. 2 (May 2022): 227–256. On the financialization of slavery, see Martin, "Slavery's Invisible Engine," 817–866; Kilbourne, *Debt, Investment, Slaves*; Boodry, "August Belmont and the World the Slaves Made," 163–179; Schermerhorn, *The Business of Slavery*, 95–123; Murphy, "The Financialization of Slavery by the First and Second Banks of the United States," 385–426.

30. *Governor's Message and Annual Reports of the Public Officers of the State, and of the Boards of Directors, Visitors, Superintendents, and Other Agents of Public Institutions or Interests in Virginia* (Richmond: Samuel Shepherd, 1849), 5; Finley, "'Cash to Corinna,'" 413.

31. "Military Celebration," *Richmond Enquirer*, June 30, 1838; "Untitled," *Richmond Enquirer*, March 6, 1829; Jeff Forret, *Williams' Gang: A Notorious Slave Trader and His Cargo of Black Convicts* (New York: Cambridge University Press, 2020), 61–65; "By Templeman & Dickinson," *Richmond Whig*, January 7, 1840; "By R. H. Dickinson & Brother," *Richmond Whig*, February 14, 1843; "By R. H. Dickinson & Bro.," *Richmond Enquirer*, February 25, 1848.

32. Peter L. Rousseau, "Jacksonian Monetary Policy, Specie Flows, and the Panic of 1837," *Journal of Economic History* 62, no. 2 (June 2003): 457–488; Jessica M. Lepler, *The Many Panics of 1837: People, Politics, and the Creation of a Transatlantic Financial Crisis* (New York: Cambridge University Press, 2013); Rothman, *Flush Times and Fever Dreams*, 292–201. For examples of the Panic's effects on the slave trade, see Newton Boley to William Crow, January 22, 1838; Thomas B. Jackson to Crow, October 9, 1839, Slave Trade Letters of William Crow, UVA.

33. "Dissolution," *Richmond Enquirer*, June 1, 1847; "The Partnership Heretofore Existing . . . ," *Richmond Enquirer*, December 5, 1844; Virginia, Vol. 43, pp. 70, 88, 109, R. G.

Dun & Co. Credit Report Volumes, Baker Library Historical Collections, Harvard Business School; Trent, *The Secret Life of Bacon Tait*, 59; "Interesting Correspondence," *Richmond Enquirer*, February 17, 1852; "Virginia Central Agricultural Society," *The American Farmer*, June 1858; "City of Richmond to wit," March 7, 1861, Cornelius Chase Family Papers, LC.

34. McInnis, *Slaves Waiting for Sale*, 76–77; Gerald G. Eggert, "Notes and Documents: A Pennsylvanian Visits the Richmond Slave Market," *Pennsylvania Magazine of History and Biography* 109, no. 4 (October 1985): 571–576; John N. Gault to Samuel Gault, December 31, 1853, John N. Gault Letter, VHS; "Copartnership Notice," *Richmond Daily Dispatch*, December 20, 1854; Tadman, *Speculators and Slaves*, 57–64; For a description of these blended firms' practices, see Deposition of D. M. Pulliam, October 9, 1855, *Tucker v. Chappell*, Halifax Co., Virginia Chancery Causes, 1855-044, LVA, as well the Hector Davis Daybooks, NYPL. On slave traders as agents of modernity, see Steven Deyle, "Rethinking the Slave Trade: Slave Traders and the Market Revolution in the South," in Barnes, Schoen, and Towers, *The Old South's Modern Worlds*, 104–119.

35. Charles W. Turner and Charles F. Turner, "The Early Railroad Movement in Virginia," *Virginia Magazine of History and Biography* 55, no. 4 (October 1947): 355–357, 360; Angus T. Johnston, "Virginia Railroads in April 1861," *Journal of Southern History* 23, no. 3 (August 1957): 312; David R. Goldfield, *Urban Growth in the Age of Sectionalism* (Baton Rouge: Louisiana State University Press, 1982), 9–28, 182–225; Majewski, *A House Dividing*, 28, 60–61.

36. W. Dennis to John E. Dennis, February 14, 1847, John E. Dennis Papers, Duke.

37. See, for example, Thomas M. Wilkinson to Dickinson, Hill & Co., February 13, 1856, Chase Papers, LC; William E. Royall to Messrs. Dickerson & Brothers, May 18, 1853, DHCRC; "Louisa Railroad," *Richmond Whig*, August 11, 1848; Benjamin Homans, *The United States Railroad Directory, for 1856* (New York: B. Homans, 1856), 73.

38. Pennington, *A Narrative of the Life of J. H. Banks*, 49. Railroad employees sometimes took direct custody of enslaved people. See Granville Bullock to Dickinson and Hill, October 8, 1860, DHCRC. See also Charles Dickens, *American Notes, For General Circulation* (London: Chapman and Hall, 1842), 17; Thomas M. Wilkinson to Dickinson, Hill & Co., February 13, 1856, Chase Papers, LC; William E. Royall to Messrs. Dickerson & Brothers, May 18, 1853, DHCRC.

39. Calvin Schermerhorn, "Capitalism's Captives: The Maritime United States Slave Trade, 1807–1850," *Journal of Social History* 47, no. 4 (Summer 2014): 897–921; Jennie K. Williams, "Trouble the water: the Baltimore to New Orleans Coastwise Slave Trade, 1820–1860," *Slavery & Abolition* 42, no. 1 (2020): 275–303; Kenneth G. Noe, *Southwest Virginia's Railroad: Modernization and the Sectional Crisis* (Urbana: University of Illinois Press, 1994), 80–83; William G. Thomas, *The Iron Way: Railroads, the Civil War, and the Making of Modern America* (New Haven, CT: Yale University Press, 2011), 32–36; Charles S. Davis, *The Cotton Kingdom in Alabama* (Montgomery: Alabama Department of Archives and History, 1939), 76; Harriet E. Amos, *Cotton City: Urban Development in Antebellum Mobile* (Tuscaloosa: University of Alabama Press, 1985), 85; Don H. Doyle, *New Men, New Cities, New South: Atlanta,*

Nashville, Charleston, Mobile, 1860–1910 (Chapel Hill and London: University of North Carolina Press, 1990), 22–50; Wendy Hamand Venet, *A Changing Wind: Commerce and Conflict in Civil War Atlanta* (New Haven, CT: Yale University Press, 2014), 5–14; Bancroft, *Slave Trading in the Old South*, 244–268, 294–300. For an example of these new connections, see Maury Brothers to Samuel Mordecai, May 4, 1857, Mordecai Papers, SHC.

40. Thomas M. Wilkinson to Dickinson, Hill & Co., April 12, 1855; W. F. Askew to Dickinson, Hill & Co., February 13, 1856, Chase Papers, LC.

41. B. M. Campbell to R. H. Dickinson, May 8, 1853, DHCRC; William W. Hall to Dickinson, Hill & Co., February 3, 1856; John Edward Robey to Dickinson, Hill & Co., February 2, 1856, Chase Papers, LC; Dickinson, Hill & Co. to Ziba Oakes, May 3, 1857, Ziba B. Oakes Papers, Boston Public Library, https://www.digitalcommonwealth.org/search/commonwealth:w3764395h (accessed January 27, 2023).

42. See, for example, Elisha Smith to R. H. Dickinson, May 12, 1853, DHCRC.

43. Seth Woodroof to Dickinson, Hill & Co., February 24, 1856, Chase Papers, LC. Emphasis in original. For the pair's longer relationship, see Samuel Reese to Dickenson & Brother, May 6, 1845, DHCRC.

44. W. J. Halleman to Dickinson Hill & Co., June 29, 1860; Alexander Flint to N. B. Hill, October 3, 1860; E. Lawrence to Dickinson Hill & Co., October 15, 1860, DHCRC.

45. Bethany Veney, *The Narrative of Bethany Veney, A Slave Woman* (Worcester: Geo. H. Ellis, 1889), 22–25, 30–31; Seth Woodroof to Dickinson, Hill & Co., February 24, 1856, Chase Papers, LC. Emphasis in original.

46. Thomas David Russell, "Sale Day in Antebellum South Carolina: Slavery, Law, Economy, and Court-Supervised Sales" (PhD diss., Stanford University, 1993), 21–152. See also John L. Boughton to Dickinson & Hill & Co., June 13, 1860, DHCRC; Kenneth M. Clark to Lewis Thompson, October 22, 1860, Lewis Thompson Papers, SHC; John Haywood to George Haywood, November 21, 1860, Ernest Haywood Collection of Haywood Family Papers, SHC; J. G. Holloway to Mary M. Pitts, February 16, 1861, Papers of the Gambrel Family, UVA; Will of Sally Felton, Rockbridge County, June 2, 1862, Papers of the Anderson Family, UVA.

47. John Kimberly to Bettie Maney, September 9, 1860, John Kimberly Papers, SHC; Johnson, *Soul by Soul*, 1–17.

48. Benjamin Drew, *A North-Side View of Slavery. The Refugee: or, The Narratives of Fugitive Slaves in Canada. Related By Themselves, with An Account of the History and Condition of the Colored Population of Upper Canada* (Boston: John P. Jewett and Company, 1856), 101, 126, 198–199.

49. Philip Southall Turner to "Dear Stephen," November 11, 1850, Philip Southall Turner Letter, VHS.

50. William Daniel Cabell to "My Beloved Wife," February 11, 1858, William Daniel Cabell Letter, VHS.

51. Samuel Spottford Clement, *Memoirs of Samuel Spottford Clement, Relating Interesting Experiences in Days of Slavery and Freedom* (Steubenville: The Herald Printing Co., 1908), 5–8; William Daniel Cabell to "My Beloved Wife," February 11, 1858, William Daniel Cabell Letter, VHS; Alfred Bates[?] to Robert W. Smith, February 20, 1856,

Robert W. Smith Papers, SHC. See also E. Hinton to Laurens Hinton, February 21, 1860, Laurens Hinton Papers, SHC; Jonathan McCalley to "Dear Wm.," January 7, 1849, Jonathan McCalley Letter, VHS; Lewis to Lucy A. Gaulden, October 28, 1860, Papers of the Palmore Family, UVA.

52. Signer Everett to Joseph Totten, March 11, 1860, Joseph Totten Papers, Caswell County Historical Association, SHC.

53. William S. Deupree to Samuel R. Fondren, June 2, 1860, Documents Relating to J. D. Fondren & Bro., Beinecke Library, Yale; Solomon Northup, *Twelve Years a Slave. Narrative of Solomon Northup, a Citizen of New York, Kidnapped in Washington City in 1841, and Rescued in 1853, from a Cotton Plantation near the Red River, in Louisiana* (Auburn: Derby & Miller, 1853), 79.

54. Gutman, *Slavery and the Numbers Game*, 124–126.

55. Henry Bibb, *Narrative of the Life and Adventures of Henry Bibb, an American Slave* (New York: Published by the Author, 1849), 41–42.

56. Henry Box Brown, *Narrative of the Life of Henry Box Brown, Written By Himself* (Manchester: Lee and Glynn, 1851), 33–34; Drew, *A North-Side View of Slavery*, 119–120.

57. Drew, *A North-Side View of Slavery*, 46.

58. Allan Kulikoff, "Uprooted Peoples: The Political Economy of Slave Migration, 1780–1840," in *The Agrarian Origins of American Capitalism* (Charlottesville: University Press of Virginia, 1992), 226–263; The precise number of enslaved people sold between Upper and Lower South remains a point of considerable disagreement. Winfield Collins put it at just under 300,000 between 1820 and 1860. Robert Fogel and Stanley Engerman suggested that of the more than 800,000 slaves in motion between Upper and Lower Souths, only 16 percent moved via sale (a total of 127,000 between 1810 and 1860, or 2,500 annually). Michael Tadman indicated that enslavers had moved a similar number of people South but argued that between 60 and 70 percent were caught up in the long-distance slave trade. Herbert Gutman and Richard Sutch raised the number transiting the South to more than one million but were unwilling to estimate how many were sold—it could have been, they argued, anywhere from 30 to 80 percent. Gutman also suggested that when local sales were accounted for, more than two million enslaved people were sold from 1820 to 1860—50,000 per year. Jonathan Pritchett, accepting Fogel and Engerman and Tadman's estimates of the total number of people moved, argued that about half of the enslaved people thus carried were sold, for a total of 343,000 sold South between 1820 and 1860. Collins, *The Domestic Slave Trade of the Southern States*, 61–67; Fogel and Engerman, *Time on the Cross*, I: 47–48; Tadman, *Speculators and Slaves*, 11–31; Herbert Gutman and Richard Sutch, "The Slave Family: Protected Agent of Capitalist Masters or Victim of the Slave Trade," in *Reckoning with Slavery: A Critical Study in the Quantitative History of American Negro Slavery*, ed. Paul A. David, Herbert G. Gutman, Richard Sutch, Peter Temin, and Gavin Wright (New York: Oxford University Press, 1976), 99–103; Gutman, *Slavery and the Numbers Game*, 124–126; Pritchett, "Quantitative Estimates of the United States Interregional Slave Trade," 467–475.

59. Huston, *Calculating the Value of the Union*, 27–29; Ransom and Sutch, "Capitalists Without Capital," 133–160.
60. Deyle, *Carry Me Back*, 40–62; Tadman, *Speculators and Slaves*, 47–108; Johnson, *Soul By Soul*, 78–116, 135–161 (quote on p. 17); Walter Johnson, "Introduction: The Future Store," in Johnson, *The Chattel Principle*, 1–31; Baptist, *The Half Has Never Been Told*, 171–259.
61. Gray, *History Agriculture in the Southern United States*, II: 696–700; Phillips, *American Negro Slavery*, 373–377; Jenny Wahl, "*Dred*, Panic, War: How a Slave Case Triggered Financial Crisis and Civil Disunion," in *Congress and the Crisis of the 1850s*, ed. Paul Finkelman and Donald R. Kennon (Athens: Ohio University Press, 2011), 177–178.
62. Edmund Ruffin, "Consequences of Abolition Agitation," *De Bow's Review* 22, no. 6 (June 1857): 588. See also Deyle, *Carry Me Back*, 177–203; Gudmestad, *A Troublesome Commerce*, 148–168, 179–189; Lightner, *Slavery and the Commerce Power*, 90–112. Though the Supreme Court upheld the trade's legitimacy in *Groves v. Slaughter* (1841), debate over Congress's exact powers continued. Lightner, *Slavery and the Commerce Power*, 71–77; Gudmestad, *A Troublesome Commerce*, 195–199; Oakes, *Freedom National*, 20–21, 27, 52–59.
63. Eric Foner, *Free Soil, Free Labor, Free Men: The Ideology of the Republican Party Before the Civil War* (New York: Oxford University Press, 1970), 83–84, 115–117; Pritchett and Calomiris, "Betting on Secession," 1–23.
64. Wahl, "*Dred*, Panic, War," 196–202; Calomiris and Pritchett, "Betting on Secession."
65. R. H. Morrison to Rufus Barringer, December 27, 1859, Barringer Family Papers, UVA.
66. Sandford R. Finney to William A. J. Finney, October 24, 1859; Philip Thomas to Jack Finney, November 19, 1859; Philip Thomas to Jack Finney, December 3, 1859, Finney Papers, Duke; Harriet Newby to Dangerfield Newby, August 16, 1859, in Rita Roberts, *I Can't Wait to Call You My Wife: African American Letters of Love and Family in the Civil War Era* (San Francisco: Chronicle Books, 2022), 50; E. H. Stokes to "Dear Thad," December 2, 1859, Chase Papers, LC; E. H. Stokes to "Dear Thad," November 12, 1859, SUSC-AAS.
67. Edward Gilliam Booth to Philip St. George Cocke, Dec. 9, 1859, Papers of Philip St. George Cocke, UVA.
68. Robert E. May, *Yuletide in Dixie: Slavery, Christmas, and Southern Memory* (Charlottesville: University of Virginia Press, 2019), 88–103.
69. W. H. Washington to Sarah T. Washington, January 12, 1860, Robert J. Washington Papers, W&M.
70. Figures from Hector Davis Account Books, Chicago History Museum; Dew, *The Making of a Racist*, 141–145.
71. Figures taken from Hector Davis Account Books, CHM; Hector Davis to "Dear Sir," January 16, 1860, Richard J. Reid Papers, UVA.
72. Redpath, *The Roving Editor*, 250.
73. John T. Foster to J. W. Gilliam, June 29, 1859, J. W. Gilliam Papers, UVA.
74. Dickinson, Hill & Co. to "Dear Sir," December 28, 1860, African-American Miscellany, Duke.

75. "Nigger Nigger Nigger!," *Southern Banner*, January 26, 1860. Ulrich B. Phillips Papers, Yale University.
76. J. Gilliam to "My Dear Mother," March 1, 1860, Gilliam Family Papers, UVA. Emphasis in original.
77. "Random Paragraphs," *New Orleans Daily Crescent*, January 30, 1860.
78. Rachel Sherman Thorndike, ed., *The Sherman Letters: Correspondence Between General and Senator Sherman from 1837 to 1891* (New York: Charles Scribner's Sons, 1894), 81.
79. "Browning, Moore & Co., Auctioneers," *Richmond Daily Dispatch*, February 16, 1860; A. Pamplin to E. C. Moore, August 17, 1860; J. J. Price to E. H. Stokes, February 8, 1860; C. B. Acriss to Browning Moore & Co., July 3, 1860; J. O. Hanfield to E. C. Moore, August 30, 1860; C. W. Parris to Browning Moore & Co., June 26, 1860; John Rucker to Browning Moore & Co., July 16, 1860; D. M. Pattie to Browning Moore & Co., April 21, 1860, Chase Papers, LC. In June, meanwhile, R. H. Davis, William S. Deupree, and S. R. Fondren formed Davis, Deupree & Co. See Broadside 1860: 23, VHS. "Fifty Negroes for Sale," *Weekly Mississippian*, September 5, 1860; "Negroes," *Memphis Daily Avalanche*, October 2, 1860; John D. Fondren to "Dear Raj[?]," July 27, 1859, Gail & Stephen Rudin Slavery Collection, Division of Rare and Manuscript Collections, Cornell University Library.
80. Thomas E. Matthews to S. R. Fondren, March 9, 1860, Chase Papers, LC; Deyle, *Carry Me Back*, 71. On New Orleans and its epidemics, see Kathryn Olivarius, *Necropolis: Disease, Power, and Capitalism in the Cotton Kingdom* (Cambridge, MA: Harvard University Press, 2022).
81. John Fraser to E. H. Stokes, February 5, 1860, Chase Papers, LC; "Trader's Bank," *Richmond Daily Dispatch*, February 21, 1860. After the war, some traders retained their banking connections. When the Commonwealth chartered the Commercial Savings Bank of Richmond in 1866, among its incorporators were former traders N. B. Hill, John B. Davis, R. D. James, and N. M. Lee. *Acts of the General Assembly of the State of Virginia, Passed in 1865-66, in the Eighty-Ninth Year of the Commonwealth* (Richmond: Allegre & Goode, Printers, 1866), 426.
82. William Freehling, *The Road to Disunion, Part II: Secessionists Triumphant, 1854–1861* (New York: Oxford University Press, 2007), 271–322; Oakes, *Freedom National*, 42–48.
83. Thomas A. Powell Jr. to W. A. J. Finney, June 25, 1860, Finney Papers, Duke.
84. Pritchett and Calomiris, "Betting on Secession," 8, 12–13; Dickinson Hill & Co. to "Dear Sir," July 21, 1860, Finney Papers, Duke.
85. Joseph Crews to Dickinson Hill & Co., June 26, 1860, DHCRC; Alex B. Barnes to David Bullock Harris, September 19, 1860, David Bullock Harris Papers, 1789–1894, Duke; W. Tompkins to William Cabell Rives, William Cabell Rives Papers, LC.
86. Betts & Gregory to "Dear Sir," July 20, 1860, R. J. Reid. Papers, 1777–1870, LVA; Davis, Deupree & Co. to Hudson Martin, September 7, 1860, Hudson Martin Papers, UVA; John S. Mosby, "Why I Fought for Virginia," *Frank Leslie's Weekly*, April 6, 1911. Even Robert E. Lee considered adding to his stock of slaves during this period. Lee to William Henry Fitzhugh Lee, July 9, 1860, George Bolling Lee Papers, VHS.

87. Betts & Gregory to "Dear Sir," September 11, 1860, Reid Papers, LVA.
88. William W. Saunders to E. H. Stokes, Undated, SUSC-AAS. See also Edward W. Jones to "My Dear Sister," December 4, 1860, Jones and Patterson Family Papers, SHC.
89. "Carolina and Virginia Negroes," New Orleans *Daily Picayune*, November 20, 1860; Receipts, H. F. Peterson to Richard L. Pugh, September 27, October 22, 1860. Peterson sold Pugh more people on November 30 (a man named Aaron) and December 14, 1860 (a woman named Martha) Receipts, Peterson to Pugh, November 30, 1860, December 14, 1860, Pugh-Williams-Mayes Family Slave Receipts, Pugh-Williams-Mayes Family Papers, Series B: LSU, Part 3, RSPEGM; H. F. Peterson to Dickinson Hill & Co., October 30, November 1, 1860, DHCRC.
90. Roscoe Briggs Heath to Lewis Edmunds Mason, October 5, 1860, Mason Family Papers, Series M: VHS, Part 5, RASP; "Threats of Disunion—Monetary Institutions," *Daily Nashville Patriot*, October 16, 1860; "The Salisbury Mass Meeting—Large Crowd," *Newbern Weekly Progress*, October 16, 1860.
91. Pritchett and Calomiris, "Betting on Secession," 12–14.
92. William J. Palmore to "My Dearest Mother," January 24, 1861, Palmore Family Papers, UVA; Betts & Gregory to "Dear Sir," November 9, 1860, Finney Papers, Duke; Hunt & James to William S. Massie, November 13, 1860, William Massie Papers, 1747–1919, DBCAH.
93. Calvin Cowles to R. R. Butter, December 1, 1860, Calvin J. Cowles Papers, NCDAH.
94. Abraham Lincoln to John A. Gilmer, December 15, 1860, Abraham Lincoln Papers, LC.
95. Harold D. Woodman, *King Cotton and His Retainers* (1968; repr. Columbia: University of South Carolina Press, 1990), 30–42, 132–153; William L. Barney, *Rebels in the Making: The Secession Crisis and the Birth of the Confederacy* (New York: Oxford University Press, 2020), 16–27.
96. See Bill of Sale, Estate of Lewis Pugh to William Grimes, February 5, 1861, Grimes Family Papers, SHC.
97. James M. Morson to William Cabell Rives, September 1, 1860; September 30, 1861, Rives Papers, LC.
98. Frederick Law Olmsted, *A Journey in the Seaboard Slave States, With Remarks on Their Economy* (New York: Dix & Edwards, 1856), 652–653 and *The Cotton Kingdom: A Traveller's Observation on Cotton and Slavery in the American Slave States* (New York: Mason Brothers, 1861), II: 233–234.
99. W. H. Pearce to John W. Gurley, December 3, 1860, John W. Gurley Papers, Series I: LSU, Part 2, RASP.
100. Barney, *Rebels in the Making*, 121–126; Moses Greenwood to Messrs. S. H. Tucker & Co., November 17, 1860, Moses Greenwood Papers, NYHS.
101. Gray, *History of Agriculture*, II: 1027.
102. See, for example, Rufus Patterson to "My Dear Father," January 12, 1861, Jones and Patterson Papers, SHC.
103. Charles Franklin Dunbar, *Economic Essays* (New York: The MacMillan Company, 1904), 299–300, 305–206; Philip S. Foner, *Business & Slavery: The New York Merchants & the Irrepressible Conflict* (Chapel Hill: University of North Carolina

Press, 1941), 214–223; Larry Schweikart, "Secession and Southern Banks," *Civil War History* 31, no. 2 (June 1985): 118–119 and *Banking in the American South from the Age of Jackson to Reconstruction* (Baton Rouge: Louisiana State University Press, 1987), 289–291. See, for example, Burton & Greenhow to William Cabell Rives, November 22, 1860, Rives Papers, LC.

104. Scott P. Marler, *The Merchants' Capital: New Orleans and the Political Economy of the Nineteenth-Century South* (New York: Cambridge University Press, 2013), 129.

105. Battle & Noble to Paul C. Cameron, October 27, November 22, 24, 1860, Cameron Family Papers, SHC; R. Taylor Scott to Fanny Scott, March 3, 1861, Keith Family Papers, 1710–1865, VHS; Kenneth M. Clark to Lewis Thompson, January 23, 1861, Thompson Papers, SHC. See also Horace L. Hunley to Robert Ruffin Barrow, November 16, 1860, Robert Ruffin Barrow Papers, Series H: Tulane University and the Louisiana State Museum Archives, RASP; Moses Greenwood to James G. Mills, December 5, 1860, Greenwood Papers, NYHS; Scott P. Marler, "'An Abiding Faith in Cotton': The Merchant Capitalist Community of New Orleans, 1860–1862," *Civil War History* 54, no. 3 (September 2008): 250–251; Milledge L. Bonham, "Financial and Economic Disturbance in New Orleans on the Eve of Secession," *Louisiana Historical Quarterly* 13 (1930): 33; William C. Tavenner to "My Dear Bettie," December 11, 1860, Cabell Tavenner Papers, 1784–1929, Duke.

106. Hunt & James to William Massie, December 29, 1860; E. E. Jefferson to Massie, December 11, 1860, Massie Papers, DBCAH.

107. Daniel Hoard Baldwin to William Baldwin, November 30, 1860, Daniel Hoard Baldwin Papers, SHC; Kenneth M. Clark to Lewis Thompson, November 26, 1860, Thompson Papers, SHC; William Ogbourne to "Dear Sister," December 14, 1860, James B. Bailey Papers, SHC. See also W. R. Fleming to James Gardner, November 17, 1860, James Gardner Papers, Georgia Archives.

108. Benjamin Blossom & Son to Daniel W. Jordan, December 8, 13, 1860, Daniel W. Jordan Papers, Duke.

109. Walthall Robertson to Mollie Robertson, November 4, 1860, Mary Overton Gentry Shaw Papers, Jackson County Historical Society, Independence, MO.

110. Moses Greenwood to W. W. Arnold, November 20, 1860, Greenwood Papers, NYHS. See also A. J. Rux to E. H. Stokes, February 7, 1861, Slavery Collection, NYHS; Paul B. Barringer to Daniel W. Barringer, December [?], 1860, Daniel Moreau Barringer Papers, SHC.

111. Peter Browne Ruffin to Thomas Ruffin, March 25, 1861, Ruffin Papers, SHC; A. J. Rux to E. H. Stokes, December 7, 1860, Slavery Collection, NYHS; A. J. Rux to E. H. Stokes, February 8, 1861, J. J. Price to E. H. Stokes, February 17, 1861, Chase Papers, LC.

112. Sales by Dickinson, Hill & Co. for D. W. Jordan, February 1861; Silas Omohundro to Jordan, February 28, 1861, Jordan Papers, Duke.

113. B. P. Crabb to Dickinson Hill & Co. November 2, 1860; B. A. Shipp to Dickinson Hill & Co., November 5, 1860; W. T. Sutherlin to Dickinson Hill & Co., November 10, 1860, DHCRC.

114. Dickinson, Hill & Co. Circular, December 28, 1860, African American Miscellany, Duke.

115. C. Fitzimmons to James Henry Hammond, October 19, 1860, Papers of James Henry Hammond, Series A: SCL, RASP.
116. "Current News," *Hancock Jeffersonian*, January 4, 1861.
117. Entry for February 1, 1861, Thomas Watson Plantation Account Book, Thomas Watson Papers, Series E: UVA, RASP; James Neblett to Sterling Neblett, November 26, 1860, Sterling Neblett Papers, Duke.
118. James W. McCrary to E. H. Stokes, November 16, 1860, Slavery Collection, NYHS.
119. James Kenan to Owen R. Kenan, February 18, 1861, Kenan Family Papers, SHC.
120. "How to Save the Union," *Cincinnati Daily Press*, November 5, 1860.
121. See, for example, Entry for February 24, 1861, Alexander Pugh Diary, Series I: LSU, Parts 1, 2, and 3, RASP.
122. "The Price of Slaves," *Plaquemines Gazette & Sentinel*, January 26, 1861; "Untitled," *New York World*, January 25, 1861.
123. Alvin F. Sanborn, ed., *Reminiscences of Richard Lathers, Sixty Years of a Busy Life in South Carolina, Massachusetts and New York* (New York: The Grafton Press, 1907), 155.
124. J. D. Wright, W. D. Hardy, and A. J. Hause to Abraham Lincoln, November 27, 1860, Lincoln Papers, LC; Joshua Lynn, "'Strange Amalgamation & General Confusion': Party Realignment as Sexual Transgression in Antebellum Political Culture," unpublished paper presented at the 2017 Annual Meeting of the Southern Historical Association. My thanks to Josh for sharing this with me.
125. Nellie Arnold Plummer, *Out of the Depths or the Triumph of the Cross* (1927; repr. New York: G. K. Hall & Co., 1997), 69–75. Quotes on p. 75.
126. F. D. Sewall to O. O. Howard, January 13, 1867, Letters Received, A-E, Jan.–May 1867, Records of the Commissioner, 41: 781/1085, RG 105, NARA M752. See also J. M. Schofield to Howard, March 2, 1867, Registers and Letters Received by the Commissioners, Indexes and Registers, Reg. 9 (40), Jan.–May 1867, Records of the Commissioner, 6: 334/371, RG 105, NARA M752.
127. George P. Rawick, ed., *The American Slave: A Composite Autobiography, Volume 9: Arkansas Narratives Parts 3 and 4* (Westport, CT: Greenwood Publishing Company, 1941, 1972), 4: 22.
128. John W. Blassingame, ed. *Slave Testimony: Two Centuries of Letters, Speeches, Interviews, and Autobiographies* (Baton Rouge: Louisiana State University Press, 1977), 394–395.
129. William J. Simmons, D. D., *Men of Mark: Eminent, Progressive and Rising* (Cleveland: Geo. M. Rewell & Co., 1887), 844.
130. George P. Rawick, Jan Hillegas, and Ken Lawrence, eds., *The American Slave: A Composite Autobiography, Supplement, Series 2, Vol. 9, Texas Narratives, Part 8* (Westport, CT: Greenwood Press, 1977), 3537.
131. Moses Greenwood to Doctor C. G. [Illegible], January [Date Uncertain], 1861; Moses Greenwood to J. N. Ember, January [7?], 1861 Greenwood Papers, NYHS.
132. "Stand Firm!" *North Carolina Standard*, November 10, 1860. See also "Bears in the Slave Market," *Commercial Advertiser*, November 13, 1860.
133. Untitled, *The Weekly Mississippian*, October 24, 1860.

134. Barney, *Rebels in the Making*, 23–33; Merritt, *Masterless Men*, 7–8.
135. Bill of Sale, H. G. Harbin to William N. Mercer, February 28, 1861, William N. Mercer Papers, Series I: LSU, Part 3, RASP; "Slaves at Buckhead," William N. Mercer Papers, Series I: LSU, Part 3, RASP. See also J. Carlyle Sitterson, "Magnolia Plantation, 1852–1862: A Decade of a Louisiana Sugar Estate," *The Mississippi Valley Historical Review* 25, no. 2 (September 1938): 198.
136. John Kimberly to Bettie Maney, November 11, 1860, Kimberly Papers, SHC.
137. A. F. Burton to "Dear Brother and Sister," January 14, March 30, 1861, Thomas W. Burton Papers, SHC; Brent Tarter, *Daydreams and Nightmares: A Virginia Family Faces Secession and War* (Charlottesville: University of Virginia Press, 2015), 26. See also Alex B. Barnes to David Bullock Harris, February 6, 1861, Harris Papers, Duke.
138. J. R. Shirley to "Mr. Dorsey," February 7, 1861, Chase Papers, LC.
139. John H. Flood to Davis, Deupree & Co., February 18, 1861, Charles F. Heartman Manuscripts of Slavery Collection, Xavier University of Louisiana Library, Digital Archives and Collections, https://cdm16948.contentdm.oclc.org/digital/collection/p16948coll6/id/6441 (accessed January 24, 2020).
140. C. D. W. to "My Beloved Brother," September 29, 1860, Lewis Neale Whittle Papers, SHC. See also H. McGinnis to Moore & Dawson, December 14, 1860, Chase Papers, LC.
141. James E. Dickinson to William Dickinson, November 11, 1860, Papers of the related Morton and Dickinson Families of Orange and Caroline Counties, Va., UVA; W. F. de Saussure to "My Dear Child," January 29, 1861, Boykin Family Papers, SHC.
142. W. A. Creasy to Betts & Gregory, February 13, 1861; A. J. Rux to E. H. Stokes, February 8, 14, 22, 1861, Chase Papers, LC.
143. Samuel Mordecai to George W. Mordecai, March 9, 1861, George W. Mordecai Papers, SHC. See also Caroline Morrill Brown, "War-Time Memories By an Old Lady Who Was Then Young," *The Magazine of Albemarle County History* 30 (1972): 30; Hunt & James to William Massie, April 25, 1861, Massie Papers, DBCAH.
144. Constitution of the Confederate States, March 11, 1861, https://avalon.law.yale.edu/19th_century/csa_csa.asp (accessed March 6, 2023); entry for March 27, 1861, in Arney Robinson Childs, ed., *The Private Journal of Henry William Ravenel 1859–1887* (Columbia: University of South Carolina Press, 1947), 57; John W. Ellis to Joseph E. Brown, January 21, 1861, in Noble J. Tolbert, ed., *The Papers of John Willis Ellis, Volume Two 1860–1861* (Raleigh, NC: State Department of Archives and History, 1964), 564; George H. Reese, ed., *Proceedings of the Virginia State Convention of 1861, February 13–May 1* (Richmond: Virginia State Library, 1965), I: 74–75. On the Confederate Constitution, see Charles R. Lee, *The Confederate Constitutions* (Chapel Hill: University of North Carolina Press, 1963). On efforts to reopen the African slave trade, see Ronald Takaki, *A Pro-Slavery Crusade: The Agitation to Reopen the African Slave Trade* (New York: Free Press, 1971); Freehling, *The Road to Disunion*, II: 168–184. On the efforts of the Secession Commissioners, see Charles B. Dew, *Apostles of Disunion: Southern Secession Commissioners and the Causes of the Civil War* (Charlottesville: University of Virginia Press, 2001).

145. Calomiris and Pritchett, "Betting on Secession," 12–13, Online Appendix, Figures A2 and A8.
146. Davis, Deupree & Co. to "Friend Fondren," February 7, 1861, Rudin Slavery Collection, Cornell; Betts & Gregory to "Dear Sir," January 5, 1861, Reid Papers, LVA.
147. "Price Advanced," *Richmond Daily Dispatch*, February 19, 1861; "Sale of Negroes and Land—Large Crowd—The Crisis, &c.," *Richmond Daily Dispatch*, February 13, 1861; Untitled, *Richmond Daily Dispatch*, March 8, 1861.
148. "Notice," *Richmond Daily Dispatch*, November 5, 1860. Several traders supported the Constitutional Union Party, including E. S. Turpin, John Frazier, and Alexander Grigsby. Grigsby even wagered $500 that Breckinridge would lose Virginia. "Political Notices," *Richmond Daily Dispatch*, November 3, 1860; "Bell and Everett in Fairfax," *Alexandria Gazette*, August 24, 1860; "Advertisement," *Alexandria Gazette*, September 29, 1860. Others claimed to have done so after the war, though these assertions must be taken with multiple grains of salt. Edward H. Stokes, Amnesty Petition, July 17, 1865; Reuben Ragland, Amnesty Petition, July 4, 1865, Case Files of Applications from Former Confederates for Presidential Pardons, 1865–67 (Amnesty Papers), RG 94: Records of the Adjutant General's Office, 1780s-1917, NARA (accessed via www.fold3.com).
149. "The Palmetto Tree," *Richmond Daily Dispatch*, March 23, 1861.
150. Samuel McDowell Moore to James D. Davidson, April 6, 1861 in Bruce S. Greenwalt, "The Correspondence of James D. Davidson, Reluctant Rebel" (MA thesis, University of Wisconsin, 1961), 41; "Local Matters," *Richmond Daily Dispatch*, April 15, 1861; James L. Apperson, Amnesty Petition, June 21, 1865, Amnesty Papers, RG 94, NARA (accessed via www.fold3.com). Apperson was, himself, a trader. "By Goddin & Apperson, Auct'rs," *Richmond Daily Dispatch*, November 4, 1862.
151. "Late News From the Rebel States," *Wheeling Daily Intelligencer*, August 17, 1861. For those who believed slavery would be safer in Virginia, see Evan Turiano, "'Prophecies of Loss': Debating Slave Flight during Virginia's Secession Crisis," *Journal of the Civil War Era* 12, no. 3 (September 2022): 338–361.
152. Bancroft, *Slave Trading in the Old South*, 165.
153. "Extracts from Teachers' Letters," *The Freedmen's Record* I, no. 5 (May 1865)
154. Steven Hahn, *The Political Worlds of Slavery and Freedom* (Cambridge, MA: Harvard University Press, 2009), 55–114.
155. T. A. Fowlkes to E. H. Stokes, April 23, 1861, Chase Papers, LC.
156. W. G. Chandler to Dickinson, Hill & Co., May 6, 1861; May 16, 1861, DHCRC.
157. Seth Woodroof to Dickinson, Hill & Co., May 7, 1861; T. R. Cherry to Dickinson, Hill & Co., May 9, 1861; J. B. Claiborne to Dickinson, Hill & Co., June 25, 1861; C. M. Price to Dickinson, Hill & Co., May 14, 1861, DHCRC.
158. "New Auction House for the Sale of Negroes," *Richmond Enquirer*, April 27, 1861; William Betts to N. B. Pleasants, March 7, 1861, Chase Papers, LC.
159. William P. Farmer to Dickinson Hill & Co., May 9, 1861, DHCRC.
160. Hunt & James to William Massie, April 25, 1861, Massie Papers, DBCAH.
161. Mel Young, *Last Order of the Lost Cause: The Civil War Memoirs of a Jewish Family from the "Old South," Raphael Jacob Moses, Major, C. S. A. 1812–1893* (Lanham, MD: University Press of America, Inc., 1995), 263.

162. W. B. Hickens[?] to Daniel J. Hartsook, June 18, 1861, Daniel J. Hartsook. Papers, 1848–1879, HL-LVA.

Chapter 2

1. Report of Maj. Gen. S. P. Heintzelman, *OR* Ser. I, Vol. 2, 40–41; "The Taking of Alexandria," *New-York Tribune*, May 25, 1861.
2. Report of Col. O. B. Willcox, *OR* Ser. I, Vol. 2, 41; "The Slave Barracoon—Capture of Cavalry," *Boston Traveler*, May 27, 1861.
3. Northup, *Twelve Years a Slave*, 41; William Still, *Still's Underground Rail Road Records* (Philadelphia: William Still, 1886), 185; C. M. Price to Dickinson Hill & Co., May 14, 1861, DHCRC.
4. Michael Ridgeway, "A Peculiar Business: Slave Trading in Alexandria, Virginia, 1825–1861" (MA thesis, Georgetown University, 1976), 150; "Report No. 104," *Index to the Reports of the Committees of the Senate of the United States for the Second Session of the Forty-First Congress. 1869–'70* (Washington, DC: Government Printing Office, 1870), 4. Price & Birch eventually re-established their business in Culpeper, Virginia. Bryan Prince, *A Shadow on the Household: One Enslaved Family's Incredible Struggle for Freedom* (Toronto: McClelland & Stewart, 2009), 211. "The Slave Barracoon—Capture of Cavalry," *Boston Traveler*, May 27, 1861.
5. "The First Slave Set Free," *Washington Evening Star*, January 11, 1901; "The War," *Boston Traveler*, May 27, 1861. My thanks to Benjamin Skolnik for sharing information on George Smith with me.
6. John G. Nicolay and John G. Hay, eds., *Complete Works of Abraham Lincoln* (New York: Francis D. Tandy Company, 1905), VI: 170; Daniel W. Crofts, *Lincoln and the Politics of Slavery: The Other Thirteenth Amendment and the Struggle to Save the Union* (Chapel Hill: University of North Carolina Press, 2016).
7. George N. Fuller, *Historic Michigan: Land of the Great Lakes. Its Life, Resources, Industries, People, Politics, Government, Wars, Institutions, Achievements, the Press, Schools and Churches Legendary and Prehistoric Lore, Volume I* (National Historic Association, 1924), 516–517; Robert Garth Scott, ed., *Forgotten Valor: The Memoirs, Journals, & Civil War Letters of Orlando B. Wilcox* (Kent: Kent State University Press, 1999), 267–268.
8. George C. Smith, Co. B., 102nd USCI, Combined Military Service Records (CMSR), RG 94, NARA.
9. Polanyi, *The Great Transformation*, 63–76, 130–162, 223–236.
10. Lightner, *Slavery and the Commerce Power*, 37–50, 71–89; Brown, *Good Wives, Nasty Wenches, and Anxious Patriarchs*, 107–136; Morgan, *Laboring Women*. On property rights and the American Founding, see, among others, Brewer, "Slavery, Sovereignty, and 'Inheritable Blood'"; Farr, "Locke, Natural Law, and New World Slavery"; Rael, *Eighty-Eight Years*, 33–41, 62–79; Huston, "Property Rights in Slavery and the Coming of the Civil War," 265; Nash, *Race and Revolution*; Gould, "The Laws of War and Peace: Legitimating Slavery in the Age of the American Revolution."

11. Lightner, *Slavery and the Commerce Power*, 37–64; Oakes, *Freedom National*, 18–29; Fehrenbacher, *The Slaveholding Republic*, 205–230.
12. George Frisbie Hoar, ed., *Charles Sumner: His Complete Works* (Boston: Lee and Shepard, 1900), 3: 126.
13. John W. Blassingame, ed., *The Frederick Douglass Papers, Series One: Speeches, Debates, and Interviews, Volume 2: 1847–54* (New Haven, CT: Yale University Press, 1982), 405–406.
14. Israel Washburn, "The Logic and the End of the Rebellion," *The Universalist Quarterly and General Review*, January 1864 (Boston: Tompkins & Co. 1864), 20; Washburn to Abraham Lincoln, January 22, 1864, Lincoln Papers, LC.
15. M. Eugene Sirmans, "The Legal Status of the Slave in South Carolina, 1670–1740," *Journal of Southern History* 28, no. 4 (November 1962): 462–473; Wiecek, "The Statutory Law of Slavery and Race in the Thirteen Mainland Colonies of British America"; Edward Rugemer, "The Development of Mastery and Race in the Comprehensive Slave Codes of the Greater Caribbean during the Seventeenth Century," *William and Mary Quarterly* 70 no. 3 (July 2013): 429–458.
16. Andrew Fede, "Legitimized Violent Slave Abuse in the American South, 1619–1865: A Case Study of Law and Social Change in Six Southern States," *American Journal of Legal History* 29, no. 2 (April 1985): 93–150; Jenny Bourne Wahl, "Legal Constraints on Slave Masters: The Problem of Social Cost," *American Journal of Legal History* 41, no. 1 (January 1997): 1–24. On amelioration and the prospect of a long-term slave system, see Willie Lee Rose, "The Domestication of Domestic Slavery," in *Slavery and Freedom*, ed. Willie Lee Rose and William W. Freeling (New York: Oxford University Press, 1982), 18–36.
17. William G. Shade, *Democratizing the Old Dominion: Virginia and the Second Party System* (Charlottesville: University of Virginia Press, 1996), 50–77, 262–291; William A. Link, *Roots of Secession: Slavery and Politics in Antebellum Virginia* (Chapel Hill: University of North Carolina Press, 2003), 11–27; Rachel N. Klein, *Unification of a Slave State: The Rise of the Planter Class in the South Carolina Backcountry, 1760–1808* (Chapel Hill: University of North Carolina Press, 1992), 257–268; Stephanie McCurry, *Masters of Small Worlds: Yeoman Households, Gender Relations, and the Political Culture of the Antebellum South Carolina Low Country* (New York: Oxford University Press, 1995), 30–36; J. Mills Thornton, *Politics and Power in a Slave Society: Alabama, 1800–1860* (Baton Rouge: Louisiana State University Press, 1978), 98–116.
18. Robin L. Einhorn, "Institutional Reality in the Age of Slavery: Taxation and Democracy in the States," *Journal of Policy History* 18, no. 1 (2006): 21–43 and *America Taxation, American Slavery* (Chicago: University of Chicago Press, 2006), 201–250.
19. Harry L. Watson, "Conflict and Collaboration: Yeomen, Slaveholders, and Politics in the Antebellum South," *Social History* 10, no. 3 (October 1985): 273–298. Quote on p. 274.
20. Hadden, *Slave Patrols*; Franklin and Schweninger, *Runaway Slaves*, 149–156; John Hope Franklin, *The Militant South, 1800–1861* (1956; repr. Urbana: University of Illinois Press, 2002), 71–79; Ryan Quintana, "Planners, Planters, and Slaves:

Producing the State in Early National South Carolina," *Journal of Southern History* 81, no. 1 (February 2015), especially 101–116; Johnson, *River of Dark Dreams*, 209–243; Susan Eva O'Donovan, "'Universities of Social and Political Change': Slaves in Jail in Antebellum America," in *Buried Lives: Incarcerated in Early America*, ed. Michele Lise Tarter and Richard Bell (Athens: University of Georgia Press, 2012), 124–148.

21. Quintana, *Making a Slave State* and "Slavery and the Conceptual History of the Early U.S. State," *Journal of the Early Republic* 38, no. 1 (Spring 2018): 77–86; Aaron Roy Hall, "Public Slaves and State Engineers: Modern Statecraft on Louisiana's Waterways, 1833–1861," *Journal of Southern History* 85, no. 3 (August 2019): 531–576 and "Slaves of the State: Infrastructure and Governance through Slavery in the Antebellum South," *Journal of American History* 106, no. 1 (June 2019): 19–46.

22. Aaron R. Hall, "'Plant Yourselves on its Primal Granite': Slavery, History and the Antebellum Roots of Originalism," *Law and History Review* 37, no. 3 (August 2019): 743–761; Donald Robinson, *Slavery and the Structure of American Politics* (New York: Harcourt Brace Jovanovitch, 1971); Leonard Richards, *The Slave Power: The Free North and Southern Domination, 1780–1860* (Baton Rouge: Louisiana State University Press, 2000), 54–82; Matthew Mason, *Slavery & Politics in the Early American Republic* (Chapel Hill: University of North Carolina Press, 2006), 51–74; John Craig Hammond, "'They Are Very Much Interested in Obtaining an Unlimited Slavery': Rethinking the Expansion of Slavery in the Louisiana Purchase Territories, 1803–1805," *Journal of the Early Republic* 23, no. 3 (Fall 2003): 353–380 and "'Uncontrollable Necessity': The Local Politics, Geopolitics, and Sectional Politics of Slavery Expansion," in Hammond and Matthew Mason, eds., *Contesting Slavery: The Politics of Bondage and Freedom in the New American Nation* (Charlottesville: University of Virginia Press, 2011), 138–160; Robert E. Bonner, *Mastering America: Southern Slaveholders and the Crisis of American Nationhood* (New York: Cambridge University Press, 2009), 3–23; Andrew Shankman, "Toward a Social History of Federalism: The State and Capitalism To and From the American Revolution," *Journal of the Early Republic* 37, no. 4 (Winter 2017): 637–649.

23. Rothman, *Slave Country*; Brian Schoen, "Positive Goods and Necessary Evils: Commerce, Security, and Slavery in the Lower South, 1787–1837," in Hammond and Mason, *Contesting Slavery*, 161–182; Brian Balogh, *A Government Out of Sight: The Mystery of National Authority in Nineteenth-Century America* (New York: Cambridge University Press, 2009), 178–184. On the functioning of the Land Office, see Malcolm J. Rohrbough, *The Land Office Business: The Settlement and Administration of American Public Lands* (New York: Oxford University Press, 1968).

24. David F. Ericson, "Slave Smugglers, Slave Catchers, and Slave Rebels: Slavery and American State Development, 1787–1842," in Hammond and Mason, *Contesting Slavery*, 183–203; Fehrenbacher, *The Slaveholding Republic*, 89–118; Kerr-Ritchie, *Rebellious Passage*; Matthew J. Clavin, *The Battle of Negro Fort: The Rise and Fall of a Fugitive Slave Community* (New York: New York University Press, 2019); Daniel Rasmussen, *American Uprising: The Untold Story of America's Largest Slave Revolt* (New York: Harper Collins, 2011), 135–147; David F. Allmendinger Jr., *Nat Turner*

and the Rising in Southampton County (Baltimore: Johns Hopkins University Press, 2014), 215; Karp, *This Vast Southern Empire*; Alice Baumgartner, *South to Freedom: Runaway Slaves to Mexico and the Road to the Civil War* (New York: Basic Books, 2020).

25. Fehrenbacher, *The Slaveholding Republic*, 205–251; Gautham Rao, "The State the Slaveholders Made: Regulating Fugitive Slaves in the Early Republic," in *Freedom's Conditions in the U.S.–Canadian Borderlands in the Age of Emancipation*, ed. Tony Freyer and Lyndsay Campbell (Durham, NC: Carolina Academic Press, 2011), 85–108 and "The Federal 'Posse Comitatus' Doctrine", 1–56.
26. Carl Paulus, *The Slaveholding Crisis: Fear of Insurrection and the Coming of the Civil War* (Baton Rouge: Louisiana State University Press, 2017), 197–234; Oakes, *Freedom National*, 8–48.
27. James D. Richardson, *A Compilation of the Messages and Papers of the Confederacy including the Diplomatic Correspondence 1861–1865* (Nashville: United States Publishing Company, 1905), I: 68.
28. Kaye, *Joining Places*, 177–208.
29. Berlin et al., *Slaves No More*, 3–76; Gerteis, *From Contraband to Freedman*; Chandra Manning, *What This Cruel War Was Over: Soldiers, Slavery, and the Civil War* (New York: Vintage Books, 2007), 73–102; Brasher, *The Peninsula Campaign and the Necessity of Emancipation*; Manning, *Troubled Refuge*, 201–231; Abigail Cooper, "'Lord, Until I Reach My Home': Inside the Refugee Camps of the American Civil War" (PhD diss., University of Pennsylvania, 2015), 198–227; Kristopher A. Teters, *Practical Liberators: Union Officers in the Western Theater during the Civil War* (Chapel Hill: University of North Carolina Press, 2018); Taylor, *Embattled Freedom*.
30. Bancroft, *Slave Trading in the Old South*, 314.
31. Stevens, *Anthony Burns*, 189–190. On slave traders and disease, see Stephen C. Kenny, "'A Dictate of Both Interest and Mercy'? Slave Hospitals in the Antebellum South," *Journal of the History of Medicine and Allied Sciences* 65, no. 1 (2010): 32–43; Robert Colby, "Waiting for Fevers to Abate: Contagion and Fear in the Domestic Slave Trade," in *The Business of Emotions in Modern History*, ed. Andrew Popp and Mandy L. Cooper (New York: Bloomsbury, 2023), 219–238.
32. Henry Guly, "Medicinal Brandy," *Resuscitation* 82, no. 7 (March 2011): 951–954; Megan L. Bever, *At War with King Alcohol: Debating Drinking and Masculinity in the Civil War* (Chapel Hill: University of North Carolina Press, 2022), 15–16.
33. Entries for April 22, 24, 25, 26, 1861, Davis Daybooks, NYPL.
34. Totals taken from the April 1860 "Sundries to Sales Acct." sections of the Hector Davis & Co. Account Books, CHM and the April 1861 "Sundries to Sales Acct." sections of the Davis Daybooks, NYPL, respectively. "By Hector Davis, Auct.," *Richmond Whig*, April 10, July 23, 1861.
35. Entries for April 4, 5, 20, 1861, Davis Daybooks, NYPL.
36. Entries for April 2, 20, 22, 24, 25, 26, ibid.
37. William P. Farmer to Dickinson Hill & Co., May 9, 1861, DHCRC. See also Seth Woodruff to Dickinson Hill & Co., May 7, 1861, in same.
38. Entries for April 6 (unnamed child), 19 (Mary), 22 (Priscilla and Nelson), 26 (Nelson), 27 (Peter), 1861, Davis Daybooks, NYPL.

39. Entry for April 25, 1861, ibid.
40. Entries for April 27, May 8, 1861, ibid.; "Louisiana Depot," *Richmond Daily Dispatch*, November 5, 1861; G. Howard Gregory, *53rd Virginia Infantry and 5th Battalion Virginia Infantry* (Appomattox: H. E. Howard, Inc., 1999), 10.
41. On red flags announcing slave auctions, see Olmsted, *A Journey in the Seaboard States*, 33–34.
42. Pritchett and Calomiris, "Betting on Secession," 8, 11–16.
43. James Henry Hammond to Christopher Memminger, May 24, 1861, James Henry Hammond Papers, LC.
44. Financial institutions appearing in Davis's books include: the Farmer's Bank of Virginia (Charlottesville, Richmond), the Traders' Bank of Richmond, the Bank of the City of Petersburg, and unspecified "NC funds" and "Baltimore" money. See entries for April 1, 5, 6, 15, 1861. Simon Guckenheim, George W. Koontz, and E. C. Moore presented the only New York checks. Entries for April 9, 13. For Davis advancing money, see, William P. Goffigon, April 1, 1861; R. L. Wade, April 8, 1861; John Strong, April 17, 1861, all Davis Daybooks, NYPL.
45. W. P. Tate[?] to "Dear Sir," April 6, 1861, Lenoir Family Papers, SHC. See also Paul B. Barringer to Daniel M. Barringer, June 14, 1861, Barringer Papers, SHC; William A. Dickinson to W. S. Pettigrew, April 19, 1861, Pettigrew Papers, SHC.
46. Charles Pettigrew to Mrs. C. S. Pettigrew, June 11, 1861, Pettigrew Papers, SHC. See also Mary A. Burton to "Dear Uncle and Aunt," September 26, 1861, Burton Papers, SHC; Sarah Hamilton Yancey to Benjamin Cudworth Yancey, November 11, 1861, Benjamin Cudworth Yancey Papers, Duke.
47. Richard Archer to Abram Barnes Archer, October 6, 1861; Archer to J. J. Person, April 1, 1862, Richard Thompson Archer Papers, Natchez Trace Collection, DBCAH.
48. Entry for July 15, 1861, John Houston Bills Diary, John Houston Bills Papers, SHC. See also Charles D. Carr & Co. to Jacob Rhett Motte, July 1861, Jacob Rhett Motte Papers, Duke.
49. James H. Iverson to William L. Mitchell, December 19, 1861, William Letcher Mitchell Papers, SHC. Stay laws—or their de facto implementation also disincentivized borrowing in this period. See for example, John H. Brown to Hamilton Brown, September 28, 1861, Hamilton Brown Papers, SHC; F. F. Forbes to James W. Bryan, July 5, 1861, Bryan Family Papers, SHC; William W. Burch to William T. Sutherlin, February 22, 1861, William Thomas Sutherlin Papers, SHC.
50. Glatthaar, *General Lee's Army*, 29–41; Stephen Davis and William A. Richards, "An Atlantan Goes to War: The Civil War Letters of Maj. Zachariah Rice," *Atlanta History* 36, no. 1 (Spring 1992): 20–40. My thanks to Pearl Young for alerting me to this source. Note, Elias W. Ferguson Papers, NCDAH; Timothy S. Huebner, "Taking Profits, Making Myths: The Slave Trading Career of Nathan Bedford Forrest," *Civil War History* 69, no. 1 (March 2023): 67–70; Brian Steel Wills, *A Battle from the Start: The Life of Nathan Bedford Forrest* (New York: Harper Collins, 1992), 45.
51. "Correspondence of the New York *Times*," *Cincinnati Daily Press*, May 9, 1861.
52. J. Gwyn to Rufus Lenoir, May 15, 1861, Lenoir Papers, SHC; William L. Barney, *The Making of a Confederate: Walter Lenoir's Civil War* (New York: Oxford University Press, 2007), 53.

53. William S. McFeely, *Grant* (New York: Norton, 1981), 82; U. S. Grant to Frederick Dent, April 19, 1861, in John Y. Simon, ed., *The Papers of Ulysses S. Grant, Volume 2: April–September 1861* (Carbondale: Southern Illinois University Press, 1969), 4; Nicholas W. Sacco, "'I Never Was an Abolitionist': Ulysses S. Grant and Slavery, 1854–1863," *Journal of the Civil War Era* 9, no. 3 (September 2019): 428. On international competition, see Sven Beckert, "Emancipation and Empire: Reconstructing the Worldwide Web of Cotton Production in the Age of the American Civil War," *American Historical Review* 109, no. 5 (December 2004): 1405–1438.

54. See, for example, Ginny McNeill Raska and Mary Lynne Gasaway Hill, eds., *The Uncompromising Diary of Sallie McNeill* (College Station: Texas A&M University Press, 2009), 100; Karen Gerhardt Fort, ed., *A Feast of Reason: The Civil War Journal of James Madison Hall* (Abilene: State House Press, 2016), 52.

55. N. H. Fennell to T. D. McDowell, July 19, 1861, T. D. McDowell Papers, SHC. Emphasis in original.

56. William Howard Russell, *The Civil War in America* (Boston: Gardner A. Fuller, 1861), 66.

57. Louis Manarin, *Richmond at War: The Minutes of the City Council 1861–1865* (Chapel Hill: University of North Carolina Press, 1966), 91, 104. Davis, Deupree & Co. does not appear on the state tax lists for this period. Auditor of Public Accounts. Administration of State Government: Revenue Assessment and Collection–Fees and Licenses. Entry 454: License Returns, Danville-Richmond, 1862, LVA.

58. Auditor of Public Accounts. Administration of State Government: Revenue Assessment and Collection–Fees and Licenses. Entry 454: License Returns, Danville-Richmond, 1862, LVA; "Dissolution of Co-Partnership," *Richmond Daily Dispatch*, November 11, 1861; Omohundro Slave Trade and Farm Accounts, 1857–1864, UVA. Martinez sees this as the most direct evidence linking slave trading with Confederate fortunes, and I am inclined to agree. Martinez, "The Slave Market in Civil War Virginia," 112.

59. Seth Woodroof to Dickinson Hill & Co., May 7, 1861; T. R. Cherry to Dickinson Hill & Co., May 9, 1861; J. B. Claiborne to Dickinson Hill & Co., June 25, 1861; C. M. Price to Dickinson Hill & Co., May 14, 1861, DHCRC.

60. J. J. M'Elrath to William A. Graham, May 15, 1861, William A. Graham Papers, SHC.

61. H. F. Peterson to Dickinson, Hill & Co., April 27, 1861, DHCRC; "Carolina and Virginia Negroes," *New Orleans Times-Picayune*, April 2, 1861.

62. May 11, 1861, New Orleans Sheriff Sales Books, 1846–1863, NOPL. They eventually sold on June 1, 1861 to Paculie Labarre.

63. Ezekiel Pickens Noble to Edward Noble, October 21, 1861, Noble Family Papers, HL.

64. "Louisiana Legislature," *New Orleans Daily Picayune*, March 1, 1861; "Lands for Sale or Exchange for Negroes," *New Orleans Times-Picayune*, April 3, 1861.

65. Laurence J. Kotlikoff, "The Structure of Slave Prices in New Orleans, 1804 to 1862," *Economic Inquiry* 17, no. 4 (October 1979): 503. On diseases in New Orleans, see Olivarius, *Necropolis*. To keep purchased people away from the urban disease climate, Walter Campbell housed them on a farm outside the city during the summer. Bancroft, *Slave Trading in the Old South*, 317; "Sale of Negroes," *New Orleans Daily*

Crescent, May 8, 1861; Deyle, *Carry Me Back*, 136; Tadman, *Speculators and Slaves*, 70–71; Freudenberger and Pritchett, "The Domestic United States Slave Trade: New Evidence," 463–465; Gerald M. Capers, *Occupied City: New Orleans Under the Federals, 1862–1865* (Lexington: University of Kentucky Press, 1965), 10–11.

66. Henry S. Gilmour to Godfrey Barnsley, June 8, 1861, in Dale A. Somers, "New Orleans at War: A Merchant's View," *Louisiana History: The Journal of the Louisiana Historical Association* 14, no. 1 (Winter 1973), 53; "New Orleans Money Market," *New Orleans Daily Crescent*, May 13, 1861.
67. "New Orleans Money Market," *New Orleans Daily Crescent*, April 1, 8, May 27, 1861.
68. "New Orleans Money Market," *New Orleans Daily Crescent*, April 22, May 6, 1861; "Remarks on the Market," *New Orleans Price-Current and Commercial Intelligencer*, June 22, 1861; William C. Thompson to Lewis Thompson, May 6, 1861; Foley, Avery & Co. to Lewis Thompson, April 18, 1861, Thompson Papers, SHC.
69. Andrew McCollam to Ellen McCollam, May 9, 1861, Andrew McCollam Papers, SHC.
70. Charles L. Dufour, *The Night the War Was Lost* (Garden City: Doubleday, 1960), 59–63. By 1862, the Union navy intercepted perhaps 40 percent of blockade runners—enough to deter most of those willing to make the attempt. Stanley Lebergott, "Through the Blockade: The Profitability and Extent of Cotton Smuggling, 1861–1865," *Journal of Economic History* 41, no. 4 (December 1981): 873. Frank L. Owsley, Sr., *King Cotton Diplomacy: Foreign Relations of the Confederate States of America*, 3rd ed. (Tuscaloosa: University of Alabama Press, 2008), 237; Stephen R. Wise, *Lifeline of the Confederacy: Blockade Running During the Civil War* (Columbia: University of South Carolina Press, 1988); James M. McPherson, *Battle Cry of Freedom: The Civil War Era* (New York: Oxford University Press, 1988), 313–314, 380–382; Craig L. Symonds, *Lincoln and His Admirals: Abraham Lincoln, the U.S. Navy, and the Civil War* (New York: Oxford University Press, 2008), 37–39, 280.
71. Moses Greenwood to Connors Harding & Co., May 13, 1861, Benjamin F. Butler Papers, LC; See also Carroll, Hay & Co. to George K. Johnson, May 29, 1861, George K. Johnson Papers, Duke. Certainly, many considered the blockade a temporary obstacle; Confederate diplomat John Slidell, for one, thought cotton exports might be blocked for five to six months before Britain and France raised the blockade. John Slidell to Edward George Washington Butler, May 30, 1861, Edward George Washington Butler Papers, Duke.
72. "Proclamation," *New Orleans Daily Crescent*, October 4, 1861; Marler, *The Merchant's Capital*, 135–139 and "'An Abiding Faith in Cotton,'" 266–268.
73. David G. Surdam, "Union Military Superiority and New Orleans's Economic Value to the Confederacy," *Louisiana History* 38, no. 4 (Autumn 1997): 400.
74. Marler, *The Merchant's Capital*, 127–135; "Monetary Affairs, *New York Times*, May 10, 1861; W. D. Urquhart to Lewis Stirling, May 2, 1861, Turnbull-Allain Family Papers, Series I: LSU, Part 4, RASP.
75. "Talk on 'Change," *New Orleans Daily Crescent*, September 26, 1862, October 23, 1861.
76. William Ashley Vaughn, "Natchez During the Civil War" (PhD diss., University of Southern Mississippi, 2001), 71

NOTES TO PAGES 57–58

77. Stephen Duncan to Alexander K. Farrar, Undated (1861), Alexander K. Farrar Papers, 1804–1865, Series I: LSU, Part 3, RASP.
78. "Untitled," *Natchez Daily Courier*, December 24, 1861.
79. Mary A. Burton to "Dear Uncle and Aunt," September 26, 1861, Burton Papers, SHC. See also Bennett Hill to Louis Covin, September 1, 1861, in Frank Anderson Chappell, *Dear Sister: Civil War Letters to A Sister in Alabama* (Huntsville: Branch Springs Publishing, 2002), 24.
80. Maud C. Fentress to David Fentress, February 3, 1862, University of North Texas Special Collections, texashistory.unt.edu/ark:/67531/metapth182714/m1/2/?q=%22negro%20property%22 (accessed August 3, 2017).
81. Sydenham Moore to Amanda Moore, February 19, 1862, Sydenham Moore Family Papers, Alabama Department of Archives and History. See also Edward Sparrow to John Perkins, January 3, 1862, John Perkins Papers, SHC.
82. Jonathan Pritchett, "New Orleans Slave Sale Data, 1856–1861," http://www.tulane.edu/~pritchet/data.html (accessed June 20, 2023). Pritchett's and Calomiris's data run through August 1861. Data from beyond that point comes from Orleans Parish Conveyance Books, Vols. 85–87, OPCO; Stanley Engerman and Robert Fogel, "New Orleans Slave Sales Sample, 1804–1862" (Ann Arbor: Inter-university Consortium for Political and Social Research), 5–7. Fogel's and Engerman's sample included 135 sales in 1860, 19 in 1861, and 15 in 1862. No other year after 1820 had fewer than 48. Pritchett and Calomiris, "Betting on Secession," 7–8.
83. "Southern Pacific Railroad Company," *New Orleans Daily Picayune*, August 4, 1861. On Confederate's aims to expand westward, see Adrian Brettle, *Colossal Ambitions: Confederate Planning for a Post–Civil War World* (Charlottesville: University of Virginia Press, 2020); Kevin Waite, *West of Slavery: The Southern Dream of a Transcontinental Empire* (Chapel Hill: University of North Carolina Press, 2021).
84. "Twenty Dollars Reward," *New Orleans Times-Picayune*, August 1, 1861; "Wanted to Purchase," *New Orleans Daily Crescent*, January 15, 1862; "Wanted to Buy For Cash Ten to Twelve Negro Men," *New Orleans Daily Crescent*, January 21, 1862; "A Valuable Slave At Auction," *New Orleans Daily Crescent*, August 26, 1861.
85. No correspondence between Dickinson, Hill & Co. and their traditional New Orleans correspondents survive past late April 1861. R. H. Dickinson to "Dear Paul," January 12, February 13, 1862, Miscellaneous File, Robert A. Brock Collection, HL-LVA.
86. "Wanted-One Hundred and Fifty Negroes For Sale," *Richmond Examiner*, October 31, 1861; Omohundro Slave Trade and Farm Accounts, UVA.
87. On Toler, see Conveyance Books, Vol. 85, June 5, 1861, OPCO. On Brittingham, see Edward Barnett (Notary), Vol. 81, Acct. 103, OPNA. A. J. Rux to E. H. Stokes, October 9, 1861, Slavery Collection, NYHS. For Brittingham's longer career, see Brittingham to R. H. Dickinson, May 20, 1853; Brittingham to Dickinson, Hill & Co., September 16, 1860; August 26, 1862, DHCRC.
88. James Augustin to J. D. B. De Bow, November 9, 1861, J. D. B. De Bow Papers, Duke.
89. Achille Chiapella to George Ulrich, December 20, 1861, Rosemonde E. & Emile Kuntz Collection: National Period, 1804–1950, Manuscripts Collection 600, La Research Collection, Howard-Tilton Memorial Library, Tulane University Digital

NOTES TO PAGES 58–59   251

Library, https://digitallibrary.tulane.edu/islandora/object/tulane:12767 (accessed August 1, 2018). Chiapella conceded that these potential buyers "ha[d] not yet come to town." Two weeks later, Chiapella successfully sold an enslaved domestic for $800. Chiapella to Ulrich, January 2, 1862, https://digitallibrary.tulane.edu/islandora/object/tulane:13097 (accessed August 1, 2018). Somers, "New Orleans at War," 62; Conveyance Books, Vol. 86, 354, 356; Vol. 87, 112, 256, 360, 405, 407–408, OPCO.

90. "From and After This Date," and "C. M. Rutherford," *New Orleans Daily Crescent*, December 27, 1861; Conveyance Books, Vol. 85, 329; Vol. 87, 253, OPCO; Edward Barnett (Notary), Vol. 81, Accts. 15, 24, 29, OPNA; Conveyance Books, Vol. 86, Nos. 241–480, 321, 380; Vol. 87, 222, 242, 243, 282, 337, 421, 439, OPCO. "Negroes for Sale," *New Orleans Daily Picayune*, March 7, 1862. On the antebellum New Orleans slave trade, see Walter Johnson, "Masters and Slaves in the Market: Slavery and the New Orleans Trade, 1804–1864" (PhD diss., Princeton University, 1995).

91. Data drawn from Conveyance Books, Vols. 85–87, OPCO, and compared to that taken from the same source by Pritchett and Calomiris, "New Orleans Slave Sale Data, 1856–1861"; Kotlikoff, "The Structure of Slave Prices in New Orleans," 501.

92. "A Vivid Picture of New Orleans," *Cleveland Morning Leader*, December 9, 1861; Sales on January 6, 7, 18, 24, 27; February 24; April 28, 1862, Orleans Parish Sheriff's Office Sales Books, Vol. 30, NOPL.

93. Joseph Bruin to John Washington III, August 8, 1845, John Washington III Manuscripts, George Washington Presidential Library at Mount Vernon, https://cdm16829.contentdm.oclc.org/digital/collection/p16829coll25/id/663 (accessed March 22, 2023). Josephine F. Pacheco, *The Pearl: A Failed Slave Escape on the Potomac* (Chapel Hill: University of North Carolina Press, 2005), 36, 120; Ridgeway, "A Peculiar Business," 103–104; "Negroes for Sale," *New Orleans Daily Picayune*, January 3, 1861.

94. "Negroes for Sale, " *New Orleans Daily Crescent*, December 27, 1861, January 14, 1862, February 18, 1862; "Negroes Arrived To-Day," *New Orleans Daily Crescent*, April 18, 1862

95. Richard Horace Browne to Sarah Browne, April 2, 1862, Richard Horace Browne Papers, SHC. Browne also served as a lawyer for the slave dealer Thomas Matthews.

96. See, among others, Edward Barnett (Notary), Vol. 80, Acct. 406, 425–427; Vol. 81, Acct. 1, 77, 79, 92, 126, 129, OPNA; Conveyance Books, Vol. 85, 153, 183, 204, 208, 295, 330, 428; Vol. 86 (1–240), 197; Vol. 86 (241–480), 243, 343, 368, 381, 382; Vol. 87, 282, 295, 349, 356, 360, 440, 455, 193, 198, 229, 240, OPCO.

97. McPherson, *Battle Cry of Freedom*, 438; Lerner, "Money, Prices, and Wages in the Confederacy," 23–25; Burdekin and Weidenmier, "Suppressing Asset Price Inflation," 420.

98. Charles Gayarré to J. D. B. De Bow, November 20, 1861, De Bow Papers, Duke. The French consul in the city noted a similar trend. Gordon Wright, "Economic Conditions in the Confederacy as Seen by the French Consuls," *Journal of Southern History* 7, no. 2 (May 1941): 208.

99. J. D. B. De Bow to Charles Gayarré, August 28, October 28, December 16, 1861, Charles E. A. Gayarré Papers, Louisiana and Lower Mississippi Valley Collections, LSU.

100. Bill of Sale, February 20, 1862, Gayarré Papers, LSU.
101. Martha De Bow to J. D. B. De Bow, December 28, 1861, De Bow Papers, Duke.
102. James M. Young to Alexander Stephens, October 29, 1861, Swann Galleries, Sale 2503, Lot 89, https://catalogue.swanngalleries.com/Lots/auction-lot/(SLAVERY-AND-ABOLITION)-[Stephens-Alexander]-The-Confederate?saleno=2503&lotNo=89&refNo=754308 (accessed June 20, 2023). This was not the first time an enslaver had consulted Stephens on the slave market. See Alexander Hamilton Stephens Letter to R. C. Daniel, December 14, 1860, UGA.
103. Totals taken from "Sundries to Sales Account," Davis Daybooks, NYPL. In 1860, by comparison, Davis had traded 404 people in January and February.
104. McPherson, *Battle Cry of Freedom*, 392–420.
105. Berlin et al., *The Wartime Genesis of Free Labor: The Lower South*, 440, 446. Butler provided a figure of $1,500 as a standard slave price and affirmed that enslaved people had been "the favorite investment for the last thirty years in the South" (444). On Butler's time in New Orleans, see Elizabeth Leonard, *Benjamin Franklin Butler: A Noisy, Fearless Life* (Chapel Hill: University of North Carolina Press, 2022), 51–83.
106. Rashauna Johnson, *Slavery's Metropolis: Unfree Labor in New Orleans during the Age of Revolutions* (New York: Cambridge University Press, 2016), 33, 38–52. Quote on p. 33. Walter Johnson explores the idea of the slave market as a space between personhood and commodity of at length in *Soul By Soul*, particularly 19–30 and 117–134. For a case study, see Johnson, "The Slave Trader, the White Slave, and the Politics of Racial Determination in the 1850s," *Journal of American History* 87, no. 1 (June 2000): 13–38.
107. See Conveyance Books, Vols. 85–87, OPCO. The United States also flexed its muscles to attack slavery and the slave trade internationally. Harris, *The Last Slave Ships*, 183–234.
108. Thomas M. Aldrich, *The History of Battery A First Regiment Rhode Island Light Artillery In the War to Preserve the Union 1861–1865* (Providence, RI: Snow & Farnham, 1904), 49; Ronald G. Watson, ed., *From Ashby to Andersonville: The Civil War Diary and Reminiscences of George A. Hitchcock, Private, Company A, 21st Massachusetts Regiment August 1862–January 1865* (Campbell, CA: Savas Publishing Company, 1997), 40; Adam Clarke Rice to Charley Rice, July 30, 1863, in Adam Clarke Rice, *The Letters and Other Writings of the Late Lieut. Adam Clarke Rice, of the 121st Regiment, N.Y. Volunteers* (Little Falls: Journal & Courier Book and Job Printing Press, 1864), 100–101.
109. Wm. W. Hall to Dickinson Hill, November 12, 1861, Charles W. and Mary Lesley Ames Papers, Minnesota Historical Society; W. W. Hall to Dickinson and Hill, January 29, 1862, Chase Papers, LC; Emma Bolt to Unknown, 1864, in Henry L. Swint, ed., *Dear Ones At Home: Letters from Contraband Camps* (Nashville: Vanderbilt University Press, 1966), 107.
110. "Ignorance and Hatred of Southeastern Virginians—A Better state of things at Portsmouth," *Cleveland Morning Leader*, May 17, 1862; Robert M. Browning Jr., *From Cape Charles to Cape Fear: The North Atlantic Blockading Squadron During the Civil War* (Tuscaloosa: University of Alabama Press, 1993), 10, 41; Charles L. Perdue

Jr., Thomas E. Baden, and Robert K. Phillips, *Weevils in the Wheat: Interviews with Virginia Ex-Slaves* (Bloomington: Indiana University Press, 1980), 135, 235, 256.

111. "The Markets of Norfolk," *The Prairie Farmer*, May 31, 1862; Perdue et al., *Weevils in the Wheat*, 256.

112. M. C. Cope, *Report of a Visit to Hampton, Norfolk & Yorktown Presented to the Executive Board of the 'Friends' Association of Philadelphia and its vicinity for the Relief of Colored Freedmen'* (Philadelphia: Ringwalt & Brown, 1863), 9–10.

113. George P. Rawick, *The American Slave*, 5: 3, 79; Rawick et al., *The American Slave... Supplement*, Series 2, 2: 1, 133.

114. Henry H. Hayne to Andrew Johnson, August 11, 1862, in Leroy P. Graf, Ralph W. Haskins, and Patricia P. Clark, eds., *The Papers of Andrew Johnson, Volume 5, 1861–1862* (Knoxville: University of Tennessee Press, 1979), 607–609.

115. Alfred Eaton to Johnson, August 25, 1862, in Graf, Haskins, and Clark, *The Papers of Andrew Johnson* 5: 631; John Cimprich, *Slavery's End in Tennessee, 1861–1865* (University: University of Alabama Press, 1985), 33–45. Quote on p. 33. Ash, *Middle Tennessee Society Transformed*, 84–95, 106–111; Berlin et al., *The Wartime Genesis of Free Labor: The Upper South*, 414; George W. Pepper, *Personal Recollections of Sherman's Campaigns in Georgia and the Carolinas* (Zanesville: Hugh Dunne, 1866), 18.

116. Berlin et al., *The Wartime Genesis of Free Labor: The Upper South*, 414–415; Jan Furman, ed., *Slavery in the Clover Bottoms: John McCline's Narrative of His Life During Slavery and the Civil War* (Knoxville: University of Tennessee Press, 1998), 51. A few slave transactions did continue in the city. "Price of Negroes at Nashville," *Wilmington Journal*, December 18, 1862; "Abduction of Negroes," *Nashville Daily Union*, September 20, 1862; Bill Carey, *Runaways, Coffles, and Fancy Girls: A History of Slavery in Tennessee* (Nashville: Clearbrook Press, 2018), 302; John David Smith, *We Ask Only for Even-Handed Justice: Black Voices from Reconstruction, 1865–1877* (Amherst: University of Massachusetts Press, 2014), 30.

117. Deyle, *Carry Me Back*, 94–97; Gerald Capers, *The Biography of a River Town: Memphis, Its Heroic Age* (Chapel Hill: University of North Carolina Press, 1939), 282; John Hallum, *The Diary of an Old Lawyer or Scenes Behind the Curtain* (Nashville: Southwestern Publishing House, 1895), 76–79; Hannah Rosen, *Terror in the Heart of Freedom: Citizenship, Sexual Violence, and the Meaning of Race in the Postemancipation South* (Chapel Hill: University of North Carolina Press, 2009), 27–28.

118. Berlin et al., *The Wartime Genesis of Free Labor: The Lower South*, 737; Oscar Derostus Ladley to Catherine Griffith Ladley, April 1, 1861, in Carl M. Becker and Ritchie Thomas, eds., *Hearth and Knapsack: The Ladley Letters, 1857–1880* (Athens: Ohio University Press, 1988), 2–3.

119. "High Prices of Negroes," *Memphis Daily Appeal*, January 16, 1862; "The War in the Southwest," *Brooklyn Daily Eagle*, May 5, 1862; Rawick, *The American Slave*, 5: 3, 79. Rawick, *The American Slave*, 7, 108.

120. "G. N. Robinson, Real Estate Broker"; "For Sale! Plantation & Thirty-Five Negroes"; "Local Matters," *Memphis Daily Avalanche*, May 24, 1862. Robinson advertised thirty enslaved people for sale—"if desired."

121. John Milton Hubbard, *Notes of a Private* (St. Louis: Nixon-Jones Printing Co., 1911), 105–106.
122. McPherson, *Battle Cry of Freedom*, 417–418; Berlin et al., *The Destruction of Slavery*, 281; Sherman to Gideon Pillow, August 14, 1862, in Brooks D. Simpson and Jean V. Berlin, eds., *Sherman's Civil War: Selected Correspondence of William T. Sherman, 1860–1865* (Chapel Hill: University of North Carolina Press, 1999), 275; "Are We to Have a New Jail," *Memphis Daily Union Appeal*, August 16, 1862.
123. Sherman to J. B. Bingham, Esq., January 26, 1864, in Simpson and Berlin, *Sherman's Civil War*, 591.
124. "Commercial Intelligence," *New Orleans Daily True Delta*, April 25, 1862; James O. Lang, "Gloom Envelops New Orleans: April 24 to May 2, 1862," *Louisiana History* 1, no. 4 (Autumn 1960): 282–289; Order to Remove the Public Stores from N. O., April 1862, Marshall McDonald Papers, Duke.
125. April 28, 1862, Orleans Parish Sheriff's Office Sales Books, Vol. 30, NOPL; "Proceedings of a Court of Inquiry, Assembled at Jackson Miss., Pursuant to Special Orders 41," *OR*, Series. I, Vol. VI, 562.
126. Capers, *Occupied City*, 145–171.
127. August Belmont to Abraham Lincoln, May 9, 1862, Lincoln Papers, LC.
128. Surdam, "Union Military Superiority and New Orleans's Economic Value to the Confederacy," 400.
129. Unknown to "My Dear Frank," June 11, 1862, Frank E. Spencer Papers, 1862–1864, Duke; Sean A. Scott, "'The Glory of the City is Gone': Perspectives of Union Soldiers on New Orleans During the Civil War," *Louisiana History* 57, no. 1 (Winter 2016): 47.
130. W. C. Corsan, *Two Months in the Confederate States: An Englishman's Travels Through the South* (Baton Rouge: Louisiana State University Press, 1996), 11, 13–14.
131. W. Mishoffer to Butler, May 20, 1862, Butler Papers, LC; Butler to Edwin Stanton, May 25, 1862, *OR*, Ser. I, Vol. XV, 440. Butler was willing to confiscate property "for the purpose of punishment and example," and would happily dispose of it, "save that where property consists in the services of slaves I shall not sell it until so ordered." C. Peter Ripley, *Slaves and Freedmen in Civil War Louisiana* (Baton Rouge: Louisiana State University Press, 1976), 44–57; William F. Messner, *Freedmen and the Ideology of Free Labor: Louisiana, 1862–1865* (Lafayette: Center for Louisiana Studies, University of Southwestern Louisiana, 1978), 6–7. For another manifestation of this spirit, see Lawrence N. Powell, *New Masters: Northern Planters During the Civil War and Reconstruction* (New Haven, CT: Yale University Press, 1980), 1–34.
132. Berlin et al., *The Destruction of Slavery*, 187–189.
133. Nathaniel P. Banks to Henry W. Halleck, January 7, 1863, Nathaniel P. Banks Papers, LC.
134. For efforts to reopen the city's commerce, see Benjamin F. Butler, *General Orders from Headquarters Department of the Gulf Issued by Major-General B. F. Butler From May 1st 1862 to the present time.* (New Orleans: E. R. Wagener, 1862), 4, 9–10; Headquarters, Department of the Gulf, *General Orders No. 112* (New Orleans: Department of the Gulf, 1864), 1; James Parton, *General Butler in New Orleans:*

History of the Administration of the Department of the Gulf in the Year 1862: With an Account of the Capture of New Orleans, and a Sketch of the Previous Career of the General, Civil and Military (New York: Mason Brothers, 1864), 407.
135. Butler, *General Orders from Headquarters*, 14.
136. "From New Orleans," *Memphis Daily Appeal*, July 19, 1862. See also William Watson, *Life in the Confederate Army Being the Observations and Experiences of an Alien in the South During the American Civil War* (London: Chapman and Hall, 1887), 439.
137. "City Intelligence," *Baltimore Daily Exchange*, April 25, 1861; Answer, November 5, 1866, Transcript of Appeal, *Walter L. Campbell* vs. *Charles Waters and Mary A. Waters*, State of Louisiana, Fourth District Court of New Orleans, No. 17,496, http://dspace.uno.edu:8080/xmlui/handle/123456789/38358 (accessed July 16, 2018); W. L. Campbell, Joseph Bruin, C. F. Hatcher, Confederate Papers Relating to Citizens or Business Firms, RG 109: War Department Collection of Confederate Records, NARA M346 (accessed via Fold3.com). H. F. Peterson to Dickinson Hill & Co., October 30, 1860, DHCRC; "Gens. Thompson's and Price's Commands," New Orleans *Daily Crescent*, December 2, 1861. Peterson may have eventually taken the oath. List of Those Taking the Oath of Allegiance, Subject File: Civil War, Dept. of the Gulf, Miscellany, 1862–1863, Butler Papers, LC.
138. Jesse Ames Marshall, *Private and Official Correspondence of Gen. Benjamin F. Butler*, Vol. 2 (Norwood, MA: The Plimpton Press, 1917), 17, 23; Butler, *General Orders from Headquarters*, 15, 30–31, 34. For the prosecution of such a case, see Edward Firory, Arian Capardi, Charles Thompson, Doctor Horentine Berta, June 13, 1863, Entry 1686, Register of the Provost Court of New Orleans, RG 393: Records of United States Army Continental Commands, Vol. IV, NARA. Those convicted were fined $1,000 or sentenced to serve time in the parish jail. Similar cases appear regularly in the register. General Orders No. 44 did except slaves brought in on the same ship, theoretically conceding the right of transit of slaves that had long underpinned the coastwise slave trade.
139. Adam Rothman, *Beyond Freedom's Reach: A Kidnapping in the Twilight of Slavery* (Cambridge, MA: Harvard University Press, 2015).
140. Russell, "Sale Day in Antebellum South Carolina," 21–86; Morris, *Southern Slavery and the Law*, 81–101; Tadman, *Speculators and Slaves*, 49–53, 119–121.
141. Morris, *Southern Slavery and the Law*, 338–353; Hadden, *Slave Patrols*, particularly 41–70; Franklin and Schweninger, *Runaway Slaves*, 149–156; Quintana, "Planners, Planters, and Slaves," especially 101–116; Johnson, *River of Dark Dreams*, 209–243. On Federal forces' role in suppressing a New Orleans slave revolt, see Rasmussen, *American Uprising*, 135–147. On the use of federal power against fugitive slaves, see Fehrenbacher, *The Slaveholding Republic*, 205–252 and R. J. M. Blackett, *The Captive's Quest for Freedom: Fugitive Slaves, The 1850 Fugitive Slave Law, and the Politics of Slavery* (New York: Cambridge University Press, 2018), 52–79.
142. A. Mygatt & Co., *A. Mygatt & Co's New Orleans Business Directory* (New Orleans: A. Mygatt & Co., 1858), 184–185 and McInnis, "Mapping the Slave Trade in Richmond and New Orleans," 116.
143. Messner, *Freedmen and the Ideology of Free Labor*, 19.

144. Berlin et al., *The Wartime Genesis of Free Labor: The Lower South*, 382; Butler to Captain Stafford, July 19, 1862, *OR* Ser. I, Vol. XV, 526, 602; Butler, *General Orders from Headquarters*, 33; Marshall, *Private and Official Correspondence*, 2: 241; Butler to Moses Bates, August 20, 1862, Entry 1738: Letters Sent, Vol. II, 310–311, RG 393, Vol. I, NARA. For an example, see Mrs. J. Keating to Nathaniel P. Banks, December 30, 1862, Entry 1920, RG 393, Vol. I, NARA; Julian Neville to H. C. Deming, November 17, 1862, Entry 1756: Department of the Gulf, Letters Received, RG 393, Vol. I, NARA; "Later from New Orleans," *New York Tribune*, December 10, 1862.

145. See, for example, W. H. Gray to Nathaniel P. Banks, January 17, 1863, Entry 1920, RG 393, Vol. I, NARA, in which Gray protests the arrest and confinement of an enslaved woman named Julia for "safe-keeping."

146. "Gen. Butler," *Pomeroy* (OH) *Weekly Telegraph*, December 5, 1862.

147. Case 6c, Henry E. Bertel, Henry E. Bertel Jr., August 14, 1863, Entry 1681: Department of the Gulf, Proceedings of the Provost Court, Vol. 1, 7–8, RG 393, Vol. IV, NARA. See also, US v. Robert H. Bell, September 30, 1863, Entry 1686: Register of the Provost Court, Vol. 235, 94, 103, RG 393, Vol. IV, NARA; US v. Robert O. Buttler, January 12, 1864, Entry 1686, Vol. 235, 335, RG 393, Vol. IV, NARA.

148. Parton, *General Butler in New Orleans*, 432.

149. Mart Bailie to Nathaniel P. Banks, January 1, 1863, Entry 1920, RG 393, Vol. 1, NARA.

150. Parton, *General Butler in New Orleans*, 532.

151. Rachel Jenkins to O. O. Howard, August 30, 1865, Letters Received, M–R, Mar.–Oct. 1865, Records of the Commissioner, 16: 654/1055, RG 105, NARA M752.

152. Parton, *General Butler in New Orleans*, 537–538.

153. Butler, *General Orders from Headquarters*, 10. For traders abandoning slave commerce, see Chester Barney, *Recollections Of Field Service With The Twentieth Iowa Infantry Volunteers, Or, What I Saw In The Army: Embracing Accounts Of Marches, Battles, Sieges And Skirmishes In Missouri, Arkansas, Mississippi, Louisiana, Alabama, Florida, Texas, And Along The Northern Border Of Mexico* (Davenport, IA: Gazette Job Rooms, 1865), 261–262; "Slavery as it is in Louisiana," *New Orleans Daily Delta*, October 29, 1862; "Home Department," *New Orleans Daily True Delta*, September 26, 1861.

154. "Dissolution of Copartnership," *New Orleans Daily Picayune*, July 3, 1862.

155. Marshall, *Private and Official Correspondence*, 2: 140; C. F. Hatcher to T. H. Bartlette, December 10, 1864, Kuntz Collection: National Period, Tulane; *Jonathan Emanuel v. Charles F. Hatcher* in J. Hawkins, *Reports of Cases Argued and Determined In the Supreme Court of Louisiana*, Vol. XIX (New Orleans: B. Bloomfield & Co., 1868), 525–526; "Wanted to Rent," *Houston Tri-Weekly Telegraph*, December 10, 1862.

156. *Louis F. Generes v. Walter L. Campbell* in Stephen K. Williams, *Cases Argued and Decided in the Supreme Court of the United States December Terms, 1870–1871, in 11, 12, 13, 14 Wallace, With Others, Book 20* (Rochester, NY: The Lawyers' Co-Operative Publishing Company, 1901), 110–111; House of Representatives Exec. Doc. No. 102, 40th Congress, 2nd Session, *Property Seized in Louisiana: Letter from*

the Secretary of War transmitting in compliance with the resolutions of the House of February 21 and March 8, 1867 in reference to property seized or taken possession of by the government in the State of Louisiana (Washington, DC: Government Printing Office, 1868), 55; "Brooms for Sale," *Daily Mississippian*, November 1, 1862; "Letter from Major Plumly," *The Liberator*, November 11, 1864.

157. Ripley, *Slaves and Freedmen in Civil War Louisiana*, 26–27; Butler to Godfrey Weitzel, October 30, 1862, *OR*, Ser. I, Vol. XV, 588.
158. Gerteis, *From Contraband to Freedman*, 66–68; Messner, *Freedmen and the Ideology of Free Labor*, 6–7; W. Mishoffer to Butler, May 20, 1862, Butler Papers, LC. Harrison, Morgan, and Lewis again fled to Union lines, where General Phelps refused to give them over a second time. Phelps to R. S. Davis, September 6, 1862, Entry 1756, RG 393, Vol. I, NARA.
159. "A Speck of Servile War," *New Orleans Daily Picayune*, August 5, 1862; Entry for August 2, 1862, Charles H. Blake Diary, MSS 262, HNOC.
160. Charles P. Roland, *Louisiana Sugar Plantations During the American Civil War* (Leiden: E. J. Brill, 1957), 32–37; Ripley, *Slaves and Freedmen in Civil War Louisiana*, 8–9.
161. Berlin et al., *Slaves No More*, 21–30; Kaye, *Joining Places*, 177–193; Joe Gray Taylor, "Slavery in Louisiana During the Civil War," *Louisiana History* 8, no. 1 (Winter 1967): 27–33.
162. John W. Phelps to Lorenzo Thomas, February 3, 1862, *OR*, Ser. I, Vol. VI, 680.
163. Robert C. Reinders and Frank D. Harding, "A Wisconsin Soldier Reports from New Orleans," *Louisiana History* 3, no. 4 (October 1962): 362.
164. Octavia V. Rogers Albert, *The House of Bondage, Or, Charlotte Brooks and Other Slaves* (New York: Hunt & Eaton, 1891), 114.
165. J. F. H. Claiborne to Benjamin F. Butler, June 3, 1862, Butler Papers, LC.
166. "More Runaways," *New Orleans Daily Picayune*, August 6, 1862.
167. Berlin et al., *Slaves No More*, 36–38; Entry for July 8, 1862, Pugh Diary, Alexander Franklin Pugh Memorandum Book, 1850–1852, and Diaries, 1859–1865, Series I: LSU, Part 1, RASP; Entry for May 31, 1862, William J. Minor Plantation Diary, Series B: LSU, Part 3, RSPEGM.
168. B. B. Muncy to J. W. Phelps, June 13, 1862; Frank H. Peck to J. W. Phelps, June 15, 1862, Entry 1756, RG 393, Vol. I, NARA.
169. K. C. Holmes to George C. Strong, October 31, 1862, Entry 1756, RG 393, Vol. I, NARA.
170. Moses Greenwood to Unknown, June 14, 1862, Moses Greenwood Papers, MSS 222, HNOC.
171. Capers, *Occupied City*, 83.
172. Butler to Godfrey Weitzel, November 2, 1862, Butler Papers, LC. Gerteis, *From Contraband to Freedman*, 67–73; Messner, *Freedmen and the Ideology of Free Labor*, 35–43.
173. Ripley, *Slaves and Freedmen in Civil War Louisiana*, 27–29; Messner, *Freedmen and the Ideology of Free Labor*, 8–9; Butler to Stanton, May 25, 1862, *OR* Ser. I, Vol. XV, 440–441.

174. *OR* Ser. I, Vol. XV, 442–447, 485–486; Edward Page Jr. to Butler, May 28, 1862; P. Haggerty to Butler, June 7, 1862; Butler to Stanton, June 18, 1862, Entry 1738, Letters Sent, Volume II, 12, 62, 114–116, RG 393, Vol. I, NARA.
175. Entries for December 19, November 12, 1862, William T. Palfrey Plantation Diary, Palfrey Family Papers, Series B: LSU, Part 6, RSPEGM.
176. Paul Vidal to the Consul of France, September 18, 1862; A. Lavisson to Butler, July 15, 1862, Butler Papers, LC.
177. R. R. Peebles to George Shepley, September 15, 1862, Petition for Return of Possessions, George Foster Shepley Papers, Maine Historical Society, https://www.mainememory.net/artifact/73960 (accessed June 22, 2023).
178. Butler to Consul Mejan, August 14, 1862, Entry 1738, Vol. II, 268, RG 393, Vol. I, NARA.
179. Thomas Williams to Mary Williams, May 22, 1862, in G. Mott Williams, ed., "Letters of General Thomas Williams, 1862," *American Historical Review* 14, no. 2 (January 1909): 318.
180. Berlin et al., *Slaves No More*, 38.
181. George H. Hepworth to Nathaniel P. Banks, April 9, 1863, Banks Papers, LC. See, for example, R. B. Brown to R. S. Dunham, February 24, 1863, Entry 1920, Bureau of Civil Affairs: Letters Received, RG 393, Vol. I, NARA.
182. George Stanton Denison to Salmon P. Chase, March 31, 1863, in George S. Denison and Samuel H. Dodson, eds., *Diary and Correspondence of Salmon P. Chase* (Washington, DC: American Historical Association, 1903), 379.
183. George H. Hepworth and E. M. Wheelock to Nathaniel P. Banks, April 10, 1863, Banks Papers, LC; John C. Rodrigue, *Reconstruction in the Cane Fields: From Slavery to Free Labor in Louisiana's Sugar Parishes 1862–1880* (Baton Rouge: Louisiana State University Press, 2001), 36–50.See also Hepworth and Wheelock to Banks, June 28, 1863, Banks Papers. Gerteis, *From Contraband to Freedman*, 72–73. Ripley, *Slaves and Freedmen in Civil War Louisiana*, 44–45. Often, they were right to be skeptical. See Antonio Jones and George Butler v. Wm. S. Stafer, Case 627, Entry 1681: Letters Sent: Office of the Judge Advocate, Provost Court, Vol. 2, 275, RG 393, Vol. IV, NARA.
184. Nathaniel P. Banks to Unknown, August 5, 1863; A. A. A. General to Unknown, September 3, 1863, Entry 1738, RG 393, Vol. I, NARA; Gerteis, *From Contraband to Freedman*, 74–75. Quote on same. Messner, *Freedmen and the Ideology of Free Labor*, 121–123.
185. Lilly Weeks to William Weeks, September 10, 1863, David Weeks and Family Collection, Series I: LSU, Part 6, RASP.
186. Warning to Gen. Shepley on Slaves, New Orleans, 1862, December 15, 1862, Shepley Papers, Maine Historical Society, https://www.mainememory.net/artifact/74541 (accessed June 22, 2023). See also "So & So" to "Dear Friend," January 2, 1863, Entry 1756, RG 393, Vol. I, NARA.
187. R. R. Barrow to John B. Petteman November 1, 1862, Butler Papers, LC. Emphasis in original.
188. Berlin et al., *Wartime Genesis of Free Labor: The Lower South*, 515.
189. Jacob Barker to Nathaniel P. Banks, August 3, 1863, Banks Papers, LC.
190. Totals drawn from Orleans Parish Conveyance Books, Vols. 85–87, OPCO.

191. Messner, *Freedmen and the Ideology of Free Labor*, 6; "For Sale or Exchange," *New Orleans Daily Picayune*, June 26, 1862; "Choice and Valuable Slaves at a Bargain," *New Orleans Daily Picayune*, July 18, 1862.
192. Orleans Parish Conveyance Books, Vol. 87, 442, 449, 527, 537, OPCO.
193. Orleans Parish Conveyance Books, Vol. 86: 241–480, 253, OPCO.
194. Orleans Parish Conveyance Books, Vol. 87, 479, 498, OPCO. On antebellum efforts to purchase family members, see Julia W. Bernier, "'Never Be Free Without Trustin' Some Person': Networking and Buying Freedom in the Nineteenth-Century United States," *Slavery & Abolition* 40, no. 2 (June 2019): 1–20.
195. Blassingame, *Slave Testimony*, 621. Williams used the savings to purchase a home.
196. Barney, *Recollections of Field Service With the Twentieth Iowa*, 233, 236.
197. "New-Orleans As It Was, and As It Is," *New York Times*, February 26, 1863.
198. George Hazen Dana to "My Dear Parents," October 12, 1863, George Hazen Dana Papers, UVA. See also John A. Bering and Thomas Montgomery, *History of the Forty-Eighth Ohio Vet. Vol. Inf. Giving a Complete Account of the Regiment From its Organization at Camp Dennison, O., in October, 1861, to the Close of the War, and Its Final Muster-Out, May 10, 1866* (Hillsboro: Highland News Office, 1880), 120.
199. "Legislative," *New Orleans Daily Delta*, December 31, 1862.
200. Totals from Orleans Parish Conveyance Books, Vols. 85–87, OPCO.
201. "General Banks and the Governmental Establishment of Slavery in New Orleans," *The Liberator*, April 3, 1863.
202. Nathaniel P. Banks to James Bowen, December 26, 1863, Entry 1844: Department of the Gulf, Provost Marshal Letters Received, Vol. 309, RG 393, Vol. I, NARA; Gerteis, *From Contraband to Freedman*, 78.
203. Deyle, *Carry Me Back*, 155.
204. Jim Barnett and H. Clark Burkett, "The Forks of the Road Slave Market at Natchez," *Journal of Mississippi History* 63, no. 3 (September 2001): 185–186; "Negroes Wanted," *Natchez Daily Courier*, May 28, 1863.
205. Ezekiel Chadwick, April 27, 1867, Registers of Complaints, Vol. 2, Aug. 1865–Dec. 1867, Wilmington Supt.–Southern Disctrict, NCFOR, 75138/249, RG 105, NARA M1909.
206. "Letter from Natchez," *Milwaukee Sentinel*, February 17, 1864.
207. Bill of Sale, John H. Phillips for B. O. Tayloe to George H. Varrell, October 5, 1861, Tayloe Family Papers, Series E: UVA, Part 1, RASP.
208. Charles Harvey Brewster to "Dear Mother," November 17, 21, 1861, in David W. Blight, ed., *When This Cruel War is Over: The Civil War Letters of Charles Harvey Brewster* (Amherst: University of Massachusetts Press, 1992), 57, 61–62.
209. Elizabeth Blair Lee to Samuel Phillips Lee, April 4, 18, 1862, in Virginia Jean Laas, ed., *Wartime Washington: The Civil War Letters of Elizabeth Blair Lee* (Urbana: University of Illinois Press, 1999), 122, 130. Joseph P. Reidy, *Illusions of Emancipation: The Pursuit of Freedom and Equality in the Twilight of Slavery* (Chapel Hill: University of North Carolina Press, 2019).
210. "From Washington," *New York Journal of Commerce*, January 15, 1863; "Local Matters," *Baltimore Sun*, June 2, 1862; "Slave Insurrection in Baltimore," *New York*

Evening Post, June 3, 1862; Berlin et al., *The Destruction of Slavery*, 372–376; "For Rent," *Baltimore Sun*, January 1, 1864.

211. L. S. Thompson, *The Story of Mattie J. Jackson; Her Parentage—Experience of Eighteen Years in Slavery—Incidents During the War—Her Escape from Slavery. A True Story* (Lawrence, MA: Sentinel Office, 1866), 15, https://docsouth.unc.edu/neh/jacksonm/jackson.html (accessed May 6, 2019).

212. *Ninety-Second Illinois Volunteers* (Freeport: Journal Steam Publishing House & Bookbindery, 1875), 59; Armstead Louis Robinson, "Day of Jubilo: Civil War and the Demise of Slavery in the Mississippi Valley, 1861–1865" (PhD diss., University of Rochester, 1976), 554; Quoted in Joseph C. Fitzharris, *The Hardest Lot of Men: The Third Minnesota Infantry in the Civil War* (Norman: University of Oklahoma Press, 2019), 43; Ronald Ray Alexander, "Central Kentucky During the Civil War, 1861–1865" (PhD diss., University of Kentucky, 1976), 235–236; Aaron Astor, *Rebels on the Border: Civil War, Emancipation, and the Reconstruction of Kentucky and Missouri* (Baton Rouge: Louisiana State University Press, 2012), 104.

213. William Truiesdale to General Rosecrans, January 14, 1863, in *OR* Ser. 1, Vol. 20, No. 2, 330. See also L. P. Brockett, *Scouts, Spies and Heroes of the Great Civil War; How They Lived, Fought, and Died for the Union Including Thrilling Adventures, Daring Deeds, Heroic Exploits, Exciting Experiences, Wonderful Escapes of Spies, Scouts and Detectives; with Anecdotes, Watchwords, Battle Cries, and Humorous and Pathetic Incidents of the War* (Philadelphia: National Publishing Co., 1911), 97.

214. Smith, *We Ask Only for Even-Handed Justice*, 30.

215. "From Fortress Monroe," *Philadelphia Press*, August 12, 1862; Berlin et al., *The Destruction of Slavery*, 89–90; Eleanor P. Cross and Charles B. Cross Jr., eds., *Child of Glencoe: Civil War Journal of Katie Darling Wallace* (Chesapeake, VA: Norfolk County Historical Society, 1983), 10; Lucy Chase to "Dear folks at home," March 4, 1863, in Swint, *Dear Ones At Home*, 59.

216. Testimony of Daniel Walters, George Wallace Court-Martial, MM-436, RG 153: Records of the Office of the Judge Advocate General, NARA.

217. Quoted in David Williams, *I Freed Myself: African American Self-Emancipation in the Civil War Era* (New York: Cambridge University Press, 2014), 126.

218. "Department of the Gulf," *New York Times*, November 22, 1863.

219. Untitled, *Chicago Tribune*, December 4, 1863.

220. "Letter from Major Plumly," *The Liberator*, November 11, 1864.

221. Gerteis, *From Contraband to Freedman*, 78.

222. Albert P. Bennett, *Debates in the Convention for the Revision and Amendment of the Constitution of the State of Louisiana Assembled at Liberty Hall, New Orleans, April 6, 1864* (New Orleans: W. R. Fish, 1864), 171.

223. "Local," *Alexandria Gazette*, May 30, 1862; "From Washington," *Alexandria Gazette*, June 18, 1862; "Prisoners Released at Washington," *Richmond Enquirer*, August 1, 1862; Bill of Sale, December 23, 1862, Rudin Slavery Collection, Cornell; Bills of Sale, January 16, 21, 1863, Charles Talbott Collection, Valentine Museum; "$100 Reward Will Be Paid," *Richmond Whig*, May 9, 1863; Receipt, December 3, 1863, Roller Family Papers, Mss1 R6498 a FA2, VHS; "$100 Reward," *Richmond Whig*,

January 29, 1864. Charles M. Price—likewise displaced from Alexandria—joined him there, selling Tift and Nelson in early 1863. George Cook to W. S. How, May 2, 1866, Registered letters received, Vol. 1, No. 1–191, Jan.–June 1866, Winchester SC, VAFOR, 184: 307/450, RG 105, NARA M1913.

Chapter 3

1. "Notice," *Daily Selma Reporter*, December 9, 1862; "The City," *Daily Selma Reporter*, November 25, 1862; John Hardy, *Selma: Her Institutions and Her Men* (Selma: Times Book and Job Office, 1879), 152; Walter M. Jackson, *The Story of Selma* (Birmingham: The Birmingham Printing Co., 1954), 522; Hannah Durkin, "Finding Last Middle Passage Survivor Sally 'Redoshi' Smith on the Page and Screen," *Slavery & Abolition* 40, no. 4 (2019): 631–658; Sylviane Diouf, *Dreams of Africa in Alabama: The Slave Ship Clotilda and the Story of the Last Africans Brought to America* (New York: Oxford University Press, 2007), 14; Receipt, John D. Ragland to Washington M. Smith, September 3, 1862, Washington M. Smith Papers, Duke. In 1859, Ragland reportedly exported at least one hundred people to the Deep South. "Untitled," *Baltimore Daily Exchange*, January 24, 1859.
2. Diouf, *Dreams of Africa in Alabama*, 17–26.
3. W. M. Smith to Robert Tyler, August 7, 1862; Smith to Christopher Memminger, August 11, 1862, File for W. M. Smith, Confederate Papers Relating to Citizens or Business Firms, RG 109, NARA M346 (accessed via Fold3.com); "Something About the Pardoned Alabamians," *Pomeroy Weekly Telegraph*, October 26, 1865; Washington Smith to "Dear Wife," August 27, 1862, Smith Papers, Duke.
4. McPherson, *Battle Cry of Freedom*, 369–422; Walter L. Fleming, *Civil War and Reconstruction in Alabama* (New York: Columbia University Press, 1905), 61–62; Megan Kate Nelson, *The Three-Cornered War: The Union, the Confederacy, and Native Peoples in the Fight for the West* (New York: Simon & Schuster, 2019).
5. "New Orleans," *Atlanta Southern Confederacy*, May 3, 1862
6. Thomas, *The Confederacy as a Revolutionary Experience*; Brian Steel Wills, "The Confederate Sun Sets on Selma: Forrest and the Defense of Alabama in 1865," in *The Yellowhammer War: The Civil War and Reconstruction in Alabama*, ed. Kenneth W. Noe (Tuscaloosa: University of Alabama Press, 2013), 71–89; John M. Strong to Hugh McCullough, November 22, 1865, Letters received, K-Y, 1865, Assistant Commissioner, Alabama, BRFAL, 1865–1872, 6: 75/928 NARA M809. On the relative security of the interior Confederacy, see (among others) William Warren Rogers, *Confederate Home Front: Montgomery During the Civil War* (Tuscaloosa: University of Alabama Press, 1999), 60–75; O'Donovan, *Becoming Free in the Cotton South*, 59–110; Smith, *Mississippi in the Civil War*, 67–72.
7. "Correspondence," *Daily Selma Reporter*, June 19, 1862.
8. Entry for July 8, 1862, in Sarah Woolfolk Wiggins, ed., *The Journals of Josiah Gorgas, 1857–1878* (Tuscaloosa: University of Alabama Press, 1995), 48; Gary W. Gallagher,

"Introduction," in *The Shenandoah Valley Campaign of 1862*, ed. Gary W. Gallagher (Chapel Hill: University of North Carolina Press, 2003), ix–xxi; Stephen W. Sears, *To the Gates of Richmond: The Peninsula Campaign* (New York: Ticknor & Fields, 1992). On the significance of the Peninsula Campaign, see Gary W. Gallagher, "A Civil War Watershed: The 1862 Richmond Campaign in Perspective," in *The Richmond Campaign of 1862: The Peninsula and the Seven Days*, ed. Gary W. Gallagher (Chapel Hill: University of North Carolina Press, 2000), 3–27.

9. David Silkenat, *Raising the White Flag: How Surrender Defined the American Civil War* (Chapel Hill: University of North Carolina Press, 2019), 55–61.
10. Kenneth Noe, *Perryville: This Grand Havoc of Battle* (Lexington: University Press of Kentucky, 2001), xiii; Earl Hess, *Civil War in the West: Victory and Defeat from the Appalachians to the Mississippi* (Chapel Hill: University of North Carolina Press, 2012), 94–103.
11. Washington M. Smith to "My Dear Wife," August 27, 1862; Receipt, John D. Ragland to Smith, September 3, 1862, Smith Papers, Duke.
12. Vincent Brown, *Tacky's Revolt: The Story of an Atlantic Slave War* (Cambridge, MA: The Belknap Press of Harvard University Press, 2020), 20. See also Elena Schneider, *The Occupation of Havana: War, Trade, and Slavery in the Atlantic World* (Chapel Hill: University of North Carolina Press, for the OIEAHC, 2018), 95, 161. A Massachusetts merchant even speculated in enslaved people during the Haitian Revolution. Entries for December 1791–February 1792, Nathaniel Cutting Journal, Massachusetts Historical Society. My thanks to Nicholas Radburn for sharing this source with me.
13. "The Courts," *Richmond Examiner*, October 17; November 27, 1862.
14. On Richmond's wartime transformation, see Thomas, *The Confederate State of Richmond*; Takagi, "Rearing Wolves to Our Own Destruction," 124–144; Ash, *Rebel Richmond*; DeCredico, *Confederate Citadel*.
15. "The Courts," *Richmond Examiner*, October 17; November 27, 1862.
16. "Sale of Negroes in Thomas," *Southern Recorder* (Milledgeville, GA), January 14, 1862. See also "High Price of Negroes," *Macon Daily Telegraph*, April 10, 1862; "Sale of Negroes," *Western Democrat*, March 18, 1862.
17. "High Prices of Negroes," *True Democrat* (Little Rock, AR), January 30, 1862; "The Demand for Negroes," *Western Democrat*, April 8, 1862.
18. "Sale of Negroes in Georgia," *New York Observer*, January 23, 1862; "General News Summary," *Springfield Republican*, February 6, 1862.
19. Sears, *To the Gates of Richmond*, 3–24.
20. William Wallace to Sarah Wallace, March 3, 1862; Wallace to "Dear Wife and Children," March 9, 1862, in John O. Holzhueter, "William Wallace's Civil War Letters: The Virginia Campaign," *The Wisconsin Magazine of History* 57, no. 1 (Autumn 1973): 39–40; Entry for June 15, 1862, in John William De Forest, *A Volunteer's Adventures: A Union Captain's Record of the Civil War* (New Haven, CT: Yale University Press, 1946), 26.
21. See, for example, Wm. P. Smith to Thomas Seddon Taliaferro, June 2, 1862, Taliaferro Family Papers, VHS; Entry for June 11, William Fanning Wickham Diary, Vol. 8, 1862–1864, Wickham Family Papers, VHS.

22. Entry for May 5, 1862, in David R. Roe, ed., *A Civil War Soldier's Diary: Valentine C. Randolph, 39th Illinois Regiment* (DeKalb: Northern Illinois University Press, 2006), 75; Brasher, *The Peninsula Campaign and the Necessity of Emancipation*, 14, 27–49, 102–124, 163–189; James Marten, "A Feeling of Restless Anxiety: Loyalty and Race in the Peninsula Campaign and Beyond," in *The Richmond Campaign of 1862*, ed. Gallagher, 121–152.
23. Williamson Murray and Wayne Wei-siang Hsieh, *A Savage War: A Military History of the Civil War* (Princeton, NJ: Princeton University Press, 2016), 173–176; Daniel E. Sutherland, *Seasons of War: The Ordeal of a Confederate Community, 1861–1865* (New York: The Free Press, 1995), 100–151.
24. Susan Emeline Jeffords Caldwell to Lycurgus Washington Caldwell, June 9, 1862, in *"My Heart is So Rebellious": The Caldwell Letters, 1861–1865*, ed. J. Michael Welton (Fauquier National Bank, 1991), 128.
25. Daniel H. Hill to "Dear Wife," February 19, 1862, Daniel Harvey Hill Papers, NCDAH.
26. Robert E. Lee to Mary Anna Custis Lee, July 11, 1862, Lee Family Papers, VHS.
27. Robert McAllister to "My Dear Daughters," April 11, 1862, in James I. Robertson Jr., ed., *The Civil War Letters of General Robert McAllister* (Baton Rouge: Louisiana State University Press, 1998), 132.
28. "Laura" to "Dr. G.," April 20, 1862, Gresham Family Papers, VHS; See also Hope W. Massie to William Massie, May 7, 1862, Massie Family Papers, VHS; Charles Morris to Mary Minor Morris, October 20, 1862, Charles Morris Papers, VHS.
29. Entries for May 6, June 10, 1862, John Armistead Selden Diary, VHS.
30. Hector Davis to A. R. Blakey, March 20, 1862, Angus R. Blakey Papers, Duke.
31. J. V. W. Vandenburgh to W. W. Rogers, June 24, 1867, Unregistered Letters Received, February 1866–October 1868, Washington and Georgetown LS, DCFOR, 17: 276, RG 105, NARA M1902.
32. Edmund Ruffin Jr. to Edmund Ruffin, October 7, 1862, Edmund Ruffin Papers, VHS; Entry for June 24, 1862, Edmund Ruffin Jr. Journal, SHC.
33. L. E. Downey to "Dear Brother," August 11, 1862, William A. Gladstone Afro-American Military Collection, LC. For a similar sentiment, see Sidney Champion to Matilda Champion, Undated (May 1863), Sidney Champion Papers, Duke.
34. A. J. Rux to E. H. Stokes, March 10, 1862; J. Wimbush Young to E. H. Stokes, April 28, 1862, Chase Papers, LC.
35. Figures from Davis Daybooks, NYPL.
36. Totals from Silas Omohundro Account Book, Omohundro Accounts, UVA.
37. Entry for May 14, 1862, Davis Daybooks, NYPL.
38. Blassingame, *Slave Testimony*, 618; Bancroft, *Slave Trading in the Old South*, 175; E. Milby Burton, *The Siege of Charleston, 1861–1865* (Columbia: University of South Carolina Press, 1970), 89–182; Entry for June 9, 1862, in Childs, *The Private Journal of Henry William Ravenel*, 147.
39. Blassingame, *Slave Testimony*, 618.
40. "Sale of Negroes," *Charleston Mercury*, April 17, 1862; George H. [Illegible] to Miss Juliet[?] G. Elliott, June 17, 1862, Edward A. Gibbes Papers, Duke.

41. James L. Petigru to Jane Petigru North, June 20, 1862, in James Petigru Carson, *Life, Letters and Speeches of James Louis Petigru, The Union Man of South Carolina* (Washington, DC: W. H. Lowdermilk & Co., 1920), 453.
42. Anne C. Bailey, *The Weeping Time: Memory and the Largest Slave Auction in American History* (New York: Cambridge University Press, 2017). Research findings by Lauren Davila suggest a still larger auction took place in Charleston in the 1830s. Jennifer Berry Hawes, "How a Grad Student Uncovered the Largest Known Slave Auction in the U.S.," *ProPublica*, June 16, 2023, https://www.propublica.org/article/how-grad-student-discovered-largest-us-slave-auction.
43. "Jos. Bryan, Real and Personal Estate Broker," *Savannah Daily Morning News*, May 16, 1862; Barry Sheehy, Cindy Wallace, and Vaughnette Goode-Walker, *Savannah: Brokers, Bankers, and Bay Lane: Inside the Slave Trade (Volume 2–Civil War Savannah)* (Austin: Emerald Book Company, 2012), 65, 75–76, 87, 99.
44. John A. Stevenson to W. C. Stevenson, March 17, 1872, John A. Stevenson Letter, MS 3810, UGA.
45. Theodorick Montfort to Maria Louisa Montfort, February 1, 1862, in Spencer B. King, ed., *Rebel Lawyer: Letters of Theodorick W. Montfort 1861–1862* (Athens: University of Georgia Press, 1965), 42.
46. Various Bills of Sale, Henry Wilink Papers, Emory.
47. Samuel Toombs, *Reminiscences of the War, Comprising a Detailed Account of the Experiences of the Thirteenth Regiment New Jersey Volunteers in Camp, on the March, and in Battle* (Highstown: Longstreet House, 1994), 197.
48. Charles I. Graves to "Aunt Mary," June 14, 1862, Charles Iverson Graves Papers, SHC.
49. William A. Link, *Atlanta, Cradle of the New South: Race and Remembering in the Civil War's Aftermath* (Chapel Hill: University of North Carolina Press, 2013), 9–12. Quote on p. 10. Venet, *A Changing Wind*.
50. "High Prices for Negroes," *Atlanta Southern Confederacy*, January 9, 1862.
51. "High Prices for Negroes," *Atlanta Southern Confederacy*, July 3, 1862.
52. Entry for July 29, 1862, in Wendy Hamand Venet, ed., *Sam Richards's Civil War Diary: A Chronicle of the Atlanta Home Front* (Athens: University of Georgia Press, 2009), 121. See also entries for August 13 and 30, September 13 and 17, 1862 (pp. 122–125).
53. L. D. Merrimon to E. H. Stokes, June 21, 1862, Chase Papers, LC.
54. Sears, *To the Gates of Richmond*, 87–145.
55. George Barnsley to Godfrey Barnsley, June 3, 1862, Godfrey Barnsley Papers, Emory.
56. J. Wimbush Young to E. H. Stokes, June 13, 1862; June 23, 1862, Chase Papers, LC.
57. Entries for May 1862, July 1862, John Fayette Dickinson Diary, VHS.
58. R. C. Ware to E. H. Stokes, June 30, 1862, Ames Papers, MHS.
59. M. H. Driver to Albert Fields, June 24, 1862, Albert Fields Papers, Emory.
60. John B. Jones, *A Rebel War Clerk's Diary* (New York: Sagamore Press, 1958), 75–84; quote on p. 82.
61. Jeremiah Morton to J. J. Halsey, May 14, 1862, Morton-Halsey Papers, Series E: UVA, Part 1, RASP.
62. A. Roane to J. D. B. De Bow, June 23, 1862, De Bow Papers, Duke. Emphasis in original.

63. Jones, *A Rebel War Clerk's Diary*, 88.
64. Clifford Dowdey, *The Seven Days: The Emergence of Lee* (1964; repr. Lincoln: University of Nebraska Press, 1993); Michael C. C. Adams, *Our Masters the Rebels: A Speculation on Union Military Failure in the East, 1861–1865* (Cambridge, MA: Harvard University Press, 1978), 114–127; Gallagher, *The Confederate War*, 85–96 and "A Civil War Watershed: The 1862 Richmond Campaign in Perspective"; Glatthaar, *General Lee's Army*, 147–149.
65. Jones, *A Rebel War Clerk's Diary*, 86.
66. Montgomery Slaughter to Robert Alexander Grinnan, December 9, 1861; Account of Benjamin Franklin Nalle, July 10, 1862, Nalle Family Papers, VHS.
67. Entries for July 17–18, October 8, 1862, Selden Diary, VHS; Nathaniel Watkins to Nannie Watkins, August 27, 1862, Nathaniel V. Watkins Papers, W&M.
68. John H. Matsui, *The First Republican Army: The Army of Virginia and the Radicalization of the Civil War* (Charlottesville: University of Virginia Press, 2017); Murray and Hsieh, *A Savage War*, 190–204; Robert K. Krick, *Stonewall Jackson at Cedar Mountain* (Chapel Hill: University of North Carolina Press, 1990); John J. Hennessy, *Return to Bull Run: The Campaign and Battle of Second Manassas* (New York: Simon & Schuster, 1993).
69. James M. McPherson, *Crossroads of Freedom: Antietam* (New York: Oxford University Press, 2002), 88–95.
70. Thomas G. Pollock to Abram D. Pollock, September 28, 1862, A. D. Pollock Papers, SHC, emphasis in original; McPherson, *Crossroads of Freedom*, 133–156; Gary W. Gallagher, "The Net Result of the Campaign Was in Our Favor: Confederate Reaction to the Maryland Campaign," in *The Antietam Campaign*, ed. Gary W. Gallagher (Chapel Hill: University of North Carolina Press, 1999), 3–43.
71. Noe, *Perryville*, xiii; Hess, *Civil War in the West*, 94–103.
72. J. Johnston Pettigrew to William Pettigrew, September 5, 1862, Pettigrew Papers, SHC.
73. J. M. Williams to "Dear Burwell," November 10, 1862, Burwell Family Papers, SHC.
74. Entry for September 21, 1862, in Wiggins, *The Journals of Josiah Gorgas*, 53.
75. D. Von Groening to Alfred Paul, September 30, 1862, D. Von Groening Letterbook, LC.
76. Ellen Mordecai to "My dear sister," August 12, 1862, Cameron Family Papers, SHC.
77. Corsan, *Two Months in the Confederate States*, 71.
78. Entry for August 10, 1862, in Jack Allen, ed., *Pen and Sword: The Life and Journals of Randal W. McGavock . . . The Political and Civil War Journals, 1853–1862* (Nashville: Tennessee Historical Commission, 1959), 661.
79. Corsan, *Two Months in the Confederate States*, 85.
80. Entries for July 30, 31, August 15, 1862, Hector Davis Daybooks, NYPL; totals taken from same. Totals from Silas Omohundro Account Book, Omohundro Slave Trade and Farm Accounts, UVA.
81. D. Von Groening to "Dear Sir," June 28, 1862, Von Groening Letterbook, LC; William T. Nelson to "Dear Sweet Wife," October 15, 1862, William T. Nelson Papers, VHS.
82. "Do You Know Him?," *Richmond Planet*, February 16, 1895.

83. Stephen Dodson Ramseur to "My Dear Brother," October 27, 1862, in George G. Kundahl, ed., *The Bravest of the Brave: The Correspondence of Stephen Dodson Ramseur* (Chapel Hill: University of North Carolina Press, 2010), 102; "$300 Reward," Salisbury (NC) *Carolina Watchman*, May 30, 1864. Thanks to Adam Domby for bringing this source to my attention.

84. R. R. Bridgers to Henry Toole Clark, September 6, 1862, Henry Toole Clark Papers, Series F: Duke, Part 3, RASP; Receipt, Jones & Slater to E. Stattman Oliver, October 29, 1862, William P. Palmer Collection, Western Reserve Historical Society.

85. Paul Jones Semmes to Emily Semmes, October 29, 1862, GLC, https://www.gilder lehrman.org/collection/glc00442 (accessed March 6, 2020).

86. "The Price of Negroes," *Richmond Whig*, October 17, 1862.

87. "High Prices for Negroes," *Macon Daily Telegraph*, November 11, 1862.

88. "The Price of Negroes," *Augusta Chronicle*, July 30, 1862.

89. "High Price of Negroes," *Yorkville Enquirer*, November 26, 1862.

90. Thomas G. Pollock to Abram D. Pollock, September 28, 1862, Pollock Papers, SHC.

91. Entry for October 16, 1862, in Edmund Ruffin, *The Diary of Edmund Ruffin, Vol. II: The Years of Hope, April 1861–June 1863* (Baton Rouge: Louisiana State University Press, 1976), 466.

92. Edward Younger, ed., *Inside the Confederate Government: The Diary of Robert Garlick Hill Kean* (New York: Oxford University Press, 1957), 100.

93. Paul Jones Semmes to Emily Semmes, October 29, 1862, GLC. Emphasis in original.

94. Entry for September 24, 1862, David Schenck Diary, SHC; Robert Colby and Mazie Clark, "'A Comfort to Her and a Relief to the Bureau': Susan Jackson's Search for Family After the Civil War," John L. Nau III Center for Civil War History, September 23, 2020, https://naucenter.as.virginia.edu/comfort-her-and-relief-bureau.

95. "The Sale of Negroes," *Charleston Mercury*, May 15, 1862; "Sale of Negroes at the Brokers' Exchange," *Charleston Daily Courier*, May 29, 1862; "By Wilbur & Son," *Charleston Daily Courier*, May 30, 1862; "City Intelligence," *Charleston Courier*, June 4, 1862; "City Intelligence," *Charleston Daily Courier*, June 5, 1862.

96. Sales and Disbursements in a/c with Winthrop & Rose, Trustees, Simon and Simon-Slave Records, SCHS; Calvin Cowles to "My Dear Wife," April 5, 1863, Calvin Cowles Papers, SHC; John Inscoe, "Mountain Masters as Confederate Opportunists: The Profitability of Slavery in Western North Carolina, 1861–1865," *Slavery and Abolition* 16, no. 1 (April 1995): 85–100.

97. David J. Logan to "My Dear Wife," July 3, 1862, in Samuel N. Thomas Jr. and Jason H. Silverman, *"A Rising Star of Promise": The Civil War Odyssey of David Jackson Logan, 17th South Carolina Volunteers* (Campbell, CA: Savas Publishing Company, 1998), 32.

98. "Negros. By Wilbur & Son"; "Estate Sale—Likely House Girl"; "Likely & Qualified Negroes," *Charleston Daily Courier*, July 11, 1862.

99. "Prices of Negros," *Charleston Mercury*, August 1, 1862.

100. "Forty Rice Field Negroes," *Charleston Daily Courier*, February 10, 1863; Entry for March 22, 1863, Margaret Ann Meta Morris Grimball Diary, SHC.

101. Sale of Negroes belonging to Ed. Wm. A. Hayne by Order Thos. R. Waring, Waring Family Papers, SCHS.

102. Julia Juvernia Verona Cotton to Julia Cotton Bethel, September 7, 1862, in VHS, "The Cotton Letters," *Virginia Magazine of History and Biography* 37, no. 1 (January 1929): 13.
103. "Rare Chance!" *Atlanta Southern Confederacy*, October 4, 1862; "Negroes for Sale"; "At the City Hotel"; "Trustee's Sale," *Atlanta Southern Confederacy*, November 2, 1862.
104. "For Sale"; "D. Mayer, Jacobe & Co."; "Thomas F. Lowe & Co.," *The Banner & Baptist*, November 8, 1862.
105. Entries for December 27, 1862 and May 2, 1863, in Venet, *Sam Richards's Civil War Diary*, 145, 174–175.
106. Mary Eliza Rose to Charles Alexander Rose, November 7, 11, 1862, Rose Family Papers, VHS; O. H. Marshall to James B. Campbell, October 16, 1862, James Butler Campbell Papers, SCHS.
107. George M. McDowell to "Dear Father," November 27, 1862, George Marshall McDowell Letter, VHS.
108. Nathaniel Watkins to Nannie Watkins, November 13, 1862; Receipt, James B. Daniel to Nathaniel Watkins, September 15, 1863, Watkins Papers, W&M.
109. Earl Hess, *Banners to the Breeze: The Kentucky Campaign, Corinth, and Stones River* (Lincoln: University of Nebraska Press, 2000), 121–176.
110. Hess, *Civil War in the West*, 110–133; Michael B. Ballard, *Vicksburg: The Campaign that Opened the Mississippi* (Chapel Hill: University of North Carolina Press, 2004), 101–155.
111. Paul Jones Semmes to Emily Semmes, October 29, 1862, GLC.
112. William Smedes to William E. Johnson, November 26, 1862, William E. Johnson Papers, SCL.
113. John K. Betterworth, *Confederate Mississippi: The People and Policies of a Cotton State in Wartime* (Baton Rouge: Louisiana State University Press, 1943), 168; Edwin H. Fay to Sarah Fay, December 21, 1862, in Bell Irvin Wiley, ed., *"This Infernal War": The Confederate Letters of Sgt. Edwin H. Fay* (Austin: University of Texas Press, 1958), 194–196.
114. "An Effect of the Proclamation, &c.," *Rutland County Herald*, August 13, 1863.
115. Thomas W. Francis to James C. Francis, March 18, 1863, in James P. Pate, ed., *When This Evil War Is Over: The Correspondence of the Francis Family, 1860–1865* (Tuscaloosa: University of Alabama Press, 2006), 119.
116. Entry for May 15, 1863, in Allen Sigler and Ruth B. Hubbard, eds., *The Civil War Diary of Col. A. J. Seay* (Kingfisher, OK: Times Publishing Co., 1958), 44.
117. Entry for September 7, 1862, in G. W. Cable, ed., "War Diary of a Union Woman in the South," *The Century Magazine* 38 (1889): 944.
118. Isaac Hall to Mary Hall, June 13, 1862, in Garnie W. McGinty, "The Human Side of War: Letters Between a Bienville Parish Civil War Soldier and His Wife," *North Louisiana Historical Association Journal* 13, nos. 2–3 (1982), 76.
119. "Died," *Richmond Whig*, January 9, 1863.
120. "Tribute of Respect," *Richmond Daily Dispatch*, January 8, 1863.
121. Figures drawn from Davis Daybooks, NYPL and Davis Account Books, CHM; "City Intelligence," *Richmond Examiner*, November 22, 1862.

122. Entry for December 27, 1862, Davis Daybooks, NYPL; "Wanted—Seventy-five Likely Young Negroes," *Daily Missouri Republican*, February 4, 1859; "$200 Reward," *Richmond Examiner*, April 13, 1864.
123. Entry for December 26, 1862, Davis Daybooks, NYPL; Bill of Sale, December 22, 1862, Sedgwick and Mussen Family Papers, Valentine Museum.
124. Entries for December 22–31, Davis Daybooks, NYPL.
125. E. H. Stokes to John Watts, December 31, 1862, Miscellaneous Documents Concerning American Slavery, 1803–1863, Houghton Library, Harvard College Library.
126. Entry for January 9, 1863, in Elizabeth Preston Allan, *The Life and Letters of Margaret Junkin Preston* (Boston: Houghton, Mifflin and Company, 1903), 159.
127. Entries for March 25 and April 4, 1863, in Alex L. Wiatt, *Confederate Chaplain William Edward Wiatt: An Annotated Diary* (Lynchburg, VA: H. E. Howard, Inc., 1994), 41, 44.
128. Roscoe Briggs Heath to Lewis Edmunds Mason, January 30, 1863, Mason Family Papers, Series M: VHS, Part 5, RASP.
129. Entry for January 8, 1863, in William Lyne Wilson, *A Borderland Confederate* (Pittsburgh: University of Pittsburgh Press, 1962), 39.
130. Lerner, "Money, Prices, and Wages in the Confederacy, 1861–1865," 24.
131. George Barnsley to Godfrey Barnsley, December 19, 1862, Barnsley Papers, Emory.
132. "High Price of Negroes," *Western Democrat*, November 25, 1862.
133. Nimrod Long to Queen Long, January 29, February 15, 1863, Nimrod William Ezekiel Long Papers, Emory. A Texan shared Long's assessment, arguing that these battles did "not lessen the price" of the enslaved "in the least." Elijah P. Petty to "Dear Daughter," February 19, 1863, in Elijah P. Petty, *Journey to Pleasant Hill: The Civil War Letters of Captain Elijah P. Petty, Walker's Texas Division CSA* (San Antonio: University of Texas Institute of Texan Cultures, 1982), 142. On the results of Fredericksburg and Stones River, see Gary W. Gallagher, "The Yanks Have Had a Terrible Whipping: Confederates Evaluate the Battle of Fredericksburg," in *The Fredericksburg Campaign: Decision on the Rappahannock*, ed. Gary W. Gallagher (Chapel Hill: University of North Carolina Press, 1995), 113–141; Murray and Hsieh, *A Savage War*, 294–296; Larry Daniel, *Conquered: Why the Army of the Tennessee Failed* (Chapel Hill: University of North Carolina Press, 2019), 71–102.
134. R. H. Dickinson to "Dear Paul," February 13, 1862, Miscellaneous File, Brock Collection, HL-LVA; Amos, *Cotton City*, 85; Charles S. Davis, *The Cotton Kingdom in Alabama* (Montgomery: Alabama Department of Archives and History, 1939), 76; W. Alvin Lloyd, *Lloyd's Southern Railroad Guide* XI, no. 2 (June 1863): 106, 123, 134; "Negroes---Negroes," *Mobile Evening News*, August 20, 1863; "Novel Reasons for Ending the Rebellion," *New York Times*, December 13, 1863.
135. One of Montgomery's slave jails stood on the site of Martin Luther King Jr.'s Dexter Avenue Baptist Church. Montgomery Museum of Fine Arts, *Spaces and Places: Views of Montgomery's Built Environment* (Montgomery, AL: Montgomery Museum of Fine Arts, 1978), 21; Equal Justice Initiative, *Slavery in America: The Montgomery Slave Trade* (Montgomery, AL: Equal Justice Initiative, 2013),

especially p. 21; Rogers, *Confederate Home Front*, 132–133; Joan Cashin, *First Lady of the Confederacy: Varina Davis's Civil War* (Cambridge, MA: The Belknap Press of Harvard University Press, 2006), 137–138.
136. Bill of Sale, B. F. Veal to John F. Boggett, September 25, 1862, Benjamin F. Veal Slave Bills of Sale, Georgia Archives.
137. William D. Battle to Gray Sills, April 12, 1863, *Spared and Shared*, https://sparedshared14.wordpress.com/2017/02/03/1863-william-david-battle-to-gray-sills/ (accessed January 30, 2018).
138. James Z. Branscomb to "Dear Sister," April 18, 1863, in Chappell, *Dear Sister*, 138.
139. A. J. Rux to E. H. Stokes, December 14, 1861, Slavery Collection, NYHS; Rux to Stokes, February 23, 1862; Receipt, Rux to J. F. Dinnis, November 13, 1863, Chase Papers, LC; S. R. Fondren to Stokes, September 29, October 13, 1863; Rux to Stokes, September 27, 1863; R. W. Booth to Stokes, September 30, 1863; J. Wimbush Young to Stokes, November 19, 1863, SUSC-AAS.
140. D. M. Prichard to Jeremiah Morton, September 12, 1862; John D. Ragland to Morton, September 2, 1863, Morton-Halsey Family Papers, Series E: UVA, Part 1, RASP. For subsequent sales, see Prichard to Morton, September 15, 1863; February 6, 1864, in same.
141. D. M. Prichard to Jeremiah Morton, August 30, 1862, Morton-Halsey Family, Series E: UVA, Part 1, RASP. For a similar enslaved response to sale, see L. Minor Blackford, *Mine Eyes Have Seen the Glory: The Story of a Virginia Lady Mary Berkeley Minor Blackford, 1802–1896* (Cambridge, MA: Harvard University Press, 1954), 205.
142. Kate Drumgoold, *A Slave Girl's Story: Being an Autobiography of Kate Drumgoold* (Brooklyn: Self-Published, 1898), 5, https://docsouth.unc.edu/neh/drumgoold/drumgoold.html (accessed May 6, 2019).
143. Thaddeus Stevens to Oliver Otis Howard, December 4, 1865, S-97 1865, Letters Received, ser. 15, Washington Headquarters, RG 105, NARA [FSSP A-7315].
144. J. H. M. McKenzie to W. Storer How, September 2, 1865, Unregistered Letters Received, ser. 4307, Winchester, Virginia SC, VAFOR, RG 105, NARA [FSSP A-8235].
145. Clement, *Memoirs of Samuel Spottford Clement*, 5–8. Quote on p. 6.
146. Hinton Graves to "My Dear Brother and Sister," March 22, 1863, Graves Papers, SHC.
147. W. H. Winn to his Family, April 2, 1863, in Mills Lane, ed., *Dear Mother: Don't Grieve About Me. If I Get Killed I'll Only Be Dead: Letters From Georgia Soldiers in the Civil War* (Savannah: Library of Georgia, Beehive Foundation, 1990), 223–224; John L'Engle to Edward L'Engle, March 14, 1863, Edward M. L'Engle Papers, SHC.
148. William A. Byrne, "The Burden and Heat of the Day: Slavery and Servitude in Savannah, 1733–1865" (PhD diss., Florida State University, 1979), 237.
149. "Price of Negroes at the South," *Richmond Examiner*, June 24, 1863.
150. Account Sales Negroes Rec'd by Robert M. Clarke, Francis M. Manning Collection, Joyner Library Special Collections, ECU.
151. "100 Negroes"; "Fifty Likely Young Negroes for Sale," *Atlanta Daily Intelligencer*, September 11, 1863.

152. "J. L. Winter & Co."; "Auction and Commission House"; "W. H. Henderson & Co."; "Slave Yard, By Robert M. Clarke," *Atlanta Southern Confederacy*, March 13, 1863; Steven Hertzberg, *Strangers Within the Gate City: The Jews of Atlanta, 1845–1915* (Philadelphia: The Jewish Publication Society of America, 1978), 22.
153. Quoted in Venet, *A Changing Wind*, 97.
154. A. J. Rux to E. H. Stokes, February 23, 1862, Chase Papers, LC; Rux to Stokes, September 11, November 19, 1863, SUSC-AAS; Solomon Cohen Ledger, Arnold and Deanne Kaplan Collection of Early American Judaica, Herbert D. Katz Center for Advanced Judaic Studies, University of Pennsylvania; "The Subscribers . . . ," *Richmond Whig*, March 27, 1863.
155. "Negroes for Sale," *Savannah Daily Morning News*, September 6, 1862; A. J. Rux to E. H. Stokes, October 3, 1863, SUSC-AAS.
156. John Berkley Grimball to Meta Grimball March 18, 1863, John Berkley Grimball Papers, Duke.
157. Robertson, Blacklock and Company to Robert F. Allston, May 9, 1863, in J. H. Easterby, ed., *The South Carolina Rice Plantation as Revealed in the Papers of Robert F. W. Allston* (Columbia: University of South Carolina Press, 2004), 426; Receipt, Louisa S. McCord to James M. Rhett, Charles H. Rhett and Roland Rhett, November 20, 1863, GLC, https://www.gilderlehrman.org/collection/glc093802 (accessed March 6, 2020). Given the Rhetts gave two receipts for payment in March 1863, it seems likely the sale took place in the spring, with a larger payment due to McCord in November. See Receipts, McCord to Charles H. Rhett, March 2, 1863, in same.
158. Mary Elliott to Emily Elliott, March 2, 1863, Elliott and Gonzales Family Papers, SHC.
159. Arthur J. L. Fremantle, *Three Months in the Southern States: April–June, 1863* (New York: John Bradburn, 1864), 191.
160. R. W. Hume to C. C. Pinckney Jr., June 29, 1863, Pinckney Family Papers, Emory.
161. Solomon Cohen Ledger, Kaplan Collection, University of Pennsylvania.
162. W. B. Fewell to Alexander F. Fewell, January 12, 1863, in Robert Harley Mackintosh Jr., ed., *"Dear Martha . . . " The Confederate War Letters of a South Carolina Soldier Alexander Faulkner Fewell* (Columbia, SC: The R. L. Bryan Company, 1976), 98; John Lynch to Bishop Patrick Lynch, February 2, 1863, Lynch Family Letters, 1858–1866, Catholic Diocese of Charleston Archives and Low Country Digital Archive, College of Charleston, http://lcdl.library.cofc.edu/content/lynch-family-letters-1858-1866 (accessed February 13, 2018).
163. McClellan Family Letter, April 6, 1863, B. H. Teague Family and Collected Papers, SCHS.
164. E. Brittingham to Dickinson & Hill, November 27, 1863, Dickinson, Hill & Co. (Richmond, Va.), Letters, 1855–1864, LVA. See also Elijah Brittingham to Dickinson Hill, August 26, 27, November 19, 1862, DHCRC.
165. S. R. Fondren to E. H. Stokes, October 12, 1863, SUSC-AAS.
166. Miles Costin to James Robertson, April 23, 1863, C. B. Heller Collection, NCDAH.
167. Inscoe, "Mountain Masters as Confederate Opportunists," 91.
168. J. Gwyn to Rufus Lenoir, February 9, 1863, Lenoir Papers, SHC.

169. "Stop the Runaways," *Asheville News*, July 17, 1862; Berlin et al., *The Destruction of Slavery*, 81; David S. Cecelski, *The Fire of Freedom: Abraham Galloway & the Slaves' Civil War* (Chapel Hill: University of North Carolina Press, 2012), 58–82. In 1860, Penland owned $5,000 in real estate and $6,500 in personal property—but only one enslaved person. Census of *1860, Division 37, Haywood, North Carolina and Census of 1860, Slave Schedules, Division 37, Haywood County*, https://www.ancestry.com/discoveryui-content/view/93265569:7668?tid=&pid=&queryId=9accf59419f63ca5638ecff4592bffe7&_phsrc=wWM3&_phstart=successSource.
170. William S. Pettigrew to Annie Pettigrew, October 8, 1862; October 1864 (likely 1862), Pettigrew Papers, SHC.
171. Jeremiah Gage to Mary M. Sanders, January 24, 1863, Gage Family Collection, Special Collections, University of Mississippi Libraries.
172. J. M. Sutherlin to W. T. Sutherlin, January 19, 1863; D. D. Hall to William Sutherlin, January 26, 1863; Silas Omohundro to William Sutherlin, January 30, 1863, William T. Sutherlin Papers, Duke.
173. Henry S. Figures to "Dear Sister," March 1, 1863, GLC, https://www.gilderlehrman.org/collection/glc00653011 2 (accessed March 6, 2020).
174. Elizabeth Barringer to Daniel W. Barringer, May 10, 15, 1863, Barringer Papers, SHC.
175. William Wirt Henry Account Book, VHS.
176. Henry K. Burgwyn to "My Dear Father," January 3, February 8, 1863, Burgwyn Family Papers, SHC.
177. Bill of Sale, Ann Moore to John W. Luke, March 31, 1863, Rudin Slavery Collection, Cornell.
178. Hsieh and Murray, *A Savage War*, 268–326; McPherson, *Battle Cry of Freedom*, 626–665; Gallagher, *The Confederate War*, 20–24 and "Lee's Army Has Not Lost Any of Its Prestige: The Impact of Gettysburg on the Army of Northern Virginia and the Confederate Home Front," in *The Third Day At Gettysburg and Beyond*, ed. Gary W. Gallagher (Chapel Hill: University of North Carolina Press, 1994), 1–30; Kent Masterson Brown, *Retreat from Gettysburg: Lee, Logistics, and the Pennsylvania Campaign* (Chapel Hill: University of North Carolina Press, 2005), 387–390; Glatthaar, *General Lee's Army*, 282–288; Allen Guelzo, *Gettysburg: The Last Invasion* (New York: Vintage Books, 2013), 453–458; Ballard, *Vicksburg*, 418–428; Charles D. Grear, " 'West of the Mississippi to Us is Nearly a Sealed Book': Trans-Mississippians and the Fall of Vicksburg," in *Vicksburg Besieged*, ed. Steven E. Woodworth and Charles D. Grear (Carbondale: Southern Illinois Press, 2020), 147–172.
179. List of Slaves Sold, 1863, Baskerville Family Papers, Series M: VHS, Part 5, RASP; Susan Wilcox to Mr. Donnan, July 8, 1863, Alexander and James M. Donnan Papers, LVA.
180. Unknown to Unknown, July 28, 1863, Weeks Collection, Series I: LSU, Part 6, RASP.
181. From Martin W. Philips (DNA, M-437, r107, f479-80) in Lynda Laswell Crist, Kenneth H. Williams, and Peggy L. Dillard, eds., *The Papers of Jefferson Davis, Volume 10: October 1863–August 1864* (Baton Rouge: Louisiana State University Press, 1999), 24.

272 NOTES TO PAGES 106–109

182. Jerome B. Yates to "Dear Ma," August 21, 1863, Confederate States of America Records, 1856–1915, DBCAH.
183. Bills of Sale, T. D. Crawford to E. S. Hammond, July 24, 1863; Hammond to James Irvin, November 10, 1863, Hammond Papers, LC. Hammond purchased two other people, William and Isaac, in the intervening months. Bills of Sale, August 26 and September 18, 1863, in same.
184. S. W. N. Feamster to "Dear Mother," July 27, 1863, Feamster Family Papers, LC.
185. Quoted in Berlin et al., *The Wartime Genesis of Free Labor: The Upper South*, 415.
186. *John A. Johnson et al v. Lucy Johnson et al*, in Joseph B. Heiskell, *Reports of Cases Argued and Determined in the Supreme Court of Tennessee, for the Middle Division, for the year 1870–71*, Volume II (Nashville: Jones, Purvis & Co., 1871), 524–525.
187. Bill of Sale, Salmon & Bledsoe to E. H. Stokes, July 10, 1863, Francis C. Brown Collection on Slavery in America, Princeton; Robert N. Trice to Stokes, July 8, 1863, Chase Papers, LC.
188. "Resumption of Business," *Richmond Whig*, September 1, 1863.
189. "Let Us Reason Together," *Houston Tri-Weekly Telegraph*, August 21, 1863. On the trans-Mississippi, see, among others, Carin Peller-Semmens, "Unreconstructed: Slavery and Emancipation on Louisiana's Red River, 1820–1880" (PhD diss., University of Sussex, 2016), 88–125; Thomas W. Cutrer, *Theater of a Separate War: The Civil War West of the Mississippi River* (Chapel Hill: University of North Carolina Press, 2017).
190. "Let Us Reason Together," *Houston Tri-Weekly Telegraph*, August 21, 1863.

Chapter 4

1. Francis W. Smith to Josiah Lilly Deans, August 17, 1863, emphasis in original; October 1, 1863, Smith Family Papers, VHS. On slave trading and Confederate morale, see Martinez, "The Slave Market in Civil War Virginia," 106–135.
2. Ramsdell, *Behind the Lines in the Southern Confederacy*; E. Merton Coulter, *The Confederate States of America, 1861–1865* (Baton Rouge: Louisiana State University Press, 1950), –149–183, 219–254, 269–300; Richard Cecil Todd, *Confederate Finance* (Athens: University of Georgia Press, 1954); Gates, *Agriculture and the Civil War*; Emory M. Thomas, *The Confederate Nation, 1861–1865* (New York: Harper Perennial, 1979, 2011), 196–214; Ball, *Financial Failure and Confederate Defeat*; John Majewski, *Modernizing a Slave Economy: The Economic Vision of the Confederate Nation* (Chapel Hill: University of North Carolina Press, 2009); Hurt, *Agriculture and the Confederacy*.
3. "Our Financial Situation," *Edgefield Advertiser*, October 14, 1863. On Gregg, see Broadus Mitchell, *William Gregg, Factory Master of the Old South* (Chapel Hill: University of North Carolina Press, 1928). Gregg himself reportedly bought people amid the secession crisis. "South Carolina," *Richmond Enquirer*, January 25, 1861.

4. Phillips, *American Negro Slavery*, 368–377; Gray, *History of Agriculture*, II: 663–667; Fogel and Engerman, *Time on the Cross*, I: 86–106; Calomiris and Pritchett, "Betting on Secession," particularly 12–16.
5. The South held perhaps $25 million in gold and silver at the war's outset, most of which the war effort immediately absorbed. Ramsdell, *Behind the Lines in the Southern Confederacy*, 10–11.
6. Phillips, *American Negro Slavery*, 368–377; Gray, *History of Agriculture*, II: 663–667, 697–700; Fogel and Engerman, *Time on the Cross*, I: 86–106; Calomiris and Pritchett, "Betting on Secession, 12–16; Huston, *Calculating the Value of the Union*, 190–232; Foner, *Free Soil, Free Labor, Free Men*, 9–38, 77–106, 313–327; Ashworth, *Slavery, Capitalism, and Politics*, I: 125–191; Merritt, *Masterless Men*, 251–322; Freehling, *The Road to Disunion*, II: 70–145, 196–253; Oakes, *Freedom National*, 1–48; Manisha Sinha, *The Slave's Cause: A History of Abolition* (New Haven, CT: Yale University Press, 2016).
7. Fogel, *Without Consent or Contract*, 86–87.
8. Stanley L. Engerman, "Chicken Little, Anna Karenina, and the Economics of Slavery: Two Reflections on Historical Analysis, with Examples Drawn Mostly from the Study of Slavery," *Social Science History* 17, no. 2 (Summer 1993): 164–166; David Potter, *The Impending Crisis, 1848–1861* (New York: Harper & Row, 1976), 238–239, 391–395; Fehrenbacher, *The Slaveholding Republic*, 266–294; Freehling, *The Road to Disunion*, II: 97–143; Karp, *This Vast Southern Empire*, 199–250; Huston, "The Pregnant Economies of the Border South, 1840–1860," 120–141. See also Starobin, *Industrial Slavery in the Old South* and Charles Dew, *Bond of Iron: Master and Slave at Buffalo Forge* (New York: Norton, 1994).
9. Fogel and Engerman estimated that had the Civil War not occurred, slave prices would have averaged an annual growth of 1.4 percent, "a figure slightly lower than the prewar trend of growth," to be sure, but still growth. Fogel and Engerman, *Time on the Cross*, I: 95–97, 103–106.
10. Berry, *The Price for Their Pound of Flesh*; Alfred H. Conrad and John R. Meyer, "The Economics of Slavery in the Antebellum South," *Journal of Political Economy* 66, no. 2 (April 1958): 95–130; Richard Sutch, "The Profitability of Slavery Revisited," *Southern Economic Journal* 31, no. 4 (April 1965): 365–377; Brown, *Good Wives, Nasty Wenches, & Anxious Patriarchs*, 107–136; Morgan, *Laboring Women* and "Partus sequitur ventrem: Law, Race, and Reproduction in Colonial Slavery," *Small Axe*, Vol. 22, no. 1 (March 2018): 1–17; Richard S. Dunn, *A Tale of Two Plantations: Slave Life and Labor in Jamaica and Virginia* (Cambridge, MA: Harvard University Press, 2014); Baptist, "'Cuffy,' 'Fancy Maids,' and 'One-Eyed Men,'" 1640–1650. For resistance to slaveholders' control over reproductive labor, see Stephanie M. H. Camp, *Closer to Freedom: Enslaved Women & Everyday Resistance in the Plantation South* (Chapel Hill: University of North Carolina Press, 2004), 60–92 and Sharla Fett, *Working Cures: Healing, Health, and Power on Southern Slave Plantations* (Chapel Hill: University of North Carolina Press, 2002), 176–177.
11. Edward Phifer, "Slavery in Microcosm: Burke County, North Carolina," *Journal of Southern History* 28, no. 2 (May 1962): 144.

12. Wright, *The Political Economy of the Cotton South*, 38, 129; Gray, *History of Agriculture*, II: 661–663.
13. John R. Sutton to R. H. Dickinson, March 8, 1864, Miscellaneous File, Brock Collection, HL-LVA.
14. William L. Barney, *The Secessionist Impulse: Alabama and Mississippi in 1860* (1974; repr. Tuscaloosa: University of Alabama Press, 2004), 219–222; Woodman, *King Cotton & His Retainers*, 201–203; Foner, *Business &*, 214–223; Schweikart, "Secession and Southern Banks," 111–125; Hurt, *Agriculture and the Confederacy*, 16; Deyle, *Carry Me Back*, 98–112; Ball, *Financial Failure and Confederate Defeat*, 65–66; Beckert, *Empire of Cotton*, 246; Gates, *Agriculture and the Civil War*, 13, 17–21, 74.
15. State of Georgia, *Annual Report of the Comptroller General, of the State of Georgia, Made to the Governor, October 20, 1861* (Milledgeville: Boughton, Nisbet & Barnes, 1861), 5–6.
16. Hurt, *Agriculture and the Confederacy*, 11–34.
17. Lerner, "Money, Prices, and Wages in the Confederacy, 1861–1865," 20, 29–30; Gates, *Agriculture and the Civil War*, 37–38, 74–77; Otto, *Southern Agriculture During the Civil War Era*, 24–45.
18. McPherson, *Battle Cry of Freedom*, 437–439; Lerner, "The Monetary and Fiscal Programs of the Confederate Government, 1861–1865," 507.
19. Gary M. Pecquet, "Public Finance in Confederate Louisiana," *Louisiana History* 29, no. 3 (Summer 1988): 264–265
20. McPherson, *Battle Cry of Freedom*, 438; Lerner, "Money, Prices, and Wages in the Confederacy," 23–25; Burdekin and Weidenmier, "Suppressing Asset Price Inflation," 420.
21. Lerner, "The Monetary and Fiscal Programs of the Confederate Government," 520. For a comparison, see David K. Thomson, *Bonds of War: How Civil War Financial Agents Sold the World on the Union* (Chapel Hill: University of North Carolina Press, 2022).
22. Ramsdell, *Behind the Lines of the Southern Confederacy*, 85.
23. Eliza Jarratt to E. H. Stokes[?], August 12, 1861, Chase Papers, LC.
24. A. J. Rux to E. H. Stokes, September 24, October 9, 1861, Slavery Collection, NYHS.
25. Maddux & Co. to Sterling Neblett, April 30, 1862, Neblett Family Papers, VHS. Emphasis in original.
26. Walter W. Lenoir to Rufus Lenoir, April 14, 1862, Lenoir Papers, SHC.
27. Alfred B. Mulligan to "My Dear Mother," January 5, 1862, in Olin Fulmer Hutchinson Jr., ed., *"My Dear Mother & Sisters": Civil War Letters of Capt. A. B. Mulligan, Co. B 5th South Carolina Cavalry—Butler's Division—Hampton's Corps 1861–1865* (Spartanburg: The Reprint Company, 1992), 6.
28. Entry for March 21, 1863, in Venet, *Sam Richards' Civil War* Diary, 169.
29. Alfred Bell to Mary Bell, August 17, 1862, Alfred W. Bell Papers, 1848–1896, Duke.
30. Walter Lenoir to Rufus Lenoir, April 24, 1862, Lenoir Papers, SHC.
31. Alfred B. Mulligan to "My Dear Mother," January 5, 1862, in Hutchinson, *"My Dear Mother & Sisters,"* 6; Frank J. Byrne, "Rebellion and Retail: A Tale of Two Merchants

in Confederate Atlanta," *The Georgia Historical Quarterly*, 79 no. 1 (April 1995), 46–47; Venet, *Sam Richards's Civil War Diary*, 120–125.
32. Mary Bell to Alfred Bell, November 20, 1862; Alfred Bell to Mary Bell, November 29, 1862; Mary Bell to Alfred Bell, December 6, 1862, Bell Papers, Duke. See also John C. Inscoe, "The Civil War's Empowerment of an Appalachian Woman: The 1864 Slave Purchases of Mary Bell," in *Discovering the Women in Slavery: Emancipating Perspectives on the American Past*, ed. Patricia Morton (Athens: University of Georgia Press, 1996), 61–81.
33. James L. Petigru to Jane Petigru North, June 20, 1862, in Carson, *Life, Letters and Speeches of James Louis Petigru*, 453.
34. William Garner to Henrietta Garner, August 4, 1862, in D. D. McBrien, ed., "Letters of an Arkansas Confederate Soldier," *Arkansas Historical Quarterly* 2, no. 1 (March 1943): 63.
35. Quoted in Kenneth Noe, *Reluctant Rebels: The Confederates Who Joined the Army after 1861* (Chapel Hill: University of North Carolina Press, 2010), 57.
36. W. L. Sharkey to Dr. Gould, June 17, 1862, Mansfield Lovell Papers, 1822–1884, HL, emphasis in original. See also Mary Hall to Isaac Hall, June 8, 1862; Isaac Hall to Mary Hall, June 21, 1862, in McGinty, "The Human Side of War," 73, 78.
37. R. C. Ware to E. H. Stokes, June 30, 1862; J. J. Adams to Stokes, August 16, 1862, Henry Easley to Stokes, September 8, 1862; March 14, 1863, Ames Papers, MHS.
38. Micajah Woods to John Rodes Woods, December 16, 1862, Micajah Woods Papers, UVA.
39. "A Chance to Invest," *Memphis Daily Appeal*, March 19, 1862; "Houses and Lots for Sale," *Raleigh Semi-Weekly Standard*, July 2, 1862; "Valuable Mills for Sale," *Raleigh Semi-Weekly Standard*, October 21, 1862; Camilla Davis to William F. Hardin, December 8, 1862, in Camilla Davis Trammell, *Seven Pines: Its Occupants and Their Letters, 1825–1872* (Houston: self-published, 1986), 177.
40. Hector Davis to A. R. Blakey, March 20, 1862, Blakey Papers, Duke; "Domestic Slave Trade," *The Friend*, January 25, 1862.
41. J. H. Burnett to E. H. Stokes, August 17, 1862, Chase Papers, LC.
42. Walter W. Lenoir to Rufus Lenoir, April 14, 1862, Lenoir Papers, SHC; Inscoe, "Mountain Masters as Confederate Opportunists," 85–100.
43. Henry K. Burgwyn to "My Dear Father," February 8, 1863, Burgwyn Papers, SHC. Emphasis in original.
44. Jesse Ruebel Kirkland to Lucinda Kirkland, October 21, 1861, in Robert G. Evans, ed., *The 16th Mississippi Infantry: Civil War Letters and Reminiscences* (Jackson: University of Mississippi Press, 2002), 32.
45. Quoted in Jason H. Silverman, Samuel N. Thomas Jr., and Beverly D. Evans IV, *Shanks: The Life and Wars of Nathan George Evans, C. S. A.* (Boston: Da Capo Press, 2002), 94, 97.
46. "'Help Me, Cassius, &c.,'" *Yorkville Enquirer*, July 1, 1863.
47. Joseph Holt to Edwin Stanton, May 24, 1864, *OR, Series II*, Vol. 7, 159–160; Howard Westwood, "The Reverend Fountain Brown: Alleged Violator of the Emancipation Proclamation," *Arkansas Historical Quarterly* 49, no. 2 (Summer 1990): 107–123.

48. Entries for June 25, July 12, October 16, 1862, in Ruffin, *The Diary of Edmund Ruffin*, Vol. II, 353, 375, 466. See also entry for June 24, 1862, Edmund Ruffin Jr. Journal, SHC.
49. Entries for June 25 and October 16, 1862, Ruffin, *The Diary of Edmund Ruffin*, Vol. II, 353, 466.
50. See, for example, "Untitled," *Wilmington Daily Journal*, January 8, 1863; Margaret Nola Burkley, "Floyd County, Georgia, During the Civil War Era" (PhD diss., Florida State University, 1998), 207.
51. Hurt, *Agriculture and the Confederacy*, 60; Ball, *Financial Failure and Confederate Defeat*, 176.
52. Ball, *Financial Failure and Confederate Defeat*, 72-73, 174; Todd, *Confederate Finance*, 64-65.
53. Lerner, "Money, Prices, and Wages in the Confederacy, 1861-1865," 2 1, 29.
54. Entry for November 29, 1862, in Childs, *The Private Journal of Henry William Ravenel*, 166; John M. Sutherlin to William T. Sutherlin, February 28, 1863, Sutherlin Papers, Duke.
55. Todd, *Confederate Finance*, 109-110.
56. James Arthur Irby, "Confederate Austin 1861-1865" (PhD diss., University of Texas at Austin, 1953), 102; "Refusing Confederate Money," *Raleigh Semi-Weekly Standard*, April 7, 1863.
57. Zack Howell to "Dear Bella," November 1, 1862, Samuel Christian Fullilove Papers, LSU-Shreveport. My thanks to Carin Peller-Semmens for pointing me to this source.
58. Walter W. Lenoir to Joseph Norwood[?], November 2, 1863, Lenoir Papers, SHC.
59. Charles Carleton Coffin, *Following the Flag* (Boston: Estes & Lauriat, 1886), 235.
60. Entries for October 3, 27, 1863, in Childs, *The Private Journal of Henry William Ravenel*, 185-186; Sarah Law Kennerly, "Confederate Juvenile Imprints: Children's Books and Periodicals Published in the Confederate States of America 1861-1865" (PhD diss., University of Michigan, 1958), 162.
61. A. J. Rux to E. H. Stokes, September 11, 1863, SUSC-AAS.
62. Wright, "Economic Conditions in the Confederacy as Seen by the French Consuls," 208.
63. W. B. Pettit to Arabella Pettit, April 9, 1863, in Charles W. Turner, ed., *Civil War Letters of Arabella Speairs and William Beverley Pettit of Fluvanna County, Virginia March 1862-March 1865*, Vol. 1, *March 1862-February 1864* (Roanoke: Virginia Lithographs & Graphics Company, 1988), 101.
64. Caleb McCurdy to J. M. McCurdy, March 6, 1863, Unknown to J. M. McCurdy, December 20, 1863, Caleb Shive McCurdy Papers, Duke. See also T. George Walton to O. Bartlett, March 20, 1863, Lenoir Papers, SHC.
65. Fragment, April 16-19, 1863, in Joseph Gregoire de Roulhac Hamilton, ed., *The Correspondence of Jonathan Worth* Vol. I (Raleigh, NC: Edwards & Broughton, 1909), 233.
66. "Negroes and Confederate Money," *Yorkville Enquirer*, August 26, 1863. See also Ervin L. Jordan Jr., *Charlottesville and the University of Virginia in the Civil War* (Lynchburg, VA: H. E. Howard, Inc., 1988), 41.
67. George C. Rable, *The Confederate Republic: A Revolution Against Politics* (Chapel Hill: University of North Carolina Press, 1994), 214-235; William J. Cooper Jr., *Jefferson Davis, American* (New York: Vintage Books, 2000), 498.

68. "Negroes and Land for Confederate Money," *Memphis Daily Appeal*, September 14, 1863; "Trade Reviving," *Memphis Daily Appeal*, September 22, 1863.
69. James C. Francis Jr. to James C. Francis, March 27, 1863, in Pate, *When This Evil War Is Over*, 121.
70. John M. Sutherlin to William T. Sutherlin, February 13, 1863; February 28, 1863, Sutherlin Papers, Duke.
71. David J. Logan to "My Dear Wife," July 30, 1863, in Thomas Jr. and Silverman, *"A Rising Star of Promise,"* 111.
72. W. Caleb McDaniel, "Involuntary Removals: 'Refugeed Slaves' in Confederate Texas," in *Lone Star Unionism, Dissent, and Resistance: Other Sides of Civil War Texas*, ed. Jesús F. de la Teja (Norman: University of Oklahoma Press, 2016), 60, 63–70; Barry A. Crouch, "Hidden Sources of Black History: The Texas Freedmen's Bureau Records as a Case Study," *Southwestern Historical Quarterly* 83, no. 3 (January 1980): 215 n 9; Paul A. Levengood, "In the Absence of Scarcity: The Civil War Prosperity of Houston, Texas," *Southwestern Historical Quarterly* 101, no. 4 (April 1998): 404–405; Randolph B. Campbell, *An Empire for Slavery: The Peculiar Institution in Texas, 1821–1865* (Baton Rouge: Louisiana State University Press, 1989), 244–245.
73. John J. Good to Susan A. Good, December 6, 1861, in Lester Newton Fitzhugh, ed., *Cannon Smoke: The Letters of Captain John J. Good, Good-Douglas Texas Battery, CSA* (Hillsboro, TX: Hill Junior College, 1971), 143. See also Goodspeed Publishing Company, *Biographical and Historical Memoirs of Southern Arkansas: Comprising a Condensed History of the State, A Number of Biographies of Its Distinguished Citizens, A Brief Descriptive History of Each of the Counties Mentioned, and Numerous Biographical Sketches of the Citizens of Such County* (Chicago: Goodspeed Publishing Company, 1890), 232.
74. John Sleeper and J. C. Hutchins, *Waco, and McLennan County, Texas: Containing a City Directory of Waco, Historical Sketches of the City and County; Biographical Sketches and Notices of a Few Prominent Citizens; Information with Regard to our Various Institutions, Organizations, Etc.* (Waco, TX: J. W. Golledge, 1876), 112; Harold B. Simpson, *Gaines' Mill to Appomattox: Waco & McClennan County in Hood's Texas Brigade* (Waco, TX: Texian Press, 1963), 233–234.
75. Fremantle, *Three Months in the Southern States*, 83; Quoted in Beverly Rowe, "He Said, She Said: Gendered Correspondence Among Texans," in *Women in Civil War Texas: Diversity and Dissidence in the Trans-Mississippi*, ed. Deborah M. Liles and Angela Boswell (Denton: University of North Texas Press, 2016), 67.
76. Levengood, "In the Absence of Scarcity," 410–412. Quote on 410.
77. Campbell, *An Empire for Slavery*, 242, 242 n 17; Levengood, "In the Absence of Scarcity," 410.
78. Rawick, *The American Slave: A Composite Autobiography*, 5, II: 232.
79. Elijah P. Petty to Margaret Petty, March 19, May 22, 1863; Elijah Petty to "Dear Daughter," February 19, March 24, 1863, in Petty, *Journey to Pleasant Hill*, 142, 153–154, 224. See also William Whateley to Nancy Whateley, December 31, 1862, in John T. Whateley, ed., *An East Texas Family's Civil War: The Letters of Nancy & William Whateley, May–December 1862* (Baton Rouge: Louisiana State University Press, 2019), 122.

80. Quoted in Rowe, "He Said, She Said," 67.
81. George Davis to "Dear Sister," February 8, 1863, in Trammell, *Seven Pines*, 192.
82. Alexander X. Byrd and W. Caleb McDaniel, "Task Force on Slavery, Segregation, and Racial Injustice Update: June 2021 on Research about Slavery," 56, https://taskforce.rice.edu/progress-reports (accessed August 1, 2023).
83. Lizzie Neblett to William Neblett, October 15, November 4, 1863, in Erika L. Murr, ed., *A Rebel Wife in Texas: The Diary and Letters of Elizabeth Scott Neblett 1852–1864* (Baton Rouge: Louisiana State University Press, 2001), 168–169, 189–191.
84. Anthony Joseph Iacono, "So Far Away, So Close to Home: Florida and the Civil War Era" (PhD diss., Mississippi State University, 2000), 143–144.
85. Inscoe, "Mountain Masters as Confederate Opportunists," 85–100.
86. Mary Bell to Alfred Bell, November 20, December 6, 1862, Bell Papers, Duke. An increasing distrust of Confederate currency shaped Bell's efforts, as the owner of another enslaved woman whom Bell considered acquiring demanded specie in payment for her.
87. Lerner, "Money, Prices, and Wages in the Confederacy, 1861–1865," 21, 24, 28–29; Richard C. K. Burdekin and Farrokh K. Langdana, "War Finance in the Southern Confederacy, 1861–1865," *Explorations in Economic History* 30 (1993): 368; Marc D. Weidenmier, "Turning Points in the U.S. Civil War: Views from the Grayback Market," *Southern Economic Journal* 68, no. 4 (2003): 882–883.
88. Blair, *Virginia's Private War*, 69–76; Thomas, *Confederate State of Richmond*, 113–114, 145–152; McCurry, *Confederate Reckoning*, 167–199.
89. Entry for September 20, 1863, in C. Vann Woodward, ed., *Mary Chesnut's Civil War* (New Haven, CT: Yale University Press, 1981), 469.
90. "Tall Price," *Raleigh Semi-Weekly Standard*, June 26, 1863.
91. "Review of the Richmond Markets," *Evansville Daily Journal*, November 13, 1863.
92. D. J. Godwin to "My Dear Uncle," November 24, 1863; Euclid Godwin to "My Dear Uncle," December 26, 1863, Borland Family Papers, W&M.
93. Rawick, *The American Slave*, 7: 83; Ronnie W. Clayton, *Mother Wit: The Ex-Slave Narratives of the Louisiana Writers' Project* (New York: Peter Lang, 1990), 24.
94. Rawick, *The American Slave*, 9, 4: 299; Rawick, *The American Slave*, 10, 5: 114.
95. Lerner, "The Monetary and Fiscal Programs of the Confederate Government," 516, 521.
96. Burdekin and Weidenmier, "Suppressing Asset Price Inflation," 420.
97. Edwin H. Fay to Sarah Fay, January 24, 1863, in Wiley, *"This Infernal War,"* 216–217.
98. Alfred Bell to Mary Bell, December 29, 1863, Bell Papers, Duke.
99. P. L. Cameron to George W. Mordecai, September 18, 1863, Mordecai Papers, SHC.
100. Pecquet, "Public Finance in Confederate Louisiana," 286; Schwab, "The Finances of the Confederate States," 50; Lerner, "Money, Prices, and Wages in the Confederacy, 1861–1865," 23–29 and "The Monetary and Fiscal Programs of the Confederate Government," 518–522.
101. Godfrey Barnsley to George Barnsley, January 14, 1864, George Scarborough Barnsley Papers, SHC.
102. Ethelred Philips to James Jones Philips, March 27, 1864, James Jones Philips Papers, SHC.

103. Farley Grubb, "The Continental Dollar: How Much Was Really Issued?" *Journal of Economic History* 68, no. 1 (March 2008): 283–291; Albert Sidney Bolles, *The Financial History of the United States, From 1774–1789: Embracing the Period of the American Revolution, Volume I* (New York: D. Appleton & Company, 1892), 117–146, 217–220; R. E. Elliott to Mrs. A. H. Elliott, April 13, 1864, Elliott and Gonzales Papers, SHC. Emphasis in the original. For Confederate skepticism, see John J. Good to Susan A. Good, December 6, 1861, in Fitzhugh, *Cannon Smoke*, 142–143; E. L. Herndon to David A. Barnes, February 3, 1864, David A. Barnes Papers, SHC.
104. Burdekin and Weidenmier, "Suppressing Asset Price Inflation," 420; Entry for March 5, 1864, in Childs, *The Private Journal of Henry William Ravenel*, 194.
105. Quoted in "Pay Day," *Western Democrat*, January 14, 1864.
106. Figures from L. C. Robards Account Books, CHM; J. Winston Coleman Jr., "Lexington's Slave Dealers and Their Southern Trade" *Filson Club History Quarterly* 12, no. 1, 1–23; Caleb W. McDaniel, *Sweet Taste of Liberty: A True Story of Slavery and Restitution in America* (New York: Oxford University Press, 2019), 58–87.
107. "Notice," *Richmond Daily Dispatch*, March 25, 1864.
108. Hill, Dickinson & Co., Tax Returns, City of Richmond, 1863–1864, Entry UD-152A, RG 109, NARA; R. A. Grinnan to Andrew Grinnan, April 13, 1864, Papers of the Grinnan and related Bryan and Tucker families of Virginia, UVA
109. John W. Cofer to "Dear Mag," May 3, 1864, Bell Irvin Wiley Papers, Emory.
110. "$100 Reward," *Raleigh Daily Progress*, March 19, 1864; "$300 Reward," *Goldsboro Messenger*, May 2, 1864.
111. W. T. Sutherlin to "Dear Major," April 5, 1864, Sutherlin Papers, Duke; S. M. Bowman to "Dear Sir," May 10, 1866, Endorsements Sent, Vol. 1–5, Nov. 1865–Dec. 1868, Winchester SC, VAFOR, 183: 46, 48/603, RG 105, NARA M1913.
112. James Graham Tate to Charles Campbell Tate, April 5, 1864, Graham-Sanders-Tate Family Papers, UVA; "Invest Your Money," *Daily South Carolinian*, March 29, 1864.
113. Kilbourne, *Debt, Investment, Slaves*, 49–74; David Silkenat, *Moments of Despair: Suicide, Divorce, & Debt in Civil War Era North Carolina* (Chapel Hill: University of North Carolina Press, 2011), 143–144, 152–154.
114. Williams, *Help Me to Find My People*, 27, 91–98, 123–124.
115. Schwab, *The Confederate States of America 1861–1865*, 106–110; Charles Kettleborough, "Moratory and Stay Laws," *The American Political Science Review* 12, no. 3 (August 1918): 458; A. H. Feller, "Moratory Legislation: A Comparative Study," *Harvard Law Review* 46, no. 7 (May 1933): 1081–1085; William L. Shaw, "The Confederate Conscription and Exemption Acts," *American Journal of Legal History* 6, no. 4 (October 1962): 400; B. F. Moore to Thomas Ruffin, September 27, 1861, Ruffin Papers, SHC.
116. Clement Evans to Allie Evans, December 19, 22, 1863; Allie Evans to Clement Evans, December 30, 1863, in Robert Grier Stephens, *Intrepid Warrior: Clement Anselm Evans, Confederate General from Georgia: Life, Letters, and Diaries of the War Years* (Dayton, OH: Morningside House, Inc., 1992), 298–315.
117. PAR Accession #21686103, Endymion D. Cornick v. William P. Morgan, et. al., Princess Anne County, Virginia, April 1861–October 1866, Series 2, Part C, RSFB; Rawick, *The American Slave*, 5, I: 185.

118. Jonathan W. White, ed., *A Philadelphia Perspective: The Civil War Diary of Sidney George Fisher* (New York: Fordham University Press, 2007), 262; John Graylet to Jane Graylet, October 20, 1862, Slave Records, Ashe County, Miscellaneous Records, NCDAH.
119. H. E. Merritt to William H. Merritt, October 15, 1862, William H. Merritt Papers, Duke; Caleb McCurdy to J. M. McCurdy, March 1, 1863, McCurdy Papers, Duke; Thomas Murray to William L. Criglar, November 3, 1863, William Louis Criglar Papers, SHC; William A. Nelson to Louisa A. Nelson March 14, 1862, W. A. Nelson Papers, SCL; Petition, James B. Campbell and Paul Remley to George Buist, June 18[?], 1861, Campbell Papers, SCHS; Roark, *Masters Without Slaves*, 83.
120. McClellan Family Letter, April 6, 1863, Teague Papers, SCHS.
121. Alfred B. Mulligan to "My Dear Mother & Sister," November 16, 1862, March 22, 29, 1863, February 21, 1864, in Hutchinson, *"My Dear Mother & Sisters,"* 55, 69, 71, 102.
122. PAR Accession #20686316, Petition of Antoinette E. Moore, 1863, Houston Co., Georgia, Series II, Part A, RSFB.
123. John S. Lewis to Mrs. Nancy Lewis, July 31, 1863, in Evans, *The 16th Mississippi Infantry*, 186.
124. Hector Harris to William Henry Haxall, April 3, 1861, Haxall Family Papers, VHS.
125. W. C. Bee to "My Dear Allen," December 1, 1862, Legare Case Papers: Litigation of C. T. Lowndes, A. M. Huger, A. Izard, 1863–1869, Campbell Papers, SCHS.
126. Drumgoold, *A Slave Girl's Story*, 4–5, 9, 39. U.S. Census, *1860, Meherrin, Brunswick, Virginia*; U.S. Census, 1860, Slave Schedule, Charlotte, Virginia, AncestryHeritageQuest.
127. Grant Taylor to Malinda Taylor, October 25, 1862, November 9, 1862, and January 19, 1864, in Ann K. Blomquist and Robert A. Taylor, eds., *This Cruel War: The Civil War Letters of Grant and Malinda Taylor* (Macon, GA: Mercer University Press, 2000), 115, 121, 217; R. H. Brooks to Telitha Brooks, June 12, 1863, in Katherine S. Holland, ed., *Keep All My Letters: The Civil War Letters of Richard Henry Brooks, 51st Georgia Infantry* (Macon, GA: Mercer University Press, 2003), 90–91.
128. PAR Accession 20186403, Petition of Allen Sims, February 9, 1864, Series II, Part A, RSFB.
129. Receipt, Wm. A. Little to Charles Bruce, January 16, 1864, Bruce Papers, LC.
130. Henry Semple to Emily Semple, October 27, 1863, Henry C. Semple Papers, Alabama Department of Archives and History.
131. McPherson, *Battle Cry of Freedom*, 671–681, 718–743; Hsieh and Murray, *A Savage War*, 336–399.
132. William A. Chunn to Lila Chunn, November 22, 1863, William Augustus Chunn Letters, Emory.
133. Gary W. Gallagher, "The Two Generals Who Resist Each Other: Perceptions of Grant and Lee in the Summer of 1864," in *Cold Harbor to the Crater: The End of the Overland Campaign*, ed. Gary W. Gallagher and Caroline E. Janney (Chapel Hill: University of North Carolina Press, 2015), 1–32; Brooks D. Simpson, "Great Expectations: Ulysses S. Grant, the Northern Press, and the Opening of the Wilderness Campaign," in *The Wilderness Campaign*, ed. Gary W. Gallagher (Chapel Hill: University of North Carolina Press, 1997), 1–35;

134. Entry for August 21, 1864, in Jones, *A Rebel War Clerk's Diary*, 412; Larry E. Nelson, *Bullets, Ballots, and Rhetoric: Confederate Policy for the United States Presidential Contest of 1864* (Tuscaloosa: University of Alabama Press, 1980); Jonathan W. White, *Emancipation, the Union Army, and the Election of 1864* (Baton Rouge: Louisiana State University Press, 2014).
135. "$500 Reward," *Raleigh Weekly Progress*, June 21, 1864; "$300 Reward," *Salisbury Daily Carolina Watchman*, July 19, 1864.
136. "$500 Reward," *Wilmington Daily Journal*, August 12, 1864; "$1000 Reward," *Daily Carolina Watchman*, December 28, 1864.
137. Lewis Warlick to Cornelia Warlick, September 13, 1864; in Mike Lawing and Carolyn Lawing, eds., *My Dearest Friend: The Civil War Correspondence of Cornelia McGimsey and Lewis Warlick* (Durham, NC: Carolina Academic Press, 2000), 182.
138. William McFall to "Dear Sister," October 9, 1864, in F. Lawrence McFall Jr., ed., *Civil War Correspondence: Letters of William and James McFall of the South Carolina Palmetto Sharpshooters* (Danville, VA: Fred Lawrence McFall Jr., 2000), 25.
139. "Steam Mills for Sale," *Yorkville Enquirer*, March 25, 1863; "Land for Sale," *Wilmington Journal*, April 30, 1863.
140. "Plantation for Sale," *Macon Daily Telegraph*, July 16, 1864.
141. *Obadiah Arnold vs. Ezekiel Trice* in N. J. Hammond, *Reports of Cases in Law and Equity, Argued and Determined in the Supreme Court of Georgia, at Atlanta, Parts of June and December Terms, 1869* Volume XXXIX (Macon, GA: J. W. Burke & Co., 1870), 511–517.
142. P. L. Cameron to George W. Mordecai, September 18, 1863, Mordecai Papers, SHC.
143. Charles Rogers to Samuel Mordecai, January 15, 1864, Mordecai Papers, SHC; Walter W. Lenoir to Rufus Lenoir, April 14, 1862, Lenoir Papers, SHC; Roark, *Masters Without Slaves*, 88–89; John Washington to Dickinson, Hill & Co., December 17, 1861, Chase Papers, LC; John L'Engle to Edward L'Engle, March 14, 1863, L'Engle Papers, SHC.
144. Theophilus Perry to Harriet Perry, January 18, 1864, in M. Jane Johansson, ed., *Widows by the Thousand: The Civil War Letters of Theophilus and Harriet Perry, 1862–1864* (Fayetteville: University of Arkansas Press, 2000), 198.
145. John Berkley Grimball, "Diary of John Berkley Grimball, 1858–1865 (Continued)," *The South Carolina Historical Magazine* 56, no. 3 (July 1955): 168 and "Diary of John Berkley Grimball, 1858–1865 (continued)," *South Carolina Historical Magazine* 56, no. 4 (October 1955): 214–216; William H. Grimball to John Berkley Grimball, February 19, 1862, Grimball Papers, Duke.
146. Augustin Taveau to Delphine Taveau, March 6, 1863, Augustin Louis Taveau Papers, Duke.
147. *Joseph McMath v. David Johnson* in R. O. Reynolds, *Reports of Cases Argued and Determined in the High Court of Errors and Appeals for the State of Mississippi*, Vol. XLI (New York: Banks Brothers, 1868), 449.
148. Gallagher, *The Confederate War*, 63–111; Glatthaar, *General Lee's Army*, 440–441; David Potter, "The Historian's Use of Nationalism and Vice Versa," in *The South and the Sectional Conflict* (Baton Rouge: Louisiana State University Press, 1968), 78–83; Reid Mitchell, "The Creation of Confederate Loyalties," in *New Perspectives on Race*

and Slavery in America: Essays in Honor of Kenneth M. Stampp, ed. Robert H. Abzug and Stephen E. Maizlish (Lexington: University Press of Kentucky, 1986), 93–108; Quigley, *Shifting Grounds*; Thomas, *The Confederate Nation*; Blair, *Virginia's Private War*; Anne Sarah Rubin, *A Shattered Nation: The Rise and Fall of the Confederacy, 1861–1868* (Chapel Hill: University of North Carolina Press, 2005); Sheehan-Dean, *Why Confederates Fought*; Phillips, *Diehard Rebels*; Colin Edward Woodward, *Marching Masters: Slavery, Race, and the Confederate Army During the Civil War* (Charlottesville: University of Virginia Press, 2015), 15–30.

149. Phillips, *Diehard Rebels*, 90–94; Brettle, *Colossal Ambitions*, 111–178.
150. Gallagher, *The Confederate War*, 106, 113–140.
151. For studies emphasizing the internal rifts within the Confederacy, see (among many others), Wesley, *The Collapse of the Confederacy*; Robinson, *Bitter Fruits of Bondage*; Hahn, *The Roots of Southern Populism*; Durrill, *War of Another Kind*; William Freehling, *The South Vs. the South: How Anti-Confederate Southerners Shaped the Course of the Civil War* (New York: Oxford University Press, 2001); McCurry, *Confederate Reckoning*.
152. Berry, *The Price For Their Pound of Flesh*, 46–57, 78–83.
153. On visions of the Confederate future, see Peter Carmichael, *The Last Generation: Young Virginians in Peace, War, and Reunion* (Chapel Hill: University of North Carolina Press, 2005), 35–58; Majewski, *Modernizing a Slave Economy*; Michael T. Bernath, "The Confederacy as a Moment of Possibility," *Journal of Southern History* 79, no. 2 (May 2013): 299–338; Adrian Brettle, "Confederate Imaginations with the Federals in the Postwar Order," *Civil War History* 65, no. 1 (March 2019): 43–72 and *Colossal Ambitions*.
154. William S. Pettigrew to Annie Pettigrew, October 3, 1862, Pettigrew Papers, SHC.
155. Walter Lenoir to Rufus Lenoir, April 14, April 24, 1862, Lenoir Papers, SHC.
156. Francis M. Coker to Sallie Coker, October 28, 1863, Francis Marion Coker Papers, UGA.
157. Ethelred Philips to "My Dear Friend," June 26, 1862, Philips Papers, SHC; Edwin H. Fay to Sarah Fay, December 21, 1862, in Wiley, *"This Infernal War,"* 196.
158. Gallagher, *The Confederate War*, 106, 113–140. Quote on p. 106; Phillips, *Diehard Rebels*, 90–94.
159. P. L. Cameron to George W. Mordecai, September 18, 1863, Mordecai Papers, SHC.
160. Virgil Sullivan Rabb to Mary Crownover Rabb, June 24, 1864, in Thomas W. Cutrer, ed., "'Bully for Fluornoy's Regiment, We Are Some Pumpkins, You'll Bet': The Civil War Letters of Virgil Sullivan Rabb, Captain, Company I," Part II, *Military History of the Southwest* 20 (Spring 1990): 68.
161. Phillips, *Diehard Rebels*, 102–134; Alex E. Spence to "Dear Father and Mother," June 7, 1864, in Mark K. Christ, ed., *Getting Used to Being Shot At: The Spence Family Civil War Letters* (Fayetteville: University of Arkansas Press, 2002), 96.
162. Berry, *The Price For Their Pound of Flesh*, 46–57, 78–83.
163. Edwin H. Fay to Sarah Fay, December 21, 1862; January 24, 1863; January 9, 1864; February 5, March 13, 1865, in Wiley, *"This Infernal War,"* 196, 216–217, 384, 424, 434.

164. James A. Forbes to John McCue, January 26, March 1, 1861, McCue Family Papers, UVA, emphasis in original; Calomiris and Pritchett, "Betting on Secession," 19–22.
165. Drumgoold, *A Slave Girl's Story*, 39. Drumgoold later described herself as having been born about 1855. U.S. Census, 1880. Brooklyn, Kings County, New York. Roll 853, page 182A, Enumeration District 202. AncestryHeritagequest; For Drumgoold's family, see Register of Persons Furnished Transportation by the Bureau, 6–7, Petersburg SC, VAFOR, 159: 4/15, RG 105, NARA M1913.
166. William Pitt Ballinger Diary, November 18, 1862, William Ballinger Papers, DBCAH.
167. John Ewing to William Austin, November 8, 1863, Papers Related to John Ewing, Papers of and Relating to Military and Civilian Personnel, RG 109, NARA.
168. M. A. Hoyt to Sally Marshall, February 7, 1863, Alan Marshall McGee Jr. Collection, ECU.
169. Henry K. Burgwyn Jr. to Henry K. Burgwyn February 8, April 21, June 13, 1863, Burgwyn Papers, SHC.
170. William Watson Jones to Phil Jones, February 18, 1863, GLC, https://www.gilderlehrman.org/collection/glc0144902 (accessed March 6, 2020). See also Joseph Bowles Learmont, *Catalogue of the Famous Library of the Late J. B. Learmont, of Montreal: Including Beautiful Manuscripts on Vellum, Valuable Incunabula and Many Rare Books on America* (New York: D. Taylor & Company, 1917), 102; John Peter Jones to "My Dear Wife," March 15, 1863, John Peter Jones Correspondence, UVA; John W. Duncan to "My Dear Wife," April 11, 1863, in John W. Duncan and Hubert L. Ferguson, "Letters of John W. Duncan, Captain Confederate States of America," *Arkansas Historical Quarterly* 9, no. 4 (Winter 1950): 301.
171. Rawick, *The American Slave*, 5, II: 195.
172. PAR Accession 20686205, Petition of Samuel Boykin, Muscogee County, Georgia, December 24, 1862–January 13, 1863, Series II, Part A, RSFB.
173. Richard Dozier to A. Robertson, December 27, 1860, Richard Dozier Papers, SHC. See also Charles William Dabney to Robert Lewis Dabney, March 16, 1863, Charles William Dabney papers, SHC.
174. George Knox Miller to "My Darling Wife," April 23, 1864, in Richard M. McMurry, ed., *An Uncompromising Secessionist: The Civil War of George Knox Miller, Eighth (Wade's) Confederate Cavalry* (Tuscaloosa: University of Alabama Press, 2007), 194–195.
175. Sam Barnes to E. H. Stokes, March 6, 1862; J. J. Adams to Stokes, August 16, 1862, Ames Papers, MHS.
176. "Negroes Wanted," *Edgefield Advertiser*, February 4, 1863. See also "Twenty-Five Likely Young Negroes for Sale at Auction," *Athens Post*, March 6, 1863; "Negroes, Negroes," *Atlanta Southern Confederacy*, April 11, 1863; "50 Likely Young Negroes For Sale," *Atlanta Daily Intelligencer*, September 11, 1863.
177. Hill, Dickinson & Co. to Iverson L. Twyman, December 2, 1863, Austin-Twyman Family Papers, Series L: W&M, Part 4, RASP.
178. Gary W. Gallagher, ed., *Fighting for the Confederacy: The Personal Recollections of General Edward Porter Alexander* (Chapel Hill: University of North Carolina Press, 1989), 257–258, 284.

179. Edward Porter Alexander to Bessie Alexander, July 26, 1863, Edward Porter Alexander Papers, SHC, emphasis in original; Alexander to "Dear Brother," July 26, 1863, Alexander and Hillhouse Family Papers, SHC.
180. Thomas L. Bondurant to Alex Bondurant, September 4, 1864, in Walbrook D. Swank, *Civil War Stories: Letters—Memoirs—Anecdotes Union and Confederate* (Shippensburg: Burd Street Press, 1996), 38.
181. Parthenia Antoinette Hague, *A Blockaded Family: Life in Southern Alabama During the Civil War* (1888; repr. Boston: Houghton Mifflin Company, the Riverside Press, Cambridge, 1971), 160–161.

Chapter 5

1. "$750 Reward," *Staunton Spectator*, May 12, 1863; "Buena Vista Furnace," *Richmond Enquirer*, July 30, 1858. On enslaved laborers in Virginia's iron industry, see Bruce, *Virginia Iron Manufacture in the Slave Era*; Samuel Sydney Bradford, "The Ante-Bellum Charcoal Iron Industry of Virginia" (PhD diss., Columbia University, 1958), 2, 114; Dew, *Ironmaker to the Confederacy* and *Bond of Iron*. For later escapes from a forge, see M. Stickler to Joseph R. Anderson, July 30, 1864, M. Stickler Letter, W&M.
2. Stephen W. Sears, *Chancellorsville* (Boston: Houghton Mifflin Harcourt, 1996), 445.
3. Dew, *Ironmaker to the Confederacy*, 80–82, 106, 147, 231.
4. Various Receipts, Jordan Family Papers, LVA.
5. Various Receipts, Tredegar Ironworks Records, LVA.
6. Potter, "The Historian's Use of Nationalism and Vice Versa"; Faust, *The Creation of Confederate Nationalism*; Gallagher, *The Confederate War*; Rubin, *A Shattered Nation*; Quigley, *Shifting Grounds*.
7. Matthew Gallman, *The North Fights the Civil War: The Home Front* (Chicago: Ivan R. Dee, 1994), 22–25; Coulter, *The Confederate States of America*, 199–200; Freehling, *The South vs. The South*, 61–64.
8. Thomas, *The Confederacy as a Revolutionary Experience*, 79–99; Raimondo Luraghi, *The Rise and Fall of the Plantation South* (New York: New Viewpoints, 1978), 83–84, 103–132; Ramsdell, *Behind the Lines of the Southern Confederacy*, especially 70–75; Vandiver, *Ploughshares Into Swords*, especially 55–83, 172–184 and "The Shelby Iron Company in the Civil War"; DeCredico, *Patriotism for Profit*, 21–71; Taylor, *Rebel Storehouse*, 44–132; McKinney, "Premature Industrialization in Appalachia: The Asheville Armory, 1862–1863"; Majewski, *Modernizing a Slave Economy*; Bonner, *Confederate Political Economy*.
9. Bernard H. Nelson, "Confederate Slave Impressment Legislation, 1861–1865," *Journal of Negro History* 31, no. 4 (October 1946): 392–410; James H. Brewer, *The Confederate Negro: Virginia's Craftsmen and Military Laborers, 1861–1865* (Durham, NC: Duke University Press, 1969); Mohr, *On the Threshold of Freedom*; Jaime Amanda Martinez, *Slave Impressment in the Upper South* (Chapel Hill: University of North Carolina Press, 2013).

10. Quintana, *Making a Slave State*; Aaron Roy Hall, "Slaves of the State," 19–46 and "Public Slaves and State Engineers," 531–576; Karp, *This Vast Southern Empire*; Rao, "The Federal 'Posse Comitatus' Doctrine," 1–56; Majewski, *Modernizing a Slave Economy*, 148–151.
11. Bruce, *Virginia Iron Manufacture in the Slave Era*; Wade, *Slavery in the Cities*, 33–40; Starobin, *Industrial Slavery in the Old South*; Dunaway, *Slavery in the American Mountain South*, 103–138; Downey, *Planting a Capitalist South*; Huston, "The Pregnant Economies of the Border South, 1840–1860," 120–144; Schermerhorn, *Money over Mastery*, 134–201.
12. Majewski, *Modernizing a Slave Economy*.
13. Luraghi, *The Rise and Fall of the Plantation South*, 5.
14. Johnson, *Soul By Soul*, 16–18, 78–116.
15. Edward Ayers, *In the Presence of Mine Enemies: War in the Heart of America, 1859–1863* (New York: Norton, 2003), xix–xx.
16. Majewski, *Modernizing a Slave Economy*, 140–161.
17. Gallman, *The North Fights the Civil War*, 22–25; Coulter, *The Confederate States of America*, 199–200; Freehling, *The South vs. The South*, 61–64; Maurice Kaye Melton, "Major Military Industries of the Confederate Government" (PhD diss, Emory University, 1978), 38.
18. Entry for April 8, 1864, in Wiggins, *The Journals of Josiah Gorgas*, 98; Thomas, *The Confederacy as a Revolutionary Experience*, 79–99; Luraghi, *Rise and Fall of the Plantation South*, 83–84, 103–132; Ramsdell, *Behind the Lines of the Southern Confederacy*, 70–75; Vandiver, *Ploughshares Into Swords*, 55–83, 172–184 and "The Shelby Iron Company in the Civil War"; DeCredico, *Patriotism for Profit*, 21–71; Taylor, *Rebel Storehouse*, 44–132; McKinney, "Premature Industrialization in Appalachia," 227–241.
19. Entry for April 8, 1864, in Wiggins, *The Journals of Josiah Gorgas*, 98.
20. Majewski, *Modernizing a Slave Economy*, 148–151.
21. Entry for April 8, 1864, in Wiggins, *The Journals of Josiah Gorgas*, 98.
22. Charles Pettigrew to Caroline Pettigrew, October 31, 1862, Pettigrew Papers; T. J. Holt to George W. Mordecai, March 5, 1863; G. P. Collins to Mordecai, March 11, 1864, Mordecai Papers; J. Gwyn to Rufus Lenoir, June 26, 1861, Lenoir Papers, all SHC; Mohr, *On the Threshold of Freedom*, 136–159.
23. Mohr, *On the Threshold of Freedom*, 136–159.
24. W. Stanley Hoole, "The Confederate Armory at Tallassee, Alabama, 1864–1865," *Alabama Review* XXV, no. 1 (January 1972): 12–13; Virginia Knapp, "William Phineas Browne, Business Man and Pioneer Mine Operator of Alabama (Part II)," *Alabama Review* III, no. 3 (July 1950): 193–205; William N. Still, "Selma and the Confederate States Navy," *Alabama Review* XV, no. 1 (January 1962): 29.
25. Richard C. Sheridan, "Production of Saltpetre from Alabama Caves," *Alabama Review* XXXIII, no. 1 (January 1980), 29; A. T. Jones et al., *Letter to Hon. Chas. B. Mitchell in Relation to The Iron Business of Alabama* (Selma: Mississippian Steam Book and Job Office, 1864), 9. Documenting the American South, https://docsouth.unc.edu/imls/shelby/shelby.html (accessed November 1, 2018).

26. Dew, *Ironmaker to the Confederacy*, 263; Martinez, *Slave Impressment in the Upper South*.

27. Dew, *Ironmaker to the Confederacy*, 22–36 and *Bond of Iron*, 98–121; Starobin, *Industrial Slavery in the Old* South, 8–25; Ronald L. Lewis, *Coal, Iron, and Slaves: Industrial Slavery in Maryland and Virginia, 1715–1865* (Westport, CT: Greenwood Press, 1979), 81–103, 191–197, 223–226. On the hiring of enslaved laborers, see Jonathan D. Martin, *Divided Mastery: Slave Hiring in the American South* (Cambridge, MA: Harvard University Press, 2004); John J. Zaborney, *Slaves for Hire: Renting Enslaved Laborers in Antebellum Virginia* (Baton Rouge: Louisiana State University Press, 2012).

28. Joseph Anderson to E. A. Goodwyn, December 5, 1862, Tredegar Ironworks Records, LVA.

29. William Mason Jr. to Dickinson Hill & Co., September 18, 1861, Chase Papers, LC; Receipts, January 4, 1865, Moore and Gatling Law Firm Papers, SHC; Robert H. McKenzie, "The Shelby Iron Company: A Note on Slave Personality after the Civil War," *Journal of Negro History* 58, no. 3 (July 1973): 343.

30. Slave Hiring Documents, January 4, 1865, Moore & Gatling Law Firm Papers, SHC.

31. See, for example, C. L. Fendall to R. H. Stuart, January 22, 1861, Richard Stuart Papers, UVA; Robert Taylor to Benjamin Temple, January 9, 1861, Harrison Family Papers, VHS; J. D. B. De Bow to Charles Gayarré, October 28, 1861, Gayarré Papers, LSU.

32. J. D. Hankins to "Dear Father & Mother," May 3, 1862, Hankins Family Papers, VHS.

33. Hector Davis to A. R. Blakey, March 20, 1862, Blakey Papers, Duke. See, for example, D. M. Prichard to Jeremiah Morton, February 6, 1864, Morton-Halsey Papers, UVA, Series E, Part 1, RASP. On hiring and control, see Martin, *Divided Mastery*, 72–103.

34. Auction Sales, Record Book, Branch & Company Records, VHS.

35. John Randolph Bryan to "My Dear Sir," January 1, 1863, Grinnan, Bryan, and Tucker Papers, UVA.

36. George P. Holman to "Dear Sir," June 4, 1863, Documents Relating to J. D. Fondren & Bro., Beinecke Library, Yale.

37. See, for example, W. H. Crenshaw to Bolling Hall, October 12, 1863, Bolling Hall Family Papers, Alabama Department of Archives and History; F. E. Duggar to "My Dear Mother," December 4, 1863, Duggar Family Letters, 1861–1865, Special Collections and Archives, Auburn; William N. Berkeley to Cynthia W. Berkeley, September 25, 1862, Berkeley Papers, UVA, Series E, Part 2, RASP.

38. Nimrod Long to "Dear Wife," January 29, 1863, Long Papers, Emory.

39. Euclid Godwin to "My Dear Uncle" (George Godwin?) December 26, 1863, Borland Family Papers, W&M.

40. Entry for October 19, 1863, in John David Smith and William Cooper Jr., eds., *Window on the War: Frances Dallam Peter's Lexington Civil War Diary* (Lexington: Lexington-Fayette County Historic Commission, 1976), 168.

41. Charles Morris to Mary Minor Morris, January 13, 1864, Morris Papers, VHS; A. M. Seabrook to "My Dear Sir," February 20, 1864, Pinckney Papers, Emory.

42. Quoted in Mohr, *On the Threshold of Freedom*, 140; Dew, *Ironmaker to the Confederacy*, 251–254.

43. Martinez, *Slave Impressment in the Upper South*, 83–85, 146–148.
44. Edwin L. Combs III, "Field or Workshop: A Study of Southern Industrial Labor in the Civil War" (PhD diss., University of Alabama, 2003), 151; James Allen to "Dear Wife," January 1, 1864, James Allen and Charles B. Allen Papers, SHC.
45. Receipt, January 24, 1863, Henry Wilink Papers, Emory.
46. Dew, *Bond of Iron*, 326. See also "$200 Reward," *Winston-Salem People's Press*, August 6, 1863. On the dichotomy between skilled and unskilled laborers, see Daina Ramey Berry, *Swing the Sickle for the Harvest Is Ripe: Gender and Slavery in Antebellum Georgia* (Urbana: University of Illinois Press, 2007).
47. "$100 Reward," *Richmond Daily Dispatch*, May 12, 1864.
48. Combs, "Field or Workshop," 148, 151–2; Knapp, "William Phineas Browne," 196.
49. Mary Elliott to Unknown, June 21, 1863, Elliott and Gonzales Papers, SHC.
50. Ella Lonn, *Salt as a Factor in the Confederacy* (University: University of Alabama Press, 1965), 16–18, 131; John Edmund Stealey, III, "Slavery and the Western Virginia Salt Industry," in *The Other Slaves: Mechanics, Artisans, and Craftsmen*, ed. James E. Newton and Ronald L. Lewis (Boston: G. K. Hall & Co., 1978), 109–134; Taylor, *Confederate Storehouse*, 55–57. See also Ethelred Philips to James Jones Philips, December 25, 1862, Philips Papers, SHC; Entry for March 2, 1863, in John Q. Anderson, ed., *Brokenburn: The Journal of Kate Stone 1861–1868* (Baton Rouge: Louisiana State University Press, 1955), 170.
51. "$200 Reward," *Daily Progress*, January 9, 1863; "$600 Reward," *Raleigh Daily Conservative*, June 20, 1864.
52. James H. Bailey, *Henrico Home Front 1861–1865 A Picture of Life in Henrico County, Virginia: Based Upon Selections from the Minute Books of the Henrico County Court* (Richmond, VA: Henrico County Civil War Centennial Commission, 1963), 152.
53. "Runaway Negroes," "Runaways," "Runaways," and "Runaways," *Richmond Daily Dispatch*, October 10, 1862.
54. Stephen Gedson Collins, "Organizing the South: Railroads, Plantations, and War" (PhD diss., Louisiana State University, 1999), 119; Robert C. Black III, *The Railroads of the Confederacy* (Chapel Hill and London: University of North Carolina Press, 1998), 29; Thomas, *The Iron Way*, 69; Larry E. Johnson, "Breakdowns from Within: Virginia Railroads During the Civil War Era" (MA thesis, University of Louisville, 2004), 115; Phillips, *American Negro Slavery*, 376; Charles W. Turner, "The Virginia Central Railroad at War, 1861–1865," *Journal of Southern History* 12, no. 4 (November 1946): 513; Starobin, *Industrial Slavery in the Old South*, 28.
55. Allen W. Trelease, "A Southern Railroad at War: The North Carolina Railroad and the Confederacy," *Railroad History* no. 164 (Spring 1991): 15.
56. Quoted in James Ford Rhodes, *History of the United States From The Compromise of 1850*, Vol. V *1864–1866* (New York: MacMillan Company, 1904), 462.
57. Wade, *Slavery in the Cities*, 48–54, 80–110, 143–208; Claudia Dale Goldin, *Urban Slavery in the American South 1820–1860: A Quantitative History* (Chicago and London: University of Chicago Press, 1976), 28–50; Genovese, *The Political Economy of Slavery*, 180–220; Fields, *Slavery and Freedom on the Middle Ground*, 40–62; David Goldfield, *Region, Race, and Cities: Interpreting the Urban South* (Baton Rouge:

Louisiana State University Press, 1997), 103–144 and *Urban Growth in the Age of Sectionalism*, 118–138; Starobin, *Industrial Slavery in the Old South*, 91–115; Randall M. Miller, "The Fabric of Control: Slavery in Antebellum Southern Textile Mills," *Business History Review* 55, no. 4 (Winter 1981), reprinted in Paul Finkelman, ed., *Articles on American Slavery*, Vol. *10: Economics, Industrialization, Urbanization, and Slavery* (New York: Garland Publishing, Inc., 1989), 301–320; Zaborney, *Slaves for Hire*, 120–148.

58. R. F. Tebault to Dickinson Hill, December 10, 1861, Ames Papers, MHS.
59. "For Sale," *Macon Daily Telegraph*, October 5, 1864; "Commercial, Agricultural, Mining and Manufacturing Items," *De Bow's Review*, December 1861.
60. Mohr, *On the Threshold of Freedom*, 154.
61. Bonner, *Confederate Political Economy*, 5; Paul Escott, *After Secession: Jefferson Davis and the Failure of Confederate Nationalism* (Baton Rouge: Louisiana State University Press, 1978), 54–134; Malcolm C. McMillan, *The Disintegration of a Confederate State: Three Governors and Alabama's Wartime Home Front, 1861–1865* (Macon, GA: Mercer University Press, 1986); Fred A. Bailey, *Class and Tennessee's Confederate Generation* (Chapel Hill: University of North Carolina Press, 1987), 77–104; Rable, *The Confederate Republic*, 132–173; Blair, *Virginia's Private War*, 55–107; Gregory P. Downs, *Declarations of Dependence: The Long Reconstruction of Popular Politics in the South, 1861–1908* (Chapel Hill: University of North Carolina Press, 2011), 15–41; McCurry, *Confederate Reckoning*, 133–156.
62. E. Merton Coulter, "The Movement for Agricultural Reorganization in the Cotton South during the Civil War," *Agricultural History* 1, no. 1 (January 1927): 3–17; James L. Nichols, "The Tax-in-Kind in the Department of the Trans-Mississippi," *Civil War History* 5, no. 4 (December 1959): 382–389; Richard D. Goff, *Confederate Supply* (Durham, NC: Duke University Press, 1969), 76–89; Thomas, *The Confederate Nation*, 190–214; Hurt, *Agriculture and the Confederacy*, 72–73, 132–136, 196–198.
63. Glatthaar, *General Lee's Army*, 200–204, 399–401; Noe, *Reluctant Rebels*, 2, 112–121. On conscription, see also Moore, *Conscription and Conflict in the Confederacy*; Patrick J. Doyle, "Replacement Rebels: Confederate Substitution and the Issue of Citizenship," *Journal of the Civil War Era* 8, no. 1 (March 2018): 3–31; John M. Sacher, *Confederate Conscription and the Struggle for Southern Soldiers* (Baton Rouge: Louisiana State University Press, 2021).
64. Abner Dawson Ford, Combined Military Service Records, Stuart's Horse Artillery, RG 109, NARA M324, fold3.com.
65. U.S. Census, *1860*, Charlotte, Virginia; Roll: M653_1340, 290, Family History Library Film: *805340*; U.S. Census, 1860, Slave Schedule, Charlotte, Virginia, AncestryHeritageQuest; Robert K. Krick, *Civil War Weather in Virginia* (Tuscaloosa: University of Alabama Press, 2007), 81.
66. Abner Dawson Ford to Mary Jane Ford, January 4, 23, February 23, 1863, Abner Dawson Ford Papers, VHS.
67. Glatthaar, *General Lee's Army*, 200–204, 399–401; Noe, *Reluctant Rebels*, 2, 112–121.
68. Quoted in Robinson, *Bitter Fruits of Bondage*, 159; Drumgoold, *A Slave Girl's Story*, 4–5, 9, 39. William House also offered one of Drumgoold's siblings as compensation to his substitute, to be given over at the war's conclusion.

69. William T. Nelson to "Dear Sweet Wife," October 8, 1862, Nelson Papers, VHS.
70. PAR #21586403, Euphrasia M. Tivis v. Benjamin Franklin Tivis, Jefferson Co., Texas, September 13, 1864, Series II, Part E, RSFB.
71. Lewis Warlick to Cornelia McGimsey, June 3, 1862, in Lawing and Lawing, *My Dearest Friend*, 87.
72. Lizzie Neblett to William Neblett, August 11, 13, 1863, in Murr, *A Rebel Wife in Texas*, 130–131, 135.
73. Kaleta Hardin to William F. Hardin, August 21, 1862, in Trammell, *Seven Pines*, 160.
74. J. A. Canon to Charles Scott, August 21, 1862, Rudin Slavery Collection, Cornell.
75. D. W. Ross to D. A. G. Ross, Unknown Date [Likely April], 1863, Ross Family Letters, 1860–1863, Special Collections and Archives, Auburn University.
76. Anthony Gene Carey, *Sold Down the River: Slavery in the Lower Chattahoochee Valley of Alabama and Georgia* (Tuscaloosa: University of Alabama Press, 2011), 62.
77. Robinson, "Day of Jubilo," 155. See also Hiring Agreement, January 21, 1863, Snider Family Slave Records, African American Miscellany, Emory. David Gleeson has recently suggested the threat of enslaved rebellion has been overstated in the arguments for the "Twenty-Negro Law." Gleeson, "The Rhetoric of Insurrection and Fear: The Politics of Slave Management in Confederate Georgia," *Journal of Southern History* 89, no. 2 (May 2023): 237–266.
78. Sam R. Watkins, *"Co. Aytch," Maury Grays, First Tennessee Regiment; or, A Side Show of the Big Show* (Nashville: Cumberland Presbyterian Publishing House, 1882), 38.
79. George C. Lester to E. H. Stokes, October 7, 1863, SUSC-AAS.
80. Byrne, "The Burden and Heat of the Day," 317.
81. For a discussion of the number of men in the Rebel service, see McPherson, *Battle Cry of Freedom*, 306–307 n 41.
82. Milton Maxcy Leverett to his mother, April 8, 1862, in Frances Wallace Taylor, Catherine Taylor Matthews and J. Tracy Power, eds., *The Leverett Letters: Correspondence of a South Carolina Family 1851–1868* (Columbia: University of South Carolina Press, 2000), 115.
83. J. Thos. R. Martin to Susan Martin, July 17, 1864, Elizabeth Perry Papers, UVA.
84. "Negro Wanted," *Winchester Daily Bulletin*, November 20, 1862; W. Henderson to Mary A. M. Henderson, May 3, 1863, J. Watson Henderson Collection, Special Collections, University of Mississippi Libraries; Robert H. Turner to Angus R. Blakey, July 20, 1864, Blakey Papers, Duke. On the use and significance of camp servants, see Woodward, *Marching Masters*, 80–103 and Kevin M. Levin, *Searching for Black Confederates: The Civil War's Most Persistent Myth* (Chapel Hill: University of North Carolina Press, 2019), 12–67.
85. "Valuable Servants At Auction," *Charleston Courier*, December 21, 1862. See also "Wanted," *The Carolina Spartan*, November 19, 1863.
86. Rebecca Christian, "Georgia and the Confederate Policy of Impressing Supplies," *Georgia Historical Quarterly* 28, no. 1 (March 1944): 1–33; Massey, *Ersatz in the Confederacy*, 55–58, 125–138; Gates, *Agriculture and the Civil War*, 22–45, 73–126; Otto, *Southern Agriculture During the Civil War Era*, 30–45; Michael Dougan, *Confederate Arkansas: The People and Policies of a Frontier State in Wartime*

(Tuscaloosa: University of Alabama Press, 1976), 105–118; Rogers, *Confederate Home Front*, 71–75; Hurt, *Agriculture and the Confederacy*, especially 60–77, 88–93, 110–127, 167–175, 191–221.

87. Herbert George Bond to Leavitt E. Bond, April 12, 1863, Herbert George Bond Letter, W&M.
88. Taylor, *Confederate Storehouse*, 83; Gates, *Agriculture and the Civil War*, 16–27; Hurt, *Agriculture and the Confederacy*, 42–50, 77–80, 115–127.
89. Emmie Johnston to "My Dear Grandmamma," December 28, 1864; Mary Elliott[?] to Emily Elliott, January 12, 1864, Elliott and Gonzales Papers, SHC.
90. James H. Embry to O. O. Howard, August 17, 1865, Registers and Letters Received, C-F, Mar.–Oct. 1865, Records of the Commissioner, 14: 841/1401, RG 105, NARA M752. See also A. E. South to General Baird, January 15, 1866, Unregistered Letters Received, ser. 3621, Assistant Commissioner, Texas, RG 105, NARA [FSSP A-3351].
91. Joseph B. Hinton to Isaiah Respess, October 5, 1864, Mary Farrow Credle Papers, SHC.
92. E. Merton Coulter, *George Walton Williams: The Life of a Southern Merchant and Banker 1820–1903* (Athens: The Hibriten Press, 1976), 83.
93. Eliza C. Ball to "My Dear Son," June 11, 1863, Ball Family Papers, SCL. For the disruptive effects of shortages, see Joseph Lovell to Mrs. W. L. Lovell, September 12, 1863, Quitman Family Papers, SHC. On enslaved people's ideas of reciprocity, see Genovese, *Roll, Jordan, Roll*, 89–91. On the Civil War experience of the people the Balls enslaved, see Edward Ball, *Slaves in the Family* (New York: Farrar, Straus and Giroux, 1998), 322–350.
94. John Colcock to James Gregorie, April 12, 1864, Gregorie and Elliott Family Papers, SHC. See also Eliza M. Smith to "Dear Children," November/December 1864, in Daniel Huger Smith, Alice R. Huger Smith, Arney R. Childs, eds., *Mason Smith Family Letters* (Columbia: University of South Carolina Press, 1950), 150.
95. "Mollie" to Lila Chunn, September 23, 1864, Chunn Letters, Emory.
96. Ethelred Philips to James Jones Philips, October 12, 1863, Philips Papers, SHC; John Bratton to Bettie Bratton, November 14, 1863; January 2, 1865, John Bratton Letters, SHC.
97. Eleanor Beverley (Meade) Platt to Rebecca Wormley Beverley Meade, December 31, 1864, Eleanor Beverley (Meade) Platt Letter, 1864, VHS.
98. See, for example, Rothman, *Flush Times and Fever Dreams*, 292–301.
99. Quoted in Byrne, "The Burden and Heat of the Day," 317.
100. William Smedes to William E. Johnson, December 15, 1860, November 26, 1862, Johnson Papers, SCL.
101. William N. Berkeley to Cynthia W. Berkeley, October 9, 1862, Berkeley Papers, Series E: UVA, Part II, RASP.
102. Alexander Galt Taliaferro to Dickinson, Hill & Co., October 10, 1862, William Booth Taliaferro Papers, W&M; "A Brief Summary of My Commission With the Army of the Confederate States of America in the Late Disastrous Civil War," Alexander Taliaferro Reminiscences, SHC; Taliaferro to Dickinson Hill & Co., October 25, November 20, 1862, DHCRC.

103. James Harvey Campbell to "My Dear Wife," May 14, 1863, James Harvey Campbell Papers, VHS. As of January 1864, Fanny remained with the family. Campbell to "My Dear Wife," January 11, 1864, in same.
104. PAR Accession 20186232, Petition of Elizabeth R. Golson, December 23, 1863, Dallas County, AL, Series II, Part A, RSFB.
105. Eliza Akin to Warren Akin, January 15, 1865, in Bell Irvin Wiley, ed., *Letters of Warren Akin: Confederate Congressman* (Athens: University of Georgia Press, 1959), 121; R. Walker Wilson to William O. George, January 22, 1865; Receipt, John B. Brockenborough to George, January 13, 1865, George Family, Papers, City of Richmond Circuit Court Records, LVA.
106. Elizabeth Fox-Genovese, *Within the Plantation Household: Black and White Women of the Old South* (Chapel Hill: University of North Carolina Press, 1988), 63, 92–145; Glymph, *Out of the House of Bondage*; Catherine Clinton, *The Plantation Mistress: Woman's World in the Old South* (New York: Pantheon Books, 1982), 16–35; Anne Firor Scott, *The Southern Lady: From Pedestal to Politics* (Chicago: University of Chicago Press, 1970), 23–44; Marli F. Weiner, *Mistresses and Slaves: Plantation Women in South Carolina, 1830–1880* (Urbana: University of Illinois Press, 1998), 23–49. On plantations as a male-directed space, see Brown, *Good Wives, Nasty Wenches, and Anxious Patriarchs*, 75–136; Walsh, *Motives of Honor, Pleasure, and Profit*; Rhys Isaac, *The Transformation of Virginia, 1740–1790* (Chapel Hill: University of North Carolina Press, 1999), 30–57; Genovese, *Roll, Jordan, Roll*, 3–25, 365–388; William Kauffman Scarborough, *The Overseer: Plantation Management in the Old South* (Baton Rouge: Louisiana State University Press, 1966); Roark, *Masters Without Slaves*, 69–76; McCurry, *Masters of Small Worlds*, 92–129, 208–238. Recent work by Stephanie Jones-Rogers urges a broader understanding of the roles women played in the system of slavery. Jones-Rogers, *They Were Her Property*.
107. Quoted in Glatthaar, *General Lee's Army*, 201. Historians have increasingly argued that the distinction between the homefront and the battlefield is an arbitrary one. Lorien Foote, "Rethinking the Confederate Homefront," *Journal of the Civil War Era* 7, no. 3 (September 2017): 445–465; Lisa Tendrich Frank, "The Union War on Women," in *The Guerilla Hunters: Irregular Conflicts During the Civil War*, ed. Brian D. McKnight and Barton A. Myers (Baton Rouge: Louisiana State University Press, 2017), 171–191; Laura Mammina, "Union Soldiers, Unionist Women, Military Policy, and Intimate Space during the American Civil War," *Civil War History* 64, no. 2 (June 2018): 146–174.
108. On changing gender roles during the Civil War, see Mary Elizabeth Massey, *Bonnet Brigades: American Women and the Civil War* (New York: Knopf, 1966), especially 197–219; Scott, *The Southern Lady*, 81–102; George C. Rable, *Civil Wars: Women and the Crisis of Southern Nationalism* (Urbana: University of Illinois Press, 1989), 50–135; Victoria Bynum, *Unruly Women: The Politics of Social and Sexual Control in the Old South* (Chapel Hill: University of North Carolina Press, 1992), 111–150; LeeAnn Whites, *The Civil War as a Crisis in Gender: Augusta, Georgia, 1860–1890* (Athens: University of Georgia Press, 1995), 15–131; Drew Gilpin Faust, *Mothers of Invention: Women of the Slaveholding South in the American Civil War* (Chapel Hill:

University of North Carolina Press, 1996), 53–79; Weiner, *Mistresses and Slaves*, 166–174; Philip N. Racine, "Emily Lyles Harris: A Piedmont Farmer During the Civil War," in *Women and War: History of Women in the United States: Historical Articles on Women's Lives and Activities*, Vol. 15, ed. Nancy F. Cott (Munich: K. G. Saur, 1993), 53–64; Laura F. Edwards, *Scarlett Doesn't Live Here Anymore: Southern Women in the Civil War Era* (Urbana: University of Illinois Press, 2000), 71–116; McCurry, *Confederate Reckoning*, 85–217; Catherine Clinton, *Stepdaughters of History: Southern Women and the American Civil War* (Baton Rouge: Louisiana State University Press, 2016), 1–74; Mary Johnston-Miller, "Heirs to paternalism: Elite women and their servants in Alabama and Georgia, 1861–1874" (PhD diss., Emory University, 1994), 69–77; Glymph, *The Women's Fight*, 19–54.

109. Glymph, *Out of the House of Bondage*, 1–18, 97–136, quotes on pp. 6–7; Entry for December 19, 1861, in Marli F. Weiner, ed., *Heritage of Woe: The Civil War Diary of Grace Brown Elmore, 1861–1868* (Athens: University of Georgia Press, 1997), 23; Susan Emeline Jeffords Caldwell to Lycurgus Washington Caldwell, June 1, 1862, in Welton, *"My Heart is So Rebellious,"* 124; Entries for March 5, 24, 1863, in Anderson, *Brokenburn*, 175, 185.

110. R. H. Thach to Lila Thach, July 27, 1863, Thach Family Papers, SHC. Emphasis in original.

111. Entry for November 26, 1862, Cushing Biggs Hassell Diary, SHC.

112. W. A. Hunter to Rebecca Hunter, July 19, 1864, in Gary Loderhose, *Far, Far From Home: The Ninth Florida Regiment in the Confederate Army* (Carmel: Guild Press, 1999), 69.

113. Abner Dawson Ford to Mary Jane Ford, April 16, 1863, Ford Papers, VHS.

114. J. J. Craig to William Sylvanus Morris, March 21, 1863, May 19, 1863, William Sylvanus Morris Papers, VHS.

115. Theodorick Montfort to Maria Louisa Montfort, February 1, 1862, in King, *Rebel Lawyer*, 42; Robert H. Turner to Angus R. Blakey, July 20, 1864, Blakey Papers, Duke; Josiah Turner to "My Dear Wife," November 8, 1863, Josiah Turner Papers, Duke.

116. William A. Nelson to "My Dear Wife," December 17, 1862; February 22, 1863, Nelson Papers, SCL.

117. Jones-Rogers, *They Were Her Property*, 123–150; Entry for August 20, 1862, Sarah Lois Wadley Diary, SHC. See also Annie Pettigrew to William Pettigrew, September 29, 1862, Pettigrew Papers, SHC.

118. Alfred Bell to Mary Bell, August 17, 1862; Mary Bell to Alfred Bell, November 20, December 6, 1862; March 26, April 15, December 8, 1864, Bell Papers, Duke; Inscoe, "The Civil War's Empowerment of an Appalachian Woman," 61–81.

119. "Extracts of Letters from Teachers," *The Freedmen's Journal* 1, no. 1 (January 1865). For a similar account, see Joseph Crosfield, *Extracts from Recent Correspondence in Relation to Fugitives From Slavery in America* (London: E. Newman, 1864), 1.

120. Baldy A. Capehart to Meeta Rhodes Armistead Capehart, February 16, 1865, Meeta Rhodes Armistead Capehart Papers, SHC.

121. Margaret Glen to Tyre Glen, January 3, 1865, Tyre Glen Papers, Duke.

122. Grimball, "Diary of John Berkley Grimball, 1858–1865 (Continued)," 166–167 and "Diary of John Berkley Grimball, 1858–1865 (continued)," 214–215; Margaret Ann Meta Morris Grimball Journal, February 13, 1863, *Journal of Meta Morris Grimball, South Carolina, December 1860–February 1866*, SHC, Documenting the American South, https://docsouth.unc.edu/fpn/grimball/grimball.html (accessed July 5, 2023); William H. Grimball to John Berkley Grimball, February 19, 1862; John Grimball to "Dear Mama," April 7, 1863; Meta Grimball to John Berkley Grimball[?], March 11, 1863, Grimball Papers, Duke.
123. Dusinberre, *Them Dark Days*, 368.
124. David Silkenat, *Driven From Home: North Carolina's Civil War Refugee Crisis* (Athens: University of Georgia Press, 2016), 113; H. B. Robinson to Daniel McIntosh, November 10, 1861, Comfort Family Papers, VHS.
125. Sternhell, *Routes of War*, especially 93–107; Silkenat, *Driven From Home*; Kaye, *Joining Places*, 177–208; Lorien Foote, *The Yankee Plague: Escaped Union Prisoners and the Collapse of the Confederacy* (Chapel Hill: University of North Carolina Press, 2016); Taylor, *Embattled Freedom*.
126. On enslaved people and the law in the antebellum South, see, among others, Ariela J. Gross, *Double Character: Slavery and Mastery in the Antebellum Southern Courtroom* (Athens: University of Georgia Press, 2006); Anne Twitty, *Before Dred Scott: Slavery and Legal Culture in the American Confluence, 1787–1857* (New York: Cambridge University Press, 2016); Kelly M. Kennington, *In the Shadow of Dred Scott: St. Louis Freedom Suits and the Legal Culture of Slavery in Antebellum America* (Athens: University of Georgia Press, 2017); Kimberly M. Welch, *Black Litigants in the Antebellum American South* (Chapel Hill: University of North Carolina Press, 2018); Tamika Y. Nunley, *At the Threshold of Liberty: Women, Slavery, and Shifting Identities in Washington, D.C.* (Chapel Hill: University of North Carolina Press, 2021).
127. Rawick, *The American Slave*, 7: Oklahoma, 198.
128. Linton Stephens to Alexander Stephens, June 8, 1863, Alexander H. Stephens Collection, Manhattanville College Library Special Collections. John eventually returned to the Stephenses. Alexander Stephens to Linton Stephens, February 22, 1864, in same.
129. "Fifty Dollars Reward," *Richmond Daily Dispatch*, December 15, 1862; "Mayor's Court—Before the Mayor," *Richmond Daily Dispatch*, March 13, 1865.
130. On antebellum kidnappings of free people of color, see McDaniel, *Sweet Taste of Liberty*; Richard Bell, *Stolen: Five Free Boys Kidnapped Into Slavery and Their Astonishing Odyssey Home* (New York: 37Ink, 2019); Jonathan Daniel Wells, *The Kidnapping Club: Wall Street, Slavery, and Resistance on the Eve of the Civil War* (New York: Bold Type Books, 2020).
131. C. Y. Savage to the General Commanding Post at Petersburg, March 26, 1863; S. G. French to Judge W. L. Joyner, October 20, 1863, John Hart Collection of Confederate Letters and Receipts, LVA; "Selling a Free Negro," *Richmond Daily Dispatch*, February 2, 1865. See also January 13–14, 1864, Richmond City, Virginia Hustings Court Minutes, No. 28, 1862–1863, LVA.

132. Brian R. Dirck, "Posterity's Blush: Civil Liberties, Property Rights, and Property Confiscation in the Confederacy," *Civil War History* 48, no. 3 (September 2002): 237–256; Rodney J. Steward, "Confederate Menace: Sequestration on the North Carolina Homefront," in Berry, *Weirding the War*, 55–60.

133. Petition for Sequestration, *Confederate States of America vs. Property of Christopher Meyers*, Confederate Court, South Carolina District, Campbell Papers, SCHS. Washington's fate is unknown.

134. Report, Francis L. Smith to James Hallyburton, November 18, 1863, Records of the Eastern Virginia District Court, 1861–1865, Brock Collection, HL.

135. Dirck, "Posterity's Blush," 247; "Speech on Slavery and State Suicide," January 8, 1864, in Graf, Haskins, and Clark, eds., *The Papers of Andrew Johnson, Volume 6, 1862–1864* (Knoxville: University of Tennessee Press, 1983), 550.

136. Sam Towler, "Monticello During the Civil War," *Magazine of Albemarle County History* 69 (2011): 45–47.

137. Byrne, "The Burden and Heat of the Day," 317; "Receiver's Sale of Negroes," *Richmond Daily Dispatch*, September 19, 1864. See also "Sale of Negro Man at Auction," *Richmond Daily Dispatch*, January 17, 1865; "Receiver's Sale of a Negro Man," *Richmond Daily Dispatch*, January 23, 1865.

138. Christopher Phillips, *The Rivers Ran Backward: The Civil War and the Remaking of the American Middle Border* (New York: Oxford University Press, 2016), 199.

139. Maria von Blücher to "Cordially loved parents," May 10, 1864, in Bruce S. Cheeseman, ed., *Maria von Blücher's Corpus Christi: Letters from the South Texas Frontier, 1849–1879* (College Station: Texas A&M Press, 2002), 144. In the end, the woman in question refused to leave Texas, sparing her human property the auction block.

140. W. T. Sherman to Gideon Pillow, August 14, 1862, in Simpson and Berlin, *Sherman's Civil War*, 276.

141. Susanna Michele Lee, *Claiming the Union: Citizenship in the Post-Civil War South* (New York: Cambridge University Press, 2014), 65. Quoted in Lee, "Claiming the Union: Stories of Loyalty in the Post-Civil War South" (PhD diss., University of Virginia, 2005), 227.

142. See, for example, Edward H. Stokes, Amnesty Petition, July 17, 1865; Reuben Ragland, Amnesty Petition, July 4, 1865, Amnesty Papers, RG 94, NARA (accessed via www.fold3.com).

143. J. Gwyn to Rufus Lenoir, February 9, 1863; Walter Lenoir to Thomas J. Lenoir, February 23, 25, 1863, Lenoir Papers, SHC. For discussions of the sale, see Gwyn to Rufus Lenoir, May 15, 1861; Walter Lenoir to Rufus Lenoir, April 14, 1862; Walter Lenoir to Thomas J. Lenoir, January 12, 1863, in same; Barney, *The Making of a Confederate*, 53, 103–105.

144. Manisha Sinha, *The Counterrevolution of Slavery: Politics and Ideology in Antebellum South Carolina* (Chapel Hill: University of North Carolina Press, 2000), 221–254; Freehling, *The Road to Disunion*, II: 271–287, 352–374; Barney, *Rebels in the Making*.

145. Mohr, *On the Threshold of Freedom*, 235–271; Bernath, "The Confederacy as a Moment of Possibility," 299–338; Brettle, *Colossal Ambitions*, 12–25.

146. Russell, "Sale Day in Antebellum South Carolina," 1–2, 21–86.
147. Frederick Douglass, *Narrative of the Life of Frederick Douglass, an American Slave* (London: G. Kershaw & Sons, 1852), 45, 47.
148. Rawick, *The American Slave*, 6: Indiana, 77–78; Morris, *Southern Slavery and the Law*, 81–99.
149. Julia Gwyn to "My dear Uncle," July 25, 1863, James Gwyn Papers, SHC.
150. Entry for December 14, 1862, in Beth G. Crabtree and James W. Patton, eds., *"Journal of a Secesh Lady": The Diary of Catherine Ann Devereux Edmondston 1860–1866* (Raleigh, NC: Division of Archives and History, 1979), 316.
151. Williams Carter Jr. to Anne Wickham, March 1, 1862, Wickham Family Papers, UVA.
152. Receipt, May 19, 1862, George Dromgoole and Richard B. Robinson Papers, Series F: Duke, Part 4, RASP. Given the similarity in their names and locations, Dromgoole may well have enslaved members of Kate Drumgoold's family. F. R. Goulding to "Dear Brother," January 12, 1864, F. R. Goulding Papers, Emory.
153. Duncan McKenzie to Duncan McLaurin, January 4, 1862, Duncan McLaurin Papers, Series F: Duke, Part 1, RASP; "Executor's Sale," *Weekly Mississippian*, January 14, 1862. See also Estate Papers, December 18, 1862, Dunkum and Sowell Family Collection, UVA; D. J. Hartsook to William Daniel Cabell, January 7, 1864, Papers of William Daniel Cabell and the Cabell and Ellet Families, UVA; Will of Sally Felton, Rockbridge County, June 2, 1862, Papers of the Anderson Family, UVA; Receipt, December 16, 1863, Charles R. Carroll Papers, SCL; Petition, Saunders Browning, Sarah Browning, Thomas Oakly, Ruffin Oakly, Lawrence Moore, and Martha Oakley to Court of Pleas & Quarter, Caswell Co., NC, April Term, 1861, Slave Records, Caswell County, Miscellaneous Records, NCDAH; George Briggs to "Dear Aunt & Unkle," January 6, 1861, George Briggs Papers, Duke.
154. Dickinson, Hill & Co. Slave Sale List, January 23, 1862, Wisconsin Historical Society.
155. J. Wimbush Young to E. H. Stokes, SUSC-AAS.
156. "Peremptory Sale of 83 Negroes," *Macon Telegraph*, February 12, 1864.
157. Aaron Astor, *Rebels on the Border: Civil War, Emancipation, and the Reconstruction of Kentucky and Missouri* (Baton Rouge: Louisiana State University Press, 2012), 104.
158. Rawick, *The American Slave*, 7: Oklahoma, 279.
159. E. H. Hunt to Thomas Hunt, December 2, 1864, Louthan Family Papers, VHS.
160. Thomas John Moore to Thomas W. Hill, November 30, 1862, in Tom Moore Craig, ed., *Upcountry South Carolina Goes to War: Letters of the Anderson, Brockman, and Moore Families, 1853–1865* (Columbia: University of South Carolina Press, 2009), 111.
161. Philip J. Schwarz, *Twice Condemned: Slaves and the Criminal Laws of Virginia* (Baton Rouge: Louisiana State University Press, 1988), 25–27, 31, 217–221; Ted Maris-Wolf, *Family Bonds: Free Blacks and Re-Enslavement Law in Antebellum Virginia* (Chapel Hill: University of North Carolina Press, 2015), 9–14, 35–37. For an example, see Forret, *Williams' Gang*.

162. December 11, 1860, May 16, December 9, 1861, December 9, 1862, July 14, 1863, Richmond City, Virginia Hustings Court Minutes, No. 28, 1862–1863, LVA.
163. Elijah P. Petty to Margaret Petty, September 23, 1862; Elijah P. Petty to "My Dear Daughter," March 24, 1863, in Petty, *Journey to Pleasant Hill*, 84, 154.
164. Entry for November 1, 1862, David Schenck Diary, SHC.
165. Roscoe Briggs Heath to Lewis Edmunds Mason, January 30, 1863, Mason Family Papers, Series M: VHS, Part 5, RASP; Jane G. North to Adele Petigru Allston, December 29, 1860, in Easterby, *The South Carolina Rice Plantation*, 172; Thomas P. Marston to Dickinson Hill & Co., November 11, 1861; L. P. Olos to Dickinson & Hill, October 3, 1861, Ames Papers, MHS.
166. Edward Porter Alexander to Bessie Alexander, July 26, 1863, Alexander Papers, SHC. See also Stephanie Jones-Rogers, "[S]he could . . . spare one ample breast for the profit of her owner': white mothers and enslaved wet nurses' invisible labor in American slave markets," *Slavery and Abolition* 38, no. 2 (April 2017): 342. R. Taylor Scott to Fanny Scott, January 3, 1861, Keith Papers, VHS; Jeremy Francis Gilmer to Mrs. J. F. Gilmer, January 4, 1863, Jeremy Francis Gilmer Papers, SHC; N. P. Callett to A. S. Lara, December 26, 1861, A. S. Lara Papers, 1856–1861, SC 0249, Special Collections, Carrier Library, James Madison University; William Birnie Jr. to William Birnie, April 5, 1863, William Birnie Papers, SHC; Bettie Maney Kimberly to John Kimberly, August 7, 1861, Kimberly Papers, SHC.
167. Randy J. Sparks, "John P. Osterhout, Yankee, Rebel, Republican," *Southwestern Historical Quarterly* 90, no. 2 (October 1986): 115, 122.
168. Margaret Cronly to Michael Cronly, January 12, 1865, Cronly Family Papers, Duke; Jedediah Hotchkiss to Nelson H. Hotchkiss, December 30, 1864, Augusta County, Virginia, Letters of the Hotchkiss Family, VS, http://valley.lib.virginia.edu/papers/A2595 (accessed July 6, 2023).
169. PAR Accession #20686208, Petition of Elizabeth C. Murphy, August 1862, Baldwin County, GA, Series II, Part A, RSFB; "For Sale," *Raleigh Daily Confederate*, October 12, 1864; Johnson, *Soul By Soul*, 1. On paternalism, see Genovese, *Roll, Jordan, Roll*, 113–158.
170. John Berkley Grimball to "My Dear Wife," March 16, 18, 1863, Grimball Papers, Duke.
171. Sarah E. Watkins to M. E. Watkins, November 26, 1860, in E. Grey Dimond and Herman Hattaway, eds., *Letters from Forest Place: A Plantation Family's Correspondence* (Jackson: University Press of Mississippi, 1993), 188.
172. M. B. Brown[?] to William Daniel Cabell, undated, but marked 1861, William Daniel Cabell and the Cabell and Ellet Papers, UVA.
173. Margaret Anderson Uhler, "Civil War Letters of Major General James Patton Anderson," *Florida Historical Quarterly* 56, no. 2 (October 1977): 169.
174. F. E. Duggar to "My Dear Mother," December 4, 1863, Duggar Letters, Auburn.
175. Woodward, *Marching Masters*, 97.
176. Entry for May 10, 1862, in Kimberly Harrison, ed., *A Maryland Bride in the Deep South: The Civil War Diary of Priscilla Bond* (Baton Rouge: Louisiana State University Press, 2006), 217.

177. Henry Walker, "Power, Sex, and Gender Roles: The Transformation of an Alabama Planter Family during the Civil War," in *Southern Families at War: Loyalty and Conflict in the Civil War South*, ed. Catherine Clinton and Nina Silber (New York: Oxford University Press, 2000), 184.
178. James Barrow to Father, December 9, 1863, in E. Merton Coulter, *Lost Generation: The Life and Death of James Barrow, C. S. A.* (Tuscaloosa: Confederate Publishing Company, 1956), 88.
179. Eliza Carrington to "Dear brother," October 22, 1861, Carrington Family Papers, VHS.
180. Charles J. Meriwether to Sterling Neblett, July 31, 1863, Neblett Papers, Duke.
181. Simeon B. Gibbons to "Dear Mother," April 8, 1861, Simeon B. Gibbons Letter, Ms2015-046, Special Collections, Virginia Tech.
182. J. F. Simms, Wm. Simms, and G. M. Simms to George W. Hamner, January 5, 1863, Hamner Family Papers, UVA.
183. William Dorsey Pender to Fanny Pender, April 26, 1863, in William W. Hassler, ed., *The General to His Lady: The Civil War Letters of William Dorsey Pender to Fanny Pender* (Chapel Hill: University of North Carolina Press, 1965), 230.
184. William Henry Terrill to George Parker Terrill, January 30, 1865; February 10, 1865, Terrill-Porterfield Families, Papers Regarding Civil War and Other Material, 1716-1994, A&M.3496, West Virginia and Regional History Center, West Virginia University.

Chapter 6

1. Ira Berlin, Joseph P. Reidy, and Leslie S. Rowland, eds., *Freedom: A History of Emancipation 1861-1867 Selected from the Holdings of the National Archives of the United States. Series II: The Black Military Experience* (New York: Cambridge University Press, 1982), 592-593; John M. Powell, CMSR, Co. E, 59th USCI, RG 94, NARA, fold3.com; Robert Cowden, *A Brief Sketch of the Organization and Services of the Fifty-Ninth Regiment of United States Colored Infantry, and Biographical Sketches* (Dayton, OH: United Brethren Publishing House, 1893), 38-39; Rosen, *Terror in the Heart of Freedom*, 23-48. On Black soldiers more generally, see Benjamin Quarles, *The Negro in the Civil War* (Boston: Little, Brown & Co., 1953); Dudley Cornish, *The Sable Arm: Negro Troops in the Union Army* (New York: Norton, 1956); James M. McPherson, *The Negro's Civil War: How Blacks Felt and Acted During the War for the Union* (New York: Vintage Books, 1965, 2003), 145-244; Mary Frances Berry, *Military Necessity and Civil Rights Policy: Black Citizenship and the Constitution, 1861-1868* (Port Washington, NY: Kennikat Press, 1977); Joseph T. Glatthaar, *Forged in Battle: The Civil War Alliance of Black Soldiers and White Officers* (New York: Free Press, 1990); Carole Emberton, "'Only Murder Makes Men': Reconsidering the Black Military Experience," *Journal of the Civil War Era* 2, no. 3 (September 2012): 369-393; Douglas R. Egerton, *Thunder at the Gates: The*

Black Civil War Regiments That Redeemed America (New York: Basic Books, 2016); Jonathan Lande, "Emancipating Masculinity: Black Union Deserters and Their Families in the Civil War South," *Journal of American History* 109, no. 3 (December 2022): 548–570.

2. Cowden, *A Brief Sketch*, 66–100; Thomas E. Parsons, *Work for Giants: The Campaign and Battle of Tupelo/Harrisburg, Mississippi, June–July 1864* (Akron, OH: Kent State University Press, 2014), 2–3, 23–25; Wills, *A Battle from the Start*, 204–215; Edwin C. Bearss, *Forrest at Brice's Cross Roads and in North Mississippi in 1864* (Dayton, OH: Morningside Bookshop, 1979), 66, 109–138. Powell does not mention his capture in his pension file, noting only that he suffered severe injuries to his chest, hip, knee, ankle, and back, as well as from diseases stemming from the march leading up to the battle. Declaration for Invalid Pension, February 26, 1898, John Powell, File 977.991, RG 15, NARA. This is not altogether surprising, for pension applications tended to be narrowly focused and to ignore any details not directly related to gaining the pension. Elizabeth A. Regosin and Donald R. Shaffer, eds., *Voices of Emancipation: Understanding Slavery, the Civil War, and Reconstruction through the U.S. Pension Bureau Files* (New York: New York University Press, 2008), 5.

3. James Henry Hammond to Unknown, July 22, 1863, Hammond Papers, LC; Caroline Wood Newhall, "'Under the Rebel Lash': Black Prisoners of War in the Civil War South" (PhD diss., University of North Carolina at Chapel Hill, 2020); Lorien Foote, *Rites of Retaliation: Civilization, Soldiers, and Campaigns in the American Civil War* (Chapel Hill: University of North Carolina Press, 2021), 49–140.

4. John M. Powell CMSR, RG 94, NARA M324, fold3.com; Powell's statement to the Freedmen's Bureau suggests he was captured later in 1864, but his service record indicates he went missing at Brices Cross Roads. Part of the confusion may stem from the fact that he was found with another formerly enslaved man and Bureau officials may have combined elements of their stories. Berlin et al., *The Black Military Experience*, 592–593.

5. Hahn, *The Political Worlds of Slavery and Freedom*, 74–79 and Steven Hahn, *A Nation Under Our Feet: Black Political Struggles in the Rural South from Slavery to the Great Migration* (Cambridge, MA: The Belknap Press of Harvard University Press, 2003), 41–43, 51–61; Camp, *Closer to Freedom*, 93–116; Kaye, *Joining Places*, 178–177–189; Susan O'Donovan, "Writing Freedom Into Slavery's Stories," in *Beyond Freedom: Disrupting the History of Emancipation*, ed. David Blight and Jim Downs (Athens: University of Georgia Press, 2017), 26–38. For the circulation of information in the broader Black Atlantic world, see, among others, Julius Scott, *The Common Wind: Afro-American Currents in the Age of the Haitian Revolution* (Brooklyn: Verso Books, 2018).

6. Blackett, *The Captive's Quest for Freedom*; Andrew Delbanco, *The War Before the War: Fugitive Slaves and the Struggle for America's Soul from the Revolution to the Civil War* (New York: Penguin Books, 2018), 189–388; Robert H. Churchill, *The Underground Railroad and the Geography of Violence in Antebellum America* (New York: Cambridge University Press, 2020), 139–232; Turiano, "'Prophecies of Loss.'"

7. For examples, see Theodore Dwight Weld, *American Slavery As It Is: Testimony of a Thousand Witnesses* (1838; repr. New York: Arno Press and the *New York Times*, 1968), 13–15, 20–24, 50–51, 53–94.
8. Harriet Jacobs, *Incidents in the Life of a Slave Girl* (Boston: Bedford/St. Martins, 2010), 103–108. Quote on p. 108.
9. Drew, *A North-Side View of Slavery*, 52.
10. Berlin et al., *Slaves No More*, 55–61; Roark, *Masters Without Slaves*, 68–108; Robinson, *Bitter Fruits of Bondage*, 37–57, 138–145, 189–195; Mohr, *On the Threshold of Freedom*, 99–234; Martinez, *Slave Impressment in the Upper South*, 45–70; McCurry, *Confederate Reckoning*, 218–309; O'Donovan, *Becoming Free in the Cotton South*, 77–110.
11. W. E. B. DuBois, *Black Reconstruction in America, 1860–1880* (1935; repr. New York: The Free Press, 1992), 55–83; McCurry, *Confederate Reckoning*, 259–262; Hahn, *A Nation Under Our Feet*, 68–115 and *The Political Worlds of Slavery and Freedom*, 55–114; P. L. Cameron to George W. Mordecai, September 18, 1863, Mordecai Papers, SHC.
12. Berlin et al., *Slaves No More*, 3–76; Gerteis, *From Contraband to Freedman*; Fields, *Slavery and Freedom on the Middle Ground*, 90–130; Freehling, *The South vs. The South*, 85–176; Oakes, *Freedom National*, 84–144, 192–223. For changing attitudes among US soldiers and civilians, see Manning, *What This Cruel War Was Over*, 73–102; Brasher, *The Peninsula Campaign and the Necessity of Emancipation*, 104–189; Cecelski, *The Fire of Freedom*, 43–137. For arguments emphasizing the complicated struggle for citizenship, see Manning, *Troubled Refuge*, 161–231; Cooper, "'Lord, Until I Reach My Home,'" 198–227; Brian Taylor, *Fighting for Citizenship: Black Northerners and the Debate over Military Service in the Civil War* (Chapel Hill: University of North Carolina Press, 2020); Holly A. Pinheiro Jr., *The Families' Civil War: Black Soldiers and the Fight for Racial Justice* (Athens: University of Georgia Press, 2022); Glymph, *The Women's Fight*, 221–250.
13. Berlin et al., *Slaves No More*, 5. See also Schwalm, *A Hard Fight for We*, 88–115; Kate Masur, "'A Rare Phenomenon of Philological Vegetation': The Word 'Contraband' and the Meaning of Emancipation in the United States," *Journal of American History* 93, no. 4 (March 2007): 1050–1084; Glymph, *Out of the House of Bondage*, 97–136; Amy Murrell Taylor, "How a Cold Snap in Kentucky Led to Freedom for Thousands: An Environmental Story of Emancipation," in Berry, *Weirding the War*, 191–214; Louis Gerteis, "Slaves, Servants, and Soldiers: Uneven Paths to Freedom in the Border States, 1861–1865," in *Lincoln's Proclamation: Emancipation Reconsidered*, ed. William A. Blair and Karen Fisher Younger (Chapel Hill: University of North Carolina Press, 2009), 170–194; Tera Hunter, *Bound in Wedlock: Slave and Free Black Marriage in the Nineteenth Century* (Cambridge, MA: The Belknap Press of Harvard University Press, 2017), 121–195. See also Reidy, *Illusions of Emancipation*, 183–190.
14. Downs, *Sick From Freedom*; Glymph, "This Species of Property," 55–71 and "Rose's War and the Gendered Politics of a Slave Insurgency in the Civil War," *Journal of the Civil War Era* 3, no. 4 (December 2013): 501–532; Cooper, "'Lord, Until I Reach My Home,'" 37–113; Rosen, *Terror in the Heart of Freedom*, 23–58; Diane Miller

Sommerville, *Aberration of Mind: Suicide and Suffering in the Civil War-Era South* (Chapel Hill: University of North Carolina Press, 2018), 122–127. On Confederate efforts to contest emancipation, see, among others, Kaye, *Joining Places*, 177–189 and Barton W. Myers, *Executing Daniel Bright: Race, Loyalty, and Guerrilla Violence in a Coastal Carolina Community* (Baton Rouge: Louisiana State University Press, 2009), 5–6, 55–62, 76–98.

15. Gregory P. Downs and Kate Masur, "Echoes of War: Rethinking Post-Civil War Governance and Politics," in *The World the Civil War Made* (Chapel Hill: University of North Carolina Press, 2015), 6; Gregory P. Downs, *After Appomattox: Military Occupation and the Ends of War* (Cambridge, MA: Harvard University Press, 2015), 39–60. On occupying Federals' ambivalence toward emancipation and its impact, see Andrew F. Lang, *In the Wake of the War: Military Occupation, Emancipation, and Civil War America* (Baton Rouge: Louisiana State University Press, 2017), 129–157, 182–209.
16. Paul B. Barringer to Daniel M. Barringer, August 19, 1862, Barringer Papers, SHC.
17. Stephen V. Ash, *When the Yankees Came: Conflict and Chaos in the Occupied South, 1861–1865* (Chapel Hill: University of North Carolina Press, 1995), 76–107. Quote on p. 95.
18. For estimates on the number of enslaved people who became free during the war, see DuBois, *Black Reconstruction*, 79; Joseph T. Glatthaar, "Black Glory: The African-American Role in Union Victory," in *Why the Confederacy*, ed. Gabor S. Boritt, *Lost* (New York: Oxford University Press, 1993), 142; Berlin et al., *The Wartime Genesis of Free Labor: The Lower South*, 77–80; Hahn, *A Nation Under Our Feet*, 82–83; Downs, *After Appomattox*, 23–35. For studies indicating enslavers' persistent power during the war, see, among others, Campbell, *An Empire for Slavery*, 231–251; O'Donovan, *Becoming Free in the Cotton South*, 59–82; Ryan M. Poe, "The Contours of Emancipation: Freedom Comes to Southwest Arkansas," *Arkansas Historical Quarterly* 70, no. 2 (Summer 2011): 109–130.
19. Allmendinger, *Nat Turner and the Rising in Southampton County*, 235.
20. M. F. Smith to Ann Nalle, December 19, 1861; M. Slaughter to Albert G. Nalle, January 1, 1862; William L. Scott Receipt, December 27, 1861; Receipt, December 28, 1861; "Expenses on Dick"; Account of Benjamin Franklin Nalle, July 10, 1862, Nalle Papers, VHS. "Orange County, Va.," Hotchkiss Map Collection, G3883.O6 186–.I9, Geography and Map Division, LC, https://lccn.loc.gov/2002627459 (accessed July 26, 2023).
21. Johnson, *River of Dark Dreams*, 209–243; Hadden, *Slave Patrols*, 172–174.
22. Camp, *Closer to Freedom*, 35–59; Franklin and Schweninger, *Runaway Slaves*, 97–123, 149–181; Hadden, *Slave Patrols*, 105–136; Johnson, *River of Dark Dreams*, 222–228.
23. Berlin et al., *The Destruction of Slavery*, 88, 339–350, 361, 362–365, 423–424.
24. Ibid., 14–22, 70–80, 114–118, 413–423.
25. Account of Benjamin Franklin Nalle, July 10, 1862, Nalle Papers, VHS.
26. For the "contagion of liberty," see Bernard Bailyn, *The Ideological Origins of the American Revolution (Fiftieth Anniversary Edition)* (Cambridge, MA: The Belknap Press of Harvard University Press, 2017), 230–246.
27. William L. Campbell to William S. Pettigrew, May 22, June 10, 1862; Angus McLeod to Pettigrew, July 31, 1862, Pettigrew Papers, SHC. Jack argued that instead of going

to the Yankees, Venus was seeking redress from Pettigrew. On the changes caused by distance from Union forces, see Ash, *When the Yankees Came*.

28. William S. Pettigrew to Kenwith Worthy, August 9, 1862; Pettigrew to Angus McLeod, August 9, 1862; William L. Campbell to Pettigrew, October 11, 1862; Pettigrew to [Blank], December 24, 1863, Pettigrew Papers, SHC. Pettigrew ultimately walked back his plan to sell Frank. Pettigrew to James Johnson, December 26, 1863, in same.

29. Notice of Sale of Slave, May 1862, Robeson County, Records Concerning Slaves and Free Persons of Color, NCDAH; Bill of Sale, Moliere Lange to Andrew J. Neal, April 3, 1862, Natchez Trace Slaves and Slavery Collection, 1793–1864, DBCAH. See also Hadden, *Slave Patrols*, 172–187; Mohr, *On the Threshold of Freedom*, 74; Laura Beecher Comer Diary, June 5, 1862, Laura Beecher Comer Papers, SHC; Albert, *The House of Bondage*, 115; H. C. Bruce, *The New Man: Twenty-Nine Years a Slave. Twenty-Nine Years a Free Man* (New York: F. Anstadt & Sons, 1895), 96; Berlin et al., *The Destruction of Slavery*, 94. On enslavers' access to jails, see William P. Smith to "My Dear Christopher," August 12, 1862, William Patterson Smith Papers, Duke. On their use of dogs in hunting fugitives, see Tyler D. Parry and Charlton W. Yingling, "Slave Hounds and Abolition in the Americas," *Past & Present* 246, no. 1 (February 2020): 69–108.

30. Morris, *Southern Slavery and the Law*, 337–343; Franklin and Schweninger, *Runaway Slaves*, 178–181.

31. "Notice," *Raleigh Weekly Standard*, November 26, 1862.

32. Mary W. Bankhead to "Uncle George," October 10 [Year Unknown], Minor Family Papers, VHS.

33. Order for Sale of a Runaway Slave, January 17, 1865, Albemarle County (Va.) Free Negro and Slave Records, 1799–1870, Local Government Records Collection, LVA.

34. R. F. Mason to Col. Latrobe, March 27, 1865, Lee Headquarters Papers, VHS.

35. George E. Lankford, *Bearing Witness: Memories of Arkansas Slavery*, 2nd ed. (Fayetteville: University of Arkansas Press, 2006), 147; Johnson, *River of Dark Dreams*, 218.

36. Jerome B. Yates to "Dear Ma," August 21, 1863, CSA Records, DBCAH. For others sending enslaved people from overrun parts of Mississippi to the Confederate interior, see H. E. Merritt to William H. Merritt, November 20, 1862, Merritt Papers, Duke; M. C. Oliver to Thomas M. Johnston, May 8, 1863, Johnston and McFaddin Family Papers, SHC; C. C. Buckner to William Dickinson, January 31, 1863, Morton and Dickinson Family Papers, UVA; Charles Elisha Taylor to "Dear Mother," December 9, 1862, Papers of Charles Elisha Taylor, UVA.

37. Edwin M. Stanton to Ambrose E. Burnside, April 29, 1863, *OR*, Ser. I, Vol. XXI, 291.

38. William A. Dobak, *Freedom By the Sword: The U.S. Colored Troops, 1862–1867* (Washington, DC: Center of Military History, United States Army, 2011), 316.

39. See, for example, Berlin et al., *The Destruction of Slavery*, 565; Sale Bond, Barren County, KY, March 16, 1863; Sale Bond, Barren County, KY, May 18, 1863, African American Miscellany, Duke.

40. E. R. Brown to Mary Baylor, September 4, 16, October 1, 1861, Harry L. and Mary K. Dalton Collection, Duke.

41. Timothy Ross Talbott, "Telling Testimony: Slavery Advertisements in Kentucky's Civil War Newspapers," *Ohio Valley History* 16, no. 3 (Fall 2016): 32, 37. See, for example, Documents Relating to the Sale of Emma and Frances Ford, American Slavery Documents, Duke.
42. William Henry Tripp to Araminta Guilford Tripp, May 20, 1862, William Henry Tripp and Araminta Guilford Tripp Papers, SHC.
43. Smith and Cooper, *A Union Woman in Civil War Kentucky*, 153.
44. Robinson, "Day of Jubilo," 256; Testimony of Morris McComb, William Yocum Court-Martial, NN-4017, RG 153, NARA. See also Edward Canby to John C. Underwood, February 7, 1864, John C. Underwood Papers, LC.
45. J. L. M. McPhail to L. C. Turner, November 14, 17, 1863, "Greenleaf Johnson," Case Files of Investigations by Levi C. Turner and Lafayette C. Baker, 1861–1866, RG 94, NARA M797; Berlin et al., *The Destruction of Slavery*, 372–376. See also Testimony of George E. H. Day, Reel 200, Records of the American Freedmen's Inquiry Commission, RG 94, NARA M619. Campbell helped bail Johnson out of jail following his arrest. "Proceedings of the Courts," *Baltimore American and Commercial Advertiser*, December 16, 1863.
46. Berlin et al., *The Destruction of Slavery*, 564, 567–569, 574, 592; Testimony of L. C. Littlefield, H. H. Hine Court-Martial, LL-2648, RG 153, NARA; W. G. Eliot to John M. Schofield, June 20, 1863, John Mc. Schofield Papers, LC. See also John Christgau, *Incident at the Otterville Station: A Civil War Story of Slavery and Rescue* (Lincoln: University of Nebraska Press, 2013).
47. Hadden, *Slave Patrols*, 183–187; Woodward, *Marching Masters*, 120–129; Glatthaar, *General Lee's Army*, 304–314.
48. See, for example, B. Randolph to Josiah Gorgas, Stanton, Va., July 15, 1863, R-681 1863, Letters Received, ser. 12, Adjutant and Inspector General's Department, RG 109, NARA [FSSP F-307]. On Black laborers see Brewer, *The Confederate Negro*; Ervin L. Jordan Jr., *Black Confederates and Afro-Yankees in Civil War Virginia* (Charlottesville: University Press of Virginia, 1995), 49–68; Martinez, *Confederate Slave Impressment in the Upper South*, 18–70, 98–131.
49. Robinson, *Bitter Fruits of Bondage*, 106–133; Martinez, *Confederate Slave Impressment in the Upper South*, 18–32. For examples, see "Notice" and "$100 Reward," *Richmond Daily Dispatch*, June 11, 1862; "Ranaway," *Richmond Daily Dispatch*, July 21, 1862; "$500 Reward," *Raleigh Daily Confederate*, June 13, 1864; "Runaway—Three Hundred Dollars Reward," *Richmond Daily Dispatch*, February 22, 1865.
50. Entry for August 23, 1861, in Woodward, *Mary Chesnut's Civil War*, 159; Jonathan Dean Sarris, *A Separate War: Communities in Conflict in the Mountain South* (Charlottesville: University of Virginia Press, 2006), 85; Richard Lewis to his mother, April 14, 1864, in Richard Lewis, *Camp Life of a Confederate Boy, of Bratton's Brigade, Longstreet's Corps, C. S. A. Letters Written by Richard Lewis, of Walker's Regiment, To His Mother, During the War* (Charleston, SC: The News and Courier Book Presses, 1883), 92.

51. Report of E. J. Allen, dated Wash., Dec. 20, 1861. Statement of a Coloured Man on the railroad to be built by the enemy between Strasburg and Winchester, George Brinton McClellan Papers, LC.
52. See Appraisement of Negroes to Work on Fortifications, 1864, Amelia County Free Negro and Slave Records, LVA; List of Appraisement of Slaves, July 1864, Fluvanna County Free Negro and Slave Records, LVA; Mims Ward, We Have Carefully Examined the Following Slaves, furnished the Confederate States . . . , 23 Feb. 1864, SCL.
53. Henry J. Brown to George W. Randolph, Lynchburg, Va., October 28, 1862, B-1275, Letters Received, ser. 5, Secretary of War, RG 109: War Department Collection of Confederate Records, NARA [FSSP F-50].
54. Mary Elliott to Emily Elliott, March 2, 1863, Elliott and Gonzales Papers, SHC. For other discussions of "demoralization," see W. Mishoffer to Benjamin F. Butler, May 20, 1862; J. F. H. Claiborne to Butler, June 3, 1862, Butler Papers, LC; Entry for July 31, 1862, Bills Diary, SHC; A. Wright to Paul Cameron, March 25, 1863, Cameron Papers, SHC; Entries for January 11–30, 1862, Louis M. DeSaussure Journal, SHC.
55. Daniel Ruggles to Col. R. S. Garnett, May 8, 1861, *OR*, Ser. I, Vol. 2, 820.
56. 12th Texas Dragoons, Receipt of an Enslaved Child Named Stephen, August 7, 1862, John L. Nau III Civil War History Collection, UVA.
57. Inventory, January 1, 1862, Farm Journal of Edward T. Tayloe, Tayloe Family Papers, Series E: UVA, Part 1 RASP.
58. Wm. Elliott to Unknown General, August 1862, Elliott and Gonzales Papers, SHC; "Runaway Negroes—Stop Them! Stop Them!," *Memphis Daily Appeal*, January 5, 1864.
59. Jerome B. Yates to "Friend Fred," January 18, 1864, CSA Records, DBCAH. See also Baldy A. Capehart to Meeta Rhodes Armistead Capehart, December 16, 1864, Capehart Papers, SHC; Entry for February 15, 1864, Belle Edmondson Diary, SHC; Charles S. Greene, *Thrilling Stories of the Great Rebellion: Comprising Heroic Adventures and Hair-Breadth Escapes of Soldiers, Scouts, Spies, and Refugees; Daring Exploits of Smugglers, Guerrillas, Desperadoes, and Others; Tales of Loyal and Disloyal Women; Stories of the Negro, Etc., Etc.* (Philadelphia: John E. Potter and Company, 1864), 280–281.
60. Judson Kilpatrick to Alfred Pleasonton, March 8, 1864, *OR*, Ser. I, Vol. 33, 183.
61. Deposition of Spencer Lloyd, May 9, 1874, Claim of Spencer Lloyd, Fairfax County, Virginia, Barred and Disallowed Case Files of the Southern Claims Commission, 1871–1880, RG 233: Records of the U.S. House of Representatives, NARA M1407 (accessed via www.fold3.com). See also Report of E. J. Allen on the Position of the Rebel Troops at Union Mills, Fairfax Co., VA., and Vicinity, Nov. 28, 1861; E. J. Allen to George B. McClellan, December 30, 1861, McClellan Papers, LC.
62. "Surrender of Harper's Ferry," *Macon Daily Telegraph*, September 23, 1862; "From Harper's Ferry," *Newark Daily Advertiser*, September 29, 1862.
63. William T. Sherman to Lorenzo Thomas, April 12, 1864, *OR*, Ser. III, Vol. 4, 225.
64. George Ingram to Martha Ingram, July 18, 1863, in Henry L. Ingram, ed., *Civil War Letters of George W. and Martha F. Ingram, 1861–1865* (College Station: Texas A&M

University Press, 1973), 56; Sarah A. Dorsey, *Recollections of Henry Watkins Allen, Brigadier-General Confederate States Army Ex-Governor of Louisiana* (New York: M. Doolady, 1866), 244.
65. P. Fishe Reed, *Incidents of the War; or the Romance and Realities of Soldier Life* (Indiana: Asher & Co., 1862), 9–10. Federal forces advancing upriver soon liberated Mingo again.
66. Manning, *Troubled Refuge*, 146.
67. Anne J. Bailey, "A Texas Cavalry Raid: Reaction to Black Soldiers and Contrabands," in *Black Flag Over Dixie: Racial Atrocities and Reprisals in the Civil War*, ed. Gregory J. W. Urwin (Carbondale: Southern Illinois Press, 2004), 28.
68. "Runaway—One Thousand Dollars Reward," *Richmond Daily Dispatch*, January 6, 1865.
69. Ted Alexander, "A Regular Slave Hunt: The Army of Northern Virginia and Black Civilians in the Gettysburg Campaign," *North and South* 4, no. 7 (September 2001): 82–89; David G. Smith, "Race and Retaliation: The Capture of African Americans during the Gettysburg Campaign," in *Virginia's Civil War*, ed. Peter Wallenstein and Bertram Wyatt-Brown (Charlottesville: University of Virginia Press, 2005), 138–140; Guelzo, *Gettysburg*, 73–74. On the campaign's legacies in the Black community, see Hilary Green, "The Persistence of Memory: African Americans and Transitional Justice Efforts in Franklin County, Pennsylvania," in *Reconciliation After Civil Wars: Global Perspectives*, ed. Paul Quigley and James Hawdon (New York: Routledge, 2018), 131–149.
70. Charles Blacknall to George Blacknall, June 18, 1863, printed in the *Carolina Watchman*, July 13, 1863, Gettysburg Library File V7-NC23, Gettysburg National Military Park Library and Research Center, Gettysburg, PA. Thanks to Hilary Green for sharing this source with me.
71. J. S. Haldeman to H. L. Sherwood, November 9, 1865; Haldeman to W. S. Howe, November 13, 1865; James Ashworth, endorsement of Haldeman to Howe, November 13, 1865; Howe to T. F. P. Crandon, December 20, 1866; Wm. Kersee, endorsement of Howe to Crandon, December 20, 1866, H-188, Registered Letters Received, ser. 3798, Assistant Commissioner, Virginia, RG 105, NARA [FSSP A-7670].
72. "Wholesale Swindling," *Charlotte Western Democrat*, August 4, 1863.
73. Guelzo, *Gettysburg*, 74.
74. Judith Kelleher Schafer, *Becoming Free, Remaining Free: Manumission and Enslavement in New Orleans, 1846–1862* (Baton Rouge: Louisiana State University Press, 2003), 127.
75. Depositions of Joseph D. Donnohue, R. M. Yates, Peter M. Everett, John A. Hannah, May 25, 1870, Benjamin Forsythe Buckner Papers, 1785–1918, Special Collections Research Center Archival Collections, University of Kentucky. My thanks to Patrick Lewis for pointing me to this source.
76. W. Storer How to Orlando Brown, September 29, 1865; How to R. S. Lacey, November 10, 1865, Augusta County, VA, Freedmen's Bureau Records, VS, http://valley.lib.virginia.edu/papers/B0523 and http://valley.lib.virginia.edu/papers/B0540 (accessed July 18, 2023).

77. Reuben Bartley Papers, VHS.
78. George S. Burkhardt, *Confederate Rage, Yankee Wrath: No Quarter in the Civil War* (Carbondale: Southern Illinois University Press, 2013), 171–172; Register of Prisoners, 1862–1865, Vol. 371, Defenses South of the Potomac, Alexandria Headquarters, Entry 1461, RG 393, Vol. IV, NARA. My thanks to Caroline Janney for sharing this with me. See also John L. Barbour to Abraham Lincoln, April 11, 1863, in *OR*, Ser. II, Vol. 5, 469–470; Hannah Johnson to Abraham Lincoln, July 31, 1863, in Berlin et al., *Freedom's Soldiers*, 106.
79. John R. Henry, April 7, 1866, Register of Letters Received, Vol. 1–2, Apr. 1865–Dec. 1868, Richmond SC, VAFOR, 164: 81/367, RG 105, NARA M1913.
80. Berlin et al., *The Black Military Experience*, 245, 247; Sharon Romeo, *Gender and the Jubilee: Black Freedom and the Reconstruction of Citizenship in Civil War Missouri* (Athens: University of Georgia Press, 2016), 60; Phillips, *The Rivers Ran Backward*, 259, 267.
81. Quoted in Harry McCorry Henderson, *Texas in the Confederacy* (San Antonio: The Naylor Company, 1955), 45.
82. Quoted in Sheehan-Dean, *Why Confederates Fought*, 113.
83. "Negro Regiments in Virginia," *Winchester Bulletin*, March 14, 1863; "The Massacres Justified—The Law of Nations," *The Danville Quarterly*, December 1864; John B. Polley to "Nellie," April 5, 1862, in Richard B. McCaslin, ed., *A Soldier's Letters to Charming Nellie by J. B. Polley of Hood's Texas Brigade* (Knoxville: University of Tennessee Press, 2008), 18.
84. "The Yankee Cavalry Raid," *Richmond Examiner*, September 10, 1863.
85. McPherson, *The Negro's Civil War*, 155–156.
86. "United States Seamen Sold into Slavery," *Milwaukee Sentinel*, May 28, 1861.
87. "Sold Into Slavery," *Pennsylvania Telegraph*, June 28, 1861.
88. John R. Taylor to Dickinson, Hill & Co., May 13, 1861, DHCRC. Taylor's refusal to sell Martin cheaply, Martin's own efforts to undercut his value, and the stalled slave market of the summer of 1861 meant that he remained unsold through at least December 1861. Taylor to Dickinson, Hill & Co., December 23, 1861, Chase Papers, LC. For African American's wartime understandings of Lincoln, see Jonathan W. White, ed., *To Address You as My Friend: African Americans' Letters to Abraham Lincoln* (Chapel Hill: University of North Carolina Press, 2021).
89. Karp, *This Vast Southern Empire*; Johnson, *River of Dark Dreams*, 303–420; Edward B. Rugemer, "Why Civil War? The Politics of Slavery in Comparative Perspective: The United States, Cuba, and Brazil," in *The Civil War as Global Conflict: Transnational Meanings of the American Civil War*, ed. David B. Gleeson and Simon Lewis (Columbia: University of South Carolina Press, 2014), 14–35.
90. William W. Freehling, *The Road to Disunion, Volume I: Secessionists At Bay 1776–1854* (New York: Oxford University Press, 1990), 77–97.
91. Slaveholders excused their own violations of these "tranquil" relations, in part, by blaming the enslaved for "betrayals." See Henry Lawrence to Hannah Lawrence, March 15, 1863, Brashear and Lawrence Family Papers, SHC; Entry for May 1, 1864, Catharine Broun Diary, Catherine Barbara Hopkins Broun Papers, SHC; Louisa

Lovell to Joseph Lovell, February 7, 1864, Quitman Papers, SHC; Nancy Weeks to Alfred Weeks, May 19, 1864, Hunter Family Papers, VHS.

92. Entry for December 14, 1862, Crabtree and Patton, *"Journal of a Secesh Lady,"* 232.
93. Charles C. Jones Jr. to Rev. C. C. Jones, July 19, 25, 1862, in Robert Manson Myers, *The Children of Pride: A True Story of Georgia and the Civil War* (New Haven, CT: Yale University Press, 1972), 934, 939–940. See also Colin Clarke to Maxwell Troax Clarke, July 22, 1862, August 10, 1862, Maxwell Troax Clarke Papers, SHC; Carolina Cook to "My Dear Brother," December 14, 1864, Cook Family Papers, SHC.
94. Micajah Woods to John Rodes Woods, June 25, July 17, 1863; John Rodes Woods to Micajah Woods, July 2, 18, 1863, Woods Papers, UVA.
95. Albert, *The House of Bondage*, 116.
96. Examination of Contrabands, William Johnson, January 1, 1862, Correspondence, McClellan Papers, LC; "Henry Dilworth," "Jim Johnson," Descriptions of Refugees, Deserters, Contrabands, Banks' Command, Entry 2223, RG 393, Vol. II, NARA; Jonathan Noyalas, *Slavery and Freedom in the Shenandoah Valley During the Civil War* (Gainesville: University Press of Florida, 2021).
97. "Amos Williams," Descriptions of Refugees, Deserters, Contrabands, Banks' Command, Entry 2223, RG 393, Vol. II, NARA.
98. Jerome B. Yates to "Dear Ma," August 21, 1863, CSA Records, DBCAH.
99. Wm. Elliott to "Dear William," August 25, 1862, Elliott and Gonzales Papers, SHC. See also John Lynch to Bishop Patrick Lynch, November 13, 1861; John Lynch to Bishop Patrick Lynch, January 22, 1862, Lynch Family Letters, 1858–1866, Catholic Diocese of Charleston Archives.
100. Joseph L. Deans to Francis W. Smith, August 24, 1862, Smith Papers, VHS.
101. William Patterson Smith to "My Dear Christopher," January 10, 1863, William Smith Papers, Duke.
102. PAR Accession #21686203, John W. Darden, Jacob Austin, and Emeline Darden Austin v. Mary J. Darden and Walter S. Darden, Southampton County, Virginia, November 1862, Series 2, Part C, RSFB.
103. Fanny Scott to Dr. Robert E. Peyton, April 23, 1862, Peyton Papers, VHS.
104. PAR Accession #21686201, Dolly A. Briggs v. Nancy E. Briggs and Caroline A. Briggs, Southampton County, Virginia, October 1862, Series 2, Part C, RSFB.
105. James M. Clifton, ed., *Life and Labor on Argyle Island: Letters and Documents of a Savannah River Rice Plantation, 1833–1867* (Savannah: The Beehive Press, 1978), 302, 342. William Dusinberre argues that Jack may have manipulated his own sale and found an intermediary to purchase him for a local plantation. Dusinberre, *Them Dark Days*, 150–152, 165.
106. Henry K. Burgwyn to "My Dear Mother," September 7, 1862, Burgwyn Papers, SHC. His uncle later decided to sell his entire plantation. Henry K. Burgwyn to "My Dear Mother," December 8, 1862, in same. For another call to sell an enslaved person whom an enslaver found threatening, see Edgeworth Bird to Sallie Bird, July 29, August 8, October 21, 1863, in John Rozier, ed., *The Granite Farm Letters: The Civil War Correspondence of Edgeworth & Sallie Bird* (Athens: University of Georgia Press, 1988), 127, 133, 154, 155 n 5.

107. Gudmestad, *A Troublesome Commerce*, 96–117; Deyle, *Carry Me Back*, 46–55.
108. Silas Omohundro to William T. Sutherlin, January 30, 1863, Sutherlin Papers, Duke.
109. Arabella Pettit to William B. Pettit, November 16, 1862, in Turner, *Civil War Letters of Arabella Speairs and William Beverley Pettit . . . Vol. 1*, 68.
110. Clement Evans to Allie Evans, August 8, 1861, in Stephens, *Intrepid Warrior*, 63.
111. R. A. Doswell to W. H. Clarke, Esq., September 15, 1863, Museum of the Confederacy, Miscellaneous African American Manuscripts, VHS.
112. Vincent Colyer, *Brief Report of the Services Rendered By the Freed People to the United States Army in North Carolina, in the Spring of 1862, after the Battle of Newbern* (New York: Vincent Colyer, 1864), 47.
113. John C. Gray Jr. to Elizabeth Gray, May 21, 1864, in John Chipman Gray and John Codman Ropes, *War Letters 1862–1865* (Boston: Houghton Mifflin Company, 1927), 339. Ironically, among Burritt's services to the United States was identifying other kidnappers. Samuel F. Du Pont to Gideon Welles, November 18, 1862, in Samuel F. Du Pont, *Official Dispatches and Letters of Rear Admiral Du Pont, U.S. Navy. 1846–48. 1861–63* (Wilmington, DE: Ferris Bros., 1883), 352–353.
114. Entry for May 1862, John Fayette Dickinson Diary, VHS.
115. Joseph Acklen to "Dear Judge," August 1, 1862, Natchez Trace Civil War Collection, DBCAH.
116. Colin Clarke to Maxwell Troax Clarke, July 22, 1862, Clarke Papers, SHC, emphasis in original. For a similar example see John Lynch to Bishop Patrick Lynch, March 17, 1862, Lynch Family Letters, Catholic Diocese of Charleston Archives.
117. William H. Grimball to John Berkley Grimball, February 19, 1862, Grimball Papers, Duke.
118. Entries for June 23 and 25, 1862, Ruffin, *The Diary of Edmund Ruffin*, Vol. II, 351–353; S. Mordecai to George W. Mordecai, 1863, Mordecai Papers, SHC. See also George P. Holman to "Dear Sir," June 4, 1963, Documents Relating to J. D. Fondren & Bro., Beinecke Library, Yale.
119. Genovese, *Roll Jordan Roll*, 113–133, especially 124–125; Johnson, *Soul By Soul*, 107–112.
120. S.H. McRae to William S. Pettigrew, January 6, 1862; Caroline Pettigrew to Mrs. C.L. Pettigrew, March 22, 1862, Pettigrew Papers, SHC.
121. S. H. McRae to William S. Pettigrew, January 6, 1862; Caroline Pettigrew to Charles Pettigrew, February 26, 1862; Caroline Pettigrew to Mrs. C. L. Pettigrew, March 22, 1862; D. G. Cowand to William S. Pettigrew, October 6, 1862; William S. Pettigrew to Annie Pettigrew, October 8, 1862, October 1864 (probably actually 1862), Pettigrew Papers, SHC. See also H. Williams to E. H. Stokes, November 21, 1862, Chase Papers, LC.
122. On resistance, see James C. Scott, *Weapons of the Weak: Everyday Forms of Peasant Resistance* (New Haven, CT: Yale University Press, 1987); Herbert Aptheker, *American Negro Slave Revolts* (New York: Columbia University Press, 1943); Raymond A. Bauer and Alice H. Bauer, "Day to Day Resistance to Slavery," *Journal of Negro History* 27, no. 4 (October 1942): 388–419; Genovese, *Roll, Jordan, Roll*, 285–324, 585–660 and *From Rebellion to Revolution: Afro-American Slave Revolts in the*

Making of the Modern World (Baton Rouge: Louisiana State University Press, 1979); Darlene Clark Hine and Kate Wittenstein, "Female Slave Resistance: The Economics of Sex," in *The Black Woman Cross-Culturally*, ed. Filomena Steady (Cambridge, MA: Harvard University Press, 1981), 289–291; Sylvia R. Frey, *Water from the Rock: Black Resistance in a Revolutionary Age* (Princeton, NJ: Princeton University Press, 1991); Camp, *Closer to Freedom*; Glymph, *Out of the House of Bondage*, 63–96. On Confederate anxieties, see Freehling, *The Road to Disunion*, II: 369–371; Steven A. Channing, *Crisis of Fear: Secession in South Carolina* (New York: Simon & Schuster, 1970); Jordan, *Tumult and Silence at Second Creek*; Link, *Roots of Secession*, 213–217; Justin Behrend, "Rebellious Talk and Conspiratorial Plots: The Making of a Slave Insurrection in Civil War Natchez," *Journal of Southern History* 77, no. 1 (February 2011): 17–52; Matthew J. Clavin, *Toussaint Louverture and the American Civil War: The Promise and Peril of a Second Haitian Revolution* (Philadelphia: University of Pennsylvania Press, 2012), 55–74; Barney, *Rebels in the Making*.

123. C. D. W. to "My Beloved Brother," September 29, 1860, Whittle Papers, SHC.
124. Bill of Sale, Abraham Bass to Herman Stein, June 9, 1862, Natchez Trace Slaves and Slavery Collection, DBCAH. See also James B. Clark to Dickinson, Hill & Co., October 26, 1861, Ames Papers, MHS; Thomas Dyer, ed., *To Raise Myself a Little: The Diaries and Letters of Jennie, a Georgia Teacher* (Athens: University of Georgia Press, 1982), 204–205; Tryphena Blanche Holder Fox to "Dear Mother," March 29, 1861 in Wilma King, ed., *A Northern Woman in the Plantation South: Letters of Tryphena Blanche Holder Fox, 1856-1876* (Baton Rouge: Louisiana State University Press, 1993), 115; William Alexander Thom to Pembroke Thom, April 26, 1863, in Catherine Thom Bartlett, ed., *"My Dear Brother": A Confederate Chronicle* (Richmond, VA: The Dietz Press, Incorporated, 1952), 92; Regosin and Shaffer, *Voices of Emancipation*, 46.
125. Entries for June 24, October 1, November 26, 1862, Hassell Diary, SHC. Hassell likely sold them to John Sedgwick, who was active in the area at the time. Receipt, J. S. Stalling to John Sedgwick, November 25, 1862, Sedgwick and Mussen Papers, Valentine Museum.
126. Colin Clark to "Dear Sallie," August 11, 1862, John L. Manning Papers, SCL. On the enslaved's alternate conceptions of their worth, see Berry, *The Price For Their Pound of Flesh*, 6, 61–70.
127. "From York River," *Richmond Daily Dispatch*, August 11, 1862; M. Deans to Mr. Smith, August 8, 1862, Smith Papers, VHS.
128. Colin Clarke to Maxwell Troax Clarke, February 7, 1864, Clarke Papers, SHC.
129. James Johnson, Fredericksburg, VA, October 25, 1866, Vol. 20, p. 377, Endorsements Sent, series 628, Assistant Commissioner, Georgia, RG 105, NARA [FSSP A-435].
130. John A. Williams to "Dear Sister," October 8, 1862, John A. Williams Papers, VHS.
131. William Grimes to Bryan Grimes, February 1, 1863; George A. Dancy to William Grimes, May 30, 1863, Grimes Papers, SHC.
132. William H. Thomson to Ruffin Thomson, August 5, 1863, Ruffin Thomson Papers, SHC; Coulter, *George Walton Williams*, 83.
133. David Bullock Harris to "My Darling Wife," January 27, 1862, Harris Papers, Duke. Naomi Cockrell to Dandridge Cockrell, October 19, 1862, in Pauline Franklin

and Mary V. Pruett, eds., *Civil War Letters of Dandridge William and Naomi Bush Cockrell, 1862–1863* (Lively: Brandylane Publishers, 1991), 20.
134. Thomas P. Jackson to John A. McDonnell, July 3, 1867, Augusta County, VAFOR, VS, http://valley.lib.virginia.edu/papers/B0418 (accessed July 18, 2023).
135. Samuel Sawyer to Oliver Otis Howard, August 8, 1866, S-259, Registered Letters Received, ser. 3379, Assistant Commissioner, Tennessee, RG 105, NARA [FSSP A-6339].
136. Lewis G. Schmidt, *A Civil War History of the 147th Pennsylvania Regiment* (Allentown: Lewis G. Schmidt, 2000), 1038.
137. Rabun Lee Brantley, *Georgia Journalism of the Civil War Period* (Nashville: George Peabody College for Teachers, 1929), 85; Ayers, *In the Presence of Mine Enemies*, 170. On the sexual abuse of mixed-race women, see, among others, Baptist, "'Cuffy,' 'Fancy Maids,' and 'One-Eyed Men,'" 1641–1649; Robinson, "Day of Jubilo," 21.
138. Fett, *Working Cures*, 169–192; Genovese, *Roll, Jordan, Roll*, 599–609; Merritt, *Masterless Men*, 179–215; Camp, *Closer to Freedom*, 60–92.
139. Sarah E. Watkins to Mrs. L. A. Walton, June 6, 1861, in Dimond and Hattaway, *Letters from Forest Place*, 232.
140. E. Donnan to Alexander Donnan, August 18, 1864, Donnan Papers, LVA.
141. J. Gwyn to Rufus Lenoir, February 9, 1863, Lenoir Papers, SHC. See also R. F. Christenbury to William A. Graham, April 6, 1861, Graham Papers, SHC.
142. Receipt, John M. Norvell to John Hartwell Cocke, August 1, 1863, Cocke Family Papers, Series E: UVA, Part 4, RASP; Ben Bell to Alfred Bell, May 30, 1864, Bell Papers, Duke. On Cocke, see Randall M. Miller, ed., *"Dear Master": Letters of a Slave Family* (Athens: University of Georgia Press, 1990).
143. Rawick, *The American Slave, Volume 6*, Alabama 346.
144. Robert H. Armistead to Dickinson & Hill, December 3, 1861, Ames Papers, MHS; P. L. Cameron to George W. Mordecai, April 5, 1861, Mordecai Papers, SHC; Entry for November 26, 1862, Hassell Diary, SHC; Kate Peddy to George Washington Peddy, March 25, 1862, in George Peddy Cuttino, *Saddle Bag and Spinning Wheel, being the Civil War letters of George W. Peddy, M. D., Surgeon, 56th Georgia Volunteer Regiment, C. S. A and his wife Kate Featherston Peddy* (Macon, GA: Mercer University Press, 1981), 75; Stephen Dodson Ramseur to "My Dear Bro.," April 25, 1863, in Kundahl, *The Bravest of the Brave*, 129; Tally Simpson to Mary Simpson, August 12, 1861, in Everson and Simpson Jr., *"Far, Far from Home,"* 60; Alexander Grinnan to "My Dear Georgia," June 25, 1862, Grinnan, Bryan, and Tucker Papers, UVA; Receipt, R. B. Williamston to William King, April 21, 1863; William King to Annie K. Leftwich King, May 24, 1863; December 18, 1863; May 4, 1864, King Family Papers, UVA.; William H. Locke to "Me Dear Wife," January 1, 1863, Civil War letters of William Herrod Locke and William Horatio Thornton, UVA; PAR Accession #21686204, Robert B. Winfree v. Robert Hatcher, Chesterfield County, Virginia, December 1862–September 1863, Series 2, Part C, RSFB; PAR Accession #20686308, Joseph E. Dent and John T. Dent, April 1863, Coweta Co., GA, Series II, Part A, RSFB; Jean V. Berlin, ed., *A Confederate Nurse: The Diary of Ada W. Bacot, 1860–1863* (Columbia: University of South Carolina Press, 1994), 158; Robert F. W. Allston to Adele Petigru Allston, April 10, 1863; Robertson, Blacklock and

Company to Robert F. Allston, May 9, 1863, in Easterby, *The South Carolina Rice Plantation*, 194, 426.
145. William J. Bailey to Dickinson & Hill, August 15, 1862, DHCRC.
146. P. M. Thompson to Dickinson Hill & Co., January 28, 1862, Chase Papers, LC; J. F. Simms, Wm. Simms, and G. M. Simms to George W. Hamner, January 5, 1863, Hamner Papers, UVA.
147. David C. Rankin, *Diary of a Christian Soldier: Rufus Kinsley and the Civil War* (New York: Cambridge University Press, 2004), 98, 110.
148. Thompson, *The Story of Mattie J. Jackson*, 11; Annie Pettigrew to William Pettigrew, September 29, 1862, Pettigrew Papers, SHC. Emphasis in the original.
149. Entry for October 27, 1863, in Harrison, *A Maryland Bride in the Deep South*, 247, 254.
150. Owen R. Kenan to Stephen Graham, September 8, 1862, Kenan Papers, SHC. See also entry for December 7, 1863, Samuel A. Agnew Diary, SHC.
151. "From Fortress Monroe," *Lowell Daily Citizen & News*, May 27, 1861.
152. Muriel Culp Barbe, *A Union Forever: An Historical Story of the Turbulent Years, 1854–1865 in the Lincoln Country and the Kansas-Missouri Border of the Old Central West, Based on Contemporary Records, Documents and Letters of Lewis Hanback, Hitherto Unpublished* (Glendale, CA: The Barbe Associates, 1949), 275–277. See also Constant C. Hanks to Mother, August 8, 1862, Constant C. Hanks Papers, Duke.
153. "Account of the Sales of the Negroes Belonging to the Estate of Flurry Seay, March–April, 1863," Louthan Papers, VHS.
154. Blassingame, *Slave Testimony*, 361–362, 699–701.
155. Burkley, "Floyd County, Georgia, During the Civil War Era," 262; "Runaways," *Richmond Daily Dispatch*, January 29, 1864.
156. Venet, *A Changing Wind*, 98.
157. "Two Hundred and Fifty Dollars Reward," *Richmond Daily Dispatch*, October 9, 1863; "$100 Reward"; "Strayed or Runaway," *Richmond Daily Dispatch*, January 6, 1864. See also S. R. Fondren to E. H. Stokes, October 12, 1863, SUSC-AAS; "$75 Reward," *Yorkville Enquirer*, August 1, 1861; "$25 Reward," *Western Democrat*, June 30, 1863; "Stop the Runaway—$75 Reward," *Raleigh Semi-Weekly Standard*, June 5, 1863; "$200 Reward," *Raleigh Daily Confederate*, June 13, 1864; "Ran Away," *Richmond Daily Dispatch*, February 22, 1865; "Runaway," *Andersonville Intelligencer*, March 9, 1865.
158. *Franklin Branch and Edward A. Clark v. William R. Wilson* in John B. Galbraith and A. R. Meek, *Reports of Cases Argued and Adjudged in the Supreme Court of Florida at Terms Held in 1867-'8-'9*, Volume XII (Tallahassee: Edward M. Cheney, 1869), 544–546.
159. Archer Anderson to Mrs. Mason, November 3, 1863, Mason Family Papers, VHS. Mason seems to have removed many of these enslaved people to South Carolina. See St. George Mason to Walter Taylor, January 6, 1864, in same.
160. Romeo, *Gender and the Jubilee*, 61.
161. *Kirksey v. Kirksey* in John W. Shepherd, *Reports of Cases Argued and Determined in the Supreme Court of Alabama During June Term, 1867, and January Term, 1868*, Volume XLI (Montgomery, AL: Barrett & Brown, 1869), 632.

NOTES TO PAGES 183-187 311

162. David P. Conyngham, *Sherman's March Through the South. With Sketches and Incidents of the Campaign* (New York: Sheldon and Company, 1865), 238; Entry for September 9, 1864, Venet, *Sam Richards's Civil War Diary*, 236.
163. Entry for November 19, 1864, in Horatio Dana Chapman, *Civil War Diary of a Forty-Niner* (Hartford, CT: Allis, 1929), 101; Sheehy et al., *Savannah: Brokers, Bankers, and Bay Lane*, 35, 65-66, 75-76, 128; Henry Bogardus to Susan Bogardus, June 13, 1865, Susan Bogardus Letter, Georgia Historical Society, Savannah, GA.
164. Glymph, *The Women's Fight*, 87.
165. Nathaniel V. Watkins to Nannie Watkins, January 8, 1865, Watkins Papers, W&M. See also Phillips, *Diehard Rebels*, 147-177.
166. Charles Coleman to Cynthia Beverly Tucker Washington Coleman, October 2, 1864, Tucker-Coleman Papers, W&M.
167. John Letcher to J. Hierholzer, November 3, 1864, John Letcher Papers, W&M.
168. E. B. Heyward to Charles Heyward, December 1(?), 1864, in Margaret Belser Hollis and Allen H. Stokes, eds., *Twilight on the South Carolina Rice Fields: Letters of the Heyward Family 1862-1871* (Columbia: University of South Carolina Press, 2010), 155-156.
169. "Our War Experiences," Cronly Papers, Duke.
170. Hill, Dickinson & Co; Lee & Bowman, Tax Returns, City of Richmond, 1863-1864, Entry UD-152A, RG 109, NARA.
171. Francis Parrish, April 27, 1868, Register of Letters Received, Vol. 1-2, Apr. 1865-Dec. 1868, Richmond SC, VAFOR, 164: 316/367, RG 105, NARA M1913
172. Eliza L. C. Tucker Harrison to Mary Jane Harrison, July 27, 1864, November 12, 1864, Harrison, Smith and Tucker Family Papers, UVA.
173. Lucilla Harrison to Alexander and James M. Donnan, December 4, 1864, Donnan Papers, LVA.
174. See, for example, John A. Campbell to William S. Pettigrew, January 24, 1865, Pettigrew Papers, SHC; Eleanor Platt to Rebecca Meade, December 31, 1864, Platt Letter, VHS.
175. Alexander F. Fewell to "Dear Father," December 15, 1864, in Mackintosh Jr., *"Dear Martha . . . ,"* 174. On converging prices, see, for example, Jedediah Hotchkiss to Nelson H. Hotchkiss, December 30, 1864, VS, https://valley.lib.virginia.edu/papers/A2595 (accessed May 3, 2023).
176. Rogers, *Confederate Home Front*, 133. "H." [James Henry Hammond?] to Maj. Gen. M. C. M. Hammond, June 19, 1864, Hammond Papers, Series A: SCL, RASP.
177. Cynthia Coleman to Charles Coleman, November 10, 1864, Tucker-Coleman Papers, W&M.
178. Lucilla Harrison to Alexander and James M. Donnan, December 4, [likely 1864], Donnan Papers, LVA.
179. George Monroe to John B. Eventon, November 8, 1864, Waller Family Papers, LVA.
180. Mary Bell to Alfred Bell, March 22, 1864, Bell Papers, Duke; Grant Taylor to Malinda Taylor, January 19, 1864, in Blomquist and Taylor, *This Cruel War*, 217.
181. Mary Blair McCarty to Harriett Boswell Caperton, January 8, 1865, McCarty Family Papers, VHS.

182. Thomas Jackson Strayhorn to Harriett Holden Nichols, August 7, 1864, in Henry McGilbert Wagstaff, "Letters of Thomas Jackson Strayhorn," *North Carolina Historical Review* 13, no. 4 (October 1936): 327.
183. Warren Akin to Eliza Akin, January 26, 1865, in Wiley, *Letters of Warren Akin*, 98; Alexander F. Fewell to Martha A. Fewell, January 1, 1865, in Mackintosh Jr., *"Dear Martha...,"* 183.
184. Lavender Ray to "My Dear Pa," December 5, 1864, February 14, 1865, Lavender Ray Papers, Emory.
185. "Extracts of Letters From Teachers," *The Freedmen's Journal* 1, no. 1 (January 1865); Cooper, "'Lord, Until I Reach My Home,'" 65, 276, 279.
186. Williams, *Help Me To Find My People*; Hunter, *Bound in Wedlock*, 165–232.

Chapter 7

1. On the aftermath of Appomattox, see Brooks D. Simpson, "Facilitating Defeat: The Union High Command and the Collapse of the Confederacy," in *The Collapse of the Confederacy*, ed. Brooks D. Simpson and Mark Grimsley (Lincoln: University of Nebraska Press, 2001), 80–103; Caroline Janney, *Ends of War: The Unfinished Fight of Lee's Army after Appomattox* (Chapel Hill: University of North Carolina Press, 2021).
2. Entry for May 15, 1865, Julia Wilbur Diary, Julia Wilbur papers (HC.MC.1158) Quaker and Special Collections, Haverford, http://triptych.brynmawr.edu/cdm/compoundobject/collection/HC_DigReq/id/9701/rec/22 (accessed September 4, 2018). Lumpkin appears to have tried dissembling in this way more than once. See Lucy N. Colman, *Reminiscences* (Buffalo: H. L. Green, 1891), 76. On the immediate aftermath of the war in Richmond, see John T. O'Brien, "Reconstruction in Richmond: White Restoration and Black Protest, April–June 1865," *Virginia Magazine of History and Biography* 89, no. 3 (July 1981): 259–281.
3. Entry for May 15, 1865, Julia Wilbur Diary, Haverford.
4. Jacobs, *Incidents in the Life of a Slave Girl*, 36–41, 48–49, 73, 105, 107–108, 126–128, 164.
5. Entry for May 18, 1865, Julia Wilbur Diary, Haverford.
6. Entry for May 31, 1865, ibid.
7. Eric Foner, *Nothing But Freedom: Emancipation and Its Legacy* (Baton Rouge: Louisiana State University Press, 1983), 6. On debates over definitions of freedom in the war's immediate aftermath, see John Hope Franklin, *Reconstruction After the Civil War* (Chicago: University of Chicago Press, 1961), 48–53; Litwack, *Been in the Storm So Long*, 221–291; Foner, *Reconstruction*, 124–136; Amy Dru Stanley, *From Bondage to Contract: Wage Labor, Marriage, and the Market in the Age of Slave Emancipation* (New York: Cambridge University Press, 1998); Dylan Penningroth, *The Claims of Kinfolk: African American Property and Community in the Nineteenth-Century South* (Chapel Hill: University of North Carolina Press, 2003), 111–161; Michael F. Fitzgerald, *Splendid Failure: Postwar Reconstruction in the American*

South (Chicago: Ivan R. Dee, 2007), 47–71; Stephen Kantrowitz, *More Than Freedom: Fighting for Black Citizenship in a White Republic, 1829–1889* (New York: Penguin, 2012); Rothman, *Beyond Freedom's Reach*; Carole Emberton, "Unwriting the Freedom Narrative: A Review Essay," *Journal of Southern History* 82, no. 2 (May 2016): 377–394; Blight and Downs, *Beyond Freedom*.

8. On the afterlives of slavery, see Hartman, *Lose Your Mother*, 6. For efforts to replicate slavery in the South following the war, see DuBois, *Black Reconstruction*, 670–709; Pete Daniel, *The Shadow of Slavery: Peonage in the South, 1901–1969* (Urbana: University of Illinois Press, 1972); Jay Mandle, *The Roots of Black Poverty: The Southern Plantation Economy after the Civil War* (Durham, NC: Duke University Press, 1978); Douglas Blackmon, *Slavery by Another Name: The Re-Enslavement of Black Americans from the Civil War to World War II* (New York: Doubleday, 2008); Kidada E. Williams, *I Saw Death Coming: A History of Terror and Survival in the War Against Reconstruction* (New York: Bloomsbury, 2023).

9. "Lynchburg Items," *Richmond Commercial Bulletin*, July 12, 1865; Untitled, *Macon Daily Telegraph*, July 25, 1865; "Local Matters," *Richmond Daily Dispatch*, January 8, 1856; Untitled, *Wheeling Daily Intelligencer*, July 18, 1865. Former trader Sidnum Grady also committed suicide after the war. Trent, *The Secret Life of Bacon Tait*, 94.

10. *Satterfield v. Spurlock*; *Spurlock v. Satterfield*; and *Satterfield v. Spurlock* in J. Hawkins, *Reports of Cases Argued and Determined in the Supreme Court of Louisiana for the Year 1869*, Volume XXI (New Orleans: Office of the Daily Republican, 1869), 772.

11. W. M. Beebee to W. W. Rogers, December 10, 1866, Letters Sent, Vol. 1–2, July 15, 1865–Sept. 12, 1868, 13: 56/322; Beebee to Rogers, January 5, 1867, Unregistered Letters Received, Part 1, 173: 20/195; Entries for January 1867, 24, Employment Registers from Wisewell Barracks, v. 1–2, Aug. 2, 1866–Aug. 10, 1868, 18: 16/84, all Washington and Georgetown LS, DCFOR, RG 105, NARA M1902; "Thompson, Millie," US Federal Census for 180, Ward 2, Augusta, Richmond Co., GA (accessed via Ancestry.com).

12. Deposition of Charles Dice, September 17, 1901; Dice to Pension Office, May 27, 1902, Charles Dice, File 634.433, RG 15, NARA; Charles Dice, CMSR, Co. C, 23rd USCI, RG 94, NARA, fold3.com; Foote, *Yankee Plague*, 107–108; John C. Inscoe and Gordon B. McKinney, *The Heart of Confederate Appalachia: Western North Carolina in the Civil War* (Chapel Hill: University of North Carolina Press, 2003), 243–253.

13. Thomas P. Jackson to John A. McConnell, April 25, 1867, Letters sent, Vol. 1–2, Mar.–June 1867, Feb.–Dec. 1868, Staunton ASC, VAFOR, 173: 20/195, RG 105, NARA M1913; Bill of sale for Jefree, 1865, UVA; Receipt, January 25, 1865, Papers of the White and Holland families of Fluvanna County, Virginia, UVA; Receipt, Dickinson Hill to E. Dromgoole, February 13, 1865, Dromgoole and Robinson Papers, Series F: Duke, Part 4, RASP.

14. C. C. Sibley to John R. Edie, June 13, 1867, Endorsements Sent, Vol. 2 (18), Sept. 27, 1866–July 24, 1868, Assistant Commissioner, North Carolina, 4: 132/206, RG 105, NARA M843.

15. George W. Pettyjohn to Davis M. Wood, March 20, 1865, in Jeff Toalson, ed., *No Soap, No Pay, Diarrhea, Dysentery & Desertion: A Composite Diary of the Last Sixteen*

Months of the Confederacy from 1864 to 1865 (New York: iUniverse, 2006), 349. See also J. G. Shepherd to T. D. McDowell, February 16, 1865, McDowell Papers, SHC.

16. Entries for December 24, 1864, February 9, 1865, Robards Account Books, CHM. Data taken from same.
17. William Henry Tripp to Araminta Guilford Tripp, February 7, 1865, Tripp Papers, SHC. See also Entry for January 1, 1865, David Schenck Diary, SHC.
18. Entry for January 28, 1865, John Houston Bills Diary, SHC. See also Bryan Grimes to "My Dear John," January 20, 1865, Grimes Papers, SHC.
19. Eldred Simkins to Eliza Simkins, January 27, 1865, Eldred J. Simkins Papers, HL.
20. Edwin H. Fay to Sarah Fay, January 1, March 13, 1865, in Wiley, *"This Infernal War,"* 409, 434.
21. I. H. Brown to Jonathan Worth, February 4, 1865, in Hamilton, *The Correspondence of Jonathan Worth*, I: 656; J. B. H. to Lt. L. B. Hereford, March 4, 1865, Rudin Slavery Collection, Cornell; Campbell, *An Empire for Slavery*, 241–242, 242 n17 and "The End of Slavery in Texas: A Research Note," *Southwestern Historical Quarterly* 88, no. 1 (July 1984): 71–80; Levengood, "In the Absence of Scarcity," 411.
22. Fort, *A Feast of Reason*, 52, 99, 116, 118, 179.
23. William D. Henderson, *Petersburg in the Civil War: War at the Door* (Lynchburg, VA: H. E. Howard, Inc., 1998), 134; Perdue et al., *Weevils in the Wheat*, 39.
24. Benjamin Cook to J. A. McDonnell, October 11, 1866, Press Copies of Letters Sent, Dec. 1865–April 1867, Richmond ASC, VAFOR, 170: 247/502, RG 105, NARA M1913; "Facts for the Freedmen's Bureau in Cumberland Co.," Registered Letters Received, Register 3, A-P, Mar.–Dec. 1868, Assistant Commissioner, North Carolina, 14: 6/1078, RG 105, NARA M843; Perdue et al., *Weevils in the Wheat*, 3.
25. John Coates, CMSR, Co. G, 23rd USCI, RG 94, NARA; Exhibit A for Deposition, John Coates to F. C. Ainsworth, John Coates, File 1377764, RG 15, NARA.
26. Roger S. Keller, ed., *Riding With Rosser, By Major General Thomas L. Rosser* (Shippensburg, PA: Burd Street Press, 1997), 68.
27. April 1865, Memoranda Book of Thomas S. Bocock, Papers of the Thornhill Family and of Thomas S. Bocock, Accession # 10612, UVA. Jaime Martinez suggests this might have been part of transaction centered primarily around wheat and other goods. Martinez, "The Slave Market in Civil War Virginia," 128.
28. Roger L. Ransom and Richard Sutch, *One Kind of Freedom: The Economic Consequences of Emancipation* (New York: Cambridge University Press, 2001), 52–55; Huston, *Calculating the Value of Union*, 27–29; Wright, *Old South, New South*, 17–21; Kilbourne, *Debt, Investment, Slaves*, 75–76.
29. Entry for October 8, 1865, in Virginia Ingraham Burr, ed., *The Secret Eye: The Journal of Ella Gertrude Clanton Thomas, 1848–1889* (Chapel Hill: University of North Carolina Press, 1990), 276.
30. Joint Select Committee to Inquire into the Condition of Affairs in the Late Insurrectionary States, *Testimony Taken by the Joint Select Committee . . . Mississippi. Volume XII* (Washington, DC: Government Printing Office, 1872), 875.
31. W. H. Foushee to William Ritchie, August 1868, Ritchie-Harrison Family Papers, W&M. Emphasis in original.

32. Quoted in McDaniel, *Sweet Taste of Liberty*, 169.
33. Amanda Laury Kleintop, "The Balance of Freedom: Abolishing Property Rights in Slaves During and After the US Civil War" (PhD diss., Northwestern University, 2018); Giuliana Perrone, "Litigating Emancipation: Slavery's Legal Afterlife, 1865–1877" (PhD diss., University of California, Berkeley, 2015), 94–128.
34. John Quincy Adams, *Narrative of the Life of John Quincy Adams, When in Slavery, and Now as a Freeman* (Harrisburg, PA: Sieg, Printer and Stationer, 1872), 8–9, https://docsouth.unc.edu/neh/adams/adams.html (accessed July 19, 2023).
35. Michael Johnson, "Looking for Lost Kin: Efforts to Reunite Freed Families after Emancipation," in Clinton, *Southern Families at War*, 23–24.
36. "The Negro Question at the West," *New York Times*, December 18, 1861.
37. Williams, *Help Me to Find My People*, 140–188; Gutman, *The Black Family in Slavery and Freedom*, 363–432; Stanley, *From Bondage to Contract*, 188–191; Penningroth, *The Claims of Kinfolk*, 163–186; Hunter, *Bound in Wedlock*, 121–195.
38. Thavolia Glymph, "Black Women and Children in the Civil War: Archive Notes," in Blight and Downs, *Beyond Freedom*, 131.
39. Amos Kendall to Nathaniel P. Banks, January 12, 1863, Banks Papers, LC.
40. Abigail Cooper, "'Away I Goin' to Find My Mamma': Self-Emancipation, Migration, and Kinship in Refugee Camps in the Civil War Era," *Journal of African American History* 102, no. 4 (October 2017): 444–467.
41. "A Colored Mechanic," *The Weekly Commonwealth* (Topeka, KS), August 12, 1863. On free people of color's struggles for security in the antebellum period, see, among others, Melvin Ely, *Israel on the Appomattox: A Southern Experiment in Black Freedom from the 1790s through the Civil War* (New York: Vintage Books, 2004); Eva Sheppard Wolf, *Almost Free: A Story about Family and Race in Antebellum Virginia* (Athens: University of Georgia Press, 2012); Kirt von Daacke, *Freedom Has a Face: Race, Identity, and Community in Jefferson's Virginia* (Charlottesville: University of Virginia Press, 2012); Warren Eugene Milteer Jr., *Beyond Slavery's Shadow: Free People of Color in the South* (Chapel Hill: University of North Carolina Press, 2021), 179–219.
42. Cynthia Nicoletti, *Secession on Trial: The Treason Prosecution of Jefferson Davis* (New York: Cambridge University Press, 2017), 272. See also Jacqueline Jones, "Wartime Workers, Moneymakers: Black Labor in Civil War-Era Savannah," in *Slavery and Freedom in Savannah*, ed. Leslie M. Harris and Daina Ramey Berry (Athens: University of Georgia Press, 2014), 141; Lee, *Claiming the Union*, 114; Toombs, *Reminiscences of the War*, 197.
43. John Woodard to Andrew Johnson, December 5, 1865, Registers and Letters Received, N-R, Oct. 1865–Feb. 1866, Records of the Commissioner, 23: 703/1140, RG 105, NARA M752.
44. Louisa Alexander to Archer Alexander, November 16, 1863, in Blassingame, *Slave Testimony*, 119.
45. "The Rebel Reign at Harper's Ferry," *Daily Missouri Democrat*, November 4, 1862.
46. "The Slaves in North Carolina," *New York Tribune*, April 17, 1862.
47. "Port Royal Correspondence of the *Tribune*," *Hartford Daily Courant*, December 24, 1861; "Local News," *St. Louis Daily Missouri Republican*, September 15, 1862.

48. "The Slave's Experience," *Boston Watchman & Reflector*, October 2, 1862.
49. Henry Hunt to BRFAL, January 29, 1867, Letters Received by Employment Agents, Jan. 19, 1866–Nov. 7, 1867, DCFOR, 18: 130/298, RG 105, NARA M1902.
50. "From the Sixteenth Vermont Regiment," *Christian Messenger*, June 18, 1863.
51. "The Lost Found," *New York Evening Post*, August 22, 1862.
52. "A Pro-Slavery Trap," *The Liberator*, May 23, 1862; Elizabeth Blair Lee to Samuel Phillips Lee, April 18, 1862, in Laas, *Wartime Washington*, 130–131.
53. "Statement of Sarah Burgess (colored)," Undated [June 1864], Union Provost Marshal's File of Papers Relating to Citizens, RG 109, NARA.
54. "Our Correspondence," *New York Evangelist*, June 1, 1865; "The Richmond Freedmen," *New York Tribune*, June 17, 1865.
55. Baden et al., *Weevils in the Wheat*, 89.
56. "Letter from Richmond," *Christian Recorder*, April 22, 1865; Edward A. Miller Jr., "Garland H. White, Black Army Chaplain," *Civil War History* 43, no. 3 (September 1997): 201–218.
57. F. N. Boney, Richard L. Hume, and Rafia Zafar, *God Made Man, Man Made the Slave: The Autobiography of George Teamoh* (Macon, GA: Mercer University Press, 1990), 115–116.
58. Manning, *Troubled Refuge*, 245–246; Smith, *We Ask Only for Even-Handed Justice*, 30. See also H. Cattey to M. F. Gallagher, Letters Received, Jan. 1867, July–Sept. 1867, Feb.–Nov. 1868, Lincolnton ASC, NCFOR, 28: 86/147, RG 105, NARA M1909.
59. On formerly enslaved people's claims on the state, see, among others, Manning, *Troubled Refuge*, 201–231; Mary Frances Berry, *My Face Is Black Is True: Callie House and the Struggle for Ex-Slave Reparations* (New York: Knopf, 2005); Lee, *Claiming the Union*, 90–132; Dale Kretz, *Administering Freedom: The State of Emancipation after the Freedmen's Bureau* (Chapel Hill: University of North Carolina Press, 2022), 14–57; Brandi C. Brimmer, *Claiming Union Widowhood: Race, Respectability, and Poverty in the Postemancipation South* (Durham, NC: Duke University Press, 2020); White, *To Address You As My Friend*.
60. N. Y. Perkins to J. B. Crenshaw, December 5, 1865, P-20, Registered Letters Received, ser. 3798, Assistant Commissioner, Virginia, RG 105, NARA [FSSP A-7702].
61. On the shortcomings of the Freedmen's Bureau, see, among others, William S. McFeely, *Yankee Stepfather: General O. O. Howard and the Freedmen* (New Haven, CT: Yale University Press, 1968); Claude F. Oubre, *Forty Acres and a Mule: The Freedmen's Bureau and Black Land Ownership* (Baton Rouge: Louisiana State University Press, 1978); William A. Richter, *Overreached on All Sides: The Freedmen's Bureau Administrators in Texas, 1865–1868* (College Station: Texas A&M Press, 1991); Paul A. Cimbala and Randall M. Miller, eds., *The Freedmen's Bureau and Reconstruction: Reconsiderations* (New York: Fordham University Press, 1999); Christopher B. Bean, *Too Great a Burden to Bear: The Struggle and Failure of the Freedmen's Bureau in Texas* (New York: Fordham University Press, 2016); Kristin Bouldin, "Contraband Camps and the Freedmen's Bureau During the Civil War and Reconstruction" (PhD diss., University of Mississippi, 2020). On freedpeople's efforts to turn the Bureau to their own purposes, see Kretz, *Administering Freedom*, 14–57 and Edward Valentin Jr.,

"Local Knowledge: Black Texans, the Freedmen's Bureau, and Military Occupation in Reconstruction Texas," *Civil War History* 67, no. 1 (March 2021): 29–55.
62. Affidavit of Kitty Young, June 20, 1866, Letters Received, Vol. 2, S-Y, Jan. 1866–Feb. 1867, Assistant Commissioner, Mississippi, 17: 714/864, RG 105, NARA M826; Fred S. Palmer to S. H. Groesbeck, March 19, 1867, Registers of Letters Received, D-S, 1867, Assistant Commissioner, Tennessee, 13: 1099/1446, RG 105, NARA M999.
63. Rachel Jenkins to O. O. Howard, August 30, 1865, Letters Received, M-R, Mar.–Oct. 1865, Records of the Commissioner, 16: 654/1055, RG 105, NARA M752. See also Mary Farmer-Kaiser, *Freedwomen and the Freedmen's Bureau: Race, Gender, and Public Policy in the Age of Emancipation* (New York: Fordham University Press, 2010).
64. E. B. Townsend to H. S. Merrell, February 26, 1866, Endorsements sent and received, vol 1–3, Apr. 1865–Dec. 1868, Virginia, Richmond SC, VAFOR, 164: 129/398, RG 105, NARA M1913.
65. Thomas P. Jackson to Orlando Brown, August 31, 1867, Augusta County, VAFOR, VS, http://valley.lib.virginia.edu/papers/B1015 (accessed July 19, 2023).
66. M. C. Vogell to Jacob F. Chur, May 13, 1868, Registered Letters Received, June 1867–Nov. 1868, Raleigh AS, NCFOR, 52: 178/206, RG 105, NARA M1909. On fears that the Bureau would encourage dependence in freedpeople, see Paul A. Cimbala, *Under the Guardianship of the Nation: The Freedmen's Bureau and the Reconstruction of Georgia, 1865–1870* (Athens: University of Georgia Press, 1997), 1–21; Farmer-Kaiser, *Freedwomen and the Freedmen's Bureau*, 35–63; Downs, *Declarations of Dependence*, 75–100; Kretz, *Administering Freedom*, 14–57.
67. E. B. Townsend to H. S. Merrell, February 26, 1866, Endorsements sent and received, vol 1–3, Apr. 1865–Dec. 1868, Virginia, Richmond SC, VAFOR, 164: 129/398, RG 105, NARA M1913.
68. F. M. H. Kendrick, January 11, 1867 and Fred S. Palmer, December 16, 1867, Registers of Letters Received, Vol. 3–5, Jan. 1867–May 1869, Assistant Commissioner, Tennessee, 6: 107, 146/398; S. H. Groesbeck to Fred S. Palmer, March 21, 1867, Letters Sent, Vol. 1–2, Jan. 1867–Dec. 1868, Assistant Commissioner, Tennessee, 4: 53/383, RG 105, NARA M999.
69. Endorsement, George F. Cook to R. S. Lacey, October 23, 1866, Registered Letters Received, April–Dec. 1866, Richmond SC, VAFOR, 166: 753/843, RG 105, NARA M1913.
70. Drumgoold, *A Slave Girl's Story*, 6; Register of Persons Furnished Transportation by the Bureau, 6–7, Petersburg SC, VAFOR, RG 105, NARA M1913.
71. John A. McDonnell to BRFAL, December 24, 1867; Endorsement, John De Forest, January 8, 1868, Unregistered Letters Received, June 1865–Dec. 1868, Winchester SC, VAFOR, 187: 253–254/378, RG 105, NARA M1913; The officer in question was likely Cyrus D. Melton. W. C. D. Melton, *Slave Schedules, Chester County, South Carolina*, US Federal Census, 1860 (accessed via Ancestry.com); Cyrus D. Melton, Amnesty Petition, November 13, 1865, "Amnesty Papers," RG 94, NARA (accessed via www.fold3.com). On De Forest's experiences, see David M. Potter, ed., *A Union Officer in the Reconstruction* (Baton Rouge: Louisiana State University Press, 1997).
72. G. R. Chandler to James A. Bates, November 23, 1866; Endorsement, Benjamin C. Cook, December 3, 1866, Unregistered Letters Received, July 1865–July 1867,

Winchester ASC, VAFOR, 191: 534/609; S. E. Goldblum, January 4, 1868, Register of Letters Received, Vols. 1–2, April 1865–Dec. 1868, Richmond SC, VAFOR, 164: 257/267, RG 105, NARA M1913.

73. Ira Ayers to Paul Hambrick, September 11, 1868, Registers of Letters Received and Endorsements Sent, Vol. 1–3, June 1866–Dec. 1868, Gordonsville Superintendent, VAFOR, 92: 428/446, RG 105, NARA M1913. Martha had also lost her son Beauregard when her enslaver hid him from her to prevent her from carrying him off in her flight. James Johnson to F. H. Haskell, July 9, 1868, Press Copies of Letters Sent, Vol. 1–2, Oct. 1867–Dec. 1868, Fredericksburg Superintendent, VAFOR, 83: 476/717, RG 105, NARA M1913.

74. J. W. Haynes to Mr. Goodyear, January 14, 1868; Robert Wyatt to M. N. Horton, May 5, 1867, Letters and Orders Received, Jan. 1867–Dec. 1868, King William Courthouse ASC, VAFOR, 99: 189–190/324, RG 105, NARA M1913.

75. C. W. Dodge to Stephen Moore, December 8, 1866, Letters Received, A-E, 1866, Newberne Superintendent-Eastern District, NCFOR, 35: 706/732, RG 105, NARA M1909; George W. Corliss to S. C. Greene, Letters Received, Vol. 5, A-G, Jan. 1868–May 1869, Assistant Commissioner, Mississippi, 23: 470/1041, RG 105, NARA M852.

76. C. V. Lanier to Col. Eddie, July 24, 1867, Miscellaneous Records, 1865–1868, Salisbury Superintendent-Western District, NCFOR, 63: 47/459, RG 105, NARA M1909; O. D. Kinman to Assistant Commissioner, November 29, 1865, Unregistered Letters Received, A-W, May–Dec. 1865, Assistant Commissioner, South Carolina, 20: 315/973, RG 105, NARA M869.

77. Wm. Lewis Tidball to William R. Morse, August 16, 1866, Letters Received, Mar. 1866–Jan. 1868, Albemarle County ASC, VAFOR 66: 243/1119, RG 105, NARA M1913. See also Augusta County Genealogical Society, *Safe-Keeping: A Glimpse Into Slave Trading in Augusta County, Virginia* (Fishersville: Augusta Co. Genealogical Society, 2013), iv.

78. Capt. Lacey to B. C. Cook, September 23, 1867, Register of Letters Received and Endorsements Sent, Sep. 1865–June 1868, Lynchburg SC, VAFOR, 108: 212/258; John A. McDonnell to Orlando Brown, April 22, 1868, Press Copies of Letters Sent Vol. 4, Oct. 1867–June 1868, Winchester SC, VAFOR, 182: 514/724, RG 105, NARA M1913.

79. Thomas P. Jackson to John A. McDonnell, July 24, 1867, Augusta County, VA, Freedmen's Bureau Records, VS, http://valley.lib.virginia.edu/papers/B1073 (accessed July 19, 2023). "Charleston," *Philadelphia Press*, March 30, 1865.

80. D. G. Connolly to J. R. Stone, October 9, 1866, Registers of Letters Received and Endorsements Sent, Vol. 1–3, June 1866–Dec. 1868, Gordonsville Supt. 4th Dist., VAFOR, 92: 113/446, RG 105 NARA M1913.

81. Thomas P. Jackson to John A. McDonnell, July 24, 1867, Augusta County, VA, Freedmen's Bureau Records, VS, http://valley.lib.virginia.edu/papers/B1073 (accessed July 19, 2023). Augusta County Genealogical Society, *Safe-Keeping*, 42; Endorsement, Benjamin C. Cook, August 27, 1866, Letters Received, Mar. 1866–Jan. 1868, Albemarle County ASC, 66: 241/1119, VAFOR, RG 105, NARA M1913; Robert Colby, "What 'The Books . . . Would Tell': Slavery, Freedom, and History in Slave Traders' Archives," *Slavery & Abolition* 43, no. 3 (September 2022): 594–612;

Capt. Lacey to B. C. Cook, September 23, 1867, Register of Letters Received and Endorsements Sent, Sep. 1865–June 1868, Lynchburg SC, VAFOR, 108: 212/258; Benjamin Cook to Paul Hambrick, May 7, 1868, Endorsements Sent, Vol. 1–5, Nov. 1865–Dec. 1868, Winchester SC, VAFOR, 183: 507/603, RG 105, NARA M1913. On Dickinson, Hill & Co.'s books, see Endorsement, Watson R. Wentworth to James Johnson, April 26, 1867; Frank A. Zutts to Paul Hambrick, May 21, 1867 of Milly Johnson to "Sir," March 26, 1867, Letters Received, ser. 2686, Hillsboro ASC, NCFOR, RG 105, NARA [FSSP A-983]; Account Book, Farmers Bank With Dickinson, Hill & Co., Museum of the Confederacy, Miscellaneous African American Manuscripts, Virginia Historical Society.

82. Thomas P. Jackson to John M. Coyle, December 23, 1867, Augusta County, VA, Freedmen's Bureau Records, VS, http://valley.lib.virginia.edu/papers/B0161 (accessed July 19, 2023). On African Americans working for slave trading firms, see Finley, *An Intimate Economy*; Colby, "'Observant of the Laws of this Commonwealth.'"

83. Thomas Jackson to Orlando Brown, August 31, 1867, Augusta County, VA, Freedmen's Bureau Records, VS, https://valley.lib.virginia.edu/papers/B1015 (accessed July 19, 2023).

84. Howard N. Rabinowitz, "From Exclusion to Segregation: Southern Race Relations, 1865–1890," *Journal of American History* 63, no. 2 (September 1976): 325–350; Rosen, *Terror in the Heart of Freedom*, 37–86; Downs, *After Appomattox*, 39–61; William A. Blair, *The Records of Murders and Outrages: Racial Violence and the Fight over Truth at the Dawn of Reconstruction* (Chapel Hill: University of North Carolina Press, 2022).

85. Andrew F. Lang, "Union Demobilization and the Boundaries of War and Peace," *Journal of the Civil War Era* 9, no. 2 (June 2019): 178–195 and *A Contest of Civilizations: Exposing the Crisis of American Exceptionalism in the Civil War Era* (Chapel Hill: University of North Carolina Press, 2022), 339–358. To see this at play in immediate postwar Richmond, see O'Brien, "Reconstruction in Richmond," 268–274.

86. James Sinclair to General Rutherford, February 21, 1867, Letters Received, C-W, 1867, Wilmington, Superintendent-Southern District, NCFOR, 70: 716/824, RG 105, NARA M1909.

87. See, for example, "Thomas S. P. Miller"; "Rachel Blunt," LS, http://www.informationwanted.org/items/show/909; http://www.informationwanted.org/items/show/198 (accessed February 20, 2017).

88. Plummer, *Out of the Depths*, 96–102.

89. "Mrs. Anna Mollie Wright reunited with her daughter, Mrs. Anna Freeman, after 29 years," LS, http://informationwanted.org/items/show/3261 (accessed February 20, 2017).

90. Margaret Young, sold and separated from her family in 1861, reunited with her son Dowen Young as Christmas gift," LS, http://informationwanted.org/items/show/2323 (accessed February 20, 2017).

91. "Emily Williams," LS, http://www.informationwanted.org/items/show/197. See also "Duff Green"; "Hannah Holland," LS, http://www.informationwanted.org/items/show/230); http://www.informationwanted.org/items/show/248 (accessed February 20, 2017).

92. "Henry Teasley," LS, http://www.informationwanted.org/items/show/389 (accessed February 20, 2017).
93. "S.M. Hightower," LS, http://www.informationwanted.org/items/show/530. See also "Information Wanted of My Daughter," *Christian Recorder*, January 4, 1883; "Peter Johnson; " "Charlotte Summers; " "Mary (Paulhill) Reynolds"; "Archey M'Cloud"; "Moultry Johnston"; "B. T Davis," LS, http://www.informationwanted.org/items/show/729); http://www.informationwanted.org/items/show/735; http://www.informationwanted.org/items/show/747; http://www.informationwanted.org/items/show/786; http://www.informationwanted.org/items/show/801; http://www.informationwanted.org/items/show/867 (accessed February 20, 2017).
94. "Mary James' sister," LS, http://www.informationwanted.org/items/show/635. See also "Mrs. Louise Brown"; "Hannah Neals," LS, http://www.informationwanted.org/items/show/626; http://www.informationwanted.org/items/show/473 (accessed February 20, 2017).
95. Rawick, *The American Slave, Volume 7*, Oklahoma, 108.
96. Perdue et al., *Weevils in the Wheat*, 153, 128.
97. "Abolition of Slavery," *Chicago Daily Tribune*, July 1, 1864; Henry Wilson, *The Death of Slavery is the Life of the Nation* (Washington, DC: H. Polkinhorn, 1864), 15.
98. "A Freedman's Speech," *Pennsylvania Freedmen's Bulletin*, March 1867. On definitions of freedom, see Eric Foner, *Reconstruction: America's Unfinished Revolution, 1863–1877* (New York: Harper & Row, 1988), 77–123.
99. Charles F. Irons, *The Origins of Proslavery Christianity: White and Black Evangelicals in Colonial and Antebellum Virginia* (Chapel Hill: University of North Carolina Press, 2008), 133–168.
100. C. H. Howard to J. A. Sladen, May 18, 1866, Registers and Letters Received, Letters Received, A-F, May–Aug. 1866, Records of the Commissioner, 31: 464–465/881, RG 105, NARA M752. On the Black church in Reconstruction, see, among others, Foner, *Reconstruction*, 88–95; Hahn, *A Nation Under Our Feet*, 230–232; Nicole Myers Turner, *Soul Liberty: The Evolution of Black Religious Politics in Postemancipation Virginia* (Chapel Hill: University of North Carolina Press, 2020).
101. Heather Andrea Williams, *Self-Taught: African American Education in Slavery and Freedom* (Chapel Hill: University of North Carolina Press, 2005); Ronald E. Butchart, *Schooling the Freed People: Teaching, Learning, and the Struggle for Black Freedom, 1861–1876* (Chapel Hill: University of North Carolina Press, 2010); Hilary Green, *Educational Reconstruction: African American Schools in the Urban South, 1865–1890* (New York: Fordham University Press, 2016); AnneMarie Brosnan, "'To Educate Themselves': Southern Black Teachers in North Carolina's Schools for the Freedpeople During the Civil War and Reconstruction Period, 1862–1875," *American Nineteenth Century History* 20, no. 3 (2019): 231–248.
102. Corey, *A History of the Richmond Theological Seminary*, 54–56.
103. Petition, Joseph Bruin to E. R. S. Canby, January 10, 1866, Union Provost Marshals' File of Papers Relating to Individual Civilians, RG 109, NARA M345; Laura Haviland, *A Woman's Life Work: Including Thirty Years' Service on the Underground Railroad and in the War* (Grand Rapids, MI: S. B. Shaw, 1897), 322; Barry A. Crouch,

"Black Education in Civil War and Reconstruction Louisiana: George T. Ruby, the Army, and the Freedmen's Bureau," *Louisiana History* 38, no. 3 (Summer 1997): 293–294.

104. "Letter from Savannah, written by Mr. Lynch, a colored preacher, of the Methodist Episcopal Church, formerly a slave, now commissioned by the National Freedman's Relief Association as a Missionary among the freed people of the department of the South," *The Anti-Slavery Reporter*, April 1, 1865; "Dear Friend," *The Pennsylvania Freedmen's Bulletin*, February 1865; Haviland, *A Woman's Life Work*, 387, 412.

105. Quoted in William B. Gould IV, ed., *Diary of a Contraband: The Civil War Passage of a Black Sailor* (Stanford, CA: Stanford University Press, 2002), 81. See also A. H. Newton, *Out of the Briars: An Autobiography and Sketch of the Twenty-Ninth Regiment Connecticut Volunteers* (Philadelphia: The A.M.E. Book Concern, 1910), 110.

106. Petition, Walter L. Campbell to E. R. S. Canby, April 9, 1866, Union Provost Marshals' File of Papers Relating to Individual Civilians, RG 109, NARA M345; William Palmer Hopkins, *The Seventh Regiment Rhode Island Volunteers in the Civil War, 1862–1865* (Providence, RI: Snow & Farnham, 1903), 131.

107. Solomon Davis to Marsena Patrick, May 8, 1865, Endorsements Sent and Received, Vol. 1–3, Apr. 1865–Dec. 1868, Richmond SC, VAFOR, 164: 27/398, RG 105, NARA M1913; John B. Davis to H. S. Merrell, Undated, Union Provost Marshals' File of Papers Relating to Individual Civilians, RG 109, NARA M345.

108. Michael B. Chesson, *Richmond After the War, 1865–1890* (Richmond: Virginia State Library, 1981), 90.

109. Foner, *Free Soil, Free Labor, Free Men*, 34; Michael Zakim, "Free Soil, Free Labor, and Free Markets: Antebellum Merchant Clerks, Industrial Statistics, and the Tautologies of Profit," in *Contested Democracy: Freedom, Race, and Power in American History*, ed. Manisha Sinha and Penny von Eschen (New York: Columbia University Press, 2007), 98–99.

110. William Tidball to William Morse, October 17, 1866, Letters sent, Vol. 1–3, Nov. 1865–June 1867, Charlottesville, Albemarle County ASC, VAFOR, 65: 173/371, NARA M1913; T. D. McAlpine to A. G. Brady, September 14, 1866, Letters Sent, Vol. 1–3, May 1866–Dec. 1868, Raleigh AS, NCFOR, 51: 18/376, NARA M1909.

111. Capt. Hillebrand to the Assistant Commissioner, Registers of letters received, Vol. 1, July 1865–Oct. 1866, Assistant Commissioner, North Carolina, BRFAL, 1862–1870, 5: 51/143, RG 105, NARA M843.

112. Welch, *Black Litigants in the Antebellum South*, 134–160.

113. Ellen Young, April 19, 1866, Registers and Letters Received, Records of the Commissioner, 4: 338/341, RG 105, NARA M742 and M752; J. M. Seavey, Undated, Letters Received, Vol. 1, Oct. 8, 1866–Feb. 4, 1867, Washington and Georgetown LS, DCFOR, 1863–1872, 15: 492/1030, RG 105, NARA M1902. See also Penningroth, *The Claims of Kinfolk*, 131–161.

114. For examples, see White, *To Address You as My Friend*, 116–135.

115. LaWanda Cox, "The Promise of Land for the Freedmen," *Mississippi Valley Historical Review* 45, no. 3 (December 1958): 413–440; Oubre, *Forty Acres and a Mule*; Julie Saville, *The Work of Reconstruction: From Slave to Wage Laborer in South Carolina,*

1860–1870 (New York: Cambridge University Press, 1994), 72–101; Penningroth, *The Claims of Kinfolk*, 131–172.

116. "A Freedman's Speech," *Pennsylvania Freedmen's Bulletin*, March 1867.
117. Quoted in O'Brien, "Reconstruction Richmond," 274.
118. George H. Pratt to Davis Tillson, January 15, 1866, Unregistered Letters Received, M-R, 1866, Assistant Commissioner, Georgia, 28: 809/1394; Report of Major William Gray, January 30, 1866, Unregistered Letters Received, G-L, 27: 31/1587, RG 105, NARA M798; Wager Swayne to O. O. Howard, September 13, 1865, Letters Received, Entered in Register 1, S, Mar.–Oct. 1865, Registers and Letters Received by the Commissioner, Records of the Commissioner, 17: 631–633/918, RG 105, NARA M752. See also Rothman, *Beyond Freedom's Reach*, 115–186.
119. Unknown to "Commissioner of the Freedmen's Bureau," April 4, 1866, Registered Letters Received, J-R, July 1865–Oct. 1866, Assistant Commissioner, North Carolina, 8: 498/1139, RG 105, NARA M843.
120. "The Steps to Reconstruction," *The Congregationalist*, April 19, 1867. On the memory of emancipation after the war, see David W. Blight, *Race and Reunion: The Civil War in American Memory* (Cambridge, MA: Harvard University Press, 2001), 24–29, 31–63, 300–337.
121. "An Address to the Loyal Citizens and Congress of the United States of America," Registers and Letters Received, Letters Received, N-R, Oct. 1865–Dec. 1866, Records of the Commissioner, 23: 593/1140, RG 105, NARA M752.
122. "Report of the Riot, May 13 at Brownsville, TN," Registers of Letters Received, D-S, 1867, Assistant Commissioner, Tennessee, 13: 1146/1446, RG 105, NARA M1999.
123. Charles Carleton Coffin, *Drum-Beat of the Nation: The First Period of the War of the Rebellion from its Outbreak to the Close of 1862* (New York: Harper & Brothers, 1888), 368.
124. Wm. Birnie to Jacob F. Cheer, March 19, 1868, Letters received, Jan 1867, Jul.–Sep. 1867, Feb.–Nov. 1868, Lincolnton ASC, NCFOR, 28: 87/147, RG 105, NARA M1909.
125. "The War in the Southwest," *Brooklyn Daily Eagle*, May 5, 1862.
126. Declaration for Original Invalid Pension, January 15, 1878, Moses Johnson, File 760855, RG 15, NARA.
127. History of Claimant's Disability, June 26, 1889, George W. Matthews, File 671055, RG 15, NARA.
128. Perdue et al., *Weevils in the Wheat*, 59. In a contraband camp near Cincinnati, enslaved people sang a different song, the lyrics of which included the verse, "Old Jeff Davis is gone to h-ll, doo dah, doo dah! He'll no more poor niggers sell." "Visit to a Camp of Contrabands," *Cincinnati Commercial*, October 24, 1862.
129. John Johnson to Richard Johnson, June 18, 1907; Mary Palmer to Richard Johnson, July 7, 1907; Deposition of Upshur Lloyd, May 17, 1907; Deposition, W. O. Edwards, March 13, 1908, Richard Johnson, File 1350583, RG 15, NARA. Besides men like Johnson who enlisted in the 7th USCI, the Lloyds' holdings in Louisiana had been scattered by the conflict. William Hopkins to Edward Lloyd, June 9, 1864, Lloyd Family Papers, Maryland Historical Society.

130. Deposition, Richard Johnson, December 12, 1906; John Johnson to Richard Johnson, June 18, 1907; Don McClain to Commissioner of Pensions, December 13, 1906, Richard Johnson, File 1350583, RG 15, NARA.
131. On enslaved people's quest for reparations, see Berry, *My Face Is Black Is True*; Ana Lucia Araujo, *Reparations for Slavery and the Slave Trade: A Transnational and Comparative History* (New York: Bloomsbury Academic, 2017); McDaniel, *Sweet Taste of Liberty*, 153–240. Slaveholders also pursued compensation for the enslaved they lost during the conflict. See Guy C. Sibley to W. E. Bibb, February 7, 1896, W. E. Bibb Papers, UVA; Amanda Laury Kleintop, "Life, Liberty, and Property in Slaves: White Mississippians Seek 'Just Compensation' for their Freed Slaves in 1865," *Slavery & Abolition* 39, no. 2 (April 2018): 383–404.
132. Steven Hahn, *A Nation Without Borders: The United States and its World in an Age of Civil Wars, 1830-1910* (New York: Viking, 2016), 275–279, 476–485.

Epilogue

1. Corey, *A History of the Richmond Theological Seminary*, 54–56; Kristen Green, *The Devil's Half Acre: The Untold Story of How One Woman Liberated the South's Most Notorious Slave Jail* (New York: Basic Books, 2022), 209–238; James River Institute for Archaeology, *Archaeological Data Recovery Investigation of the Lumpkin's Jail Site (44HE1053) Richmond, Virginia, Volume I: Research Report*. 23–41, https://www.dhr.virginia.gov/pdf_files/SpecialCollections/Lumpkin%27s%20Jail%20data%20recovery%20report%20vol.%201%20(research).pdf (accessed June 9, 2022).
2. Tadman, *Speculators and Slaves*, 211–221 and "The Reputation of the Slave Trader in Southern History and the Social Memory of the South"; Gudmestad, *A Troublesome Commerce*, 169–201. For an example, see Daniel R. Hundley, *Social Relations in our Southern States* (New York: Henry B. Price, 1860), 139–145.
3. G. J. Rains to James Seddon, November 18, 1864, *OR* Ser.1, Vol. 42, No. 3, 1220.
4. Michael B. Chesson, "Richard Henry Dickinson (1811 or 1812–1873)," *Dictionary of Virginia Biography*, Library of Virginia (1998–), http://www.lva.virginia.gov/public/dvb/bio.asp?b=Dickinson_Richard_Henry (accessed June 12, 2023); N. B. Hill to Dr. Gwathmey, February 28, 1870, Gwathmey Papers, Series M: VHS, Part 3, RASP.
5. "John B. Davis," *Southern Planter and Farmer*, July 1876.
6. JRI, *Archaeological Data Recovery* . . . , 48–129; Abigail Tucker, "Digging Up the Past at a Richmond Jail," *Smithsonian Magazine*, March 2009, https://www.smithsonianmag.com/history/digging-up-the-past-at-a-richmond-jail-50642859/ (accessed June 22, 2022).
7. Hacker, "A Census-Based Count of the Civil War Dead," 307–348; Downs, *Sick From Freedom*, 95–119; Faust, *This Republic of Suffering*; Nelson, *Ruin Nation*; Lisa M. Brady, *War Upon the Land: Military Strategy and the Transformation of Southern Landscapes During the American Civil War* (Athens: University of Georgia Press, 2012); Brian Allen Drake, ed., *The Blue, the Gray, and the Green: Toward an*

Environmental History of the Civil War (Athens: University of Georgia Press, 2014); Mauldin, *Unredeemed Land*; Joan E. Cashin, *War Stuff: The Struggle for Human and Environmental Resources in the American Civil War* (New York: Cambridge University Press, 2018); Marten, *Sing Not War*; Jordan, *Marching Home*; Brian Craig Miller, *Empty Sleeves: Amputation in the Civil War South* (Athens: University of Georgia Press, 2015); Sarah Handley Cousins, "'Wrestling at the Gates of Death': Joshua Lawrence Chamberlain and Nonvisible Disability in the Post–Civil War North," *Journal of the Civil War Era* 6, no. 2 (June 2016): 220–224.

8. Theda Skocpol, *Protecting Soldiers and Mothers: The Political Origins of Social Policy in the United States* (Cambridge, MA: The Belknap Press of Harvard University Press, 1992); Richard F. Bensel, *Yankee Leviathan: The Origins of Central State Authority in America* (New York: Cambridge University Press, 1991); Gaines Foster, *Ghosts of the Confederacy: Defeat, the Lost Cause, and the Emergence of the New South* (New York: Oxford University Press, 1987); Nina Silber, *The Romance of Reunion: Northerners and the South, 1865–1900* (Chapel Hill: University of North Carolina Press, 1993); Alan Nolan, "The Anatomy of the Myth," in *The Myth of the Lost Cause and Civil War History*, ed. Gary Gallagher and Alan Nolan (Bloomington: University of Indiana Press, 2000), 11–34; Blight, *Race and Reunion*; Caroline Janney, *Burying the Dead But Not the Past: Ladies' Memorial Associations and the Lost Cause* (Chapel Hill: University of North Carolina Press, 2008) and *Remembering the Civil War: Reunion and the Limits of Reconciliation* (Chapel Hill: University of North Carolina Press, 2013); W. Fitzhugh Brundage, *The Southern Past: A Clash of Race and Memory* (Cambridge, MA: The Belknap Press of Harvard University Press, 2005); M. Keith Harris, *Across the Bloody Chasm: The Culture of Commemoration Among Civil War Veterans* (Baton Rouge: Louisiana State University Press, 2014); Kytle and Roberts, *Denmark Vesey's Garden*.

9. Painter, "Slavery as Soul Murder," 15-39.
10. Entry for April 22, 1863, Julia Wilbur Diary, Haverford.
11. Patricia Sullivan, "Like We Descended From Hitler," *Washington Post*, February 8, 2018, https://www.washingtonpost.com/local/virginia-politics/like-we-descended-from-hitler-coming-to-terms-with-a-slave-trading-past/2018/02/07/3d65b0bc-f48a-11e7-b34a-b85626af34ef_story.html?utm_term=.418cfa3b59dc; Edward Ball, "Retracing Slavery's Trail of Tears," *Smithsonian Magazine*, https://www.smithsonianmag.com/history/slavery-trail-of-tears-180956968/ (accessed June 16, 2019); Anne C. Bailey, "They Sold Human Beings Here," *New York Times*, February 12, 2020.

Select Bibliography

Manuscript Sources Consulted

Alabama Department of Archives and History
  Bolling Hall Family Papers (online)
  Sydenham Moore Family Papers (online)
  Henry C. Semple Papers (online)

American Antiquarian Society
  Slavery in the United States Collection, 1703–1905 (online)

Special Collections and Archives, Auburn University
  Duggar Family Letters (online)
  Ross Family Letters (online)

Boston Public Library
  Ziba B. Oakes Papers (online)

Chicago History Museum
  Hector Davis Account Books
  L. C. Robards Account Books

Catholic Diocese of Charleston Archives and Low Country Digital Archive, College of Charleston
  Lynch Family Letters, 1858–1866 (online)

Rare Book & Manuscript Library, Columbia University
  Frederic Bancroft Papers

Division of Rare and Manuscript Collections, Cornell University Library
  Gail & Stephen Rudin Slavery Collection (online)

David M. Rubenstein Rare Book and Manuscript Library, Duke University
  African American Miscellany
  American Slavery Documents
  Alfred W. Bell Papers
  Angus R. Blakey Papers
  George Briggs Papers
  Edward George Washington Butler Papers

Sidney Champion Papers
Henry Toole Clark Papers (microfilm)
Cronly Family Papers
Harry L. and Mary K. Dalton Collection
J. D. B. De Bow Papers
John E. Dennis Papers
George Dromgoole and Richard B. Robinson Papers (microfilm)
William A. J. Finney Papers
Edward A. Gibbes Papers
Tyre Glen Papers
John Berkley Grimball Papers
Constant C. Hanks Papers
David Bullock Harris Papers
George K. Johnson Papers
Daniel W. Jordan Papers
Caleb Shive McCurdy Papers
Marshall McDonald Papers
Duncan McLaurin Papers (microfilm)
William H. Merritt Papers
James A. Mitchell Papers (microfilm)
Jacob Rhett Motte Papers
Sterling Neblett Papers
Washington M. Smith Papers
William Patterson Smith Papers
Frank E. Spencer Papers
William T. Sutherlin Papers
Augustin Louis Taveau Papers
Cabell Tavenner Papers
Josiah Turner Papers
Benjamin Cudworth Yancey Papers

Joyner Library Special Collections, East Carolina University
Francis M. Manning Collection
Alan Marshall McGee, Jr. Collection

Rose Library Special Collections, Emory University
African American Miscellany
Godfrey Barnsley Papers
William Augustus Chunn Letters
Albert Fields Papers
F. R. Goulding Papers
Nimrod William Ezekiel Long Papers
Pinckney Family Papers
Lavender Ray Papers
Bell Irvin Wiley Papers
Henry Wilink Papers

George Washington Presidential Library at Mount Vernon
John Washington III Manuscripts (online)

Georgia Archives
James Gardner Papers
Benjamin F. Veal Slave Bills of Sale

Georgia Historical Society
Susan Bogardus Letter, MS 1122

Gettysburg National Military Park Library and Research Center
Gettysburg Library File V7-NC23

Gilder Lehrman Institute for American History
Gilder Lehrman Collection

Baker Library Historical Collections, Harvard Business School
R. G. Dun & Co. Collection

Houghton Library, Harvard College Library
Miscellaneous Documents Concerning American Slavery, 1803–1863

Quaker and Special Collections, Haverford College
Julia Wilbur Papers (online)

Historic New Orleans Collection
Charles H. Blake Diary, MSS 262
Moses Greenwood Papers, MSS 222

Huntington Library, San Marino, CA
Robert A. Brock Collection
Mansfield Lovell Papers
Noble Family Papers
Eldred J. Simkins Papers

Jackson County Historical Society (Independence, MO)
Mary Overton Gentry Shaw Papers

Special Collections, Carrier Library, James Madison University
A. S. Lara Papers

Special Collections Research Center Archival Collections, University of Kentucky
Benjamin Forsythe Buckner Papers, 1785–1918

Library of Congress
Nathaniel P. Banks Papers
Bruce Papers
Benjamin F. Butler Papers

Cornelius Chase Family Papers
Feamster Family Papers
William A. Gladstone Afro-American Military Collection (online)
James Henry Hammond Papers
Abraham Lincoln Papers (online)
George Brinton McClellan Papers (online)
William Cabell Rives Papers
John Mc. Schofield Papers
D. Von Groening Letterbook
John C. Underwood Papers

Library of Virginia
Albemarle County (Va.) Free Negro and Slave Records, 1799–1870
Amelia County Free Negro and Slave Records
Auditor of Public Accounts Records
Robert A. Brock Collection (microfilm)
Dickinson, Hill & Co. (Richmond, Va.), Letters, 1855–1864
Alexander and James M. Donnan Papers
Fluvanna County Free Negro and Slave Records
George Family, Papers
Halifax Co., Virginia Chancery Causes
John Hart Collection of Confederate Letters and Receipts, 1860–1868
Daniel J. Hartsook. Papers, 1848–1879 (microfilm)
Jordan Family Papers
R. J. Reid. Papers, 1777–1870
Richmond City, Virginia Hustings Court Minutes (microfilm)
Tredegar Ironworks Records
Waller Family Papers, 1799–1867

Louisiana and Lower Mississippi Valley Collection, Louisiana State University
Alexander K. Farrar Papers, 1804–1865 (microfilm)
Charles E. A. Gayarré Papers
John W. Gurley Papers (microfilm)
William N. Mercer Papers (microfilm)
William J. Minor Plantation Diary (microfilm)
Palfrey Family Papers (microfilm)
Alexander Pugh Diary (microfilm)
Pugh-Williams-Mayes Family Papers (microfilm)
Turnbull-Allain Family Papers (microfilm)
David Weeks and Family Collection (microfilm)

Northwest Louisiana Archives, Louisiana State University-Shreveport
Samuel Christian Fullilove Papers

Maine Historical Society
George Foster Shepley Papers (online)

Manhattanville College Library Special Collections
   Alexander H. Stephens Collection

Maryland Historical Society
   Lloyd Family Papers

Massachusetts Historical Society
   Nathaniel Cutting Journal

Minnesota Historical Society
   Charles W. and Mary Lesley Ames Papers

New Orleans Public Library
   New Orleans Sheriff Sales Books, 1846–1863

New-York Historical Society
   Moses Greenwood Papers
   Slavery Collection

New York Public Library
   Hector Davis Daybooks

North Carolina Department of Archives and History
   Ashe County, Miscellaneous Records, 1801–1954 C.R.006.928.2
   Caswell County, Miscellaneous Records, 1775–1900, C.R.020.928.5
   Calvin J. Cowles Papers
   Elias W. Ferguson Papers
   C. B. Heller Collection
   Daniel Harvey Hill Papers
   Robeson County, Records Concerning Slaves and Free Persons of Color, 1856–1867, C.R.083.928.5

Orleans Parish Conveyance Office (New Orleans, LA)
   Orleans Parish Conveyance Books

Orleans Parish Notarial Archives (New Orleans, LA)
   Edward Barnett (Notary), Vol. 81

Special Collections, Princeton University Library
   Francis C. Brown Collection on Slavery in America

South Caroliniana Library, University of South Carolina
   Ball Family Papers
   Charles R. Carroll Papers
   Papers of James Henry Hammond (microfilm)
   William E. Johnson Papers
   John L. Manning Papers
   W. A. Nelson Papers

Mims Ward, We Have Carefully Examined the Following Slaves, furnished the Confederate States..., 23 Feb. 1864

South Carolina Historical Society
James Butler Campbell Papers
Simon and Simon-Slave Records
B. H. Teague Family and Collected Papers
Waring Family Papers

Southern Historical Collection, Wilson Library, University of North Carolina, Chapel Hill
Samuel A. Agnew Diary
Edward Porter Alexander Papers
Alexander and Hillhouse Family Papers
James Allen and Charles B. Allen Papers
James B. Bailey Papers
Daniel Hoard Baldwin Papers
Rice C. Ballard Papers
David A. Barnes Papers
George Scarborough Barnsley Papers
Daniel Moreau Barringer Papers
John Houston Bills Papers
William Birnie Papers
Boykin Family Papers
Brashear and Lawrence Family Papers
John Bratton Letters
Catherine Barbara Hopkins Broun Papers
Hamilton Brown Papers
Richard Horace Browne Papers
Bryan Family Papers
Burgwyn Family Papers
Thomas W. Burton Papers
Burwell Family Papers
Cameron Family Papers
Meeta Rhodes Armistead Capehart Papers
Maxwell Troax Clarke Papers
Laura Beecher Comer Papers
Cook Family Papers
Calvin Cowles Papers
Mary Farrow Credle Papers
William Louis Criglar Papers
Charles William Dabney papers
Louis M. DeSaussure Journal
Richard Dozier Papers
Belle Edmondson Diary
Elliott and Gonzales Family Papers
Jeremy Francis Gilmer Papers
William A. Graham Papers

Charles Iverson Graves Papers
Gregorie and Elliott Family Papers
Margaret Ann Meta Morris Grimball Diary
Grimes Family Papers
James Gwyn Papers
Cushing Biggs Hassell Diary
Ernest Haywood Collection of Haywood Family Papers
Laurens Hinton Papers
Johnston and McFaddin Family Papers
Jones and Patterson Family Papers
Kenan Family Papers
John Kimberly Papers
Edward M. L'Engle Papers
Lenoir Family Papers
Andrew McCollam Papers
T. D. McDowell Papers
William Letcher Mitchell Papers
Moore and Gatling Law Firm Papers
George W. Mordecai Papers
Mordecai Family Papers
John Perkins Papers
Pettigrew Family Papers
James Jones Philips Papers
A. D. Pollock Papers
Quitman Family Papers
Edmund Ruffin, Jr. Journal
Thomas Ruffin Papers
David Schenck Diary
Robert W. Smith Papers
William Thomas Sutherlin Papers
Alexander Taliaferro Reminiscences
Thach Family Papers
Lewis Thompson Papers
Ruffin Thomson Papers
Joseph Totten Papers, Caswell County Historical Association
William Henry Tripp and Araminta Guilford Tripp Papers
Sarah Lois Wadley Diary
Lewis Neale Whittle Papers
Trist Wood Papers

Digital Collections and Archives, Tufts University
Dickinson, Hill & Co. Records and Correspondence

Hargrett Rare Book and Manuscript Library, University of Georgia
Francis Marion Coker Papers
Alexander Hamilton Stephens Letter to R. C. Daniel, December 14, 1860
John A. Stevenson Letter

Special Collections, University of Mississippi Libraries
Gage Family Collection
J. Watson Henderson Collection

University of North Texas Special Collections
Maud C. Fentress to David Fentress, February 3, 1862 (online)

Herbert D. Katz Center for Advanced Judaic Studies, University of Pennsylvania
Arnold and Deanne Kaplan Collection of Early American Judaica

Dolph Briscoe Center for American History, University of Texas, Austin
Richard Thompson Archer Papers
William Ballinger Papers, 1815–1909
Confederate States of America Records, 1856–1915
William Massie Papers
Natchez Trace Civil War Collection
Natchez Trace Slaves and Slavery Collection, 1793–1864

Howard-Tilton Library, Tulane University, and the Louisiana State Museum Archives
Rosemonde E. & Emile Kuntz Collection: National Period, 1804–1950 (online)
Robert Ruffin Barrow Papers (microfilm)

Albert and Shirley Small Special Collections Library, University of Virginia
Papers of the Anderson Family
Barringer Family Papers
Berkeley Papers (microfilm)
W. E. Bibb Papers
Bill of sale for Jefree, 1865
Papers of William Daniel Cabell and the Cabell and Ellet Families
Cocke Family Papers (microfilm)
Papers of Philip St. George Cocke
Slave Trade Letters of William Crow
George Hazen Dana Papers
Dunkum and Sowell Family Collection
Papers of the Gambrel Family
J. W. Gilliam Papers
Gilliam Family Papers
Graham-Sanders-Tate Family Papers
Papers of the Grinnan and related Bryan and Tucker families of Virginia
Hamner Family Papers
Harrison, Smith and Tucker Family Papers
John Peter Jones Correspondence
King Family Papers
Civil War letters of William Herrod Locke and William Horatio Thornton
Hudson Martin Papers
McCue Family Papers

Papers of the related Morton and Dickinson Families of Orange and Caroline Counties, Va.
Morton-Halsey Papers (microfilm)
John L. Nau III Civil War History Collection
Papers of the Palmore Family
Elizabeth Perry Papers
Omohundro Slave Trade and Farm Accounts
Richard J. Reid Papers
Richard Stuart Papers
Tayloe Family Papers (microfilm)
Papers of Charles Elisha Taylor
Papers of the Thornhill Family and of Thomas S. Bocock
Thomas Watson Papers (microfilm)
Papers of the White and Holland families of Fluvanna County, Virginia
Wickham Family Papers
Micajah Woods Papers

Valentine Museum (Richmond, VA)
Robert Lumpkin Account Book
Sedgwick and Mussen Family Papers
Charles Talbott Collection

Virginia Museum of History and Culture
Reuben Bartley Papers
Baskerville Family Papers
Branch & Company Records
Broadside 1860: 23
William Daniel Cabell Letter
James Harvey Campbell Papers
Carrington Family Papers
Comfort Family Papers
John Fayette Dickinson Diary
Abner Dawson Ford Papers
John N. Gault Letter
Gresham Family Papers
Gwathmey Papers (microfilm)
Hankins Family Papers
Harrison Family Papers
Haxall Family Papers
William Wirt Henry Account Book
Hunter Family Papers
Keith Family papers
Lee Family Papers
Lee Headquarters Papers
George Bolling Lee Papers
Louthan Family Papers
Mason Family Papers (microfilm)
Massie Family Papers

Jonathan McCalley Letter
McCarty Family Papers
George Marshall McDowell Letter
Minor Family Papers
Charles Morris Papers
William Sylvanus Morris Papers
Museum of the Confederacy, Miscellaneous African American Manuscripts
Nalle Family Papers
Neblett Family Papers
William T. Nelson Papers
Peyton Family Papers
Eleanor Beverley (Meade) Platt Letter
Roller Family Papers
Rose Family Papers
Edmund Ruffin Papers
John Armistead Selden Diary
Smith Family Papers
Taliaferro Family Papers
Philip Southall Turner Letter
Wickham Family Papers
John A. Williams Papers
Wyllie Family Papers

Special Collections, Virginia Tech
Simeon B. Gibbons Letter

Earl Gregg Swem Library, College of William & Mary
Austin-Twyman Family Papers (microfilm)
Herbert George Bond Letter
Borland Family Papers
John Letcher Papers
Ritchie-Harrison Family Papers
M. Stickler Letter
Tucker-Coleman Papers
Robert J. Washington Papers
Nathaniel V. Watkins Papers

National Archives and Records Administration, Washington, DC
Record Group 15: Records of the Department of Veterans Affairs
Record Group 94: Records of the Adjutant General's Office, 1780s–1917
Record Group 105: Records of the Bureau of Refugees, Freedmen, and Abandoned Lands
Record Group 109: War Department Collection of Confederate Records
Record Group 153: Records of the Office of the Judge Advocate General
Record Group 233: Records of the U.S. House of Representatives
Record Group 393: Records of United States Army Continental Commands

West Virginia and Regional History Center, West Virginia University
Terrill-Porterfield Families, Papers Regarding Civil War and Other Material

Western Reserve Historical Society
    William P. Palmer Collection

Wisconsin Historical Society
    Dickinson, Hill & Co. Slave Sale List

Beinecke Library, Yale University
    Documents Relating to J. D. Fondren & Bro.

Yale University Library
    Ulrich B. Phillips Papers

Index

For the benefit of digital users, indexed terms that span two pages (e.g., 52–53) may, on occasion, appear on only one of those pages.

1st Michigan Infantry, 45–47
7th United States Colored Infantry, 209, 210
23rd United States Colored Infantry, 171–72, 193
59th United States Colored Infantry, 160–61

African Americans
   And the search for family during and after the Civil War, 197–205
   See also Enslaved people.
Alabama, 139
   Antebellum slave trading in, 24
   Slave trading in during the secession crisis, 37, 38, 41
   Wartime slave trading in, 54, 59–60, 64–65, 78–80, 94, 99–101, 104, 105–6, 113, 116–17, 122–23, 130, 131, 139, 140, 143, 147, 154, 157–58, 173, 177–78, 180, 183, 186–87, 207
Alexander, Edward Porter, 130–31, 156
Alexandria, Virginia, 22, 39, 45–47, 46*f*, 47*f*, 50–51, 77, 190–91, 206, 215
Alfred (enslaved man), 156–57
Ancker, G. V., 94, 120–21, 193
Anderson, Joseph R., 134, 137
Ann (enslaved woman), 103
Antietam, Battle of, 90–91
Appomattox, Surrender at, 189, 192
Arkansas, 113, 114, 117, 127–28, 143–45, 154–56, 166, 169–70
Atlanta Campaign, 123, 127–28, 183–84
Atlanta, Georgia, 24, 53–54, 74–75, 87*f*, 87–88, 94–96, 98, 101–2, 107, 112–13, 127–28, 131, 136–37, 139, 140–41, 148, 160–61, 180–81, 182–84, 200

Augusta, Georgia, 24, 93, 102–3, 124, 136–37, 192–93, 201

Ball, Charles, 21–22
Baltimore, Maryland, 24–26, 39, 74, 168, 200
Banks, Jourden, 24
Banks, Nathaniel P., 66–67, 71–73, 75–76
Barber, Henry and Peyton, 201–2
Baton Rouge, Louisiana, campaign against, 96
Bell, Alfred and Mary, 112–13, 118, 119–20, 149, 186–87
Betts & Gregory, 34, 41, 42, 43–44
Betts, William, 33. See also Betts & Gregory.
Benjamin Blossom & Son, 36
Birch, James H., 45–46. See also Price, Birch & Co.
Blockade of the Confederacy, 50, 56–58, 79, 111
Blount & Dawson, 86–87, 86*f*, 94–96, 183–84
Border States, 136. See also Kentucky, Maryland, and Missouri.
   Wartime slave trading in, 39, 45, 73–74, 97, 120, 139, 166–68, 167*f*, 171, 182, 205–6
Bowman, S. M., 120–21. See also Lee & Bowman
Brices Crossroads, Battle of, 160–61
Brittingham, Elijah, 58, 103, 193
Brown, John, 30–32, 83
Bruin, Joseph, 58–60, 66–67, 77, 98, 206, 215
Bryan, Alexander, 86, 183–84, 206
Bryan, Joseph, 86

INDEX

Bryant (enslaved man), 133–34
Buena Vista Furnace, 133–34, 139
Bureau of Refugees, Freedmen, and Abandoned Lands, 9, 192–93, 200–4, 206–8, 211
Burgwyn, Henry King, 105, 113–14, 129–30, 175–76
Butler, Benjamin F., 60–61, 65–70

Cameron, Paul, 119–20, 125, 127, 162
Campbell, Bernard M., 24–26, 74, 168
Campbell, Walter L., 66–67, 68–69, 74, 206–7
Carson, James E., 203–4
Chancellorsville, Battle of, 104–5, 133, 158
Charleston, South Carolina, 24–26, 37–39, 43, 55f, 80, 85, 94, 102–3, 107, 113, 114, 116, 136–37, 140, 143–45, 151, 172, 175, 182, 193, 203, 205, 213–14
Chattanooga, Tennessee, 85, 123
Chickamauga, Battle of, 123
Civil War
    Beginning of, 43
    Causes of, 30–32, 49–50, 164
    See also specific battles and campaigns.
Clark, John, 168
Clarke, Robert, 74–75, 94–96, 101–2, 182–83, 200
Clotilda, 78
Coal mining, 136–37, 139–40
Coates, John, 194–95, 196f, 209
Cohen, Solomon, 94–96, 98, 101–2
Columbia, South Carolina, 120–21, 124, 183–84
Confederate States of America
    And individual slave traders, 42–43, 52, 53–54, 55–56
    And the suppression of enslaved flight, 163–66, 169–71, 173–78
    Armies of, 168–71
    Collapse of, 1–3, 189, 192–97
    Conscription in, 53–54, 141–43
    Cotton embargo, 50
    Creation of, 42–43
    Currency, 59, 111–13, 115–16, 118–21, 186–87
    Civilian life in, 145–52
    Hiring of enslaved people in, 137–39, 186
    Impressment of goods, 141, 145
    Impressment of enslaved laborers, 168–69
    Industrialization in, 136–40, 141
    Infrastructure in, 140–41
    Loyalty to, 151–52
    Military affairs, 45, 60, 79–80, 89–91, 96, 99, 105, 108, 110–11, 123–24, 127–28, 160–61, 183–84, 186, 189, 193
    Mobilization for war, 133–35, 136–47
    Monetary Policy, 59, 111–12, 115–16, 118–20, 139
    Perceived strength of, 82–84, 85–97, 98–99, 103–6, 108, 109–10, 113–15, 123–25, 126–32, 138, 139, 184–87
    Nationalism in, 126–28, 184
    Protection of the slave trade, 49–50, 58–60, 74–75, 77, 80–81, 82–106, 150, 152–55, 163–73, 183
    Shortages in, 53, 145–46
    Taxation, 111–12, 120, 145, 159, 186
Conscription. See Confederate States of America.
Cooper, Mrs. (enslaved woman), 190–91, 197, 203
Corinth, battles for, 91, 96–97
Cotton Kingdom
    Emergence of, 5–6, 21–24
    Wartime slave trade to, 55–60, 94, 96–97, 103–4
Courts, 26–28, 67, 68, 121, 122–23, 135, 151, 152–53, 154–55, 166–67, 192
Crawford, Frazer & Co., 101–2
Cuba, 66–67, 207–8
Culpeper, Virginia, 83–84, 243

Daniel (enslaved man), 163–64
Dardin, Joe, 187–88
Davis, Deupree & Co., 41, 42, 55, 106
Davis, Hector, 20, 23, 26, 29, 32, 33, 51–52, 53, 55, 59–60, 84–85, 92, 94, 98, 102, 137–38, 192, 203, 212–13, 220
Davis, Jefferson, 49–50, 198
Davis, John B., 33, 92, 212–13
Davis, Robert H., 92, 182–83. See also Davis, Deupree & Co.
Davis, Solomon, 33, 103, 182–83, 206–7
De Bow, J. D. B., 59–60, 89–90, 137–38

Democratic Party, 23, 30, 33, 90–91, 123–24
Deupree, William S., 29, 33, 212–13. See also Davis, Deupree & Co.
Devil's Half Acre, 1–6, 4f–5f, 51, 189–90, 200, 206, 212, 213–14, 214f, 215
Dice, Charles, 1–2, 193, 209, 210
Dick (enslaved man), 90, 163–64
Dickinson, Hill & Co., 17–18, 19f, 20–21, 32, 33–34, 37, 43–44, 45, 51–52, 55, 58, 90, 98, 102–3, 110–11, 120, 130, 141, 147, 151, 164, 173, 182, 184, 189–90, 203–4, 206–7, 210, 212–13
  Formation of, 23–24
  Trading Methods, 23–26
Dickinson, Richard H., 20, 22–24, 58, 154, 203–4, 212–13
Douglass, Frederick, 21–22, 48, 153–54
Driver, Mickleberry, 89
Drumgoold, Kate, 101, 122–23, 129, 142, 201–2

Early's Raid, 171, 186
Election of 1860, 14, 33, 34, 35–36, 37–38, 39–40, 204–5
Election of 1864, 123–24, 124f, 126
Ellen (enslaved woman), 99, 138
Elviry (enslaved woman) and children, 142, 148
Emancipation
  And the Confederate military, 168–70
  As a revolution, 71–72, 162
  Compensated, 74
  Economic effects, 195–97
  In Alabama, 183
  In the District of Columbia, 73–74, 200
  In Florida, 176–77, 182–83
  In Georgia, 174, 180–81, 182–84
  In Kansas, 197
  In Kentucky, 166–68, 182
  In the Lower Mississippi River Valley, 69–72, 122, 146–47, 170, 174–75, 177, 197–98, 202–3, 204–5
  In Maryland, 74, 166–67, 200
  In Missouri, 197–98
  In North Carolina, 103, 105, 113–14, 126–27, 176–77, 178–79, 180, 182, 190–91, 199, 202–3, 204
  In South Carolina, 114, 125, 177, 182, 199, 202, 203
  In Tennessee, 63–64, 65, 198, 201–2
  In Texas, 202–3
  In Virginia, 83–84, 92, 133–34, 139–40, 145, 149–50, 163–64, 166–67, 168–69, 174–75, 177–78, 179–80, 182–83, 186, 187–88, 199, 200–2, 203–4
Emancipation Proclamation, 85, 90–91, 93–94, 114–15, 146–47
Enslaved People
  Antebellum prices offered for, 18, 20, 21–22, 23, 30, 32–38, 39–42, 43–44, 195–97
  Anticipated future value of, 41, 126–30, 194
  Monetary Value of, 6–7, 20
  Pursuit of freedom, see Emancipation.
  Wartime prices offered for, 51–59, 60–61, 64–65, 70, 73–74, 75–76, 80, 82–83, 84–85, 87–89, 90, 91–97, 98–99, 100, 101–6, 108, 111, 112–17, 119, 120, 122, 126–28, 129–31, 142, 152–53, 154, 155, 156, 157, 161, 166, 168–69, 172, 177, 183–84, 186–87, 193–94, 195–97, 198
  See also individual enslaved people.
Evans, Clement, 121, 176

Fay, Edwin, 96–97, 119–20, 127, 128–29, 194
Florida, 33–34, 101, 118, 120, 127, 146, 148, 157–58, 182–83
Fondren, Samuel F., 29, 33, 98
Food
  Cultivation of, 141, 146
  Inflation and, 118–19, 139
  Shortages of, 38, 111, 139, 145–46, 159, 162, 177, 181, 186
Ford, Abner Dawson, 141–42, 148
Forrest, Nathan Bedford, 53–54, 65, 160–61
Fort Monroe, 62, 69, 74–75, 83, 182, 187–88
Forts Henry and Donelson, 60
Foster, Thomas, 38–39, 68–69, 72
Frank (enslaved man, Virginia), 81–82
Frank (enslaved man, North Carolina), 165

Franklin & Armfield, 22–24, 45, 177, 215
Fredericksburg, Virginia, 81, 96, 163–64, 169–70, 173–74
　Battle of, 99
Freedmen's Bureau. See Bureau of Refugees, Freedmen, and Abandoned Lands.
Free people of color, 68, 72, 137, 150–51, 153, 156, 170–71, 172, 176, 198
Fremantle, Arthur, 102–3, 117
Fugitives from Slavery. See Emancipation.
Fugitive Slave Act, 49

Galveston, Texas, 24, 79
Gayarré, Charles, 59–60
George (enslaved man), 163–64
Georgia, 18–19, 21–22, 24–26, 41, 42, 43–44, 53–54, 82–83, 86–88, 89, 92–93, 94, 100–2, 104, 105–6, 111, 112–13, 120, 122, 123–25, 127, 130, 131, 137, 141, 143, 145–46, 147, 148, 150, 169–70, 174, 175–76, 180, 182–83, 187, 192–93, 195, 208–9
Gettysburg Campaign, 102–3, 105–6, 108, 116–17, 118–19, 129–31, 154, 174
　And the capture of enslaved people, 101, 170–71
Glasgow (enslaved man), 165
Gloucester County, Virginia, 98–99, 171–72, 175, 177, 179–80
Goldsboro, North Carolina, 103–4, 200–1
Gorgas, Josiah, 79–80, 91, 136–37
Grant, Ulysses S., 54, 60, 96, 105, 123–24, 130–31, 166, 180, 189
Greensboro, North Carolina, 94, 210–11
Greenwood, Moses, 35–36, 37, 39–40, 56–57, 69–70
Griffin (enslaved man), 78–80
Grimball family, 102, 125, 150, 156–57, 177
Gwyn, James, 54, 103, 181

Hall, William W., 24–26, 62
Hammond, James Henry, 37–38, 52–53, 105–6, 161
Hargrove, James, 192
Harpers Ferry, Virginia, 30–32, 161–62, 168–69, 170, 198–99

Hatcher, Charles, 33, 55–56, 66–67, 68–69, 186
Henry (enslaved man), 174
Hill, Charles B., 20, 23–24, 33, 55. See also Dickinson, Hill & Co.
Hill, Dickinson & Co. See Dickinson, Hill & Co.
Hill, Nathaniel B., 20, 23–24, 42–43, 189–91, 212–13. See also Dickinson, Hill & Co.
Hills, Alfred C., 76
Hiring of enslaved people, 28, 57–58, 68, 89, 99, 117, 118, 134, 137–39, 140, 143–45, 148–49, 161, 165, 186
Holmes, Benjamin, 85
Houston, Texas, 24, 117, 118

Indian Removal, 5–6, 18–19, 21, 22, 49
Industrial Revolution, 21
Inflation, 59, 82–83, 85, 87–88, 93–94, 99, 101, 106–7, 109, 111–13, 115–16, 118–20, 121–22, 138, 145, 186–87
Iron production, 79, 101, 133–34, 136–37, 138, 139–40
Iuka, Battle of, 96

Jacobs, Harriet, 161–62, 190, 215
Jack (enslaved man), 165
Jackson, Susan, Anderson, and Priscilla, 94, 204
Jackson, Thomas J., 79–80, 89–91, 92, 98–99, 198–99
James, R. D., 203–4
Jeff (enslaved man), 68
Jenkins, Rachel, 68, 201
Jerry (enslaved man), 133–34
Joe (enslaved man), 103
Joe (enslaved woman), 89
John (enslaved man), 103
Johnson, Andrew, 63–64, 151, 208
Johnson, Richard, 210–11
Jones, John B., 89–90, 123–24
Jones & Slater, 92–93
Jordan, Daniel, 36, 37
Jordan, Samuel, 133–34

Kansas, 20, 197, 198
Kentucky, 29, 39, 73–74, 79–80, 91, 97, 120, 139, 145, 151–52, 166–68, 167f, 171, 182, 201–2

INDEX

King, John H., 81–82
Knoxville, Tennessee, 115–16, 148–49, 201–2

Lee & Bowman, 184, 193
Lee, N. M., 84–85, 168–69, 203–4, 209.
    See also Lee & Bowman.
Lee, Robert E., 2, 79–80, 83–84, 123–24, 133, 189
Lester, Angeline, 143, 144*f*
Lenoir family, 54, 112–14, 115–16, 127, 152–53
Lexington, Kentucky, 139, 167–68, 171, 201–2, 206–7
Lincoln, Abraham, 19–20, 31*f*, 33–34, 35–36, 37–40, 43–44, 45–46, 48, 51, 66, 82–83, 90–91, 93–94, 123–24, 124*f*, 126, 166, 173, 181–82, 198, 204–5
Long, Nimrod and Queen, 99, 138
Louisiana, 32–33, 35–36, 52, 56–57, 58, 60–61, 66–73, 75–77, 96, 100, 105–7, 111–12, 117, 127–28, 148, 157–58, 170, 173, 177, 179, 181–82, 192, 210–11
    See also Emancipation in the Lower Mississippi Valley, New Orleans.
Louisville, Kentucky, 91, 151–52, 168
Lumpkin, Mary, 4–5, 206, 212
Lumpkin, Robert, 1–6, 15–16, 22–23, 33, 51, 189–91, 193, 212
Lynchburg, Virginia, 26, 41, 105–6, 120, 147, 154–55, 169, 192, 193

Macon, Georgia, 24, 93, 136–37
Manuel (enslaved man), 104–5
Manufacturing, 136–40, 141
March to the Sea, 180, 187
Maria (enslaved woman), 78–80
Martin (enslaved man), 173–74
Maryland, 21–22, 29, 39, 45–46, 73–74, 79–80, 166–67, 168, 171, 193, 204–6, 210–11
Maryland Campaign, 1862, 79–80, 198–99
Meinhard Brothers, 86, 102
Melinda (enslaved woman), 51
Memminger, Christopher, 52–53, 111–12
Meria (enslaved woman), 104–5
Memphis, Tennessee, 24, 50–51, 53–54, 64–65, 160, 201, 208–9
Miles, Josh, 62–63, 63*f*

Mississippi, 9, 21–22, 32–33, 35, 41, 53, 58, 60, 64–65, 68–69, 70, 73, 79, 82–83, 91, 94, 96–97, 100, 103–4, 105–6, 112, 113, 114, 119, 122, 126, 129, 142, 146–47, 154, 157, 160–61, 162, 166, 170, 174–75, 181, 195, 201, 202–3
    See also Emancipation in the Lower Mississippi Valley.
Missouri, 37, 39, 74, 117, 154, 168, 169–70, 171, 181–82, 198, 204–5
Mitchell, James, 22
Mobile, Alabama, 28–29, 43, 68–69, 80, 99–100, 183–84
Montgomery, Alabama, 24, 99–100, 104, 105
Mordecai family, 41, 91–92, 127
Morton, Jeremiah, 89–90, 100–1
Mulligan, Alfred, 112–13

Nalle Family, 90, 163–64
Nashville, Tennessee, 24, 60, 62–64, 74–75, 200
Natchez, Mississippi, 22, 24, 57, 73
Nelly (enslaved woman), 156–57
Nelson (enslaved child), 51–52
Nelson (enslaved man), 51
New Orleans, Louisiana, 8–9, 21–22, 24–26, 28–29, 32–34, 35–36, 37, 38–39, 41, 42, 52, 68
    Fall of, 60–61
    Financial Crisis in, 35–36, 39–40, 66
    Union occupation of, 60–61, 65–73
    Wartime slave trade in, 55–60, 65–67, 68–69, 72–73, 75–76, 93, 171, 181–82, 197–98, 206
Ned (enslaved man), 17–20
Norfolk, Virginia, 24–26, 62, 74–75, 141, 187–88, 191*f*
North Carolina, 17–19, 28, 30–32, 34, 39–40, 42, 53–54, 165
    Reconstruction in, 204
    Wartime slave trade in, 1–2, 53–54, 80, 82–83, 84–85, 92–93, 94, 98, 99, 101–2, 103–5, 112–14, 116, 118, 119–20, 122, 124–25, 126–27, 129–30, 140–41, 142, 145, 148, 149–50, 152–53, 154, 156, 165, 170–71, 175–77, 178–79, 180, 181, 182, 184, 190–91, 193, 194–95, 199, 200–1, 202–3, 204, 206–7, 208–9, 210

INDEX

Oakes, Ziba B., 24–26, 102–3
Omohundro, Silas, 22–23, 37, 55, 58, 84–85, 92, 104, 176, 212–13
Overland Campaign, 123, 127–28, 180

Panic of 1857, 30–32, 37–38, 111
Panic of 1860, 34–44, 57–58
Paternalism, 28–30, 100–1, 156–58, 173–74, 177–78, 181
Peninsula Campaign, 60, 62, 83–85, 88, 114–15, 177–78
Perryville, Battle of, 91
Petersburg, Virginia, 94, 98, 105, 124, 138, 143–45, 146, 150–51, 166, 177–78, 186, 194–95, 201–2, 204, 207
　Siege of, 2, 123–24, 130–31, 143–45, 166, 186
　The Crater, 171–72, 189, 193, 194–95
Peterson, Henry F., 34, 55–56, 66–67
Petigru, James, 85, 113
Pettigrew family, 53, 91, 103, 126–27, 130–31, 165, 178–79, 181–82
Plummer, Miranda, 39, 204–5
Pope, Mary, 149–50, 187–88
Portsmouth, Virginia, 62
Powell, John, 160–62
Price, Birch & Co., 45–47, 46f, 47f, 243
Price, Charles M., 45. See also Price, Birch & Co.

Ragland, John D., 78, 80, 100–1
Ragland, Reuben, 98
Railroads, 17, 24, 57–58, 80, 81, 87–88, 91, 94–96, 122, 126–27, 139, 140–41, 174
Raleigh, North Carolina, 17–18, 101, 104–5, 119, 199, 207
Ravenel, William, 115–16, 120
Ray, Lavender, 187
Reconstruction, 191, 200–9
Redoshi, 78–79
Refugees
　From slavery. See Emancipation.
　From Union occupation, 70, 86–87, 94, 111, 113–14, 117, 137–38, 145, 146, 147, 150, 165, 166, 176
Republican Party, 19–20, 30–32, 31f, 33, 46, 49–50, 208

Richards, Samuel, 87–88, 94–96, 112–13, 183–84
Richmond, Virginia, 4f, 170, 184
　As a site of Black family reunions, 200–1
　Fall of, 1–3, 189–92, 204
　Financial Crisis in, 36, 37
　Hiring of enslaved people in, 137–38
　Hustings Court, 155
　Manufacturing, 133–34
　Reconstruction in, 203–4, 207–8
　Slave Trading, antebellum, 1–3, 18, 19f, 22–26, 27f, 28, 29, 30–32, 33–34, 37, 38–39, 41, 42, 43–44
　Slave trading, landscape, 212, 213–14
　Wartime slave trade, 51–52, 55, 59–60, 77, 78, 80, 81–82, 84–85, 88–94, 98–99, 100–2, 103–4, 110–11, 113, 114–15, 119, 120–21, 126–27, 130, 133, 134, 140, 142, 145, 147, 148–49, 150–51, 155, 156, 158, 164, 165–66, 168–69, 170–72, 174–75, 176–77, 178–80, 182, 184–88, 190–91, 191f, 193, 194–95, 198–99, 200–1, 202, 203, 207, 209, 210
Riggs, John S., 94, 143–45
Robards, Lewis C., 120, 193–94, 206–7
Ruffin, Edmund, 30–32, 93–94, 114–15, 177–78
Ruffin, Edmund Jr., 84, 150–51
Ruffin, Thomas, 17–20
Rux, A. J., 37, 41, 84–85, 100, 112

Saltworks, 140
Sandy (enslaved man), 133–34
St. Louis, Missouri, 39, 98, 197–98
Sarah (enslaved woman), 78–80
Savannah, Georgia, 36, 86–88, 101–2, 139–40, 146, 148–49, 183–84, 206
Sectional Crisis, 30–34
Secession, 34, 42, 53–54, 64–65, 106, 129, 137–38, 172, 198, 203
　As a defense of slavery, 29–30, 49–50
　As a financial crisis, see Panic of 1860.
　Of Virginia, 42–43, 45, 51, 169–70, 173, 179
Second Bull Run, Battle of, 79–80, 90–91
Sedgwick, John R., 98, 308

Selden, John Armistead, 84, 90
Selma, Alabama, 78–79, 136–37, 140
Selma Naval Works, 137
Semmes, Paul, 92–93, 94, 96–97
Seven Days' battles, 79–80, 90, 94, 113, 164, 202
Shelby Iron Company, 137, 139
Shenandoah Valley, 26, 60, 98–99, 101, 124, 133–34, 158, 170–71, 174–75, 180, 186, 193, 194, 201–2
Shenandoah Valley Campaign, 1862, 79–80, 89–90, 174–75
Shenandoah Valley Campaign, 1864, 186
Sheriffs, 49, 55–56, 58, 65–66, 67, 153, 163–64, 165–66
Sherman, William T., 32–33, 65, 97, 105, 124–25, 127–28, 139, 160–61, 170, 180, 183–84, 187
Shiloh, Battle of, 60
Simmons, Betty, 39, 40f
Slave patrols, 18–19, 49, 67–68, 69, 71, 163–64, 165–66, 172–73
Slave Trade, Atlantic, 5–6, 21–22, 42, 78
Slave Trade, Domestic
    Communication networks and, 24–26, 27f
    Financing of, 34–36, 53
    Historians and, 7, 9–10, 213
    Local trade, 28–30
    Nineteenth century changes to, 23–24
    Origins of, 5–7, 20–21
    The Secession Crisis and, 30–44, 111
    State support for, 9–10, 28, 47–49
    Transportation and, 22, 24
Slave Trade, Wartime
    And Confederate Nationalism, 127–32, 184
    And debt, 54, 67, 96, 121–23, 150–51, 152–55, 194
    And Emancipation, 12–13, 84, 113–14, 160–63, 164–65, 174–88
    Aboard ships, 172
    And Confederate enlistment, 53–54
    And contingency, 135
    And continuity from the antebellum years, 135, 152–56
    And gender roles, 147–50
    As a hedge against inflation, 113–15, 116–21, 124–26, 186–87
    As a means of defining freedom, 191, 205–8
    And loyalty, 151–52, 176–77
    And mobility in the CSA, 150–51
    As a sign of Confederate confidence, 103–5
    And statemaking, 134–36
    Confederate state support for, 10–11, 65, 67, 80–81, 103–4, 153–54, 162–63, 165, 168–72
    Effects on postbellum life, 191–92, 197–208
    Effects of Panic of 1860 on, 53
    Effects of Union occupation upon, 60–77
    End of, 192–97
    Estimates of scale, 8–9, 197
    In women and children, 126, 128–30
    And mobilization for war, 133–35, 136–47
    Prices, 98–99, 103, 106, 110, 114–15, 116, 119
    Speculation through, 11, 101, 102–3, 106–7, 108–9, 117–18, 119–21, 126–32, 170, 194
    Symbolism of its demise, 72–73, 205–7
Smedes, William, 96–97, 146–47
Smith, George C., 45–48
Smith, Washington M., 78–80
Southampton County, Virginia, 149–50, 175–76, 183, 187–88
South Carolina, 32, 33–34, 36, 37–38, 41, 60, 79, 85, 88, 93, 94, 96, 102–3, 109, 112, 114, 115, 116, 120–21, 122, 124–25, 130, 142, 143–45, 146, 148–49, 150, 154–55, 169–70, 172, 180, 182, 184, 186–87, 194, 199, 202, 207
    Secession of, 34
Staunton, Virginia, 194–95, 201–2, 203
Stephens, Alexander, 59–60, 150–51
Stokes, E. H., 30–32, 38, 43–44, 55, 88–89, 92, 98, 102, 106, 113–14, 120–21, 175, 209
Stones River, Battle of, 99, 152–53
Substitutes, 141–43, 144f
Sumner, Charles, 48

344 INDEX

Sutherlin family, 104, 115, 116–17, 176

Taveau, Augustin, 125
Taylor, John R., 173–74
Templeman, Henry N., 22–23
Tennessee, 22, 34, 53, 60–61, 64, 68–69, 79, 84–85, 100, 101, 106, 113, 115–16, 148–49, 151–52, 171–72, 180, 193, 194, 198, 201, 208
   Secession of, 53–54
Texas, 54, 57, 68–69, 106–7, 113, 114–15, 117–18, 129–30, 142–43, 151–52, 155–56, 157, 170, 172, 174–75, 194, 195–98, 202–3, 208–9
Thompson, Millie, 192–93
Three fifths clause, 10, 49
Trans-Mississippi, 94, 106–7, 127–28
   See also Texas, Arkansas, and Missouri
Tredegar Ironworks, 133–34, 136–37, 138, 139
"Twenty-Negro Law," 143

Union Military
   And fugitives from slavery, 45–47, 61–65, 68, 160, 162, 167–68
   And the slave trade, 74
   See also specific battles.
United States Colored Troops, 3, 46–47, 71, 160–61, 171–72, 193, 207–8, 209, 210

Veney, Bethany, 26
Venus (enslaved woman), 165
Vicksburg, Mississippi, 39–40, 97, 146–47, 174–75
Vicksburg Campaign, 96–97, 105–6, 107, 108, 116–17, 118–19, 123, 146–47, 166

Virginia, 30–33, 34, 35, 36, 37–38, 39–44, 45–46, 51–52, 58, 59–60, 62, 69, 73–74, 77, 78–80, 81–82, 83–85, 88–89, 90–94, 96, 98–99, 100, 102, 103–6, 108, 110–11, 112, 113, 114, 116, 119, 120–21, 122–23, 124, 129, 130, 131, 133–34, 139–42, 143–45, 147, 148, 149–50, 151, 154–55, 156, 157–58, 159, 163–64, 166, 167–68, 169–70, 171–72, 173–75, 176, 177, 179–81, 182, 183, 186–87, 193–97, 202–3, 205, 206, 208, 209–10
   Antebellum slave trade in, 22–26, 28–30. See also individual cities and localities.
   Invasions of, 45–47, 83–84, 123, 127–28, 180
   Occupation of, 45–47, 62, 167–68

Washington, Booker T., 19–20
Washington, DC, 24–26, 48, 73–74, 166, 168–69, 192–93, 199–200
Watkins, Nathaniel V., 96
Westover (plantation), 84, 90
White, Garland, 3, 200
Wilbur & Son, 85, 94
Wilbur, Julia, 189–90, 215
Wilink, Henry, 86–87, 139–40
Wilmington, NC, 79, 80, 103, 206–7
Women. See Slave trade, wartime and gender.
Woodroof, Seth, 26, 37, 43
Woods family, 113, 174
Wylly, George, 86–87, 101–2

Young, Kitty, Dallas, and Laura, 201–2
Young, J. Wimbush, 84–85, 88–89, 100